The Victorian Design Book

A Complete Guide to Victorian House Trim

 Lee Valley Tools Ltd.

Lee Valley Tools Ltd.
1080 Morrison Drive
Ottawa, Ontario K2H 8K7

Canadian Cataloguing in Publication Data
Main entry under title:
  Victorian Design Book
  R.   Originally published: Universal design book containing official price
  lists, illustrating mouldings, balusters, stairwork . . .; official price list
  adopted by the Wholesale Sash, Door, and Blind Manufacturers
  Association, October 15th, 1903. Chicago. |1904|
  Includes the Official Moulding Book, adopted March 1, 1897, revised
  May 2, 1901. Chicago, n.d.
  Includes Index.
  ISBN 0-9691019-5-3 (bound)
  ISBN 0-9691019-6-1 (pbk)
1. Woodwork — United States — Catalogs. 2. Woodwork — Canada —
Catalogs. i. Wholesale Sash, Door, and Blind Manufacturers Association.
ii. Title: Universal design book. iii. Title: Official moulding book.
TH1155.V53 1984
729'.38'0218 C84-090159-3

Printed and bound in Canada

Introduction

The Association for Preservation Technology is pleased to make this Universal Design Book available to the carpenters, architectural conservators, historians, architects and other lovers of early architecture who want to know more of our Victorian and Edwardian past. It is our hope that not only will you find a joy of discovery in these pages, but also we hope this book transmits some sense of how we came to have the richness of architectural detail we had at the end of the nineteenth and the beginning of the twentieth century in North America. Doors, stained glass windows, moldings, railings — it's all here. Just take out your order pad . . . Oh, that we could still be so fortunate.

The original volume from which we prepared this reprint was used at a lumber yard in St. John, New Brunswick and is dated 1904 on its cover. It is noted as the "Official Price List Adopted by the Wholesale Sash, Door and Blind Manufacturers' Association of the Northwest, October 15th, 1903." The clear implication is that this book was in use in both the United States and Canada at the turn of the century, and for those who are looking for a national identity in stylistic architectural elements, it is an obvious conclusion that Canadians and Americans were drawing from the same source.

How many of these catalogues were available? We don't know. The few libraries in the United States and Canada that had copies of this book in their indexes, were unable to find the volume on their shelves. We trust that this limited reprinting will bring fresh insight into our architectural history and help refill those empty shelves for future generations.

On a personal note I would like to thank Leonard Lee of Lee Valley Tools, Ottawa, Ontario for his efforts and business support in publishing this book. Without his help this edition would have been far costlier and fewer in number. It is his valued and generous contribution to all of us.

Also, I would like to thank Ray Maybee of Moncton, New Brunswick who gave this book to me in 1976. He is a generous man who has always shared his knowledge. A gift such as this is treasured, and on behalf of the many new readers of The Universal Design Book, I extend to Ray our appreciation and say thank you.

Richard O. Byrne

This book is published under the auspices of the Association for Preservation Technology and has been reproduced in major part from the original copy owned by Richard O. Byrne, Director, Preservation Services, Preservation Partnership, New Bedford, Massachusetts. Mr. Byrne served as a Director of APT for a number of years.

UNIVERSAL
Design Book

1904

Lawton Co., Ltd.,
St. John, N. B.

UNIVERSAL
DESIGN BOOK

CONTAINING

OFFICIAL PRICE LISTS.

ILLUSTRATING

MOULDINGS,
BALUSTERS, STAIR WORK,
CORNER BLOCKS,
BRACKETS,
HEAD BLOCKS, SPINDLES,
BASE BLOCKS,

Windows, Doors, Blinds

COLUMNS, FRAMES,
MANTELS,
INTERIOR FINISH,
MILL WORK
OF EVERY DESCRIPTION,
LEADED
ART GLASS,
WHEEL CUT GLASS,
WINDOW GLASS,
VENETIAN BLINDS,
SLIDING BLINDS,
GRILLES.

Official Price List Adopted by the Wholesale Sash, Door and Blind Manufacturers'
Association of the Northwest, October 15th, 1903.

INTRODUCTORY

FTER examining this, our new catalogue, we are confident you will agree with us that it is the most complete book of its kind ever issued. No effort has been spared by us to make it attractive, comprehensive and best adapted to the convenience and requirements of the trade.

We wish to call particular attention to the many new designs and ideas contained therein, and at the same time to emphasize the fact that our facilities for furnishing all kinds of mill work are unsurpassed.

We solicit your orders and will endeavor to handle them in a manner that will be satisfactory to you.

Write us for any desired information and we will be pleased to be of service to you.

INDEX

▼ ▼ ▼ ▼ ▼

PAGE

Altar Rail 230
Angle Beads 234
Art Glass .... 340 to 362
Balls (turned) 235

BALUSTERS—

    Outside Porch 190–197
    Stair 148–163
Base Corners 234

BLINDS—

    Door 134
    Extras 129
    Inside Folding 128
    Outside, Twelve and Eight Light 126
    Outside, Four and Two Light and Pantry 127
    Sliding 130
    Sliding, List Prices 131
    Venetian 132
    Venetian, List Prices 133
    Water Closet 134–135
    Swing and Saloon Door Blinds 135

BLOCKS—

    Base 143
    Corner 141
    Head 142
    Stock 140
    Prices of 141
Brackets 186–187–188–189
Brackets (composition) 289
Capitals (composition) .... 274 to 289
Cap Trim for Inside Doors and Windows 175–176–177
Carvings 236–237–238–239
China Closets 290
Church Furniture 230–232
Church Seats 232
Church Windows 41–214–229–355
Church Window Frames 214
Columns 192–193–194–195–196–197
Corner Beads 234
Crestings 178
Cupboard Doors 62
Dimension Shingles 199
Directions for Ordering 7

DOORS—

    Church 228–229
    Cupboard 62
    Door Blinds 134
    Door Measurements 364
    Five Panel, Bead and Cove 54
    Five Cross Panel 53
    Five Panel, O G 53
    Four Panel Flush Moulded 55
    Four Panel, O G 52
    Front Doors 59–60–61
    Front Doors, Cottage .... 73 to 114
    Grained Doors 70–71
    Interior Doors and Finish 92
    Inside Doors 93–94–95–96
    Lattice Doors 125
    O G Sash Doors 57–58
    Painted Sash Doors 56 66–68
    Side Lights 63
    Store Doors 120–121–122–123–124

INDEX —*Continued*.

DOORS—*Continued.*   PAGE
  Stickings, Details of 50–51
  Table, of Square Feet 364
  Table, 1¾ inch 63
  Vestibule Doors 86–90–115–119
  Water Closet 134–135
Door Extras 64–65
Dowels 235
Drapery 178
Drops 235
Fence Posts Caps 182
Finials 178

FRAMES—
  Church 214
  Gable 42–43
  Plain Drip Cap, Moulded Cap and Fancy 212–213
  Frame Price List 215
  Gable Frames 42–43
  Gable Ornaments 178–180–181

GLASS—
  Art Glass, Leaded in Colors ....341 to 356
  Art Glass, Sand Blast ....327 to 332
  Enamel and Fancy ....338 to 340
  Geometric Chipped and Ground 339
  Leaded Beveled Plate' ....357 to 361
  Leaded Colored, for Church Windows 355
  Leaded Plain D. S. (no color) 362
  Mitred Beveled Plate 357
  Plate Glass Price List ....315 to 325
  Table of Measurements 363
  Window Glass Price List ....305 to 314
Grades of Sash, Doors and Blinds 6
Grained Doors 70–71
Grilles ....240 to 251
Leaded Beveled Plate ....357 to 361
Leaded Colored Art Glass ....341 to 356

MANTELS—
  Cuts of ....252 to 267
  Andirons 273
  Fenders and Fire Sets 268–269–270–271–272
Mitred Beveled Plate 357

MOULDINGS—
  Embossed ....218 to 227
  Ordinary ....366 to 415
  Ordinary Moulding Price List 415–416
  Turned Beads 216–217

NEWELS—
  Outside Porch 194–195
  Stair 164–165
Painted Doors 56–66–68
Paneled Wainscoting 174
Parquetry ....291 to 304
Pew Ends 231
Pickets 182
Picture Mouldings, Embossed 218

PORCH WORK—
  Balls and Dowels 235
  Balusters 190
  Brackets 186–187–188–189
  Columns 192–193–194–195–196–197
  Corinthian and Ionic Columns 194–195–196
  Elevations 200–201–202–203
  Newels 194–195
  Rails 183–184–185
  Spindles 191
  Views 204–205–206–207–208–209–210–211

PAGE

Portiere Work .... 240 to 251
Pulpits 233
Rosettes (Turned) 235
Sand Blast Glass .... 327 to 332

SASH—

Attic 21–42–43
Barn 21
Cellar 20
Cottage Front .... 22 to 28–33 to 36
Cupboard 62
Gable 42–43
Hot Bed 21
Landscape with Leaded Toplights 33–34–35–36
Queen Anne 30
Stall 21
Store 136–137–138–139
Storm 29
Sash Extras 44–45–46–47
Shingles, Square and Fancy Butt 199
Side Lights for Doors 63
Sink and Table Legs 234
Spindles 191

STAIR WORK—

Balusters 148–163
Brackets 166
Elevations 149–156–167–169
Ground Plans 157
Interiors 170–171–172–173
Newels (Angle and Platform) 164–165
Newels (Starting) 165
Price List 162
Rails 145–146–147–158–161
Store Doors 120–121–122–123–124
Store Fronts 136–137–138–139
Table and Sink Legs 234
Table 1¾ Doors 63
Tracery 178
Turned Work .... 190 to 199

TRANSOMS—

Circle Top 32
Cottage Front 22–28
Gothic Top 32
One and Two Lights 18–19
Queen Anne 31
Segment Top 32
Verandas .... 200 to 212
Verge Boards 179
Wainscoting (Paneled) 174
Water Closet Doors 134–135
Weather Strips 49

WINDOWS—

Church 41–214–229–355
Circle Face (Bow or Bent) 48
Circle Top 9
Cottage Front .... 22–28–148 to 152
Four Light, Check Rail 12–13
Gothic and Peak Head 41
Landscape with Leaded Top Lights 33–34–35–36
Queen Anne 38–39 40
Segment Top 9
Triple Front Windows 37
Twelve and Eight Light, Plain Rail 10
Twelve and Eight Light, Check Rail 11
Two Light, Check Rail 13–14–15–16
Two and Four Light Pantry 17
Window Extras 44–45–46–47
Window Frames 212–213
Wood Carpet .... 291 to 304

Official Grades of Sash, Doors and Blinds.

Adopted by the Wholesale Sash, Door and Blind Manufacturers'
Association of the Northwest.

DOORS.

AAA. Oil Finish Doors.—Material for AAA. Oil Finish Doors must be Clear, no white sap admitted. Workmanship must be good.

AA. Oil Finish Doors.—Material for AA. Oil Finish Doors must be Clear, with the exception that white sap will be admitted, not to exceed twenty-five (25) per cent of the face of any one piece. Workmanship must be good.

A. Doors.—Material in A. Doors must be Clear, with the exception that water stains and small pin knots not exceeding one-fourth (¼) inch in diameter may be admitted. No piece to contain more than two (2) such defects and no door more than five (5) such defects on each side; white sap not considered a defect. Workmanship must be good.

B. Doors.—Material in B. Doors may contain knots not to exceed one (1) inch in diameter, and blue sap showing on both sides not to exceed fifty (50) per cent in any one piece of the door and gum spots showing on one (1) side of a piece only and other slight defects, shall not exceed ten (10) in number on each side and each white pine stile, bottom and lock rail must contain at least one (1) and not to exceed three (3) such defects; plugs admitted and not regarded as a defect. Slight defects in workmanship admitted.

C. Doors.—Material in C. Doors may contain all stained sap and small worm holes and fine shake; also knots not exceeding one and three-fourths (1¾) inches in diameter. Twenty (20) defects may be allowed on each side, also slight defects in workmanship.

Each piece of white Pine in a No. C Door must contain a defect. Not more than six (6) defects allowed in any one piece.

D. Doors.—D Doors are regarded as a cull door and must contain large coarse knots and may contain rot, worm holes, shake and other serious defects.

A Standard Door may be through tennon, blind tennon or dowelled.

WINDOWS.

Check Rail **Windows may** contain two (2) knots three-eighths (⅜) inch in diameter or one red knot five-eighths (⅝) inch in diameter in each piece of a window. White sap and not over thirty-three and one-third (33 1-3) per cent blue sap may be admitted in any one window. Workmanship must be good.

Plain Rail **Windows** and Sash may contain blue sap and small knots.

BLINDS.

No. 1. Outside Blinds must be made of Clear lumber, except that small, sound pin knots, water stain and white sap may be admitted. Workmanship must be good.

WOODS ADMISSIBLE.

Woods other than Michigan, Wisconsin and Minnesota White Pine admitted in Doors, Blinds and Windows, except in Oil Finish Goods.

DIRECTIONS FOR ORDERING.

Valuable time will be saved us in serving our patrons by their close observance of the following directions:

Unless otherwise specified, or covered by standing instructions to the contrary, we will understand all orders as calling for **REGULAR WESTERN STYLES OF GOODS,** as described in this Catalogue.

The universal rule in ordering mill work is to give the width first and then the height.

WINDOWS AND SASH.

A—The term Sash indicates a single piece.

B—The term Window means two pieces, an upper and a lower Sash, made with either plain or check rail.

C—In ordering regular sizes of Sash or Windows, give size of glass and number of lights and thickness; if a Window, whether check or plain rail; state whether open or glazed, and if glazed, whether with single or double strength glass.

D—In ordering odd sizes, give the size of opening to be filled and describe as above.

E—When measurements are given in inches, it usually indicates the glass size, and we will so understand it; when given in feet and inches the outside measure or opening is understood.

F—In ordering Segment or Circle-head Sash and Windows, give the number of style desired (see page 9) and the radius of Circle or Segment. If no number or proper description is given in ordering, we will substitute for Circle Head Style No. 2, and for Segment Head Style No. 4, using our regular radius, which is the width of the Sash for Segment Heads and one-half the width of Sash for Circle Heads.

DOORS.

G—In ordering always give width, height, thickness, number of panels and quality. If full instructions are not given, to save time in shipment, we assume that our Standard Door, 1⅜ inch, Four Panel O. G. No. 1 quality is desired, and will fill order accordingly.

H—If other than Four Panel O. G. Doors are required, for panel Doors give number and arrangement of panels and style of Sticking; for Sash Doors give number of style desired; indicate whether open or glazed, and if glazed, style of glazing.

I—Where Moulded Doors are required state whether flush or raised mould is desired, and if to be moulded on one or two sides.

BLINDS.

In Ordering, Specify Whether Outside (O. S.) or Inside (I. S.) Blinds are Wanted.

J—**OUTSIDE BLINDS.** In ordering Outside Blinds, if regular, give size of glass and number of lights in window for which they are intended, the size of opening to be filled, if odd; give thickness and state if rolling slats (R. S.), stationary slats (S. S.), or half rolling and half stationary slats (½ R. S., ½ S. S.) are required. If other than these styles are required, order must so state.

K—The regular opening for Outside Blinds is one (1) inch longer than Check Rail Windows of corresponding glass size. Where Blinds of extra length for brick buildings are desired, order must so state, and Blinds will then be made two (2) inches longer than sash opening.

L—Our Standard Blinds are 1⅛ inch thick, full rolling slats made for regular openings, as above described. When not otherwise specified we assume this to be the style desired, and fill orders accordingly.

M—**INSIDE BLINDS.** In ordering it is best to give exact outside measure of opening to be filled. Give thickness, number of folds and state if all panels, all slats or half panel and half slats, giving sketch of any unusual arrangement of panels.

N—If Blinds are to be cut, state how many times and give distance from top of window to center of meeting rail.

O—If Blinds are to fold into pockets, give size of pockets.

P—State quality, whether No. 1, for paint or oil finish.

Q—When description of window only is given, as in ordering O. S. Blinds, we furnish our standard measurement of Inside Blinds, which is the same as the check rail window opening, 1⅛ inch thick, four fold where practicable, made to cut once at check rail.

MOULDINGS.

R—In ordering, give numbers as shown in this catalogue and name kind of wood. If other styles than are shown herein are required, furnish detail or sketch with correct measurements.

S—Unless otherwise instructed, we will fill orders with our Standard Mouldings, No. 1 Paint Quality, in miscellaneous long lengths, 10, 12, 14 and 16 feet long.

FRAMES.

T—In ordering, state whether for Outside or Inside Frames.

U—For Window Frames give size, thickness and full description of window, stating whether for frame, brick or veneer buildings. If for frame or brick veneer building, give width of studding. If for brick building give thickness of wall. State if frames are desired with or without pulleys.

V—For Outside Door Frames give size and thickness of Door, and state whether frames are required with stops or with rabbeted jambs, and if sill is to be Pine or Oak. If for frame building give width of studding; if for brick building, give thickness of wall.

W—For Inside Door Frames give size and thickness of Door and width and thickness of jambs; state whether stops or rabbeted jambs are required, and advise if thresholds are desired.

WE ASSUME that the numbers of designs in orders or Bills for estimate, refer to this Catalogue unless otherwise specified.

CIRCLE and SEGMENT TOP WINDOWS.

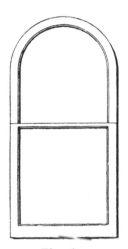

Fig. 1

Circle inside and outside.

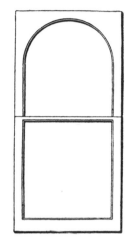

Fig. 2

Circle outside, Square inside.

In ordering Segment or Circle-head Sash and Windows, give the number of style desired and the radius of Circle or Segment. If no number or proper description is given in ordering, we will substitute for Circle Head Style No. 2, and for Segment Head Style No. 4, using our regular radius, which is the width of the Sash for Segment Heads and one-half the width of Sash for Circle Heads.

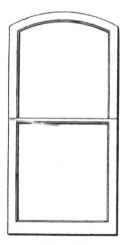

Fig. 3

Segment inside and outside.

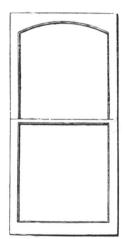

Fig. 4

Segment outside, Square inside.

The above windows can be filled with any number of lights required. Always give radius of segment, otherwise they will be made regular radius, which is width of window.

For prices see sash extras, pages 44 to 47.

PLAIN RAIL WINDOWS.

Eight Lights, 1⅛-in. Thick.

Size of Glass.			Price, Open.	Price, Glazed.	Size of Opening.				Weight, Open.	Weight, Glazed.
8	x	10	$0.69	$2.60	1	8½ x 3		9¼	5	10
		12	.76	3.10			4	6	5	12
		14	.85	3.65			5	2	7	14
		16	.95	4.05			5	10	8	19
9	x	12	.78	3.25	1	10½ x 4		6	6	14
		14	.87	3.70			5	2	7	17
		16	.97	4.35			5	10	9	20
10	x	12	.82	3.40	2	0½ x 4		6	8	15
		14	.90	3.80			5	2	8	18
		16	1.00	4.40			5	10	9	20
		18	1.10	5.10			6	6	10	23
12	x	14	.95	4.45	2	4½ x 5		2	9	19
		16	1.06	4.95			5	10	11	22
		18	1.15	5.70			6	6	12	25½

PLAIN RAIL WINDOWS.

Twelve Lights, 1⅛-in. Thick.

Size of Glass.			Price, Open.	Price, Glazed.	Size of Opening.				Weight, Open.	Weight, Glazed.
7	x	9	$0.75	$3.25	2	1 x 3		5½	5	13
8	x	10	.80	3.40	2	4 x 3		9¼	6	14
		12	.88	3.95			4	6	8	18
		14	.97	4.85			5	2	8	19
9	x	12	.96	4.30	2	7 x 4		6	9	20
		13	1.00	5.05			4	10	9	21
		14	1.05	5.10			5	2	9	22
		15	1.10	5.40			5	6	9	24
		16	1.16	5.70			5	10	9	26
		18	1.26	6.80			6	6	10	28
10	x	12	1.02	4.70	2	10 x 4		6	9	21
		14	1.11	5.25			5	2	9	23
		15	1.16	5.85			5	6	10	24
		16	1.20	6.10			5	10	10	26
		18	1.30	7.00			6	6	10	29
		20	1.42	8.05			7	2	11	31
12	x	14	1.23	6.95	3	4 x 5		2	10	25
		16	1.33	7.65			5	10	10	28
		18	1.42	8.30			6	6	10	31

For sash extras see pages 44 to 47.

CHECK RAIL WINDOWS.

Eight Lights.   1⅜ in. thick.

Size of Glass.			Price Open.	Price Glazed	Size of Opening.				Weight Open.	Weight Glazed.
9	x	12	$ .91	$3.50	1	11 x 4		6	8	17
		14	1.01	3.95			5	2	9	18
		16	1.13	4.65			5	10	9	19
10	x	12	.95	3.60	2	1 x 4		6	9	18
		14	1.05	4.00			5	2	11	19
		16	1.17	4.70			5	10	12	22
		18	1.28	5.65			6	6	13	24
		20	1.41	6.20			7	2	13	26
12	x	14	1.11	4.70	2	5 x 5		2	11	23
		16	1.23	5.20			5	10	12	24
		18	1.34	5.75			6	6	13	27
		20	1.48	7.00			7	2	14	30
14	x	16	1.32	6.20	2	9 x 5		10	13	28
		18	1.43	6.75			6	6	14	31
		20	1.57	7.45			7	2	15	35
		22	1.83	9.00			7	10	16	37
		24	2.10	10.00			8	6	17	40

CHECK RAIL WINDOWS.

Twelve Lights.   1⅜ in. thick.

Size of Glass.			Price Open.	Price Glazed.	Size of Opening.				Weight Open.	Weight Glazed.
8	x	10	$ .93	$3.60	2	4½ x 3		10	8	19
		12	1.03	4.35			4	6	8	20
		14	1.13	5.15			5	2	9	22
9	x	12	1.12	4.55	2	7½ x 4		6	10	22
		13	1.17	5.30			4	10	10	24
		14	1.22	5.35			5	2	11	24
		15	1.28	6.00			5	6	11	25
		16	1.34	6.30			5	10	11	27
10	x	12	1.19	4.95	2	10½ x 4		6	11	23
		14	1.29	5.50			5	2	12	26
		15	1.35	6.30			5	6	12	27
		16	1.40	6.40			5	10	13	29
		18	1.51	7.30			6	6	13	32
		20	1.65	8.40			7	2	14	34
12	x	14	1.44	7.30	3	4½ x 5		2	14	28
		16	1.55	8.00			5	10	14	30
		18	1.66	8.75			6	6	14	32
		20	1.80	9.75			7	2	14	36

For sash extras see pages 44 to 47.

CHECK RAIL WINDOWS.

Four Lights. 1⅜ in. Thick.

Size of Glass.	Price Open.	Price Glazed, S. S.	Price Glazed, D. S.	Size of Opening.	Weight Open.	Weight Gl. S. S.	Weight Gl. D. S.
10 x 16	$0.80	$3.00	----------	2 1 x 3 2	5½	18	---------
18	.80	3.15	...	3 6	5½	18	......
20	.80	3.20	----------	3 10	6	19	....
22	.86	3.55	----------	4 2	6	19	....
24	.90	3.65	------	4 6	7	21	....
26	.95	4.05	----------	4 10	7	21	...
28	1.00	4.25	--------	5 2	8	22	.
30	1.06	4.75	----------	5 6	8	22	--------
32	1.12	5.20	----------	5 10	9	23	---------
34	1.19	5.85	------	6 2	9	24	---------
36	1.23	6.10	----------	6 6	9	25	-------
12 x 16	.86	3.35	--------	2 5 x 3 2	6	18	---------
18	.86	3.50	---- ----	3 6	6	19	---------
20	.86	3.55	----------	3 10	6	19	---------
22	.92	4.05	-------	4 2	6	19	--- ---
24	.96	4 30	----------	4 6	7	21	---------
26	1.01	4.60	----------	4 10	7	21	---------
28	1 06	4.80	----------	5 2	9	22	--------
30	1.12	5.35	---------	5 6	10	24	---------
32	1.18	5.60	----------	5 10	12	25	---------
34	1.25	6.20	----------	6 2	12	26	---------
36	1.29	6.25	----------	6 6	12	27	---------
38	1.38	6.90	----------	6 10	13	28	--------
40	1.43	7.45	----------	7 2	13	30	---------
42	1.53	7.90	.. ..	7 6	14	31	---------
44	1.69	8.95	----------	7 10	14	32	---------
46	1.82	9.55	.. -------	8 2	15	33	---------
48	1.96	9.80	----------	8 6	15	35	---------
14 x 20	1.04	4.35	----------	2 9 x 3 10	10	22	------
22	1.04	4.75	----------	4 2	10	22	---------
24	1.04	4.80	----------	4 6	11	23	---------
26	1.09	5 35	----------	4 10	11	23	---------
28	1.14	5.55	----------	5 2	12	24	---------
30	1.20	6.05	----------	5 6	12	26	--------
32	1.26	6.35	$9.45	5 10	12	28	31
34	1.33	7.10	10.00	6 2	13	28	31
36	1.37	7.15	10.60	6 6	13	30	33
38	1.46	8.15	11.00	6 10	13	30	33
40	1.51	8.25	11.70	7 2	14	31	34
42	1.61	9.70	12.85	7 6	14	32	35
44	1.77	9.95	13.15	7 10	15	33	36
46	1.90	10.75	14.20	8 2	15	34	37
48	2.04	11.80	15.30	8 6	16	36	39
15 x 20	1.10	5.05		2 11 x 3 10	10	23	26
22	1.10	5.35		4 2	11	23	26
24	1.10	5.60	7.35	4 6	11	24	27
26	1.15	6.15	8.20	4 10	11	24	27
28	1.20	6.35	8.95	5 2	12	25	28
30	1.26	6.70	9.45	5 6	12	27	30
32	1.31	7.05	10.00	5 10	12	29	32

(Continued on next page.)

CHECK RAIL WINDOWS.

(*Continued.*)

Four Lights. 1⅜ in. Thick.

Size of Glass.	Price Open.	Price Glazed S. S.	Price Glazed D. S.	Size of Opening.	Weight Open.	Weight Gl. S. S.	Weight Gl. D. S.
15 x 34	$1.38	$7.85	$10.60	2 11 x 6 2	13	29	32
36	1.42	8.50	11.55	6 6	13	31	33
38	1.51	8.65	11.70	6 10	13	31	33
40	1.56	9.60	12.80	7 2	14	32	35
42	1.66	10.35	13.80	7 6	14	33	36
44	1.82	10.60	14.05	7 10	15	34	37
46	1.95	12.40	16.25	8 2	15	35	39
48	2.09	12.65	16.50	8 6	16	37	40

When ordering Windows, always say if wanted glazed or open.
For less than stock quantities on sizes not listed an extra 10 per cent will be charged.
Irregular and intermediate sizes in stock quantities, same list as next larger listed size, both open and glazed.
All Check Rail Windows plowed and bored.
For sash extras see pages 44 to 47.

CHECK RAIL WINDOWS.

Two Lights. 1¾ in. thick.

Size of Glass.	Price Open.	Price Glazed, S. S.	Price Glazed, D. S.	Size of Opening.	Weight Open.	Weight Gl. S. S	Weight Gl. D. S.
16 x 20	$0.83	$3.15	$4.05	1 8⅛ x 3 10	5	17	19
22	.83	3.30	4.25	4 2	5	17	19
24	.83	3.35	4.50	4 6	5	19	21
26	.88	3.90	5.20	4 10	5	19	21
28	.93	3.95	5.50	5 2	7	21	23
30	.99	4.10	5.80	5 6	8	22	24
32	1.04	4.35	6.15	5 10	9	23	25
34	1.11	4.85	6.60	6 2	10	24	26
36	1.15	5.05	6.80	6 6	10	24	26
18 x 20	.83	3.35	4.40	1 10⅛ x 3 10	6	18	26
22	.83	3.70	4.95	4 2	6	18	20
24	.83	3.75	5.15	4 6	6	20	22
26	.88	4.00	5.40	4 10	6	20	22
28	.93	4.15	6.00	5 2	8	22	24
30	.99	4.25	6.10	5 6	9	24	27
32	1.04	4.50	6.45	5 10	0	24	27
34	1.11	5.20	7.10	6 2	10	25	28
36	1.15	5.50	7.60	6 6	10	25	29
38	1.23	6.15	7.90	6 10	11	26	29
40	1.28	6.60	8.50	7 2	11	26	29
20 x 20	.83	3.70	4.95	2 0⅛ x 3 10	7	19	21
22	.83	3.85	5.05	4 2	7	19	21
24	.83	3.90	5.10	4 6	7	21	23
26	.88	4.10	5.35	4 10	7	21	23
28	.93	4.35	5.70	5 2	8	22	25
30	.99	4.65	6.10	5 6	8	22	25
32	1.04	5.10	6.75	5 10	9	23	26
34	1.11	5.45	7.20	6 2	9	24	27

(*Continued on next page.*)

CHECK RAIL WINDOWS.

(Continued.)

Two Lights, 1⅜ in. thick.

Size of Glass.	Price, Open.	Price Glazed, S. S.	Price Glazed, D. S.	Size of Opening.	Weight, Open.	Weight, Gl. S. S.	Weight, Gl. D. S.
20 x 36	$1.15	$5.80	$7.55	2 0⅛ x 6 6	10	25	28
38	1.23	6.50	8.40	6 10	11	26	30
40	1.28	6 70	8.70	7 2	11	26	30
22 x 20	.86	3.95	5.15	2 2⅛ x 3 10	7	19	22
22	.86	4.05	5.35	4 2	7	19	22
24	.86	4.10	5.40	4 6	7	22	26
26	.91	4.30	5.70	4 10	7	22	26
28	.96	4.60	6.05	5 2	8	23	27
30	1.02	5.05	6.70	5 6	8	23	27
32	1.07	5.45	7.25	5 10	10	24	28
34	1.14	6.10	7.90	6 2	10	25	29
36	1.18	6.25	8.55	6 6	10	25	29
38	1.26	7.00	9.10	6 10	11	26	30
40	1.31	7.80	10.10	7 2	11	26	30
42	1.41	8.35	10.75	7 6	11	28	32
44	1.56	9.35	12.10	7 10	12	30	34
46	1.69	9.55	12.30	8 2	12	31	35
48	1.83	9.80	12.55	8 6	13	33	38
24 x 18	.89	3.90	5.25	2 4⅛ x 3 6	6	20	22
20	.89	4.15	5.65	3 10	7	21	23
22	.89	4.30	5.90	4 2	7	22	26
24	.89	4.50	5.95	4 6	8	23	26
26	.94	4.55	6.05	4 10	8	23	26
28	.99	5.00	6.65	5 2	9	24	27
30	1.05	5.40	7.20	5 6	10	24	27
32	1.10	5.75	7.45	5 10	12	25	28
34	1.17	6.25	8.15	6 2	12	25	28
36	1.21	6.30	8.20	6 6	12	27	30
38	1.29	7.80	10.05	6 10	12	28	31
40	1.34	7.85	10.15	7 2	13	29	33
42	1.44	9.15	11.90	7 6	13	29	33
44	1.59	9.40	12.15	7 10	14	30	34
46	1.72	9.60	12.35	8 2	14	30	34
48	1.86	12.00	15.10	8 6	15	31	35
26 x 20	.98	4.45	6.05	2 6⅛ x 3 10	7	21	23
22	.98	4.65	6.35	4 2	7	22	26
24	.98	4.85	6.70	4 6	8	23	26
26	.98	5.25	7.00	4 10	10	23	26
28	1.03	5.90	7.70	5 2	11	24	27
30	1.09	6.10	8.00	5 6	12	25	28
32	1.14	6.20	8.10	5 10	12	26	30
34	1.21	7.30	9.45	6 2	13	27	31
36	1.25	7.35	9.55	6 6	13	28	32
38	1.33	8.15	10.65	6 10	13	28	32
40	1.38	8.20	10.70	7 2	14	30	34
42	1.48	9.20	11.95	7 6	14	30	34
44	1.63	10.45	13.70	7 10	15	32	36
46	1.76	11.85	14.95	8 2	15	32	36

(Continued on next page.)

CHECK RAIL WINDOWS.
(*Continued.*)

Two Lights, 1⅜ in. Thick.

Size of Glass.	Price Open.	Price Glazed S. S.	Price Glazed D. S.	Size of Opening.	Weight Open	Weight Gl. S. S.	Weight Gl. D. S.
26 x 48	$1.90	$12.05	$15.20	2 6⅛ x 8 6	16	34	39
28 x 24	1.07	5.40	7.45	2 8⅛ x 4 6	9	24	27
26	1.07	5.95	7.80	4 10	11	24	27
28	1.07	6.10	8.00	5 2	11	26	30
30	1.13	6.15	8.10	5 6	12	27	31
32	1.18	7.25	9.40	5 10	12	28	32
34	1.25	7.70	10.00	6 2	12	28	32
36	1.29	8.10	10.60	6 6	13	30	34
38	1.37	8.20	10.70	6 10	14	30	34
40	1.42	8.30	10.80	7 2	15	32	36
42	1.52	10.30	12.90	7 6	15	32	37
44	1.67	11.15	14.15	7 10	16	34	38
46	1.80	11.90	15.00	8 2	16	35	39
48	1.94	13.15	16.70	8 6	17	36	40
30 x 24	1.20	5.90	8.20	2 10⅛ x 4 6	10	24	27
26	1.20	6.60	9.00	4 10	12	25	28
28	1.23	6.65	9.05	5 2	12	27	31
30	1.23	7.70	10.45	5 6	13	28	32
32	1.23	8.00	10.50	5 10	13	28	33
34	1.30	8.10	10.60	6 2	13	28	33
36	1 34	8.15	10.65	6 6	14	29	34
38	1.42	9.10	11.85	6 10	14	29	34
40	1.47	9.75	12.80	7 2	15	30	35
42	1.57	11.00	14.00	7 6	15	30	35
44	1.72	11.25	14.20	7 10	16	31	36
46	1.85	13.00	16.55	8 2	16	31	36
48	1.99	13.20	16.80	8 6	17	32	38
50	2.14	13.45	17.05	8 10	18	34	40
32 x 24	1.47	6.75	8.55	3 0⅛ x 4 6	12	25	28
26	1.47	7.15	9.20	4 10	12	26	30
28	1.50	8.20	10.50	5 2	12	28	32
30	1.50	9.35	12.10	5 6	13	28	33
32	1.50		12.15	5 10	14	29	34
34	1.57		12.20	6 2	14	29	34
36	1.62		13.80	6 6	14	29	34
38	1.70		14.90	6 10	14	29	34
40	1.76		16.00	7 2	15	30	35
42	1.86		16.15	7 6	15	30	35
44	2.02		18.80	7 10	15	30	35
46	2.15		19.00	8 2	16	31	36
48	2.33		19.30	8 6	17	32	38
50	2.45		19.80	8 10	18	34	40
34 x 24	1.54	7.65	9.75	3 2⅛ x 4 6	12	25	28
26	1.54	8.65	11.05	4 10	13	27	31
28	1.57	8.70	11.10	5 2	12	28	32
30	1.57	9.45	12.20	5 6	13	28	33
32	1.57		12.25	5 10	14	29	34
34	1.65		13.85	6 2	14	29	34
36	1.70		14.90	6 6	14	30	34

(*Continued on next page.*)

CHECK RAIL WINDOWS.
(Continued.)

Two Lights. 1⅜ in. Thick.

Size of Glass.	Price Open.	Price Glazed S. S.	Price Glazed D. S.	Size of Opening.	Weight Open.	Weight Gl. S. S.	Weight Gl. D. S.
34 x 38	$1.78		$15.05	3 2⅛ x 6 10	15	30	35
40	1.83		16.10	7 2	15	31	35
42	1.94		18.65	7 6	15	31	35
44	2.12		18.95	7 10	16	32	36
46	2.25		19.20	8 2	17	32	38
48	2.41		19.75	8 6	18	34	40
50	2.57		23.65	8 10	19	35	41
36 x 24	1.76	$8.25	10.35	3 4⅛ x 4 6	12	27	30
26	1.76	9.30	11.70	4 10	13	28	32
28	1.80	10.10	12.85	5 2	13	30	34
30	1.80	10.15	12.90	5 6	14	30	34
32	1.80		14.35	5 10	14	30	34
34	1.87		15.45	6 2	14	30	34
36	1.91		15 55	6 6	15	31	35
38	2.00		19.05	6 10	15	31	35
40	2.05		19.10	7 2	16	32	37
42	2.17		19.35	7 6	16	32	37
44	2.33		19.60	7 10	17	33	38
46	2.48		23.75	8 2	19	35	41
48	2.64		24.05	8 6	20	36	43
50	2 80		25.45	8 10	20	36	43
40 x 24	1.98		12.05	3 8⅛ x 4 6	13	29	32
26	1.98		13.15	4 10	14	30	33
28	2.02		13.25	5 2	15	32	35
30	2.02		14.70	5 6	15	32	36
32	2.02		15.70	5 10	16	32	36
34	2.09		15.85	6 2	16	32	36
36	2.14		19.30	6 6	16	32	36
38	2.22		19.45	6 10	16	33	37
40	2.28		19.50	7 2	17	33	38
42	2.39		23 60	7 6	19	35	41
44	2.55		23.90	7 10	20	36	43
44 x 30	2.23		17.10	4 0⅛ x 5 6	16	31	36
32	2.23		19.45	5 10	16	31	36
34	2.31		19.55	6 2	17	32	38
36	2.35		19.65	6 6	19	35	41
38	2.45		23.70	6 10	19	35	41
40	2.50		23.80	7 2	21	37	44
42	2 61		27.10	7 6	21	37	44
44	2.77		27.40	7 10	22	39	46
48 x 30	2.46		19.85	4 4⅛ x 5 6	19	33	39
32	2.46		19.90	5 10	17	32	38
34	2.53		20.25	6 2	19	35	41
36	2.58		23.95	6 6	20	36	43
38	2.67		25.25	6 10	21	37	44
40	2.72		25.35	7 2	21	38	45
42	2.83		27.50	7 6	23	40	50
44	3.00		35.30	7 10	24	42	56

Irregular and intermediate sizes, in stock quantities, same list as next larger listed size, both open and glazed.
For less than stock quantities, on sizes not listed, an extra 10 per cent will be charged.
For additional sash extras see pages 44 to 47.

PANTRY CHECK RAIL WINDOWS.

Two Lights, 1⅜ Inch Thick.

One Light Wide.

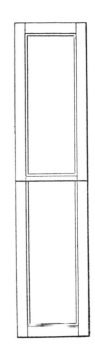

Size of Glass.	Price, Open.	Price, Glazed.	Size of Opening.	Weight Open.	Weight Glazed.
12 x 20	$0.73	$3.05	1 4⅛ x 3 10	6	13
24	.73	3.25	4 6	6	13
26	.78	3.80	4 10	6	13
28	.83	3.85	5 2	7	14
30	.89	4.00	5 6	7	14
32	.94	4.25	5 10	8	15
34	1.01	4.75	6 2	8	15
36	1.05	4.95	6 6	8	15
14 x 20	.76	3.10	1 6⅛ x 3 10	9	16
24	.76	3.30	4 6	9	16
26	.81	3.85	4 10	9	16
28	.86	3.90	5 2	10	17
30	.92	4.05	5 6	10	17
32	.97	4.30	5 10	11	19
34	1.04	4.80	6 2	11	19
36	1.08	5.00	6 6	12	21

PANTRY CHECK RAIL WINDOWS.

Four Lights, 1⅜ Inch Thick.

One Light Wide.

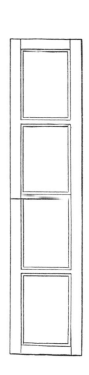

Size of Glass.	Price, Open.	Price, Glazed.	Size of Opening.	Weight Open.	Weight Glazed.
12 x 14	.85	3.85	1 4⅛ x 5 2	7	17
16	.96	4.25	5 10	8	18
18	1.07	4.95	6 6	9	20

All Check Rail Windows plowed and bored.

For Sash extras see pages 44 to 47.

BENT OR SWELL FACE WINDOWS.

For Square Head Open Sash or Windows Bent or Swell Face add to net price of Sash of same size or thickness, as follows: For sash or windows 3 ft. 4 in. wide or under if radius is 8 feet or less for single one-light sash $1.50 net; for two-light windows $3.00 net. For sash or windows wider than 3 ft. 4 in. and not wider than 6 ft. for single one-light sash add $2.00 net, and for two-light windows $4.00 net. If radius is greater than 8 ft. deduct 20 per cent from above figures.

TRANSOMS.

One and two lights, 1⅜ in. thick.

 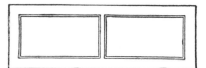

Size of Opening.	Price, Open.	Price, Glazed. Two Light.	Price, Glazed. One Light.	One Light, Glazed. Double Strength.	Weight, Glazed, S. S.	Weight, Glazed, D. S.
2- 6 x 10	$0.47		$1.65		6	
12	.47		1.85		6	
14	.47		1.95		6	
16	.50		2.15		6½	
18	.56		2.40		6½	
20	.63		2.80		7	
2- 8 x 10	.50		1.75		6	
12	.50		1.95		6	
14	.50		2.05		6½	
16	.53		2.25		6½	
18	.57		2.55		7	
20	.63		2.85		7	
22	.69		3.15		8	
24	.75		3.40		8	
2-10 x 14	.51		2.10		6½	
16	.57		2.45		1½	
18	.60		2.70		7	
20	.64		2.95		7	
22	.70		3.20		8	
24	.76		3.55		8	
3- 0 x 14	.57		2.40		6½	
16	.60		2.65		7	
18	.64		2.95		7½	
20	.71		3.25		8	
22	.77		3.50		8	
24	.83		4.00		9	
3- 6 x 14	.65	$2.70	2.75	$3.40	9	10
16	.68	2.95	3.00	3.75	9	10
18	.74	3.25	3.40	4.25	9½	10½
20	.79	3.65	3.75	4.75	10	11
22	.79	3.90	4.00	5.05	10	11
24	.86	4.40	4.40	5.50	11	12½
3- 8 x 14	.71	2.85	3.00	3.65	9	10
16	.77	3.20	3.40	4.20	9	10
18	.83	3.50	3.75	4.65	10	11
20	.89	3.95	4.30	5.35	10	11
22	.95	4.30	4 60	5.75	10	11½
24	1.01	4.80	5.00	6.30	11	12½
4- 0 x 14	.88	3.30		4.30	10	11
16	.93	3.65		4.75	10	11
18	.93	3.95		5.15	11	12
20	1.00	4.30		5.85	11	12

(Continued on next page.)

TRANSOMS.

One and two lights, 1⅜ in. thick.—*Continued.*

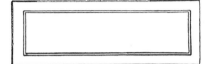 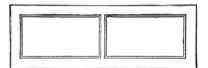

Size of Opening.	Price, Open.	Price, Glazed, Two Light.	Price, Glazed, One Light.	One Light, Glazed. Double Strength.	Weight, Glazed, S. S.	Weight, Glazed, D. S.
4- 0 x 22	$1.00	$4.75		$6.55	11	12
24	1.07	5.20		7.20	11	12½
4- 4 x 14	1.00	3.70		4.80	11	12
16	1.00	4.05		5.15	11	12
18	1.04	4.40		5.95	12	12
20	1.04	4.65		6.70	12	12
22	1.12	5.20		7.40	12	13
24	1.12	5.55		7.45	12	13
4- 6 x 14	1.04	4.00		5.50	11	12
16	1.04	4.30		5.65	12	13
18	1.07	4.60		6.35	11	12½
20	1.07	5.10		6.75	11	12½
22	1.15	5.45		7.45	12	13
24	1.15	5.80		8.65	12	13
5- 0 x 14	1.12	4.30		6.25	12	13½
16	1.12	4.60		6.60	12	13½
18	1.15	5.10		7.50	13	14½
20	1.15	5.50		8.05	11	12½
22	1.22	6.00		8.95	11	12½
24	1.22	6.25		9.95	12	13½
26	1.29	6.65		10.10	12	13½
5- 6 x 18	1.29	5.85		8.85	12	13½
20	1.29	6.20		9.15	13	14½
22	1.36	6.60		10.30	13	14½
24	1.36	7.30		10.35	14	15½
26	1.43	7.85		12.35	15	16½
28	1.43	8.10		12.40	12	13½
30	1.50	8.75		12.75	14	16
6- 0 x 20	1.43	6.80		9.90	15	17
22	1.50	7.30		11.10	16	18
24	1.50	7.65		12.55	17	19
26	1.57	8.45		12.70	18	20
28	1.57	8.95		15.15	19	23
30	1.65	10.40		15.30	20	24
32	1.72	10.55		17.45	25	39
34	1.86	11.70		17.70	26	33

For open transoms 1¾ inch thick add 50 per cent. to 1⅜ inch open list.
For glazed transoms 1¾ inches thick add 66⅔ per cent of open 1⅜ inch list to glazed list.
For prices on segment and circle tops and other extras see pages 44 to 47.
For special designs of transoms see page 31.

CELLAR SASH.

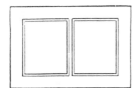 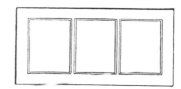

Two Lights.

Size of Glass.	Thickness.	Price Open.	Price Single Glazed.	Price Double Glazed.	Size of Opening.	Weight Open.	Weight Glazed.
10 x 12	1⅜	$0.43	$1.75	$2.75	2 1 x 16	4	6
14	"	.43	1.80	2.80	18	4	6
16	"	.50	2.10	3.30	20	4	6
18	"	.57	2.35	3.70	22	5	8
12 x 12	"	.50	2.00	3.15	2 5 x 16	5	8
14	"	.50	2.15	3.40	18	5	8
16	"	.57	2.40	3.80	20	5	8
18	"	.57	2.60	4.15	22	6	9
20	"	.65	2.90	4.60	24	6	9
22	"	.70	3.20	5.05	26	------	------
24	"	.75	3.50	5.60	28	------	------
26	"	.82	3.80	6.05	30	------	------
28	"	.90	4.05	6.35	32	------	------
14 x 16	"	.65	2.80	4.40	2 9 x 20	5	8
18	"	.65	2.95	4.70	22	5	8
20	"	.72	3.20	5.05	24	6	11
22	"	.72	3.45	5.50	26	6	11
24	"	.79	3.75	5.95	28	6	12

Three Lights.

Size of Glass.	Thickness.	Price Open	Price Single Glazed.	Price Double Glazed.	Size of Opening.	Weight Open.	Weight Glazed.
7 x 9	1⅛	$0.43	$1.60	$2.50	2 1 x 13	4	6
8 x 10	"	.43	1.75	2.75	2 4 x 14	4	6
12	"	50	2.00	3.10	16	4	6
9 x 12	"	.50	2.05	3.20	2 7 x 16	4	7
13	"	.50	2.15	3.40	17	4	7
14	"	.50	2.20	3 50	18	5	8
16	"	.57	2.50	3.95	20	5	8
10 x 12	"	.50	2.15	3.40	2 10 x 16	5	8
14	"	.57	2.45	3.85	18	5	8
16	"	.57	2.75	4.40	20	5	8
12 x 12	"	.57	2.55	4.05	3 4 x 16	6	9
14	"	.65	2.95	4.70	18	6	10
16	"	.65	3.10	4.95	20	6	10

For open 3-light cellar sash made 1⅜-inch thick, add 15 per cent to 1⅛-inch open list.

For glazed 3-light cellar sash made 1⅜-inch thick, add 20 per cent of 1⅛-inch open list to 1⅛ in. glazed list   For sash extras see pages 44 to 47.

BARN SASH.

Four Light.

Size of Glass.	Thickness.	Price Open.	Price Glazed.
8 x 10	1⅛	$0.43	$1.95
9 x 12	"	.50	2.35
14	"	.50	2.50
10 x 12	"	.50	2.45
14	"	.57	2.80
16	"	.57	3.15
12 x 14	"	.65	3.40
16	"	.65	3.60

Six Light.

7 x 9	1⅛	$0.60	$2.65
8 x 10	"	.63	2.95
10 x 12	"	.78	3.85

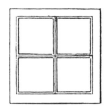

STALL SASH.

One Light.

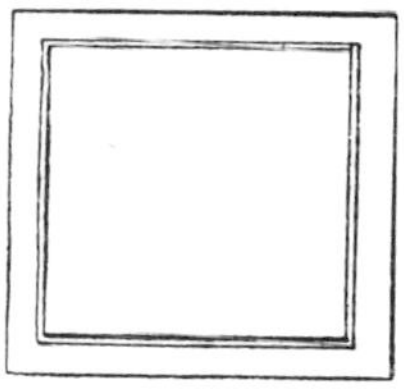

Size of Glass.	Thickness.	Price Open.	Price Glazed.
8 x 10	1⅛	$0.35	$1.15
10 x 12	"	.43	1.45
14	"	.50	1.60
12 x 16	"	.57	1.95

HOT BED SASH.

Made for 7-inch glass.

Size of Opening.	Thickness.	Price Open.	Price Glazed.
3 0 x 6 0	1⅜	$2.30	$8.55
3 0 x 6 0	1¾	3.45	10.25

For 8 inch glass.

3 4 x 6 0	1⅜	$2.40	$9.05
3 4 x 6 0	1¾	3.60	10.85

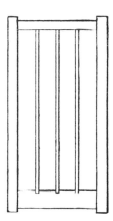

ATTIC SASH.

Three Inch Bottom Rail.

Size of Glass.	Thickness.	Price Open.	Price Glazed.
18 x 20	1⅜	$0.65	$2.70
20 x 20	"	.68	2.95
24	"	.70	3.20
24 x 24	"	.72	3.60
28	"	.77	3.95

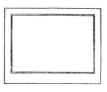

COTTAGE FRONT CHECK RAIL WINDOWS.

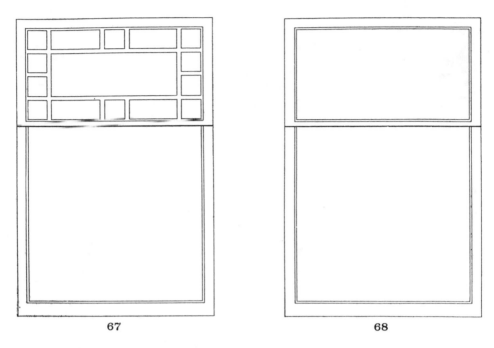

67　　　　　　　　68

COTTAGE FRONT SINGLE SASH.

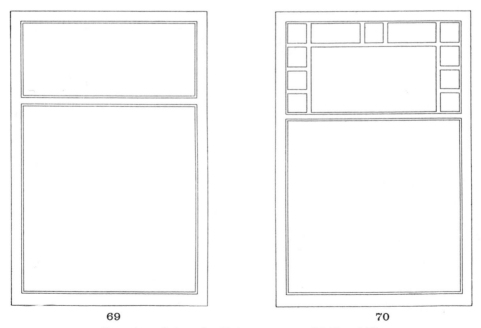

69　　　　　　　　70

For prices of above in all sizes, see pages 25, 26 and 27.

COTTAGE FRONT SASH and TRANSOMS.

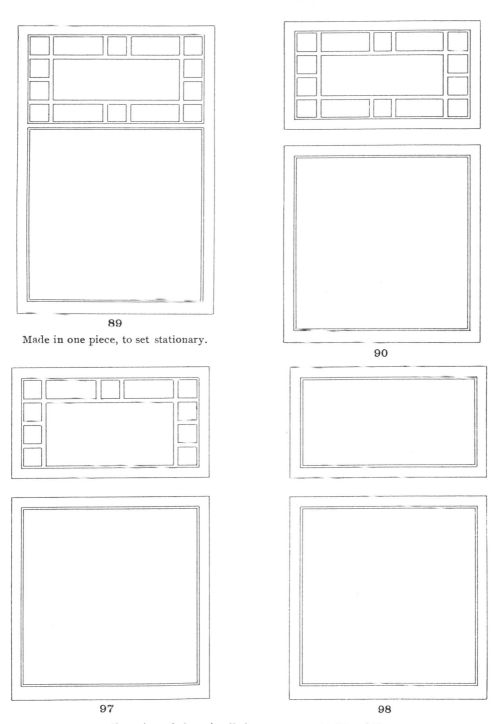

89

Made in one piece, to set stationary.

90

97

98

For prices of above in all sizes, see pages 26, 27 and 28.

COTTAGE FRONT CHECK RAIL WINDOWS.

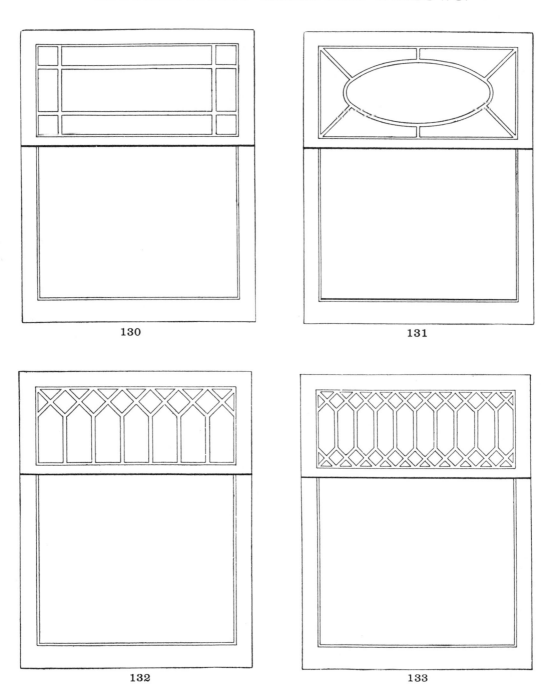

130

131

132

133

For prices of above in all sizes, see pages 26, 27 and 28

PRICES ON COTTAGE FRONT SASH and WINDOWS.

SIZE.	Top Light.	Bottom Light.	No. 67—1⅜		No. 68—1⅜		No. 69—1⅜	
			Open.	Glazed.	Open.	Glazed.	Open.	Glazed.
3- 8 x 5- 2	40 x 16	40 x 40	$3.72	$18.70	$2.22	$16.00	$2.55	$16.60
5- 6	40 x 16	40 x 44	3.72	20.75	2.22	18.05	2.55	18.65
5-10	40 x 16	40 x 48	3.72	21.35	2.22	18.65	2.55	19.25
6- 2	40 x 18	40 x 50	3.80	21.80	2.30	19.10	2 65	19.70
3-10 x 5- 2	42 x 16	42 x 40	3.83	20.95	2.33	18.25	2.68	18.90
5- 6	42 x 16	42 x 44	3.83	22.60	2.33	19.90	2.68	20.50
5 10	42 x 16	42 x 48	3.83	22.65	2.33	19.95	2 68	20.55
6- 2	42 x 20	42 x 48	3.92	23.65	2.42	20.95	2.78	21.60
4- 0 x 5- 2	44 x 16	44 x 40	3.95	22.05	2.45	19.35	2 82	20.00
5- 6	44 x 16	44 x 44	3.95	23.70	2.45	21.00	2.82	21.65
5-10	44 x 18	44 x 46	3 95	24.30	2.45	21.60	2.82	22.25
6- 2	44 x 18	44 x 50	4.04	28.40	2.54	25.70	2.93	26.40
6- 6	44 x 22	44 x 50	4.09	29.55	2.59	26.85	2 98	27.55
4- 4 x 5- 2	48 x 16	48 x 40	4.21	24.35	2.71	21.65	3 12	22.35
5- 6	48 x 18	48 x 42	4.21	25.85	2 71	23 15	3.12	23.85
5-10	48 x 18	48 x 46	4.21	29.75	2.71	27.05	3.12	27.80
6- 2	48 x 18	48 x 50	4.28	32.50	2 78	29.80	3.20	30.55
6- 6	48 x 20	48 x 52	4.34	32.60	2.84	29.90	3.27	30.70
4- 6 x 5- 2	50 x 16	50 x 40	4.21	24.95	2.71	22.25	3.12	22.95
5- 6	50 x 16	50 x 44	4.21	29.90	2.71	27.20	3.12	27.90
5-10	50 x 16	50 x 48	4.21	32.50	2.71	29.80	3.12	30.55
6- 2	50 x 18	50 x 50	4.28	33 10	2.78	30.40	3.20	31.15
6- 6	50 x 22	50 x 50	4.34	34.30	2.84	31.60	3.27	32.35
4- 8 x 5- 2	52 x 16	52 x 40	4.44	29 55	2.94	26.85	3.38	27.65
5- 6	52 x 18	52 x 42	4 44	31.35	2.94	28.65	3.38	29.45
5-10	52 x 18	52 x 46	4.44	34.00	2.94	31.30	3.38	32.10
6- 2	52 x 20	52 x 48	4.53	35.25	3.03	32.55	3.48	33.35
6- 6	52 x 20	52 x 52	4.57	36.80	3 07	34.10	3.53	34 90
5- 0 x 5- 6	56 x 16	56 x 44	4 68	35.55	3.18	32.85	3.66	33.70
5-10	56 x 16	56 x 48	4.68	37.00	3.18	34.30	3.66	35.20
6- 2	56 x 20	56 x 48	4.77	38 75	3 27	36.05	3 76	30 95
6- 6	56 x 20	56 x 52	4.82	41.20	3.32	38.50	3.82	39.40
7- 2	56 x 24	56 x 56	4.97	49.15	3.47	46.45	3.99	47.40

All Cottage Front Sash and Windows are glazed with D. S. glass.   If glazed with white chipped, enameled or colored glass (any color except Ruby) add 40 cents per square foot of glass measure to glazed list.   If Ruby, add 70 cents per square foot to glazed list.

For prices of 1¾-inch sash and windows, see sash extras page, 44 to 47.

PRICES ON COTTAGE FRONT SASH and WINDOWS.

Size	Top Light.	Bottom Light.	No. 70—1⅜.		No. 89—1⅜.		No. 130—1⅜.	
			Open.	Glazed.	Open.	Glazed.	Open.	Glazed.
3- 8 x 5- 2	40 x 16	40 x 40	$3.75	$18.75	$4.05	$19.30	$3.12	$17.65
5- 0	40 x 16	40 x 44	3.75	20.80	4.05	21.35	3.12	19.65
5-10	40 x 16	40 x 48	3.75	21.40	4.05	21.95	3.12	20.25
6- 2	40 x 18	40 x 50	3.85	21.85	4.15	22.40	3.20	20.70
3-10 x 5- 2	42 x 16	42 x 40	3.88	21.05	4.18	21.60	3.23	19.85
5- 6	42 x 16	42 x 44	3.88	22.65	4.18	23.20	3.23	21.50
5-10	42 x 16	42 x 48	3.88	22.70	4.18	23.25	3.23	21.55
6- 2	42 x 20	42 x 48	3.98	23.75	4.28	24.30	3.32	22.55
4- 0 x 5- 2	44 x 16	44 x 40	4.02	22.15	4.32	22.70	3.35	20.95
5- 6	44 x 16	44 x 44	4.02	23.80	4.32	24.35	3.35	22.60
5-10	44 x 18	44 x 46	4.02	24.40	4.32	24.95	3.35	23.20
6- 2	44 x 18	44 x 50	4.13	28.55	4.43	29.10	3.44	27.30
6- 6	44 x 22	44 x 50	4.18	29.70	4.48	30.25	3.49	28.45
4- 4 x 5- 2	48 x 16	48 x 40	4.32	24.55	4.62	25.05	3.61	23.25
5- 6	48 x 18	48 x 42	4.32	26.05	4.62	26.55	3.61	24.75
5-10	48 x 18	48 x 46	4.32	29.95	4.62	30.50	3.61	28.65
6- 2	48 x 18	48 x 50	4.40	32.75	4.70	33.25	3.68	31.45
6- 6	48 x 20	48 x 52	4.47	32.85	4.77	33.40	3.74	31.55
4- 6 x 5- 2	50 x 16	50 x 40	4.32	25.15	4.62	25.65	3.61	23.85
5- 6	50 x 16	50 x 44	4.32	30.10	4.62	30.60	3.61	28.80
5-10	50 x 16	50 x 48	4.32	32.70	4.62	33.25	3.61	31.45
6- 2	50 x 18	50 x 50	4.40	33 35	4.70	33.85	3.68	32.05
6- 6	50 x 22	50 x 50	4.47	34.55	4.77	35.05	3.74	33.20
4- 8 x 5- 2	52 x 16	52 x 40	4.58	29.80	4.88	30.35	3.84	28.45
5- 6	52 x 18	52 x 42	4.58	31.60	4.88	32.15	3.84	30.30
5-10	52 x 18	52 x 46	4.58	34.25	4.88	34.80	3.84	32.90
6- 2	52 x 20	52 x 48	4.68	35 50	4.98	36.05	3.93	34.15
6- 6	52 x 20	52 x 52	4.73	37.10	5.03	37.60	3.97	35.70
5- 0 x 5- 6	56 x 16	56 x 44	4.86	35.85	5.16	36.40	4.08	34.45
5-10	56 x 16	56 x 48	4.86	37.35	5.16	37.90	4.08	35.95
6- 2	56 x 20	56 x 48	4.96	39.10	5.26	39.65	4.17	37.65
6- 6	56 x 20	56 x 52	5.02	41.55	5.32	42.10	4 22	40.15
7- 2	56 x 24	56 x 56	5.19	49.55	5.49	50.10	4.37	48.10

All Cottage Front Sash and Windows are glazed with D. S. glass. If glazed with white chipped, enameled or colored glass (any color except Ruby) add 40 cents per square foot of glass measure to glazed list. If Ruby, add 70 cents per square foot to glazed list.

For prices of 1¾-inch sash and windows, see sash extras Nos. 95 and 96, page 47.

PRICES ON COTTAGE FRONT SASH and WINDOWS.

SIZE.	Top Light.	Bottom Light	No. 131—1⅜		No. 132—1⅜		No. 133—1⅜	
			Open.	Glazed.	Open.	Glazed.	Open.	Glazed.
3- 8 x 5- 2	40 x 16	40 x 40	$6.92	$24.50	$6.62	$23.95	$12.62	$34.75
5- 6	40 x 16	40 x 44	6.92	26.50	6.62	25.95	12.62	36.75
5-10	40 x 16	40 x 48	6.92	27.10	6.62	26.55	12.62	37.35
6- 2	40 x 18	40 x 50	7.00	27.55	6.70	27.00	12.70	37.80
3-10 x 5- 2	42 x 16	42 x 40	7.03	26.70	6.73	26.15	12.73	36.95
5- 6	42 x 16	42 x 44	7.03	28.35	6.73	27.80	12.73	38.60
5-10	42 x 16	42 x 48	7.03	28.40	6.73	27.85	12.73	38.65
6- 2	42 x 20	42 x 48	7.12	29.40	6 82	28.85	12.82	39.65
4- 0 x 5- 2	44 x 16	44 x 40	7.15	27.80	6.85	27 25	12.85	38.05
5- 6	44 x 16	44 x 44	7.15	29.45	6.85	28.90	12.85	39.65
5-10	44 x 18	44 x 46	7.15	30.05	6.85	29.50	12.85	40.30
6 2	44 x 18	44 x 50	7.24	34.15	6.94	33.60	12.94	44.40
6- 6	44 x 22	44 x 50	7.29	35 30	6.99	34 75	12.99	45.55
4- 4 x 5- 2	48 x 16	48 x 40	7.41	30.10	7.11	29.55	13 11	40.35
5- 6	48 x 18	48 x 42	7.41	31.60	7.11	31.05	13 11	41.85
5-10	48 x 18	48 x 46	7.41	35 50	7.11	34.95	13.11	45.75
6- 2	48 x 18	48 x 50	7.48	38.25	7.18	37.75	13.18	48.55
6- 6	48 x 20	48 x 52	7.54	38.40	7.24	37.85	13.24	48.65
4- 6 x 5- 2	50 x 16	50 x 40	7.41	30.70	7.11	30.15	13.11	40.95
5- 6	50 x 16	50 x 44	7.41	35.05	7.11	35.10	13.11	45.90
5-10	50 x 16	50 x 48	7.41	38.30	7.11	37.75	13.11	48.55
6- 2	50 x 18	50 x 50	7.48	38.85	7.18	38.35	13.18	49.15
6- 6	50 x 22	50 x 50	7.54	40.05	7.24	39.50	13.24	50.30
4- 8 x 5- 2	52 x 16	52 x 40	7.64	35 30	7.34	34.75	13.34	45.55
5- 6	52 x 18	52 x 42	7.64	37.10	7.34	36.60	13.34	47.40
5-10	52 x 18	52 x 46	7.64	39.75	7.34	39.20	13.34	50.00
6- 2	52 x 20	52 x 48	7.73	41.00	7.43	40.45	13.43	51.25
6- 6	52 x 20	52 x 52	7.77	42.55	7.47	42.00	13.47	52.80
5- 0 x 5- 6	56 x 16	56 x 44	7.88	41.30	7.58	40.75	13.58	51.55
5-10	56 x 16	56 x 48	7.88	42.75	7.58	42.25	13 58	53.05
6- 2	56 x 20	56 x 48	7.97	44.50	7.67	43.95	13.67	54.75
6- 6	56 x 20	56 x 52	8.02	46.95	7.72	46 45	13.72	57.25
7- 2	56 x 24	56 x 56	8.17	54.95	7.87	54.40	13.87	65.20

All Cottage Front Sash and Windows are glazed with D. S. glass. If glazed with white chipped, enameled or colored glass (any color except Ruby) add 40 cents per square foot of glass measure to glazed list. If Ruby, add 70 cents per square foot to glazed list.

For prices of 1¾-inch sash and windows, see sash extras No. 95 and 96, page 47.

COTTAGE FRONT SASH.

One Light, 1⅜ inch.

Size of Sash	Size of Glass	Price Open	Price Glazed D. S.
3- 8 x 3-10	40 x 40	$1.74	$12.00
4- 2	44	1.77	14.10
4- 6	48	1.81	14.80
4-10	52	1.86	18.45
5- 2	56	1.92	20.95
5- 6	60	1.99	21.10
4- 0 x 3-10	44 x 40	1.98	15.10
4- 2	44	2.01	16.75
4- 6	48	2.05	20.75
4-10	52	2.10	23.50
5- 2	56	2.16	23.60
5- 6	60	2.22	25.20
5-10	64	2.28	27.65
4- 4 x 3-10	48 x 40	2.21	16.40
4- 2	44	2.24	21.40
4- 6	48	2.28	24.10
4-10	52	2.33	24.20
5- 2	56	2.39	25.80
5- 6	60	2.45	28.25
5-10	64	2.51	30.70
4- 6 x 3-10	50 x 40	2.32	17.20
4- 2	44	2.35	22.20
4- 6	48	2.39	24.40
4-10	52	2.44	26.50
5- 2	56	2.50	28 95
5- 6	60	2.57	29.10
5-10	64	2.63	31.50
5- 0 x 4- 2	56 x 44	2.69	26.05
4- 6	48	2 73	27.60
4-10	52	2.78	30.05
5- 2	56	2.84	36 60
5- 6	60	2.91	36.75
5-10	64	2.97	36.85

For Open Transom No. 90, Front Sash, 1⅜ inch thick, add $1.50 to price of one Light Open Transom of same size. If glazed with plain glass, add $2.00 to price of one light Transom of same size glazed with plain glass.

For Open Transom No. 97, Front Sash, 1⅜ inch thick, add $1.20 to price of a one light Open Transom of same size. If glazed with plain glass, add $1.60 to price of a one light Transom of same size glazed with plain glass.

If Transom No. 90 and No. 97 are glazed with White Chipped, Enameled or colored glass (any color except Ruby) add 40 cents per square foot of glass measure to glazed list. If Ruby, add 70 cents list per square foot to glazed list.

For prices of 1¾ inch sash, see sash extras pages 44 to 47.

GLAZED STORM SASH.

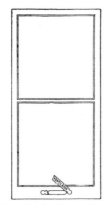

Two-Light Storm Sash.
Bottom rail ventilator open.

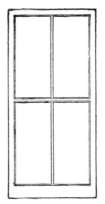

Four-Light Storm Sash.

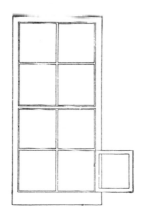

Eight-Light Storm Sash,
Swing light ventilator.

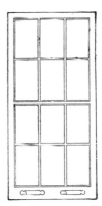

Twelve-Light Storm Sash.
Double ventilator.

STORM SASH.

1⅛-inch Storm Sash, same price as 1⅜-inch Check Rail Window same opening.

1⅜-inch Open Storm Sash, add 15 per cent. to 1⅜ Check Rail Open list. For glazed add 20 per cent. to 1⅜ Check Rail Open list.

For Ventilators in top or bottom rail, add 10 cents net.

For Swing Light, add 40 cents net.

PLEASE NOTICE.

Our regular Storm Sash are made with 2¼-inch stiles. 3-inch stiles, when so specified, will be furnished without extra charge. We can make one or more Ventilators in bottom rail of each sash as per cuts above.

IF VENTILATORS ARE WANTED, ORDER MUST SO STATE.
PLACE YOUR ORDER FOR STORM SASH EARLY.

149

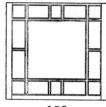

150

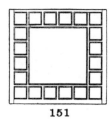

151

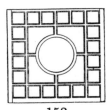

152

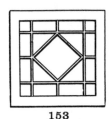

153

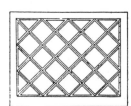

154

QUEEN ANNE SASH.

149. For open, 1⅜ inch thick add 12 cents list for each marginal light to price of a one-light open sash of same size. If glazed with plain glass add 17 cents list for each marginal light to price of a one-light sash of same size, glazed with plain glass.

150. For open, 1⅜ inch thick add $1.85 to half the list price of a two-light window, of similar size. For glazed, add $2.55 to glazed list.

151. For open, 1⅜ inch thick add 12 cents list for each marginal light to price of a one-light open sash of same size. If glazed with plain glass add 17 cents list for each marginal light to price of a one-light sash of same size, glazed with plain glass.

152. For open, 1⅜ inch thick add $7.45 to half the list price of a two-light window of similar size. For glazed add $9.95 to glazed list.

153. For open, 1⅜ inch thick add $2.80 to half the list price of a two-light window of similar size. For glazed, add $3.80 to glazed list.

154. For open, 1⅜ inch thick add 24 cents list for each light to price of one-light open sash of same size. If glazed with plain glass add 36 cents list for each light to price of a one-light sash of same size, glazed with plain glass.

For prices on sash 1¾ inch thick, see sash extras Nos. 95 and 96, page 47.

Prices on Queen Anne Sash are for less than stock quantities (Note "a," Sash extras.)

If above sash are glazed with white chipped, enameled or colored glass (any color except ruby) add 40 cents per square foot of glass measure to glazed list. If ruby add 70 cents per square foot to glazed list.

QUEEN ANNE TRANSOMS.

155. For open, $1\frac{3}{8}$ inch thick, add 24 cents list for each light to price of one light open transom of same size. If glazed with plain glass add 36 cents list for each light to price of a one-light transom same size, glazed with plain glass

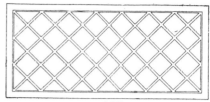

155

156. For open, $1\frac{3}{8}$ inch thick, add $6.00 to list price of $1\frac{3}{8}$ inch one-light transom of same size. For glazed, add $8.05 to glazed list.

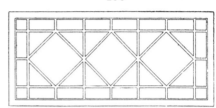

156

157. For open, $1\frac{3}{8}$ inch thick, add 12 cents list for each marginal light to price of a one-light open transom of same size. If glazed with plain glass add 17 cents list for each light to price of a one-light transom of same size, glazed with plain glass.

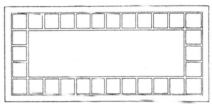

157

158. For open, $1\frac{3}{8}$ inch thick, add 24 cents list for each light to price of a one-light open transom of same size. If glazed with plain glass add 36 cents list for each light to price of a one-light transom of same size, glazed with plain glass.

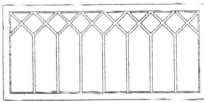

158

159. For open, $1\frac{3}{8}$ inch thick, add 24 cents list for each light to price of one-light open transom of same size. If glazed with plain glass add 36 cents list for each light to price of a one-light transom of same size, glazed with plain glass.

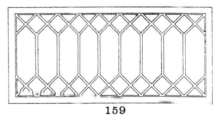

159

160. For open $1\frac{3}{8}$ inches thick, add $1.10 to list price of one-light transom of same size. For glazed, add $1.45 to glazed list.

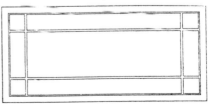

160

For open transoms, $1\frac{3}{4}$ inches thick, add 50 per cent to list of $1\frac{3}{8}$ open transoms.
For glazed transoms, $1\frac{3}{4}$ inches thick, add $66\frac{2}{3}$ per cent of $1\frac{3}{8}$ open list to glazed list.
If above transoms are glazed with white chipped or colored glass (any color except ruby) add 40 cents per square foot of glass measure to glazed list. If ruby, add 70 cents per square foot to glazed list.
Prices on Queen Anne transoms are for less than stock quantities. (Note "a," Sash Extras.)

TRANSOMS.

SEGMENT, CIRCLE TOP and GOTHIC
GLAZED PLAIN GLASS.

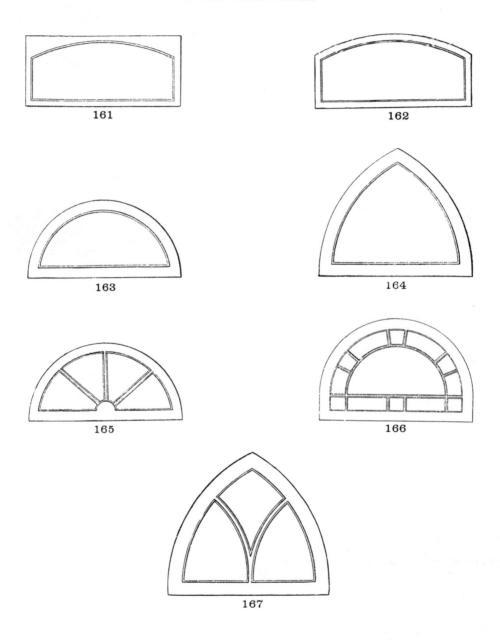

161

162

163

164

165

166

167

For prices see sash extras, pages 44 to 47. Paragraph 1 to 40.

FRONT WINDOW with LEADED ART GLASS in TOP SASH.

Design A.

(Made in 2 pieces.)

Write us for prices, specifying size wanted.   Regular check rail window.

FRONT WINDOW with LEADED ART GLASS in TOP SASH.

Design B.

(Made in 2 pieces.)

Write us for prices, specifying size wanted.

LANDSCAPE SASH with LEADED ART GLASS in TOP LIGHT.

Design C.

(Made in 1 piece.)

Write us for prices, specifying size wanted.

LANDSCAPE SASH with LEADED ART GLASS in TOP LIGHT

Design D.

(Made in 1 piece.)

Write us for prices, specifying size wanted.

TRIPLE FRONT WINDOWS.

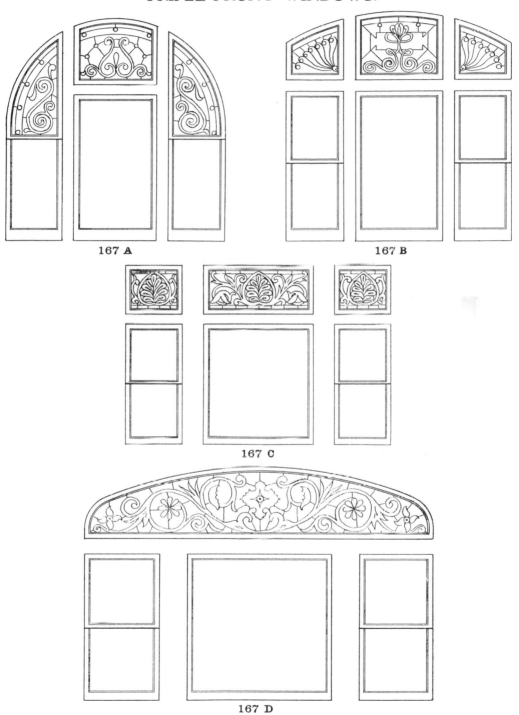

167 A   167 B

167 C

167 D

Send for prices, giving outside measures and thickness of each check rail window, single sash and transoms; and when ordering also give width of mullions, thickness of transom bar in frame, and if circular or segment top, the radius.

QUEEN ANNE WINDOWS.

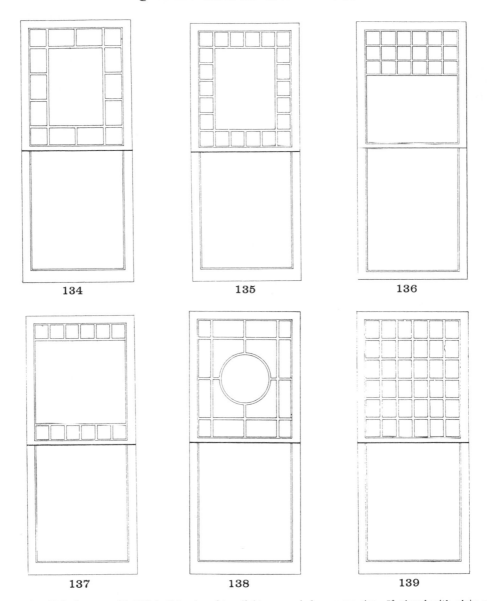

134   135   136

137   138   139

No. 134. 1⅜-inch open, add $1.70 to list price of two-light open window, same size. If glazed with plain glass add $2.30.

No. 135. For 1⅜-inch open, add 12 cents list for each marginal light to price of two-light open window same size. If glazed with plain glass add 17 cents list for each marginal light to price of two-light window, same size, glazed with plain glass.

No. 136. For 1⅜-inch open, add 12 cents list for each marginal light to price of two-light open window, same size If glazed with plain glass add 17 cents list for each marginal light to price of two-light window, same size, glazed with plain glass.

No. 137. For 1⅜-inch open, add 12 cents list for each marginal light to price of two-light open window, same size. If glazed with plain glass add 17 cents list for each marginal light to price of two-light window, same size, glazed with plain glass.

No. 138. 1⅜-inch open, add $6.25 to list price of two-light window, same size, For glazed add $8.35.

No. 139. 1⅜-inch open, add 12 cents list for each light to price of two-light open window of same size. If glazed with plain glass add 17 cents list for each light to price of a two-light window, same size, glazed with plain glass.

QUEEN ANNE WINDOWS.

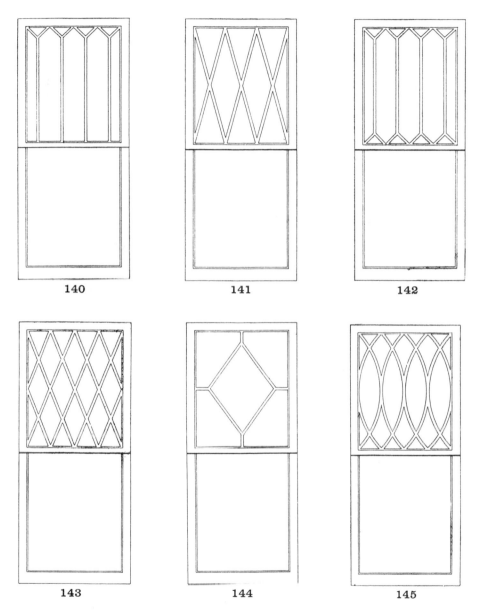

No. 140. For 1⅜-inch open, add 24 cents list for each light to price of two-light open window of same size. If glazed with plain glass add 36 cents list for each light to price of a two-light window same size, glazed with plain glass.

No. 141. For 1⅜-inch open, add 24 cents list for each light to price of two-light open window of same size. If glazed with plain glass add 36 cents list for each light to price of a two-light window same size, glazed with plain glass.

No. 142. For 1⅜-inch open, add 24 cents list for each light to price of two-light open window of same size. If glazed with plain glass add 36 cents list for each light to price of a two-light window same size, glazed with plain glass.

No. 143. For 1⅜-inch open, add 24 cents list for each light to price of two-light open window of same size. If glazed with plain glass add 36 cents list for each light to price of a two-light window, same size, glazed with plain glass.

No. 144. For 1⅜-inch open windows add $1.75 to list of two-light windows of same size. If glazed, add $2.35 to glazed list.

No. 145. For 1⅜-inch open, add $2.10 for each segment bar to list of two-light open window of same size. If glazed with plain glass add $3.00 for each segment bar to list of two-light window, same size, glazed with plain glass.

QUEEN ANNE WINDOWS.

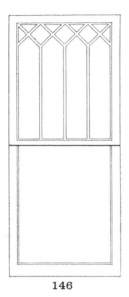

146

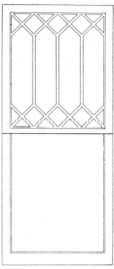

147

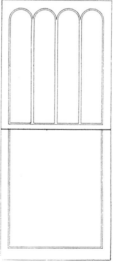

148

No. 146. For 1⅜-inch open add 24 cents list for each light to prices of two-light open window of same size.   If glazed with plain glass add 36 cents list for each light to price of a two-light window, same size, glazed with plain glass.

No. 147. For 1⅜-inch open, add 24 cents list for each light to price of two-light open window of same size.   If glazed with plain glass add 36 cents list for each light to price of a two-light window, same size, glazed with plain glass.

No. 148. For 1⅜-inch open, add 80 cents list for each light to price of two-light open window of same size.   If glazed with plain glass add $1.10 list for each light to price of a two-light window, same size, glazed with plain glass.

For open windows 1¾ inches thick, add 50 per cent. to list of 1⅜-inch open windows.

For glazed windows 1¾ inches thick, add 66⅔ per cent. to list of open 1⅜ open·list to glazed list.

If above windows are glazed with white chipped ,enameled or colored glass (any color except Ruby) add 40 cents per square foot of glass measure to glazed list.   If Ruby add 70 cents per square foot to glazed list.

GOTHIC and PEAK HEAD WINDOWS.

168	169	170
171	172	172½

For prices of above windows see sash extras, pages 44 to 47.

For 1¾ inch open windows, like above, add 50 per cent to above prices.

For 1¾ inch glazed windows add 66⅔ per cent of 1⅜ open list to glazed list.

If above windows are glazed with enamel, white chipped or colored cathedral glass, add 70 cents. per square foot to list price of same window glazed with plain glass.

GABLE FRAMES and SASH.

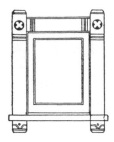

Sash No. 173
Frame No. 3047

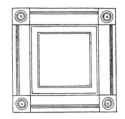

Sash No. 174
Frame No. 3048

Sash No. 175
Frame No. 3049

Sash No. 176
Frame No. 3050

Sash No. 177
Frame No. 3051

Sash No. 178
Frame No. 3053

List Price, Sash 1⅜ Inches Thick and Frame.

SASH No.	Size of Opening.			Price Open.	Price Glazed. Plain.	FRAME No.	4 Inch Studing. Price
173	2	0 x 2	5	$0.70	$3.20	3047	$3.00
174	2	0 x 2	5	.70	3.20	3048	2.50
175	2	0 x 2	0	4.18	7.65	3049	4.20
176	2	0 x 2	5	2.45	5.55	3050	3.80
177	2	0 x 2	0	6.25	9.50	3051	4.20
178	2	0 x 2	5	1.55	4.35	3053	5.00

Sash open and glazed subject to sash discount only.

Frame price subject to special discounts.

We ship above sash glazed with plain glass unless order calls for colored.

Add 40 cents per square foot extra to list price if glazed colored glass.

GABLE FRAMES and SASH.

Sash No. 179
Frame No. 3179

Sash No. 180
Frame No. 3182

Sash No. 181
Frame No. 3181

Sash No. 182
Frame No. 3180

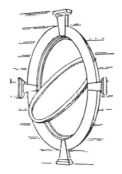

Sash No. 183
Frame No. 3183

Sash No. 184
Frame No. 3184

List Prices, Sash 1⅜ Inches Thick and Frame.

SASH No.	Size of Opening.	Price Open.	Price Glazed Plain	FRAME No.	4 Inch Studing. Price.
179	2 0 x 1 2	$7.00	$10.00	3179	$6.25
180	2 0 x 2 2	9.00	17.50	3180	4.00
181	2 0 x 2 0	6.00	7.25	3181	7.50
182	1 8 x 2 8	3.65	7.50	3182	5.25
183	1 8 x 2 8	4.90	9.30	3183	5.60
184	1 8 x 2 8	9.00	17.75	3184	5.60

Sash open and glazed subject to sash discount only.

Frame price subject to special discounts.

We ship above sash glazed with plain glass unless order calls for colored.

Add 40 cents per square foot extra to list price if glazed colored glass.

SASH EXTRAS.

NOTE—(A). The term "stock quantities," wherever used in this list, means 5 or more Doors, and 10 or more Windows, Sash or Blinds, of one size, kind and quality.

NOTE—(B). Irregular and intermediate sizes, in stock quantities, same list as next larger listed size, both open and glazed. For less than stock quantities on sizes not listed, an extra 10 per cent will be charged.

NOTE—(C). Where no provision is made for price on quantities less than 10, use stock quantity price and add 10 per cent to the amount thus created.

	ADD TO LIST For 10 or More.	For Less Than 10

SEGMENT HEAD.

No. 1. For Segment Head Windows and Transoms, Fig. 3 and 4 and Nos. 161 and 162, 1⅜ inches thick, 3 feet 4 inches in width and under, open........$ 85 $1.00
No. 2. For the same, 1⅜ inches thick, glazed 1.15 1.40
No. 3. For the same, 1¾ inches thick, open 1.30 1.55
No. 4. For the same, 1¾ inches thick, glazed 1.75 2.10
No. 5. For Segment Head Windows and Transoms, Fig. 3 and 4 and No. 161 and 162, 1⅜ inches thick, over 3 feet 4 inches in width and not over 5 feet in width, open............ 1.45 1.75
No. 6. For the same, 1⅜ inches thick, glazed 1.95 2.35
No. 7. For the same, 1¾ inches thick, open 2.15 2.60
No. 8. For the same, 1¾ inches thick, glazed 2.90 3.50

CIRCLE HEAD.

No. 9. For Half Circle Head (inside and outside) Fig. 1, and No. 163, 1⅜ inches thick, 3 feet 4 ins. in width and under, open. 1.75 2.10
No. 10. For the same, 1⅜ inches thick, glazed 2.35 2.80
No. 11. For the same, 1¾ inches thick, open 2.60 3.10
No. 12. For the same, 1¾ inches thick, glazed 3.50 4.20
No. 13. For Half Circle Head (inside and outside), Fig. 1, and No. 163, 1⅜ inches thick, over 3 feet 4 inches in width and not over 5 feet in width, open 2.85 3.40
No. 14. For the same, 1⅜ inches thick, glazed 3.80 4.55
No. 15. For the same, 1¾ inches thick, open 4.30 5.15
No. 16. For the same, 1¾ inches thick, glazed 5.75 6.90

No. 17. For Half Circle Head (Circle outside and square inside) 1⅜ inches thick, 3 feet 4 inches in width and under, open 2.15 2.60
No. 18. For the same, 1⅜ inches thick, glazed 2.90 3.50
No. 19. For the same, 1¾ inches thick, open 3.25 3.90
No. 20. For the same, 1¾ inches thick, glazed 4.35 5.20
No. 21. For Half Circle Head (Circle outside and square inside) 1⅜ inches thick, over 3 feet 4 inches in width and not over 5 feet in width, open..... 4.00 4.80
No. 22. For the same, 1⅜ inches thick, glazed 5.35 6.40
No. 23. For the same, 1¾ inches thick, open 6.00 7.20
No. 24. For the same, 1¾ inches thick, glazed 8.00 9.60

GOTHIC AND PEAK HEAD.

No. 25. For Gothic and Peak Head Windows and Transoms No. 164, 168 and 171, 1⅜ inches thick, 3 feet 4 inches in width and under, open................ 1.75 2.10
No. 26. For the same, 1⅜ inches thick, glazed 2.35 2.80
No. 27. For the same, 1¾ inches thick, open 2.60 3.10
No. 28. For the same, 1¾ inches thick, glazed 3.50 4.20
No. 29. For Gothic and Peak Head Windows and Transoms No. 164, 168 and 171, 1⅜ inches thick, over 3 feet 4 inches and not over 5 feet in width, open.. 2.85 3.40
No. 30. For the same, 1⅜ inches thick, glazed 3.80 4.55
No. 31. For the same, 1¾ inches thick, open 4.30 5.15
No. 32. For the same, 1¾ inches thick, glazed 5.75 6.90

SASH EXTRAS—*Continued.*

	ADD TO LIST	
	For 10 or More.	For Less Than 10

No. 33. For Gothic and Peak Head Windows and Transoms No. 167, 169 and 172, 1⅜ inches thick, 3 feet 4 inches in width and under, open.............. 3.50   4.20

No. 34. For the same, 1⅜ inches thick, glazed 4.70   5.65

No. 35. For the same, 1¾ inches thick, open 5.25   6.30

No. 36. For the same, 1¾ inches thick, glazed 7.00   8.40

No. 37. For Gothic and Peak Head Windows and Transoms No. 167, 169 and 172, 1⅜ inches thick, over 3 feet 4 inches and not over 5 feet in width, open.. 5.75   6.90

No. 38. For the same, 1⅜ inches thick, glazed 7.70   9.25

No. 39. For the same, 1¾ inches thick, open 8.60 10.30

No. 40. For the same, 1¾ inches thick, glazed ....,.....11.50 13.80

LONGER THAN LIST.

No. 41. For open list on 1⅜-in. windows longer than listed sizes, add to the open list of longest windows of same description for each additional 4 inches in height or fraction thereof........ .25 list Note C

WIDER THAN LIST.

No. 42. For open list on 1⅜-inch 2-light windows wider than listed sizes, add to the open list of a 30-inch 2-light window of same height (see Rule 41) for each additional 4 inches in width or fraction thereof.. .25 list Note C

No. 43. For open list on 1⅜-inch 4-light windows wider than listed sizes, add to the open list of a 15-inch 4-light window of same height (see Rule 41) for each additional 4 inches in width or fraction thereof.. .25 list Note C

No. 44. For open list on 1⅜-inch 8-light windows, wider than listed sizes, add to the open list of a 14-inch 8-light window of same height (see Rule 41) for each additional 4 inches in width or fraction thereof.. .25 list Note C

No. 45. For open list on 1⅜-inch 12-light windows wider than listed sizes, add to the open list of a 12-inch 12-light window of same height (see Rule 41) for each additional 4 inches in width or fraction thereof.. .25 list Note C

COTTAGE FRONT WINDOWS.

No. 50. For Cottage Front Windows open, not otherwise provided for, make list according to Rule 42 plus an additional 10 per cent.

No. 51. For Bead Stops in Cottage Front Windows and Sash, per foot............. .02 list .02½

SINGLE SASH LIST.

No. 52. For list on 1⅜-inch Single Sash, open, with 2, 4, 8 or 12 lights of same glass sizes as listed windows, add to price of open windows, same size........ .15 list .20

For the same, glazed, add to price of Glazed Windows .... .20 list .25

No. 53. For list on 1⅜-inch Single Sash, open, with 1, 2, 4 or 6 lights of same glass sizes as listed windows, add to price of half window, open, same size .... .15 list .20

For the same, glazed, add to price of half window glazed .... .20 list .25

No. 54. To make Open Sash list on 1⅜-in. Transoms, Cellar, Barn, Attic and Stall Sash and other Single Sash containing 4 rectangular lights or less, not otherwise provided for in this list, figure the united inches (width and length added) of the outside glass measurement, when 70 united inches or less, per inch.... .01½ list .01¾

No. 55. For the same, when glass measurement is over 70 united inches and not over 100 united inches, per inch .... .02 list .02½

SASH EXTRAS—*Continued.*

	ADD TO LIST For 10 or More.	For Less Than 10

No. 56. For the same, when glass measurement exceeds 100 united inches, per inch. .02½ list .03

No. 57. For more than 4 lights in above sash add for each light .... .07 list Note C

No. 58. For Circle Sash add list for two half circles to the list of a Sash of the same size, as provided in Rules 52 to 57, and 9 to 24 inclusive.

FOLDING SASH LIST.

No. 59. For Folding Sash in pairs, figure each Sash as per Rules Nos. 52 to 57, and add if rabbeted .... .10 net .15

RECTANGULAR AND DIAMOND LIGHTS.

No. 60. For 1⅜-inch Open Sash or Windows with marginal or numerous rectangular lights containing 12 united inches or less, add for each light............. .10 list Note C

No. 62. For 1⅜-inch Open Sash or Windows, with marginal or numerous rectangular lights containing over 12 united inches, add for each light .... .07 list Note C

No. 64. For 1⅜-inch open marginal light windows, with Segment, Half Circle, Gothic or Peak Head, add twice amount shown by the rules for similar heads and for each marginal light.... .10 list Note C

No. 66. For open Windows and Sash 1⅜ in. thick made with diamond or irregular shaped lights formed by straight bars, add per light. .20 list Note C

WIDE STILES AND RAILS.

No. 68. For Stiles wider than 2¼ inches, for each ¼ inch or fraction thereof, add to list if open................ 5% 15%
If glazed, add of open list to glazed list.............. 7% 20%

No. 69. For Bottom Rails wider than 3⅜ inches and

	ADD TO LIST For 10 or More.	For Less Than 10

not over 4½ inches, add to list, if open............... .15 list Note C
Add to list if glazed...... .20 list Note C

No. 70. For 1½ inch check rails for 1⅜-inch check windows, add to list, if open .... .20 list Note C
Add to list, if glazed...... .27 list Note C

No. 71. For 1¾ inch check rails for 1¾-inch check windows, add to list, if open.. .30 list Note C
Add to list, if glazed...... .40 list Note C

ODD WIDTH GLASS.

No. 72. For Open Windows made for glass 11 inches wide, same price as 12 inch. Note C

No. 73. For Open Windows made for glass 13 or 13½ inches wide, same price as 14 inch .... Note C

O G LUGS.

No. 74. For O G Lugs, 1⅜ Windows, open, add to list for each sash with lugs.... .15 list Note C

No. 75. For the same 1⅜ inches thick, glazed, add to glazed list.............. .20 list Note C

OIL FINISH.

No. 76. For open Windows, Sash or Transoms, prepared for oil finish, add to open list .... 20% Note C

No. 77. For the same, glazed, add of the open to the glazed list .... 30% Note C

GLAZING.

No. 78. For glazing with AA glass, add 10 per cent to glazed list price.

No. 79. In figuring glazing of unlisted glazed sash with marginal or divided lights, either diamond, square, peak or otherwise, when glazed with sheet glass, figure as though the sash contained but one light single or double strength, as may be specified.

SASH EXTRAS—*Continued*.

15 AND 18 LIGHT WINDOWS.	ADD TO LIST	
	For 10 or More.	For Less Than 1
No. 80. For 15-light Windows, open or glazed, add to list of 12 light............	25%	Note C
No. 81. For 18-light Windows, open or glazed, add to list of 12 light............	50%	Note C

STORM SASH.

No. 82. 1⅛-inch Storm Sash, same price as 1⅜ Check Rail Windows, same opening.

No. 83. 1⅜-inch Open Storm Sash, add to 1⅜ Check Rail, open list............   15%   Note C

No. 84. For 1⅜-inch glazed Storm Sash, add of the open 1⅜ inch list to 1⅜ inch glazed Window list..   20%   Note C

No. 85. For Ventilators in top or bottom rail, add each.   .10 net   .12 net

No. 86. For Swing Light, add ....   .40 net   .50 net

No. 87. For 1⅛ in. Storm Sash made with 3 in. stiles, add ....   .05 net   .07

No. 88. For 1⅛ in. Storm Sash, with 3 in. O G stiles, add ....   .12 net   .15

No. 89. For 1⅛ in. Storm Sash, painted Black outside, add ....   .08 net   .12

STORE SASH.

No. 90. 3½ inch Stiles, 4½ inch bottom rail, per lineal foot 1⅜ inch list.........   .20

1¾ inch list..............   .30

No. 91. For price on Paneling, see under Store Doors.

THICKNESS.

	ADD TO LIST	
	For 10 or More.	For Less Than 10

No. 92. For 1⅛ inch 2 and 4-light Windows, plain rail, deduct from 1⅜ inch Check Rail open list..............   10%

No. 93. 1⅛ Check Rail Windows, same price as 1⅜-inch Check Rail Windows.   Note C

No. 94. 1⅜ inch Plain Rail Windows, same price as 1⅜-inch Check Rail Windows ....   Note C

No. 95. For price of Open Sash, Windows, Transoms or Sash Extras 1¾ in. thick, add to the 1⅜ in. open list ....   50%   Note C

No. 96. For price of Glazed Sash, Windows, Transoms, or Sash Extras, 1¾ inches thick, add, of the 1⅜ inch open list to the 1⅜ inch glazed list ....   66 2-3%   Note C

No. 97. For price of Open Sash, Windows, Transoms or Sash Extras, 2¼ inches thick, add to 1¾ inch open list ....   100%   Note C

For the same, glazed, add, of the open to the glazed list ....   133 1-3%   Note C

CIRCLE-FACE WINDOWS.

When ordering, give radius measured to outside of top sash, and say whether frames are made with square jambs like detail A, or radiating jambs like detail B.

A full size paper pattern of sill sent will prevent errors.

If made like detail B give distance measured straight across between jambs from outside edges of the top sash.

DETAIL A.

DETAIL B.

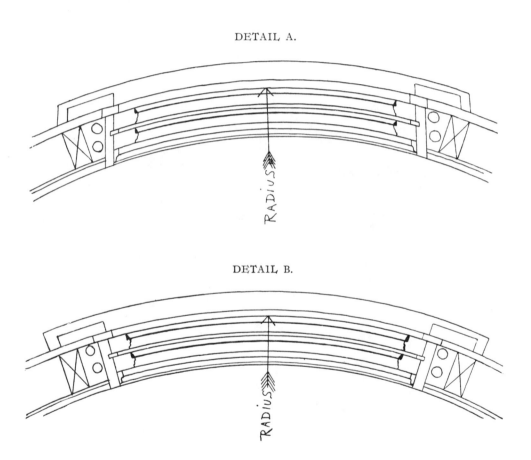

For Square Head Open Sash or Windows Bent or Swell Face add to net price of Sash of same size or thickness, as follows: For sash or windows 3 ft. 4 in. wide or under, if radius is 8 feet or less for single one light sash $1.50 net; for two-light windows $3.00 net. For sash or windows wider than 3 ft. 4 in. and not wider than 6 ft. for single one-light sash add $2.00 net, and for two-light windows $4.00 net. If radius is greater than 8 ft. deduct 20 per cent. from above figures.

WEATHER STRIPS.

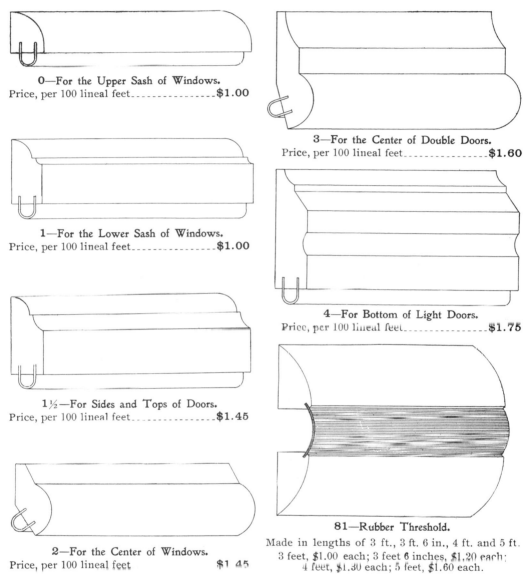

0—For the Upper Sash of Windows.
Price, per 100 lineal feet................$1.00

1—For the Lower Sash of Windows.
Price, per 100 lineal feet................$1.00

1½—For Sides and Tops of Doors.
Price, per 100 lineal feet................$1.45

2—For the Center of Windows.
Price, per 100 lineal feet $1 45

3—For the Center of Double Doors.
Price, per 100 lineal feet................$1.60

4—For Bottom of Light Doors.
Price, per 100 lineal feet................$1.75

81—Rubber Threshold.
Made in lengths of 3 ft., 3 ft. 6 in., 4 ft. and 5 ft.
3 feet, $1.00 each; 3 feet 6 inches, $1.20 each;
4 feet, $1.30 each; 5 feet, $1.60 each.

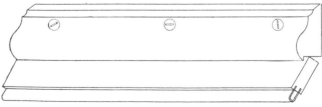

80—Spring Door Bottom.
Two sizes, 2 feet 8 inches and 3 feet.   Price per dozen............$6.50

SECTIONS OF STICKING.

For Solid Moulded Doors.

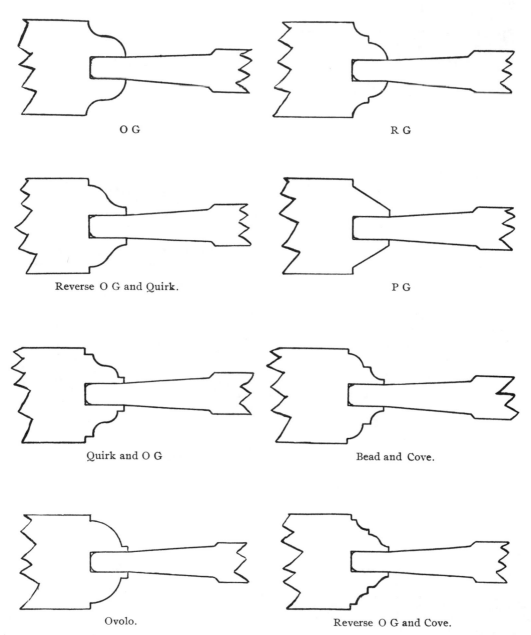

O G

R G

Reverse O G and Quirk.

P G

Quirk and O G

Bead and Cove.

Ovolo.

Reverse O G and Cove.

Our standard sticking for stock doors is the O G, and unless otherwise specified, all orders are entered accordingly.

SECTIONS OF MOULDED DOORS.

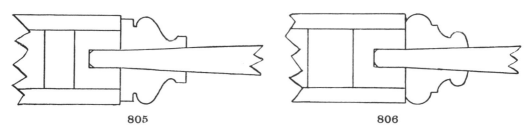

805   806

Showing styles of flush mouldings.

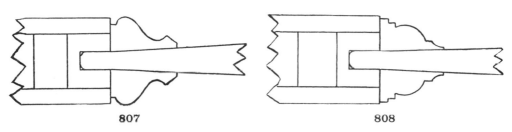

807   808

Showing styles of flush mouldings.

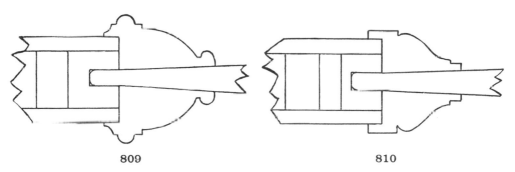

809   810

Showing styles of raised mouldings.

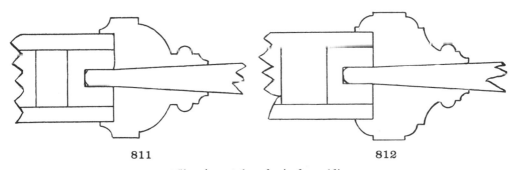

811   812

Showing styles of raised mouldings.

In ordering, give style of moulding required, referring to numbers on this page.

200

200—O. G. FOUR-PANEL DOORS.

RAISED PANELS BOTH SIDES.

SIZE.	Thickness, Inches.	Price A Quality.	Price B Quality.	Price C Quality	SIZE.	Thickness, Inches.	Price A Quality.	Price B Quality.	Price C Quality.
2 0 x 6 0	1⅛	$4.35	$4.15	$3.25	2 10 x 6 10	1⅜	$7.15	$6.45	$4.90
2 6 x 6 0	"	4.95	4.75		3 0 x 6 10	"	7.90	7.15	
2 8 x 6 0	"	5.35	5.05		2 0 x 7 0	"	7.00	6.30	
3 0 x 6 0	"	5.65	5.35		2 4 x 7 0	"	7.15	6.45	
2 4 x 6 4	"	4.90	4.65		2 6 x 7 0	"	7.20	6.55	
2 0 x 6 6	"	4.80	4.60		2 8 x 7 0	"	7.45	6.70	
2 6 x 6 6	"	5.05	4.80	3.90	2 10 x 7 0	"	7.75	7.00	
2 6 x 6 8	"	5.25	4.95		3 0 x 7 0	"	7.90	7.15	5.65
2 8 x 6 8	"	5.35	5.05	4.15	2 6 x 7 6	"	8.40	7.60	
2 10 x 6 10	"	6.25	5.95	4.75	2 8 x 7 6	"	8.70	7.80	
3 0 x 7 0	"	7.00	6.70	5.50	2 10 x 7 6	"	9.00	8.10	
2 0 x 6 0	1⅜	5.05	4.50	3.60	3 0 x 7 6	"	9.40	8.50	
2 4 x 6 0	"	5.50	4.95		2 6 x 8 0	"	9.90	8.95	
2 6 x 6 0	"	5.70	5.10		2 8 x 8 0	"	10.20	9.25	
2 8 x 6 0	"	6.00	5.40		3 0 x 8 0	"	10.90	9.85	
3 0 x 6 0	"	6.45	5.80		3 0 x 8 6	"	12.40	11.20	
2 4 x 6 4	"	5.50	4.95		3 0 x 9 0	"	14.25	12.70	
2 6 x 6 4	"	5.70	5.10		2 6 x 6 6	1¾	8.55	7.70	
2 0 x 6 6	"	5.35	4.80		2 8 x 6 8	"	9.00	8.10	
2 4 x 6 6	"	5.70	5.10		2 10 x 6 10	"	10.75	9.70	
2 6 x 6 6	"	5.70	5.10	4.05	2 6 x 7 0	"	10.80	9.75	
2 8 x 6 6	"	6.00	5.40		2 8 x 7 0	"	11.20	10.10	
2 10 x 6 6	"	6.90	6.25		2 10 x 7 0	"	11.65	10.50	
3 0 x 6 6	"	7.05	6.40		3 0 x 7 0	"	11.85	10.70	
2 0 x 6 8	"	5.70	5.10		2 6 x 7 6	"	12.60	11.35	
2 4 x 6 8	"	5.85	5.25		2 8 x 7 6	"	13.05	11.75	
2 6 x 6 8	"	6.00	5.40		2 10 x 7 6	"	13.50	12.15	
2 8 x 6 8	"	6.00	5.40	4.30	3 0 x 7 6	"	14.10	12.70	
2 10 x 6 8	"	7.15	6.45		2 6 x 8 0	"	14.85	13.40	
3 0 x 6 8	"	7.75	7.00		2 8 x 8 0	"	15.30	13.80	
2 0 x 6 10	"	6.40	5.80		3 0 x 8 0	"	16.35	14.75	
2 4 x 6 10	"	6.55	5.85		3 0 x 8 6	"	18.60	16.75	
2 6 x 6 10	"	6.70	6.00		3 0 x 9 0	"	21.40	19.30	
2 8 x 6 10	"	6.90	6.25						

For door extras see table of door extras, pages 64 and 65.

O. G. FOUR-PANEL INCH DOORS.
RAISED PANELS ONE SIDE.

SIZE.	Thickness, Inches.	Price A Quality	Price B Quality.	Price C Quality
2 0 x 6 0	1	$3.10	$2.75	$2.35
2 4 x 6 4	"	3.45	3.25	
2 0 x 6 6	"	3.30	3.10	
2 6 x 6 6	"	3.45	3.25	2.65
2 8 x 6 8	"	3 90	3.70	3.00

Inch Doors finish up about 1⅜ inch thick and have Bevel Raised Panels one side.
For Door Extras see pages 64–65.

O G 5-PANEL DOORS.

201

201

Size of Opening.				A Quality, 1⅜ in. thick.	B Quality 1⅜ in. thick.	A Quality, 1¾ in. thick.	B Quality 1¾ in. thick.
2	6	x	6	6	$6.00	$5.40	$8.85	$8.00
2	6	x	6	8	6.30	5.70	9.30	8.40
2	8	x	6	8	6.30	5.70	9.30	8.40
2	6	x	6	10	7.00	6.30	10.35	9.35
2	8	x	6	10	7.20	6.55	10.65	9.60
2	10	x	6	10	7.45	6.75	11.05	10.00
2	6	x	7	0	7.50	6.85	11.10	10.05
2	8	x	7	0	7.75	7.00	11.50	10.40
2	10	x	7	0	8.05	7.30	11.95	10.80
3	0	x	7	0	8.20	7.45	12.15	11.00
2	6	x	7	6	8.70	7.90	12.90	11.65
2	8	x	7	6	9.00	8.10	13.35	12.05
2	10	x	7	6	9.30	8.40	13.80	12.45
3	0	x	7	6	9.70	8.80	14.40	13.00
3	0	x	8	0	11.20	10.15	16.65	15.05
3	0	x	8	6	12.70	11.50	18.90	17.05
3	0	x	9	0	14.55	13.00	21.70	19.60

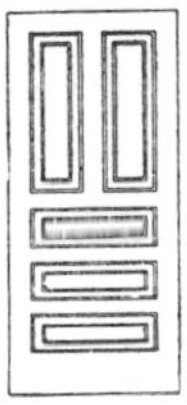

201½

O G 5-CROSS PANEL DOORS.

202½

202½

Size of Opening				A Quality 1⅜ in. thick	B Quality 1⅜ in. thick	A Quality 1¾ in. thick	B Quality 1¾ in. thick
2	6	x	6	6	$6.30	$5.70	$9.15	$8.30
2	6	x	6	8	6.60	6.00	9.60	8.70
2	8	x	6	8	6.60	6.00	9.60	8.70
2	6	x	6	10	7.30	6.60	10.65	9.65
2	8	x	6	10	7.50	6.85	10.95	9.90
2	10	x	6	10	7.75	7.05	11.35	10.30
2	6	x	7	0	7.80	7.15	11.40	10.35
2	8	x	7	0	8.05	7.30	11.80	10.70
2	10	x	7	0	8.35	7.60	12.25	11.10
3	0	x	7	0	8.50	7.75	12.45	11.30
2	6	x	7	6	9.00	8.20	13.20	11.95
2	8	x	7	6	9.30	8.40	13.65	12.35
2	10	x	7	6	9.60	8.70	14.10	12.75
3	0	x	7	6	10.00	9.10	14.70	13.30
3	0	x	8	0	11.50	10.45	16.95	15.35
3	0	x	8	6	13.00	11.80	19.20	17.35
3	0	x	9	0	14.85	13.30	22.00	19.90

For doors made with three cross panels below and two vertical panels above, in stock quantities, same list as five cross panel doors. (See Note "c," Door Extras.) For door extras see pages 64-65.

202

BEAD and COVE 5-PANEL DOORS.

202

Size					A Quality 1⅜ in. Thick	B Quality 1⅜ in. Thick.	A Quality 1¾ in. Thick	B Quality 1¾ in. thick.
2	6	x	6	6	$6.20	$5.60	$9.05	$8.20
2	6	x	6	8	6.50	5.90	9.50	8.60
2	8	x	6	8	6.50	5.90	9.50	8.60
2	6	x	6	10	7.20	6.50	10.55	9.55
2	8	x	6	10	7.40	6.75	10.85	9 80
2	10	x	6	10	7.65	6.95	11.25	10.20
2	6	x	7	0	7.70	7.05	11.30	10.25
2	8	x	7	0	7.95	7.20	11.70	10.60
2	10	x	7	0	8.25	7.50	12.15	11.00
3	0	x	7	0	8.40	7.65	12.35	11.20
2	6	x	7	6	8.90	8.10	13.10	11.85
2	8	x	7	6	9.20	8.30	13.55	12.25
2	10	x	7	6	9.50	8.60	14.00	12.65
3	0	x	7	6	9.90	9.00	14.60	13.20
3	0	x	8	0	11.40	10.35	16.85	15.25
3	0	x	8	6	12.90	11.70	19.10	17.25
3	0	x	9	0	14.75	13.20	21.90	19.80

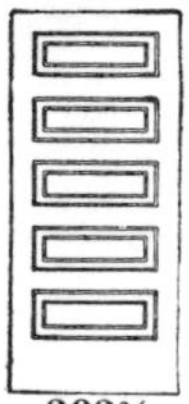

202¾

BEAD and COVE 5-CROSS PANEL DOORS.

202¾

Size					A Quality, 1⅜ inches thick.	B Quality, 1⅜ inches thick.	A Quality, 1¾ inches thick.	B Quality, 1¾ inches thick
2	6	x	6	6	$6.50	$5.90	$9.35	$8.50
2	6	x	6	8	6.80	6.20	9.80	8.90
2	8	x	6	8	6.80	6.20	9.80	8.90
2	6	x	6	10	7.50	6.80	10.85	9.85
2	8	x	6	10	7.70	7.05	11.15	10.10
2	10	x	6	10	7.95	7.25	11.55	10.50
2	6	x	7	0	8.00	7.35	11.60	10.55
2	8	x	7	0	8.25	7.50	12.00	10.90
2	10	x	7	0	8.55	7.80	12.45	11.30
3	0	x	7	0	8.70	7.95	12.65	11.50
2	6	x	7	6	9.20	8.40	13.40	12.15
2	8	x	7	6	9.50	8.60	13.85	12.55
2	10	x	7	6	9.80	8.90	14.30	12.95
3	0	x	7	6	10.20	9.30	14.90	13.50
3	0	x	8	0	11.70	10.65	17.15	15.55
3	0	x	8	6	13.20	12.00	19.40	17.55
3	0	x	9	0	15.05	13.50	22.20	20.10

For door extras see pages 64 and 65.

4-PANEL MOULDED DOORS.

Flush or Sunk Moulding.

203

Size of Opening.			Moulded One Side, 1⅜ in. Thick.	Moulded Two Sides, 1⅜ in. Thick.	Moulded One Side, 1¾ in. Thick.	Moulded Two Sides, 1¾ in. Thick.
2	6 x 6	6	$6.75	$7.45	$9.80	$10.55
2	6 x 6	8	7.15	7.80	10.35	11.20
2	8 x 6	8	7.15	7.80	10.35	11.20
2	10 x 6	10	8.35	9.10	12.15	13.05
2	6 x 7	0	8.50	9.30	12.40	13.35
2	8 x 7	0	8.70	9.55	12.80	13.75
2	10 x 7	0	9.00	9.85	13.25	14.20
3	0 x 7	0	9.15	10.00	13.45	14.40
2	6 x 7	6	9.85	10.75	14.30	15.35
2	8 x 7	6	10.15	11.05	14.75	15.80
2	10 x 7	6	10.45	11.35	15.25	16.30
3	0 x 7	6	10.80	11.70	15.85	16.90
3	0 x 8	0	12.45	13.45	18.25	19.35
3	0 x 8	6	14.10	15.15	20.70	21.95

4-PANEL MOULDED DOORS.

Raised Moulding.

204

Size of Opening.			Moulded One Side, 1⅜ in. Thick.	Moulded Two Sides, 1⅜ in. Thick.	Moulded One Side, 1¾ in. Thick.	Moulded Two Sides, 1¾ in. Thick.
2	6 x 6	6	$7.80	$9.15	$11.05	$12.55
2	6 x 6	8	8.25	9.60	11.70	13.40
2	8 x 6	8	8.25	9.60	11.70	13.40
2	10 x 6	10	9.55	11.05	13.55	15.35
2	6 x 7	0	9.75	11.40	14.00	15.90
2	8 x 7	0	10.00	11.65	14.40	16.30
2	10 x 7	0	10.30	11.95	14.85	16.75
3	0 x 7	0	10.45	12.10	15.05	16.95
2	6 x 7	6	11.25	13.05	16.00	18.10
2	8 x 7	6	11.55	13.35	16.45	18.55
2	10 x 7	6	11.85	13.65	17.00	19.10
3	0 x 7	6	12.25	14.05	17.60	19.70
3	0 x 8	0	13.95	15.90	20.15	22.35
3	0 x 8	6	15.85	17.95	22.80	25.30

For Door Extras, see pages 64 and 65.

PAINTED SASH DOORS.

1⅜ Inches Thick.

Size.					210—4 Light.		211—2 Light.	
					Open.	Glazed.	Open.	Glazed.
2	6	x	6	6	$3.75	$6.30	$3.75	$6.30
2	8	x	6	8	3.90	6.85	3.90	7.05
2	10	x	6	10	4.30	7.70	4 30	7.85
3	0	x	7	0	4.65	8.40	4.65	8.95

Size.					212—1 Light.		212½—1 Light, 3-pan.	
					Open.	Glazed.	Open.	Glazed.
2	6	x	6	6	$3.75	$7.20	$3.95	$7.10
2	8	x	6	8	3.90	8.10	4.10	7.55
2	10	x	6	10	4.30	9.25	4.50	8.90
3	0	x	7	0	4.65	10.50	4.85	9.85

213—2 Light, Circle Top.

Size.					213	
					Open.	Glazed.
2	6	x	6	6	$4.65	$6.85
2	8	x	6	8	4.80	8.20
2	10	x	6	10	5.20	8.95
3	0	x	7	0	5.55	10.05

For Beads around glass in 1-light Painted Sash Doors, add 20 cents to above list.
For Grained Sash Doors, add 10 cents net to price of Painted Sash Doors.
For unpainted D quality sash doors deduct 60c list.

O G 4-PANEL DOORS.

D Quality and Painted.

Size.					Thick.	D Quality.	Painted.
2	0	x	6	0	13-16	$1.70	$2.30
2	6	x	6	6	"	2.00	2.60
2	8	x	6	8	"	2.15	2.75
2	0	x	6	0	1⅛	2.30	2 90
2	6	x	6	6	"	2.60	3.20
2	8	x	6	8	"	2.75	3.35
2	10	x	6	10	"	3.15	3 75
3	0	x	7	0	"	3.50	4.10
2	0	x	6	0	1⅜	2.45	3.05
2	6	x	6	6	"	2.75	3.35
2	8	x	6	8	"	2.90	3.50
2	10	x	6	10	"	3.30	3.90
3	0	x	7	0	"	3.65	4.25

5-panel D quality and Painted Doors, 5 cents net more than 4-panel. Grained Doors, 10 cents net more than Painted Doors.

O G SASH DOORS.

Raised Panels, Two Sides.

210 and 211.   List Prices, 1⅜ Inches Thick.

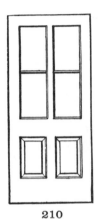

210

Size of Opening.	210 Open.	210 Glazed.	211 Open.	211 Glazed.
2 6 x 6 6	$6.20	$8.75	$6.20	$8.75
2 8 x 6 8	6.50	9.45	6.50	9.65
2 10 x 6 10	7.65	11.05	7.65	11.20
2 6 x 7 0	7.70	10.65	7.70	11.70
2 8 x 7 0	7.95	11.35	7.95	11.95
3 0 x 7 0	8.40	12.15	8.40	12.70
3 0 x 7 6	9.90	14.35	9.90	15.55
3 0 x 8 0	11.40	16.05	11.40	17.55

211

Sash Doors, 1½ inch thick, in stock quantities, same price as 1⅜ inch. For less than stock quantities, add 10 per cent.

For price of 1¾ inch O G Sash Doors, add the difference between 1⅜ and 1¾ inch O G Four-Panel Doors, same size, see table on page 63.

Irregular and intermediate sizes, in stock quantities, same list as next larger listed size. For less than stock quantities, on sizes not listed, an extra 10 per cent will be charged.

212 and 212½.   Raised Panels, Two Sides.

List Prices, 1⅜ Inches Thick.

212

Size of Opening.	212 Open.	212 Gl. D. S.	212½ Open.	212½ Gl. D. S.
2 6 x 6 6	$6.20	$9.65	$6.50	$9.65
2 8 x 6 8	6.50	10.70	6.80	10.25
2 10 x 6 10	7.65	12.60	7.95	12.35
2 6 x 7 0	7.70	12.65	8.00	11.55
2 8 x 7 0	7.95	12.95	8.25	12.60
3 0 x 7 0	8.40	14.25	8.70	13.70
3 0 x 7 6	9.90	16.80	10.20	16.20
3 0 x 8 0	11.40	18.45	11.70	18.65

212½

For price of 1¾ inch O G Sash Doors, add the difference between 1⅜ and 1¾ inch O G Four-Panel Doors, same size, see table on page 63.

Irregular and intermediate sizes, in stock quantities, same list as next larger listed size. For less than stock quantities, on sizes not listed, an extra 10 per cent will be charged.

O G SASH DOORS.

Raised Panels, Two Sides.

213 and 214. List Prices, 1⅜ Inches Thick.

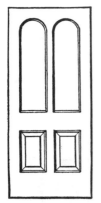

213

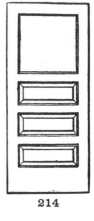

214

SIZE.	213 Open.	213 Glazed.	214 Open.	214 Gl. D. S.
2 6 x 6 6	$7.35	$9.55	$6.80	$9.20
2 8 x 6 8	7.65	11.05	7.10	10.05
2 10 x 6 10	8.80	12.55	8.25	11.90
2 6 x 7 0	8.85	13.05	8.30	11.60
2 8 x 7 0	------	------	8.55	11.90
3 0 x 7 0	9.55	14.05	9.00	13.40
3 0 x 7 6	11.05	16.05	10.50	15.60
3 0 x 8 0	12.55	17.95	12.00	18.05

For price of 1¾-inch O G Sash Doors add the difference between 1⅜ and 1¾-inch Four Panel O G Doors same size, see table, page 63.

Irregular and intermediate sizes, in stock quantities, same list as next larger listed size.

For less than stock quantities on sizes not listed, an extra 10 per cent will be charged.

215 and 215½. Raised Panel, Two Sides.

List Price, 1⅜ Inches Thick.

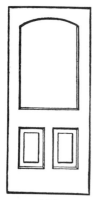

215

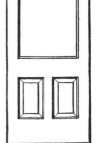

215½

SIZE.	215 Open.	215 Gl. D. S.	215½ Open.	215½ Gl. D. S.
2 6 x 6 6	$7.35	$11.10	$7.35	$11.10
2 8 x 6 8	7.65	12.25	7.65	12.25
2 10 x 6 10	8.80	14.10	8.80	14.10
2 6 x 7 0	8.85	14.20	8.85	14.20
3 0 x 7 0	9.55	15.85	9.55	15.85
3 0 x 7 6	11.05	18.40	11.05	18.40
3 0 x 8 0	12.55	20.05	12.55	20.05

For price of 1¾-inch O G Sash Doors add the difference between 1⅜ and 1¾-inch O G Four Panel Doors same size, see table on page 63.

Irregular and intermediate sizes, in stock quantities, same list as next larger listed size.

For less than stock quantities, on sizes not listed, an extra 10 per cent will be charged.

FRONT DOORS.

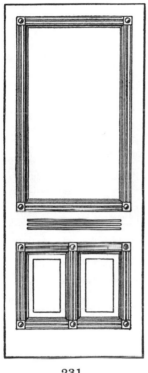

231

233

List Price 1⅜ Inches Thick.

Size of Opening.					231		233	
					Open	Glazed D. S.	Open	Closed D. O.
2	8	x	6	8	$ 9.45	$14.05	$10.95	$15.55
2	10	x	6	10	10.60	15.90	12.10	17.40
2	8	x	7	0	11.05	16.35	12.55	17.85
3	0	x	7	0	11.65	17.95	13.15	19.45
3	0	x	7	6	13.50	20.85	15.00	22.35
3	0	x	8	0	15.40	22.90	16.90	24.40

For prices of 1¾-inch doors, in stock quantities, add to above list the difference between 1⅜ and 1¾-inch O. G. four-panel doors, same size, see table on page 63.

Irregular and intermediate sizes, in stock quantities, same list as next larger listed size.

For less than stock quantities, on sizes not listed, an extra 10 per cent will be charged.

FRONT DOORS.

253

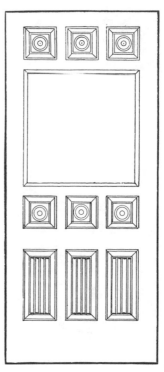

298

List Price, 1⅜ Inches Thick.

Size of Opening.				253		298	
				Open.	Glazed, D. S.	Open.	Glazed, D. S.
2	8 x 6	8		$13.80	$18.40	$8.20	$10.95
2	10 x 6	10		14.95	20.25	9.30	12.90
2	8 x 7	0		15.55	20.90	9.60	13.15
3	0 x 7	0		16.00	22.05	10.05	13.95
3	0 x 7	6		17.50	24.85	11.55	16.95
3	0 x 8	0		19.00	26.50	13.05	19.15

For price of 1¾ inch doors, in stock quantities, add to above list the difference between 1⅜ and 1¾ inch four-panel O. G. doors, same size, see table on page 63.

Irregular, and intermediate sizes, it stock quantities, same list as next larger listed size.

For less than stock quantities on sizes not listed, an extra 10 per cent will be charged.

FRONT DOORS.

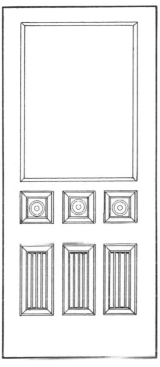

307   406

List Price, 1⅜ Inches Thick.

Size of Opening.				307		406	
				Open	Glazed, D. S.	Open.	Glazed, D. S.
2	8 x 6	8		$7.75	$12.45	$7.75	$12.45
2	10 x 6	10		8.85	14.20	8.85	14.20
2	8 x 7	0		9.15	14.50	9.15	14.50
3	0 x 7	0		9.60	15.70	9.60	15.70
3	0 x 7	6		11.10	18.45	11.10	18.45
3	0 x 8	0		12.60	20.10	12.60	20.10

For price of 1¼ inch door, in stock quantities add to above list the difference between 1⅜ and 1¼ inch four panel O G. doors, same size, see table page 63.

Irregular and intermediate sizes, in stock quantities, same list as next larger listed size.

For less than stock quantities, on sizes not listed, an extra 10 per cent will be charged.

CUPBOARD DOORS and SASH.

LIST FOR CUPBOARD DOORS.

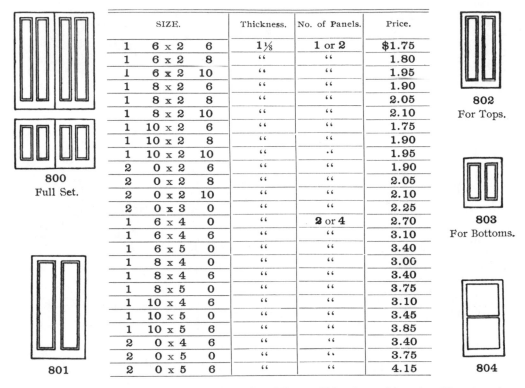

	SIZE.			Thickness.	No. of Panels.	Price.
1	6 x 2		6	1⅛	1 or 2	$1.75
1	6 x 2		8	"	"	1.80
1	6 x 2		10	"	"	1.95
1	8 x 2		6	"	"	1.90
1	8 x 2		8	"	"	2.05
1	8 x 2		10	"	"	2.10
1	10 x 2		6	"	"	1.75
1	10 x 2		8	"	"	1.90
1	10 x 2		10	"	..	1.95
2	0 x 2		6	"	"	1.90
2	0 x 2		8	"	"	2.05
2	0 x 2		10	"	"	2.10
2	0 x 3		0	"	"	2.25
1	6 x 4		0	"	2 or 4	2.70
1	6 x 4		6	"	"	3.10
1	6 x 5		0	"	"	3.40
1	8 x 4		0	"	"	3.00
1	8 x 4		6	"	"	3.40
1	8 x 5		0	"	"	3.75
1	10 x 4		6	"	"	3.10
1	10 x 5		0	"	"	3.45
1	10 x 5		6	"	"	3.85
2	0 x 4		6	"	"	3.40
2	0 x 5		0	"	"	3.75
2	0 x 5		6	"	"	4.15

800 Full Set.

801

802 For Tops.

803 For Bottoms.

804

Less than five, 10 per cent extra.   No Cupboard Door will be charged less than 75 cents net.
1⅛ inch Cupboard Doors No. 2, 5 per cent less than above prices.
⅞ inch Cupboard Doors, 80 per cent of 1⅛ inch Cupboard Door list.
Rabbeting, 10 cents per pair, net.

CUPBOARD SASH.

Usual sizes made, two light each, ⅞ and 1⅛ thick:

1-4x4-0	1-4x5-6	1-6x5-0	1-8x4-8
1-4x4-6	1-6x4-0	1-6x5-6	1-8x5-0
1-4x4-8	1-6x4-6	1-8x4-0	1-8x5-6
1-4x5-0	1-6x4-8	1-8x4-6	

WRITE FOR PRICES.

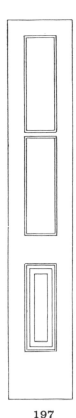

SIDE LIGHTS FOR DOORS.

WITH MOULDED PANEL BELOW.

Width and Height.				Thickness.	Price per Pair, Unglazed.	Price per Pair, Glazed.
12	x	6	6	1⅜	$5.50	$7.45
12	x	6	8	"	5.65	7.60
12	x	6	10	"	5.80	8.20
12	x	7	0	"	5.95	8.35
12	x	7	6	"	6.25	9.15
14	x	6	6	"	5.70	7.90
14	x	6	8	"	5.85	8.05
14	x	6	10	"	6.00	8.40
14	x	7	0	"	6.15	8.55
14	x	7	6	"	6.45	9.40
14	x	8	0	"	6.90	10.00

For 1¾-inch thick, in stock quantities (Note "a"), add 50 per cent. For less than stock quantities, add 10 per cent to the price thus made.

Prices are for either two or three lights in each sash.

10-inch same price as 12-inch. Subject to door discount.

State in ordering whether two or three lights are wanted.

For O G deduct $1.05 per pair from above list.

197

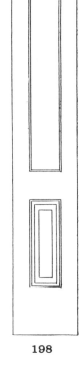

198

1¾-INCH DOOR TABLE.

Differences between 1⅜ and 1¾ inch Four-Panel Doors:

SIZE.					O G Doors A Quality.	O G Doors B Quality
2	6	x	6	6	$2.85	$2.60
2	8	x	6	8	3.00	2.70
2	10	x	6	10	3.60	3.25
2	8	x	7	0	3.75	3.40
2	10	x	7	0	3.90	3.50
3	0	x	7	0	3.95	3.55
2	8	x	7	6	4.35	3.95
2	10	x	7	6	4.50	4.05
3	0	x	7	6	4.70	4.20
3	0	x	8	0	5.45	4.90
3	0	x	8	6	6.20	5.55
3	0	x	9	0	7.15	6.40

See No. 14 and Note C, Door Extras, page 64.

DOOR EXTRAS.

NOTE—(a). The term "stock quantities," wherever used in this list, means 5 or more Doors and 10 or more Windows, Sash or Blinds of one size, kind or quality.

NOTE—(b). Irregular and intermediate sizes, in stock quantities, same list as next larger listed size. For less than stock quantities, on sizes not listed, an extra 10 per cent will be charged.

NOTE—(c) Where no provision is made for price on quantities less than 5, use stock quantity price and add 10 per cent to the amount thus created.

WIDTH.

	For 5 or more.	For less than 5.
No. 1. For Doors over 3 feet in width up to 3 feet 6 inches, add to list of 3 foot Door, same height........	20%	Note C
No. 2. For Doors over 3 feet 6 inches in width and not wider than 4 feet, add to list of 3 foot Door, same height.	50%	Note C
No. 3. For Doors over 4 feet in width and not wider than 5 feet, add to list of price of a 3 foot Door, same height.	100%	Note C
No. 4. For Doors over 5 feet in width and not exceeding 5 feet 6 inches wide, add to list price of two 3 foot Doors, same height........	15%	Note C
No. 5. For Doors over 5 feet 6 inches in width, and not exceeding 6 feet wide, add to list price of two 3 foot Doors, same height........	25%	Note C
No. 6. For Doors over 6 feet in width, and not exceeding 6 feet 6 inches wide, add to list price of two 3-foot Doors, same height.........	50%	Note C
No. 7. For Doors 6 feet 6 inches wide and not exceeding 7 feet in width, add to list price of two 3 foot Doors, same height........	65%	Note C

HEIGHT.

	For 5 or more.	For less than 5.
No. 10. Doors over 9 feet long and not exceeding 10 feet, add to the difference in the list between 8-foot and 9-foot listed doors........	10%	Note C

THICKNESS.

	For 5 or more.	For less than 5.
No. 14. For prices of 1¾-inch Front and Cottage Doors, add to list the difference between 1⅜ and 1¾-inch O G Four-Panel Doors, same size .... (See table on page 63.)		Note C
No. 15. For Doors 1⅞ inches thick add to 1¾ inch list..	30%	Note C

	For 5 or more.	For less than 5.
No. 16. For Doors 2¼ inches thick (made single or double thick) add to 1¾ inch list.	50%	Note C
No. 17. For Doors 2½ inches thick (made single or double thick) add to 1¾ inch list	60%	Note C

PANELS.

No. 20. Beveled Panels for Doors are standard.

No. 21. Doors over 3 feet up to 3 feet 6 inches, may be made 3 panels wide.

No. 22. Doors over 3 feet 6 inches, up to 4 feet, may be made 3 or 4 panels wide.

No. 23. Doors over 4 feet and up to 5 feet, may be made 4 panels wide.

No. 24. Doors over 5 feet up up to 7 feet, may be made 5 or 6 panels wide.

No. 25. For Graduated Panels, add per door.........	$1.50 list	Note C
No. 26. For wide doors made with less panels than specified in Nos. 21 to 24, extra price.		
No. 27. Additional panels in Doors O. G., P. G., or other solid mould sticking, each..	.30 list	Note C
No. 28. Solid Mould Sticking Doors with panels part horizontal and part vertical, add to list of cross panel doors with same number of panels	.30 list	Note C
No. 29. For extra panels over four in Flush Moulded Door No. 203, 1⅜ inches thick, flush moulding one side, add for each extra panel	.60 list	Note C
No. 30. For extra panels over four in Flush Moulded Door No. 203, 1⅜ inches thick, flush moulding two sides, add for each extra panel...	.80 list	Note C

DOOR EXTRAS—*Continued.*

	For 5 or more.	For less than 5.
No. 31. For extra panels over four in Flush Moulded Door No. 203 1¾ inches thick, flush moulding one side, add for each extra panel..	.65 list	Note C
No. 32. For extra panel over four in Flush Moulded Door No. 203 1¾ inches thick, flush moulding two sides, add for each extra panel...	.90 list	Note C
No. 33. For extra panels in Raised Moulded Doors, add to difference in list between O. G. and Flush Moulded Doors of same description..	100%	Note C

STICKING.

	For 5 or more.	For less than 5.
No. 40. For Ovolo or P. G. Five-Panel Doors use Bead and Cove Five Panel list...		Note C
No. 41. For P. G., Ovolo, Cove and Bead or Bead and Cove sticking four panel, add to list on four panel O. G. doors	.20 list	Note C
No. 42. Solid mould sticking on back side of Cottage Front Doors is standard.		

CHAMFERED DOORS.

No. 50. For price of Machine Chamfered Doors No. 207, use list on Flush Moulded Doors 203		Note C

RAISED MOULDED DOORS.

No. 55. For price of raised moulded doors, add to difference between O. G. and Flush Moulded Doors of same size	100%	Note C
No. 56. For Circle Top Raised Moulded Sash or Panel Doors, add to list for each side Moulded ....$0.23 list	Note C	

OIL FINISH.

	For 5 or more.	For less than 5.
No. 60. AAA Doors 3-0 x 9-0 and under, free from sap, machine smoothed for oil finish, add to "A" door list.	3.00 list	Note C
No. 61. For AAA Doors 3-0 x 9-0 and under, free from sap, hand smoothed for oil finish, add to "A" door list.	3.90 list	Note C
No. 62. For AA selected stock Doors, machine smoothed for oil finish, add to "A" door list	.75 list	Note C

GLASS BEADS.

	For 5 or more.	For less than 5.
No. 65. For Beads around glass in one light square top sash Doors add........ (This does not include regular listed Cottage Doors.)	.08 net	.10
No. 66. For Beads around glass in square-head Sash Doors with two or more lights add for each light....	.06 net	.08

ASTRAGALS AND RABBETING.

	For 5 or more.	For less than 5.
No. 70. For Double Astragal for Sliding Doors 1¾ inches thick add	.50 net	.60
No. 71. For Double Astragal for Sliding Doors 2¼ or 2½ inches thick add........	.75 net	.90
No. 72. For Single Astragal for Folding Doors 1¾ inches thick add	.25 net	.30
No. 73. For Single Astragal for Folding Doors thicker than 1¾ inches, add.......	.40 net	.50
No. 74. For Astragal joint on solid for Doors 1¾ inches thick in pairs, add per pair.	.30 net	.35
No. 75. For Astragal joint on solid for Doors thicker than 1¾ inches, add per pair....	.45 net	.55
No. 76. For Rabbeting Stock Doors on solid, per pair...	.30 net	.35
No. 77. For Rabbeting and Beading Folding Doors, made extra width for rabbeting, add per pair........	.50 net	.60

BANDING.

	For 5 or more.	For less than 5.
No. 80. For Banding Sliding Doors two sides add per lineal foot around opening of each door..............	.04 net	.05

CIRCLE TOP, ETC.

	For 5 or more.	For less than 5.
No. 85. For 1⅜-in. solid moulded doors, Circle Top, Eliptic, Gothic or Peak Head, either single or in pairs, add for each door....	4.35 list	Note C
No. 86. For the same, 1¾ inches thick	6.55 list	Note C
No. 90. Irregular and intermediate sizes, in stock quantities, same list as next larger listed size. For less than stock quantities, on sizes not listed, an extra 10 per cent will be charged.		

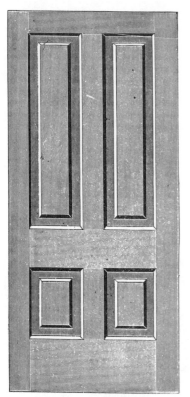

4-Panel, O G Painted.

PAINTED DOORS.

WITH GLOSS FINISH.

Our Painted Doors are well manufactured, shellaced and painted two coats of light colored paint.

They are good sellers and it will pay you to carry them in stock.

All of our Painted Doors are carefully crated before shipping to avoid damage in transit.

We manufacture these doors in the following sizes, which we always have on hand ready for prompt shipment:

FOUR-PANEL PAINTED DOORS.

2- 6x6- 6, 1⅛.
2- 8x6- 8, 1⅛.
2- 6x6- 6, 1⅜.
2- 8x6- 8, 1⅜.

PAINTED SASH DOORS.

2- 6x6- 6, 1⅜.
2- 8x6- 8, 1⅜.

For List Prices on Painted Doors, see page 56.

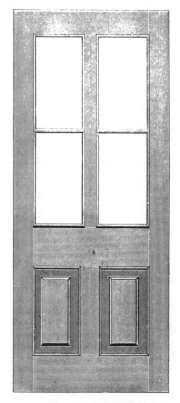

210. Painted.

PAINTED DOORS.

WITH GLOSS FINISH.

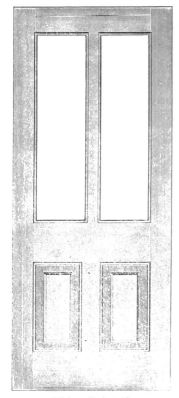

211. Painted.

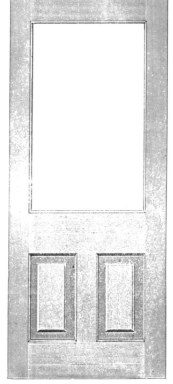

212. Painted.

213. Painted.

For List Prices see page 56.

FANCY PAINTED COTTAGE DOORS.

A 1

A 2
Glazed Plain.

A 3
Glazed Sand Blast.

A 4
Glazed Sand Blast.

These Doors always in stock and can be shipped promptly, but in the following sizes only :
2-6 x 6-6, 1⅜.   2-8 x 6-8, 1⅜.   2-10 x 6-10, 1⅜   2-8 x 7-0, 1⅜.   3-0 x 7-0, 1⅜.
For net prices see our Discount Sheet.

Oak Grained Doors

4-Panel, O G Grained.

OAK GRAINED DOORS.

Our Oak Grained Doors are un-excelled.   They are painted two coats, best lead and oil paint, and are carefully oil finished.

Doors finished by our process have all the appearance of the genuine oak, at a much lower cost.

For prices on Grained Doors see our Discount Sheet.

210.   Grained.

211 Grained.

OAK
GRAINED
DOORS

212 Grained.

We carry in stock the following:

FOUR-PANEL
GRAINED DOORS.

    2- 6x6- 6, 1⅛.
    2- 8x6- 8, 1⅛.
    2- 6x6- 6, 1⅜.
    2- 8x6- 8, 1⅜.

GRAINED
    SASH DOORS.

    2- 6x6- 6, 1⅜.
    2- 8x6- 8, 1⅜.

213 Grained.

These Doors are carefully crated to avoid damage in shipment . . . .

To The Trade

We illustrate in this catalogue a complete line of Fancy Front Doors and Special Millwork. We take special pride in producing the best line of doors on the market; up to date in style, quality and workmanship. Our increased facilities enable us to serve our customers even better than in the past. We can glaze any door in this catalogue with

Maze   **Cathedral**
Florentine   **Enamel**
Figure No. 1 or 2
White Chip
or any Fancy Glass

We will be pleased to send samples of glass if desired.

OUR SPECIAL COTTAGE DOORS.

Monarch **A**

Mon**a**rch **B**

Can be glazed plain D. S. or designs of glass as shown on pages 326 to 340.

OUR SPECIAL COTTAGE DOORS.

Monarch E   Venus

Can be glazed plain D. S. or designs of glass as shown on pages 326 to 340.

OUR SPECIAL COTTAGE DOORS.

Vixen

Carnival

Can be glazed plain D. S. or designs of glass as shown on pages 326 to 340.

OUR SPECIAL COTTAGE DOORS.

Moonstone   Imp

Can be glazed plain D. S. or designs of glass as shown on pages 326 to 340.

OUR SPECIAL COTTAGE DOORS.

Best   Ruby

Can be glazed plain D. S. or designs of glass as shown on pages 326 to 340.

OUR SPECIAL COTTAGE DOORS.

Extra   Better

Can be glazed plain D. S. or designs of glass as shown on pages 326 to 340.

OUR SPECIAL COTTAGE DOORS.

Good   Diamond

Can be glazed plain D. S. or designs of glass as shown on pages 326 to 340.

OUR SPECIAL COTTAGE DOORS.

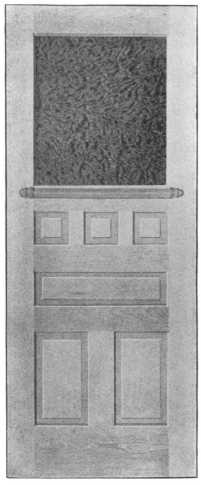

Pearl

Opal

Can be glazed plain D. S. or designs of glass as shown on pages 326 to 340.

OUR SPECIAL COTTAGE DOORS.

United A

United B

Can be glazed plain D. S. or designs of glass as shown on pages 326 to 340.

OUR SPECIAL COTTAGE DOORS.

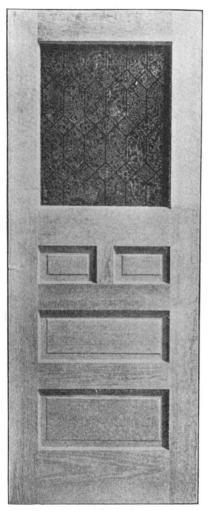

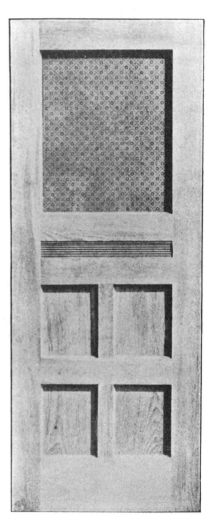

United D   United E

Can be glazed plain D. S. or designs of glass as shown on pages 326 to 340.

OUR SPECIAL COTTAGE DOORS.

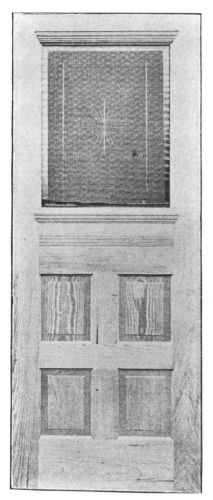

United F

United G

Can be glazed plain D. S. or designs of glass as shown on pages 326 to 340.

OUR SPECIAL COTTAGE DOORS.

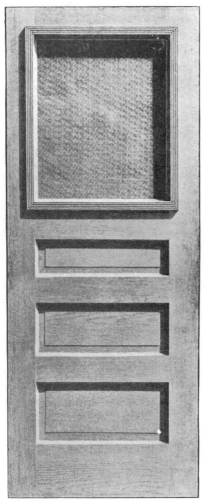

United **H**

Winner

Can be glazed plain D. S. or designs of glass as shown on pages 326 to 340

INSIDE DOORS.

I 693

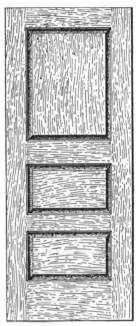

J 693

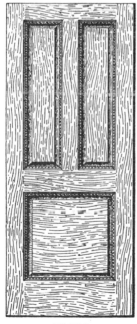

K 693

L 693

We make these Doors to order, Veneered in any of the Cabinet Woods, or if desired, in solid White Pine or Hardwood.

For finish, style and reliable qualities, our work cannot be excelled.

VESTIBULE DOORS.

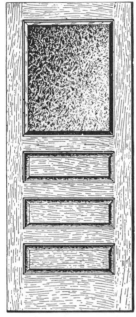

M 693

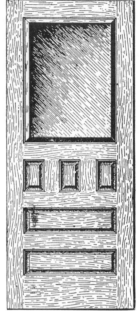

N 693

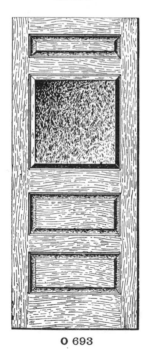

O 693

P 693

These special doors we make to order in any size. Made in white or yellow Pine or any of the hardwoods. We are prepared to glaze these doors with sand blast, polished bevel plate, or leaded art glass of handsome design.

Nothing made superior to the quality of our work.

SPECIAL FRONT DOORS.

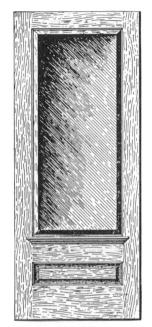

Q 693

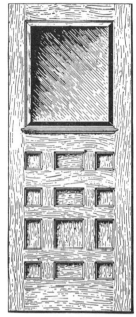

R 693

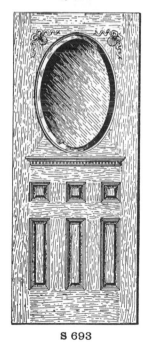

S 693

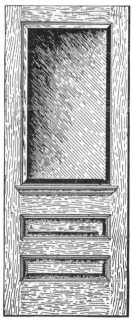

T 693

Built to order either solid or veneered in hardwood. Can also be made in white or yellow Pine and Cypress. We build them right, using only first class material and work out all details with exactness, the carvings executed in the highest style of art

Our veneered doors are made from selected stock, chosen for its beauty of grain and uniformity of color. For finish, style and enduring quality, we guarantee them equal to any made.

SPECIAL FRONT DOORS

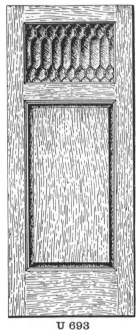

U 693

V 693

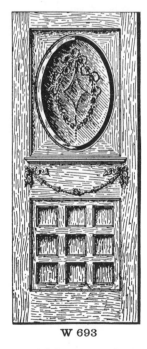

W 693

X 693

These special doors we make to order in any size. Made in white or yellow Pine or any of the hardwoods.   We are prepared to glaze these doors with sand blast, polished bevel plate, or leaded art glass of handsome design.

Nothing made superior to the quality of our work.

SPECIAL FRONT DOORS.

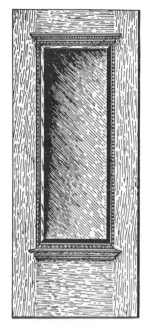

Y 693

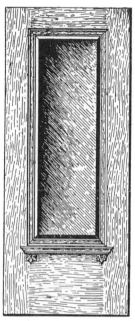

Z 093

A B 693

CD 693

Built to order either solid or veneered in hardwood. Can also be made in white or yellow Pine and Cypress. We build them right, using only first class material and work out all details with exactness, the carvings executed in the highest style of art.

Our veneered doors are made from selected stock, chosen for its beauty of grain and uniformity of color. For finish, style and enduring quality, we guarantee them equal to any made.

SPECIAL FRONT DOORS

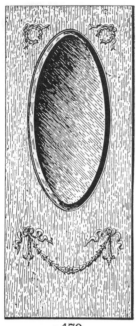

470

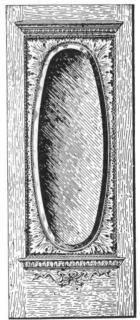

471

472

473

These special doors we make to order in any size. Made in white or yellow Pine or any of the hardwoods. We are prepared to glaze these doors with sand blast, polished bevel plate, or leaded art glass of handsome design.

Nothing made superior to the quality of our work.

Mill Work

We give special attention to orders for this class of work. Our new mill is equipped with the latest improved machinery and appliances and we are prepared to execute all orders for turned work, carving, stair work and fine interior finish, promptly and at prices that will be satisfactory to our customers

INTERIOR DOORS and FINISH.

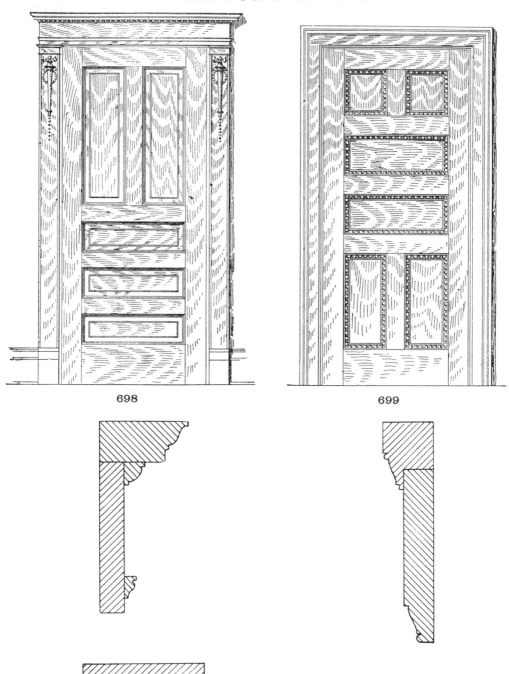

698

699

WRITE FOR PRICES.

INSIDE DOORS.

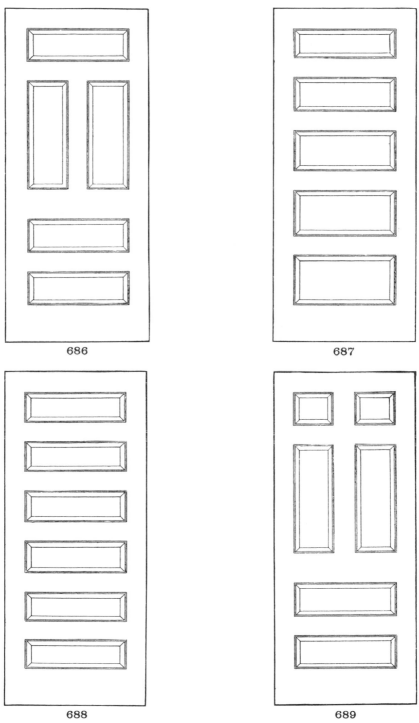

686

687

688

689

Doors of above styles we make to order either solid hardwood or veneered.

INSIDE DOORS

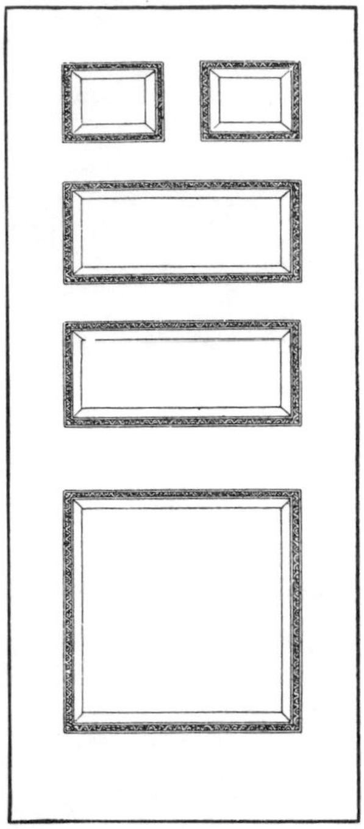

690

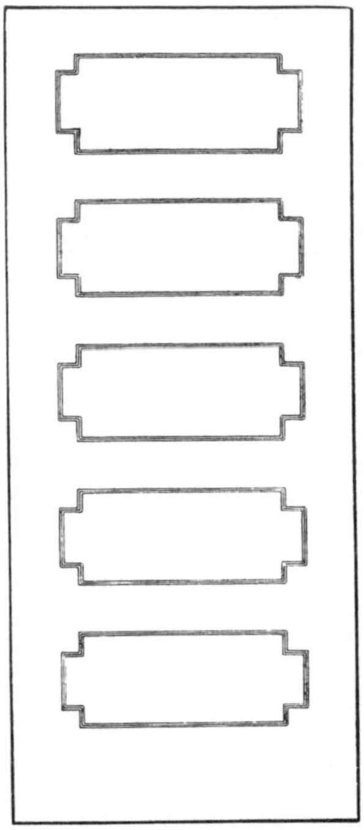

691

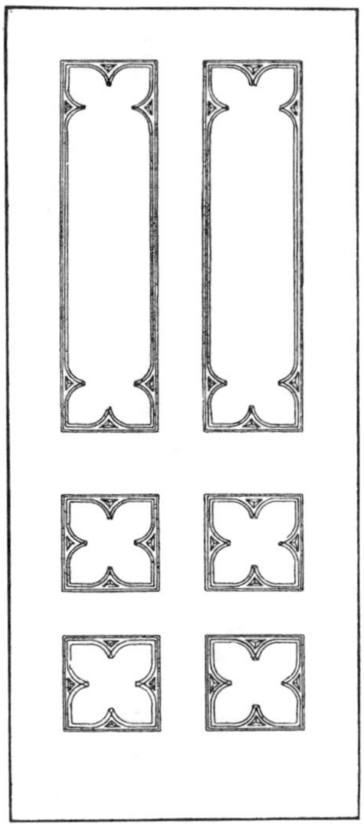

692

693

Our veneered doors are made from selected stock, chosen for its beauty of grain and uniformity of color.

INSIDE DOORS.

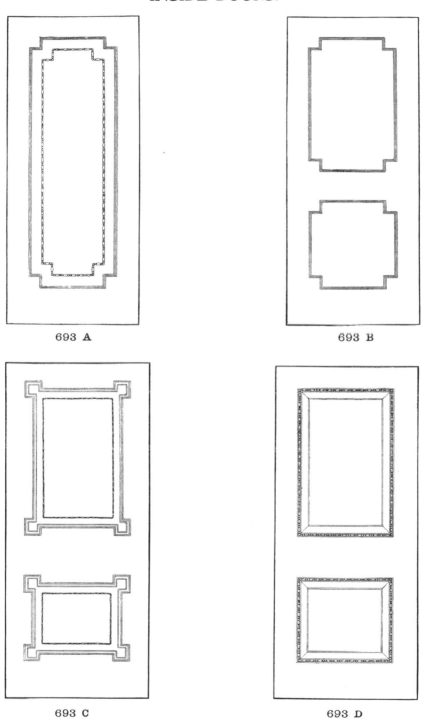

693 A   693 B

693 C   693 D

These doors can be made flush or raised moulding or solid stuck.   See pages 50 and 51 for sections.

INSIDE DOORS.

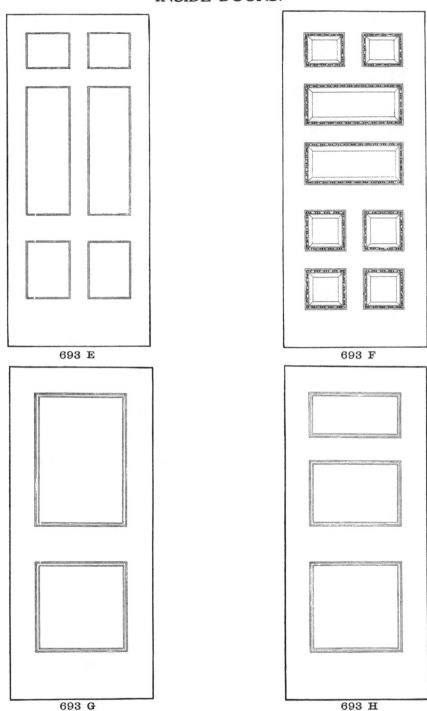

693 E   693 F

693 G   693 H

We make these Doors to order, Veneered in any of the Cabinet Woods, or if desired, in solid White Pine or Hardwood.

For finish, style and reliable qualities, our work cannot be excelled.

SPECIAL FRONT DOORS.

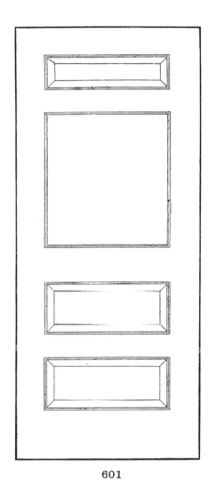

600   601

These special doors we make to order in any size. Made in white or yellow Pine or any of the hardwoods. We are prepared to glaze these doors with sand blast, polished bevel plate, or leaded art glass of handsome design.

Nothing made superior to the quality of our work.

SPECIAL FRONT DOORS.

602

603

These special doors we make to order in any size.   Made in white or yellow Pine or any of the hardwoods.   We are prepared to glaze these doors with sand blast, polished bevel plate, or leaded art glass of handsome design.

Nothing made superior to the quality of our work.

SPECIAL FRONT DOORS.

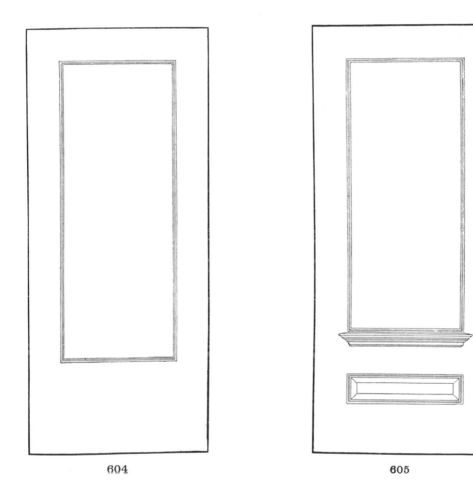

604   605

Built to order either solid or veneered in hardwood. Can also be made in white or yellow Pine and Cypress.

We build them right, using only first class material and work out all details with exactness, the carvings executed in the highest style of art.

Our veneered doors are made from selected stock, chosen for its beauty of grain and uniformity of color.

For finish, style and enduring quality, we guarantee them equal to any made.

SPECIAL FRONT DOORS.

606

607

These special doors we make to order in any size. Made in white or yellow Pine or any of the hardwoods. We are prepared to glaze these doors with sand blast, polished bevel plate, or leaded art glass of handsome design.

Nothing made superior to the quality of our work.

SPECIAL FRONT DOORS.

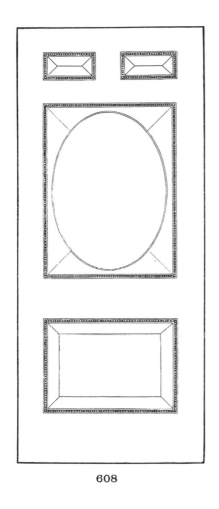

608

609

Built to order either solid or veneered in hardwood. Can also be made in white or yellow Pine and Cypress.

We build them right, using only first class material and work out all details with exactness, the carvings executed in the highest style of art.

Our veneered doors are made from selected stock, chosen for its beauty of grain and uniformity of color

For finish, style, and enduring quality, we guarantee them equal to any made.

SPECIAL FRONT DOORS.

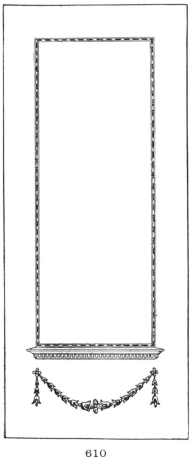

610

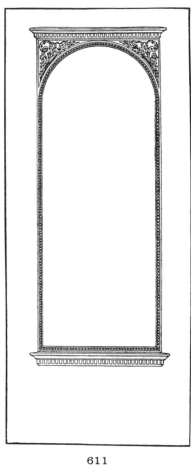

611

These special doors we make to order in any size. Made in white or yellow Pine or any of the hardwoods. We are prepared to glaze these doors with sand blast, polished bevel plate, or leaded art glass of handsome design.

Nothing made superior to the quality of our work.

SPECIAL FRONT DOORS.

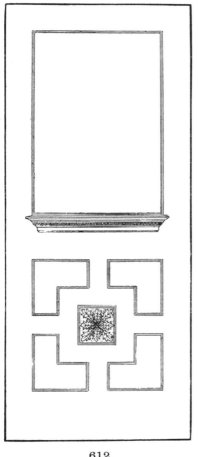

612 613

Built to order either solid or veneered in hardwood. Can also be made in white or yellow Pine and Cypress.

We build them right, using only first class material and work out all details with exactness, the carvings executed in the highest style of art.

Our veneered doors are made from selected stock, chosen for its beauty of grain and uniformity of color.

For finish, style and enduring quality, we guarantee them equal to any made.

SPECIAL FRONT DOORS.

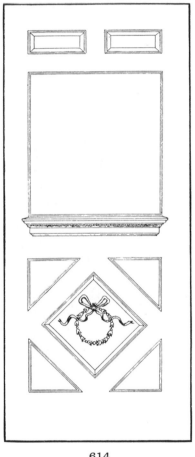

614

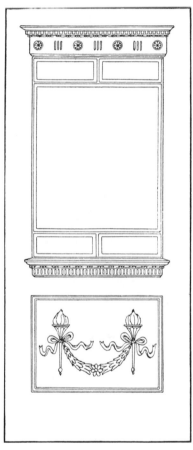

615

These special doors we make to order in any size.   Made in white or yellow Pine or any of the hardwoods.   We are prepared to glaze these doors with sand-blast, polished bevel plate, or leaded art glass of handsome design.

Nothing made superior to the quality of our work.

SPECIAL FRONT DOORS.

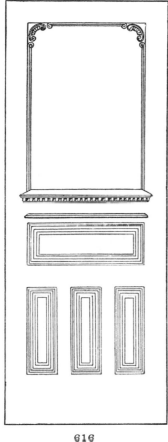

616

617

Built to order either solid or veneered in hardwood. Can also be made in white or yellow Pine and Cypress.

We build them right, using only first class material and work out all details with exactness, the carvings executed in the highest style of art.

Our veneered doors are made from selected stock, chosen for its beauty of grain and uniformity of color.

For finish, style and enduring quality, we guarantee them equal to any made.

SPECIAL FRONT DOORS.

618

619

These special doors we make to order in any size.   Made in white or yellow Pine or any of the hardwoods.   We are prepared to glaze these doors with sand blast, polished bevel plate, or leaded art glass of handsome design.

Nothing made superior to the quality of our work.

SPECIAL FRONT DOORS.

702

703

Bead and Cove Sticking.

SIZE.		PRICES OF 702.		PRICES OF 703.		Add for 1¾ Inches Thick.
		Open.	Glazed. D. S.	Open.	Glazed, D. S.	
2 8 x 6 8	1⅜	$7.50	$10.30	$7.45	$10.20	$3.00
2 10 x 6 10	"	8.65	11.95	8.55	11.85	3.60
2 8 x 7 0	"	8.95	12.25	8.85	12.15	3.75
3 0 x 7 0	"	9.40	13.30	9.30	13.20	3.95
3 0 x 7 6	"	10.90	15.60	10.80	15.55	4.70

If wanted veneered in any of the hardwoods consult our discount sheet for prices.
Sizes not listed, extra price.

SPECIAL FRONT DOORS.

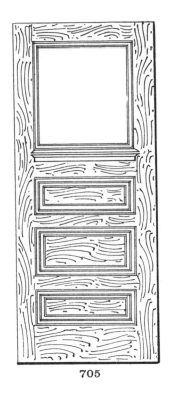

704   705

Bead and Cove Sticking.

SIZE		PRICES OF 704.		PRICES OF 705.		Add for 1¾ inches Thick
		Open.	Glazed, D. S.	Open.	Glazed, D. S.	
2 8 x 6 8	1⅜	$7.35	$10.50	$7.80	$10.95	$3.00
2 10 x 6 10	"	8.50	12.40	8.95	12.85	3.60
2 8 x 7 0	"	8.80	12.40	9.25	12.85	3.75
3 0 x 7 0	"	9.25	13.95	9 70	14 40	3.95
3 0 x 7 6	"	10.75	16.05	11.20	16.50	4.70

If wanted veneered in any of the hardwoods consult our discount sheet for prices.
Sizes not listed, extra price.

SPECIAL FRONT DOORS.

706

707

Bead and Cove Sticking.

SIZE			PRICES OF 706.		PRICES OF 707.		Add for 1¾ inches Thick.
			Open	Glazed, D. S	Open	Glazed, D. S.	
2 8 x 6 8	1⅜		$7.15	$10.90	$8.25	$12.00	$3.00
2 10 x 6 10	"		8 25	13.00	9.40	14.10	3.60
2 8 x 7 0	"		8.55	13.30	9.70	14.40	3.75
3 0 x 7 0	"		9.00	14.35	10.15	15.45	3.95
3 0 x 7 6	"		10.50	16.80	11.65	17.95	4.70

If wanted veneered in any of the hardwoods consult our discount sheet for prices.
Sizes not listed, extra price.

SPECIAL FRONT DOORS.

708   709

Bead and Cove Sticking.

SIZE				PRICES OF 708.		PRICES OF 709.		Add for 1¾ inches Thick.
				Open	Glazed, D. S.	Open	Glazed, D. S.	
2	8 x 6	8	1⅜	$8.40	$12.15	$8 70	$11.50	$3.00
2	10 x 6	10	"	9 55	14.25	9.85	13 15	3.60
2	8 x 7	0	"	9 85	14.55	10.15	13 45	3.75
3	0 x 7	0	"	10.30	15.60	10 60	14.50	3.95
3	0 x 7	6	"	11.80	18.10	12.10	16.80	4.70

If wanted veneered in any of the hardwoods consult our discount sheet for prices.
Sizes not listed, extra price.

SPECIAL FRONT DOORS.

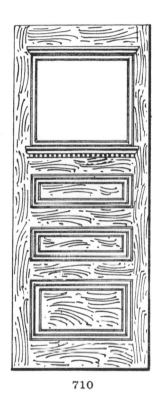

710

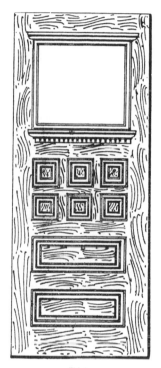

711

Bead and Cove Sticking.

SIZE.		PRICES OF 710.		PRICES OF 711.		Add for 1¾ inches Thick.
		Open.	Glazed, D. S.	Open.	Glazed, D. S.	
2 8 x 6 8	1⅜	$8.70	$11.50	$9.15	$11.95	$3.00
2 10 x 6 10	"	9.85	13.15	10.30	13.60	3.60
2 8 x 7 0	"	10.15	13.45	10.60	13.90	3.75
3 0 x 7 0	"	10.60	14.50	11.05	14.95	3.95
3 0 x 7 6	"	12.10	16.80	12.55	17.25	4.70

If wanted veneered in any of the hardwoods consult our discount sheet for prices.
Sizes not listed, extra price.

SPECIAL FRONT DOORS.

FLUSH MOULDED ONE SIDE.

712

713

SIZE.				PRICES OF 712.		PRICE OF 713.	Add for 1¾ inches Thick.
				Open.	Glazed, D. S.		
2	8 x 6	8	1⅜	$18.00	$20.80	$16.50	$3.00
2	10 x 6	10	"	19.15	22.45	17.65	3.60
2	8 x 7	0	"	19.45	22.75	17.95	3.75
3	0 x 7	0	"	19.90	23.80	18.40	3.95
3	0 x 7	6	"	21.40	26.10	19.90	4.70

If wanted veneered in any of the hardwoods consult our discount sheet for prices.
Sizes not listed extra price.

SPECIAL FRONT DOORS.

FLUSH MOULDED ONE SIDE.

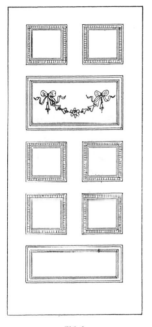

714

715

SIZE.			PRICES OF 714.	PRICES OF 715.	Add for 1¾ inches Thick.
2	8 x 6	8	1⅜	$16.50	$16.50	$3.00
2	10 x 6	10	"	17.65	17.65	3.60
2	8 x 7	0	"	17.95	17.95	3.75
3	0 x 7	0	"	18.40	18.40	3.95
3	0 x 7	6	"	19.90	19.90	4.70

If wanted veneered in any of the hardwoods consult our discount sheet for prices.
Sizes not listed, extra prices.

SPECIAL FRONT DOORS.

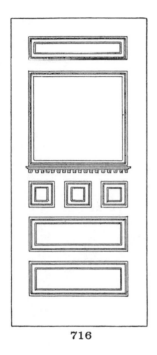

716

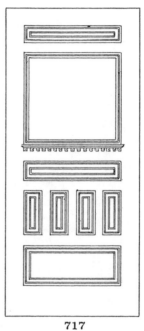

717

Bead and Cove Sticking.

SIZE.			PRICES OF 716.		PRICES OF 717.		Add for 1¾ inches Thick.
			Open.	Glazed, D. S.	Open.	Glazed, D. S.	
2	8 x 6	8	1⅜	$8.55	$11.35	$8.70	$11.50	$3.00
2	10 x 6	10	"	9.70	13.00	9.85	13.15	3.60
2	8 x 7	0	"	10.00	13.30	10.15	13.45	3.75
3	0 x 7	0	"	10.45	14.35	10.60	14.50	3.95
3	0 x 7	6	"	11.95	16.65	12.10	16.80	4.70

If wanted veneered in any of the hardwoods consult our discount sheet for prices.
Sizes not listed, extra price.

FRONT and VESTIBULE DOORS.

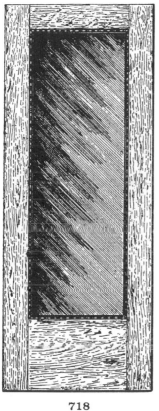

718

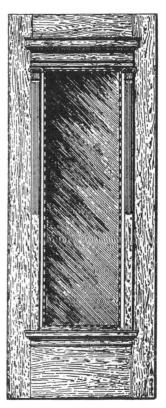

719

SIZE.		PRICES OF 718.		PRICES OF 719.		Add for 1¾ inches Thick.
		Open.	Glazed	Open.	Glazed	
2 8 x 6 8	1⅜	$9.00	Prices Furnished on Application	$19.50	Prices Furnished on Application	$3.00
2 10 x 6 10	"	10.30		20.80		3.60
2 8 x 7 0	"	10.75		21.25		3.75
3 0 x 7 0	"	11.35		21.85		3.95
3 0 x 7 6	"	13.15		23.65		4.70

In writing for glazed prices on these doors state with what kind of glass they are to be glazed.
Sizes not listed, extra price.
If wanted veneered in any of the hardwoods consult our discount sheet for prices.
Made to order only.

FRONT and VESTIBULE DOORS.

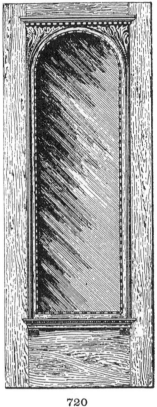

720　　　　　　　　　　　　721

SIZE.		PRICES OF 720.		PRICES OF 721.		Add for 1¾ inches Thick.
		Open.	Glazed.	Open.	Glazed.	
2 8 x 6 8	1⅜	$26.25	Prices Furnished on Application	$34.90	Prices Furnished on Application	$3.00
2 10 x 6 10	"	27.55		36.30		3.60
2 8 x 7 0	"	28.00		36.90		3.75
3 0 x 7 0	"	28.60		37.35		3.95
3 0 x 7 6	"	30.40		39.40		4.70

In writing for glazed prices on these doors state with what kind of glass they are to be glazed.
If wanted veneered in any of the hardwoods consult our discount sheet for prices.
Size not listed, extra price.
Made to order only.

FRONT and VESTIBULE DOORS.

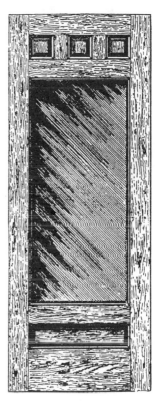

722

723

SIZE.			PRICES OF 722.		PRICES OF 723.		Add for 1¾ inches Thick.
			Open.	Glazed.	Open.	Glazed.	
2	8 x 6	8	1⅜	$10.75		$7.75		$3.00
2	10 x 6	10	"	11.85	Prices Furnished on Application	8.85	Prices Furnished on Application	3.60
2	8 x 7	0	"	12.15		9.15		3.75
3	0 x 7	0	"	12.60		9.60		3.95
3	0 x 7	6	"	14.10		11.10		4.70

In writing for glazed prices on these doors state with what kind of glass they are to be glazed. If wanted veneered in any of the hardwoods consult our discount sheet for prices. Made to order only.

FRONT and VESTIBULE DOORS.

724

725

SIZE.				PRICES OF 724.		PRICES OF 725.		Add for 1¾ inches Thick.
				Open.	Glazed.	Open.	Glazed.	
2	8 x 6	8	1⅜	$19.50	Prices Furnished on Application	$18.00	Prices Furnished on Application	$3.00
2	10 x 6	10	"	20.65		19.15		3.60
2	8 x 7	0	"	20.95		19.45		3.75
3	0 x 7	0	"	21.40		19.90		3.95
3	0 x 7	6	"	22.90		21.40		4.70

In writing for glazed prices on these doors, state with what kind of glass they are to be glazed.
If wanted veneered in any of the hardwoods consult our discount sheet for prices.
Made to order only.

FRONT and VESTIBULE DOORS.

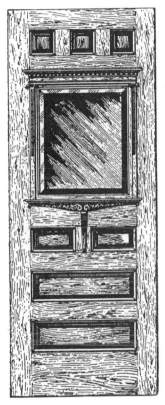

726

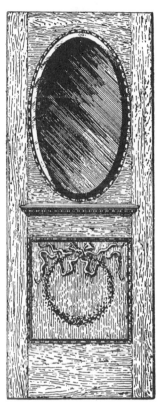

727

SIZE.				PRICES OF 726.		PRICES OF 727.		Add for 1¾ inches Thick.
				Open.	Glazed.	Open.	Glazed.	
2	8 x 6	8	1⅜	$18.00		$24.00		$3.00
2	10 x 6	10	"	19.15	Prices Furnished on Application	25.15	Prices Furnished on Application	3.60
2	8 x 7	0	"	19.45		25.45		3.75
3	0 x 7	0	"	19.90		25.90		3.95
3	0 x 7	6	"	21.40		27.40		4.70

In writing for glazed prices on these doors, state with what kind of glass they are to be glazed. We are prepared to furnish these handsome front doors or any modification of them in pine or any of the hardwoods, both solid and veneered. Specify style of glazing wanted.

STORE DOORS.

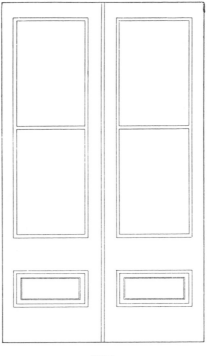

780

Moulded panels outside, O G finish inside.

List price per pair.

Size of Opening.	1⅜ Thick.		1¾ Thick.	
	Per Pair Open.	Per Pair Glazed D. S.	Per Pair Open.	Per Pair Glazed D. S.
5 0 x 7 0	$16.15	$26.25	$23.35	$33.45
7 6	18.30	30.75	26.70	39.15
8 0	20.40	33.15	30.30	43.05
8 6	24.40	38.40	35.80	49.80
6 0 x 7 6	20.35	37.65	29.75	47.05
8 0	22.20	39.55	33.10	50.45
8 6	24.80	44.35	37.20	56.75
9 0	28.50	48.05	42.75	62.30

For doors 2¼ inches thick (see Note 16 Door Extras.)

Above doors are not made for shutters.   For door extras see pages 64-65.

STORE DOORS.

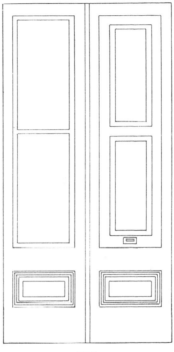

781

Moulded panel outside, O. G. finish inside for shutters.

List price per pair.

Size of Opening	Per Pair, Open, 1⅜ Thick		Per Pair, Open, 1¾ Thick		Add to open list either thickness for Glazing D. S. Glass, 2 lights each door
	Sash Rabbeted on for Shutters	Shutters Fitted and Trimmed	Sash Rabbeted on for Shutters	Shutters Fitted and Trimmed	
5-0 x 7-0	$21.15	$29.40	$28.35	$36.60	$9.45
7-6	23.35	32.20	31.75	40.60	11.55
8-0	25.45	35.10	35.35	45.00	11.55
8-6	29.40	39.40	40.80	50.80	12.75
9-0	31.50	42.00	44.75	55.25	14 05
6-0 x 9-0	33.50	44.50	47.75	58.75	19.60

For 2¼ nches thick see rule 16 Door Extras.

SPECIAL STORE DOORS.

783

Size of Opening.	1⅜ Thick.		1¾ Thick.	
	Per Pair Open.	Per Pair Glazed D. S.	Per Pair Open.	Per Pair Glazed D. S.
5 0 x 7 0	$16.75	$28.30	$23.95	$32.30
7 6	18.90	32.80	27.30	41.20
8 0	21.00	35.20	30.90	45.20
8 6	25.00	40.45	36.40	51.85
6 0 x 7 6	20.95	41.20	30.35	50.60
8 0	22.80	43.10	33.70	54.00
8 6	25.40	47.90	37.80	60.30
9 0	29.10	51.60	43.35	65.85

For 2¼ inches thick see rule 16 Door Extras.

SPECIAL STORE DOORS.

783½

Size of Opening.				1¾ Thick.	
				Per Pair Open.	Per Pair Glazed D. G.
5	0 x 7	0		$41.00	$64.85
		7	6	43.00	71.25
		8	0	45.60	75.40
		8	6	51.25	107.75
6	0 x 7	6		45.60	82.50
		8	0	48.25	89.10
		8	6	51.25	115.50
		9	0	55.00	128.75

For 2¼ inches thick see rule 16 Door Extras.

SPECIAL STORE DOORS.

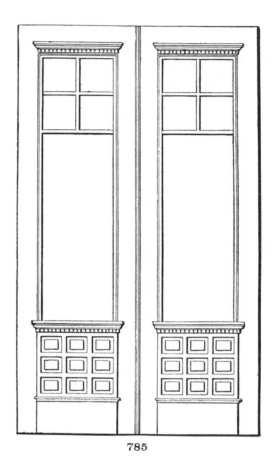

785

Size of Opening.				1¾ Thick.	
				Per Pair Open.	Per Pair Glazed D. S.
5	0 x 7	0		$45.50	$69.35
		7	6	47.50	75.75
		8	0	50.10	79.90
		8	6	55.75	112.25
6	0 x 7	6		50.10	87.00
		8	0	52.75	93.60
		8	6	55.75	120.00
		9	0	59.50	133.25

For 2¼ inches thick see rule 16 Door Extras.

LATTICE DOORS.

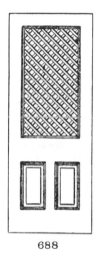

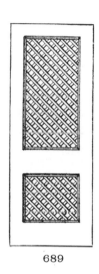

688   689

Size	Price 688		Price 689	
	1⅜ Thick	1¾ Thick	1⅜ Thick	1¾ Thick
2- 8 x 6- 8	$5 75	$ 8.35	$ 6.55	$ 9.25
2- 10 x 6- 10	6.50	9.70	7.15	10.00
2- 8 x 7- 0	6.70	10.00	7.50	10.80
3- 0 x 7- 0	7.10	10.50	7.80	11.30
3- 0 x 7- 6	7.80	11.85	8.60	12.65
3- 0 x 8- 0	8.75	13.45	9.55	14 25
3- 0 x 8- 6	9.90	15.35	10.70	16.15

For Door Extras, see pages 64-65.

OUTSIDE BLINDS.

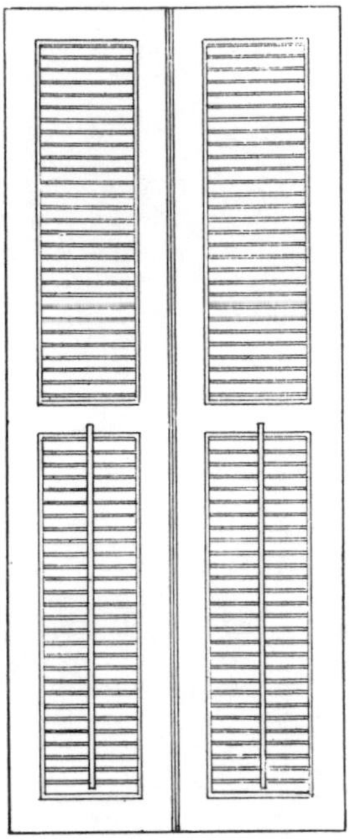

EIGHT-LIGHTED WINDOWS.

Size of Glass.	Price, Rolling Slats.	Price, Stationary or Half Stationary Slats.		Size of Opening.			Weight.	
	1⅛ thick.	1⅛ thick.	1⅜ thick.				1⅛ in.	1⅜ in.
9x12	$1.90	$2.15	$2.60	1	11 x 4	7	15	19
14	2.10	2.35	2.85		5	3	16	20
16	2.35	2.60	3.15		5	11	18	22
10x12	1.90	2.15	2 60	2	1 x 4	7	16	20
14	2 10	2.35	2.85		5	3	18	22
16	2.35	2.60	3.15		5	11	20	25
18	2.65	2.90	3.50		6	7	22	27
20	2.90	3.15	3.80		7	3	23	29
12x14	2.10	2.35	2.85	2	5 x 5	3	20	25
16	2 35	2.60	3.10		5	11	23	29
18	2.65	2.90	3.50		6	7	24	30
20	2.90	3.15	3.80		7	3	26	32

For 1⅜-inch rolling slat blinds in stock quantities deduct 20c list from 1⅜ stationary slat blinds. Size of blinds measure same as check rail windows, with the addition of 1 inch to bottom rail for sub-sill frame, which can be cut off if necessary. Our regular stock rolling slat blinds are made with O G stiles. We make square stiles on rolling slat blinds only on special orders. Stationary and half stationary blinds are made with square stiles.

For blind extras see page 129.

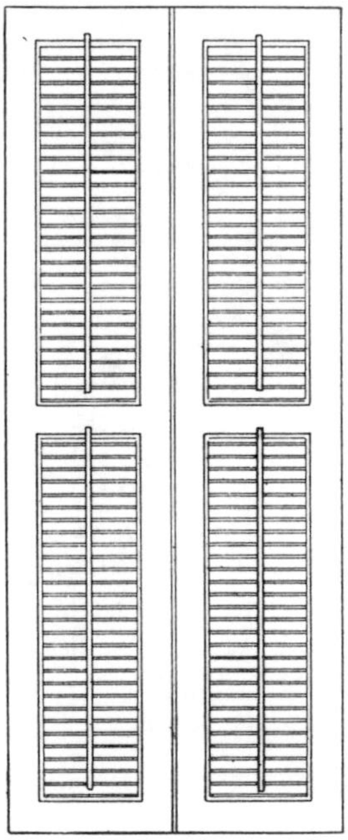

Half Stationary and Half Rolling Slats.

TWELVE-LIGHTED WINDOWS.

Size of Glass.	Price, Rolling Slats.	Price, Stationary or Half Stationary Slats.		Size of Opening.			Weight.	
	1⅛ thick.	1⅛ thick.	1⅜ thick.				1⅛ in.	1⅜ in.
8x10	$1.65	$1.90	$2.30	2	4½ x 3	11	14	18
12	1.90	2.15	2.60		4	7	16	20
14	2.10	2.35	2.85		5	3	18	22
9x12	2.10	2.35	2.85	2	7½ x 4	7	18	22
13	2.20	2.45	2.95		4	11	19	24
14	2.25	2.50	3.00		5	3	20	25
15	2.45	2.70	3.25		5	7	21	25
16	2.50	2.75	3.30		5	11	23	29
10x12	2.20	2.45	2.95	2	10½ x 4	7	20	25
14	2.35	2.60	3.15		5	3	22	27
15	2.50	2.75	3.30		5	7	23	29
16	2.65	2.90	3.50		5	11	25	31
18	2.95	3.20	3.85		6	7	27	34
20	3.25	3.50	4.20		7	3	30	37

Rolling Slats.

OUTSIDE BLINDS. FOUR-LIGHTED WINDOWS.

Size of Glass.	Price Rolling Slats.	Price Stationary or Half Stationary Slats.		Size of Opening.		Weight.	
	1⅛ thick	1⅛ thick	1⅜ thick			1⅛ in.	1⅜ in.
12 x 20	$1.65	$1.90	$2.30	2 5 x 3	11	14	18
22	1.70	1.95	2.35	4	3	15	19
24	1.90	2.15	2.60	4	7	16	20
26	2.00	2.25	2.70	4	11	17	21
28	2.10	2.35	2.85	5	3	18	23
30	2.25	2.50	3.00	5	7	19	24
32	2.35	2.60	3.15	5	11	20	25
34	2.50	2.75	3.30	6	3	22	28
36	2.65	2.90	3.50	6	7	23	29
38	2.85	3.10	3.75	6	11	24	30
40	2.90	3.15	3.80	7	3	25	31
14 x 24	2.10	2.35	2.85	2 9 x 4	7	20	25
26	2.20	2.45	2.95	4	11	20	25
28	2.25	2.50	3.00	5	3	22	27
30	2.45	2.70	3.25	5	7	23	29
32	2.50	2.75	3.30	5	11	24	30
34	2.85	3.10	3.75	6	3	26	32
36	2.90	3.15	3.80	6	7	27	34
38	3.10	3.35	4.05	6	11	28	35
40	3.15	3.40	4.10	7	3	30	37
42	3.35	3.60	4.35	7	7	32	40
44	3.50	3.75	4.50	7	11	33	41
46	3.70	3.95	4.75	8	3	34	42
48	3.75	4.00	4.80	8	7	36	45

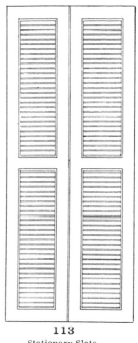

113
Stationary Slats.

For 15-inch glass, see No. 3 blind extras.
Irregular and intermediate sizes, in stock quantities, same price as next larger listed size.
For less than stock quantities, on sizes not listed, an extra 10 per cent will be charged.

OUTSIDE BLINDS.—TWO-LIGHTED PANTRY WINDOWS.—1⅛-inches thick.

Size of Glass.	Price Single Blind.	Size of Opening.	Weight	Size of Glass.	Price Single Blind.	Size of Opening.	Weight
12 x 24	$1.25	1 4⅛ x 4 7	8	14 x 24	$1.40	1 6⅛ x 4 7	9
26	1.40	x 4 11	9	26	1.45	4 11	10
28	1.40	x 5 3	10	28	1.60	5 3	11
30	1.45	x 5 7	10	30	1.65	5 7	12
32	1.60	x 5 11	11	32	1.65	5 11	13
34	1.70	x 6 3	12	34	1.85	6 3	14
36	1.85	x 6 7	13	36	1.90	6 7	14

Blinds for two-lighted windows, with glass 20, 22 or 24 inches wide, same price as blinds for four lighted windows with 12-inch glass, same height.

Blinds for two-lighted windows, with glass 26 or 28 inches wide, same price as blinds for four-lighted windows with 14-inch glass, same height.

Blinds for two-lighted windows, with glass 30 inches wide, same price as blinds for four-lighted windows with 15-inch glass, same height. (See No. 3, blind extras.)

Blinds for windows with 34-inch glass and longer made three panels high unless otherwise ordered. Sizes not listed, extra price.

All blinds for four-light pantry windows same price as two-light, same height.

Irregular and intermediate sizes, in stock quantities, same price as next larger listed size.

For less than stock quantities, on sizes not listed, an extra 10 per cent will be charged.

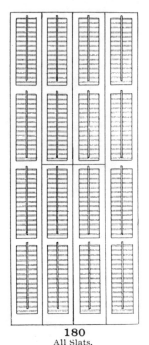

180
All Slats.

INSIDE BLINDS.

DIRECTIONS FOR ORDERING.

First—In all cases give the exact outside measure of Blinds wanted.

Second—Give the number of folds.

Third—State if Blinds are to be all slats, or half panels and half slats.

Fourth—State distance from top of window to center of meeting rail of sash, or where Blinds are to be cut.

Fifth—Give thickness of Blinds.

Sixth—If Blinds fold in pockets, give size of pockets.

Seventh—State if Blinds are to be painted or finished in oil.

Eighth—If for oil finish, extra price.

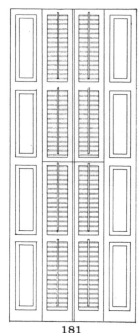

181
½ Panels, ½ Slats.

1⅛-inch thick all slats, all panels, or a combination of both.   Per Lin. Ft.

2-fold, 2 feet wide and under	$1.00
3-fold, 2 feet 11 inches wide and under	1.25
4-fold, 2 feet 11 inches wide and under	1.50
4-fold, over 2 feet 11 inches and not over 3 feet 5 inches	1.75
5-fold, over 2 feet 11 inches and not over 3 feet 5 inches	2.00
6-fold, 3 feet 5 inches to 4 feet 5 inches, inclusive	2.50
8-fold, 4 feet 4 inches to 5 feet 5 inches, inclusive	3.00

⅞-inch inside blinds 5 per cent less than 1⅛ inch.

The above prices are for White Pine.

If for oil finish **add** 20 per cent to above prices.

If hardwood, such as Cherry, Ash, Maple, or Black Walnut are wanted, we **charge** extra price.

We **make Inside Blinds that** are not excelled, either in workmanship or style, in any market.

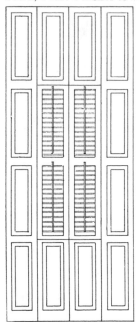

182
¾ Panel

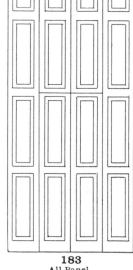

183
All Panel.

BLIND EXTRAS.

NOTE—(a). The term "stock quantities," wherever used in this list, means 5 or more Doors and 10 or more Windows, Sash or Blinds, of one size, kind and quality.

NOTE—(b). Irregular and intermediate sizes, in stock quantities, same list as next larger listed size. For less than stock quantities, on sizes not listed, an extra 10 per cent will be charged.

NOTE—(c). Where no provision is made for price on quantities less than 10, use stock quantity price and add 10 per cent to the amount thus created.

	For 10 or more.	For less than 10.
No. 1. Window and Door Blinds wider than listed sizes, for every 4 inches or fractional part thereof, add	15%	Note C
No. 2. Window and Door Blinds longer than listed sizes, for every 2 inches or fractional part thereof, add for 1⅛ inch Blinds...$	.25 list	Note C
Add for 1⅜ inch Blinds..	.30 list	Note C
No. 3. For Blinds for 15 inch glass, 4-lights, add to list price of Blinds same length for 14 inch glass....	10%	Note C
No. 4. Blinds for 2-light Windows, with glass 20, 22 or 24 inches wide, same price as Blinds for 4-light Windows with 12-inch glass, same height.		
No. 5. Blinds for 2-lighted Windows, with glass 26 or 28 inches wide, same price as Blinds for 4-lighted Windows with 14-inch glass, same height....		
No. 6. Blinds for 2-lighted Windows, with glass 30 inches wide, same price as Blinds for 4-lighted Windows with 15-in. glass, same height		Note C
No. 7. Blinds for 34-inch glass and longer, made in three panels, unless otherwise ordered.		
No. 8. For Blinds, 1⅜-inch, rolling slats, deduct from price of 1⅜ inch stationary slat Blinds, same size..	.20 list	Note C
No. 9. Our Regular Stock Rolling Slat Blinds are made with O G Stiles.		

	For 10 or more.	For less than 10.
No. 10. We make Square Stiles on Rolling Slat Blinds only on special orders.		
No. 11. Stationary and Half Stationary Blinds are made with Square Stiles.		
No. 12. For Mullion Blinds, add to price of a pair of Blinds same size.........	10%	Note C
No. 13. For Segment Head Blinds, add	2.25 list	3.00 list
For Circle Head—Circle Corners—Gothic or Eliptic Head Blinds, add.........	3.75 list	5.00 list
No. 14. For Solid Mould Panel Shutters, add to list of Stationary Slat Blinds, same size and thickness....	25%	Note C
No. 15. For Solid Mould Panel Shutters, add to list of Stationary Slat Blinds of same thickness	25%	Note C
No. 16. For Shutters Bead and Butt 1 side, Flush Moulded 1 side, add to list of Stationary Slat Blinds same thickness	45%	Note C
No. 17. For Blinds with Stiles over 1¾ inches wide, add for every half inch or fractional part thereof for 1⅛ inch Blinds..........	.25 list	Note C
For 1⅜ inch Blinds, add..	.30 list	Note C
No. 18. In ordering, state if Blinds are to be a pair or single piece, to each opening.		
No. 19. All Door Blinds are made in pairs and rabbeted, same as Window Blinds, unless otherwise ordered.		
No. 20. For Blinds made in one piece, add	10%	Note C

INSIDE SLIDING BLINDS.

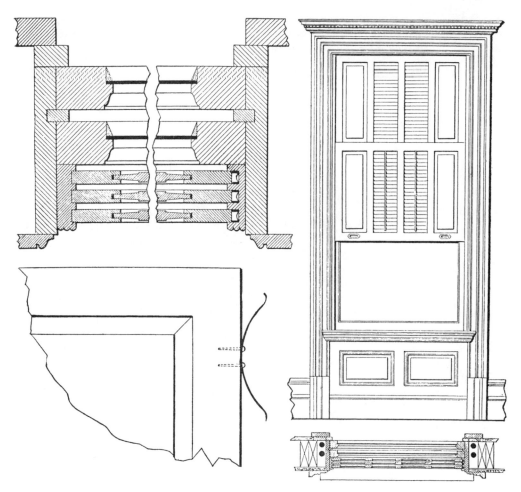

Above section shows that no special frame is required to use our sliding blinds. The guideway is fastened on pulley stile, acting as a stop for the sash,

These sliding blinds are made ½-inch in thickness, and though constructed of light material possess great strength and lasting qualities.

Can be closed with the window raised and cannot blow open or rattle, thus giving the best medium of ventilation.

They do not interfere with curtains or window ornaments, and admit light and air from any part of the window.

These blinds are specially made to order in the white or finished complete; either varnished in the natural colors of the different woods or stained and varnished, or wood filled and cabinet or rubbed finish. All trimmings and hardware we furnish, which is included in the price of blinds given on page 131.

LIST PRICE INSIDE SLIDING BLINDS.

Per lineal foot in height, including Guideways and all necessary Hardware.

WOOD AND FINISH

White Pine, Poplar, Cypress, Basswood, Spruce and Yellow Pine.	2 DIV. 12 to 22 in.	3 DIV. 16 to 29 in.	4 DIV. 21 to 37 in.	5 DIV. 26 to 46 in.	6 DIV. 30 to 54 in.
In White (no finish)	$0.65	$0.75	$0.85	$1.00	$1.15
Varnish Finish (2 coat)	.75	.90	1.05	1.20	1.40
Varnish Finish (3 coat)	.80	.95	1.15	1.30	1.55
Oil Rubbed Cabinet Finish	.85	1.05	1.20	1.40	1.65

Plain Oak, Common Ash, Red Gum (Hazel), Maple, and Chestnut.					
In White (no finish)	.75	.85	1.00	1.10	1.25
Varnish Finish (3 coat)	.90	1.05	1.25	1.50	1.75
Oil Rubbed Cabinet Finish	1.00	1.20	1.40	1.60	1.85

Quartered Oak, Butternut, Quartered Sycamore, California Red Wood and White Ash.					
In White (no finish)	.85	.95	1.10	1.25	1.40
Varnish Finish (3 coat)	1.00	1.15	1.35	1.60	1.85
Oil Rubbed Cabinet Finish	1.10	1.30	1.50	1.75	2.00

Black Walnut, Cherry, Curly Birch, and Bird's Eye Maple					
In White (no finish)	1.00	1.10	1.30	1.60	1.90
Varnish Finish (3 coat)	1.15	1.30	1.55	1.85	2.15
Oil Rubbed Cabinet Finish	1.25	1.45	1.65	2.00	2.40

Mahogany.					
In White (no finish)	1.10	1.25	1.45	1.80	2.10
Varnish Finish (3 coat)	1.25	1.50	1.75	2.10	2.45
Oil Rubbed Cabinet Finish	1.35	1.65	1.90	2.30	2.70

For combination of woods average the prices of the several woods.

Convex Blinds _____$4.00 per window extra.
Gothic, Segment, Oval or Circle Tops_____ 2.00   "   "   "
Extra Heavy Lifts, Bronze or Old Copper (put on with screws)_____10 cents each.
Drop Pulls, Bronze or Old Copper_____15   "   "
Concealed Metal Operator, per division_____12   "   "

PLEASE NOTE—That above list prices include all necessary Hardware or Trimming, and in comparing cost with folding blinds or other makes of sliding blinds, this should be taken into consideration. **Above prices subject to discount.**

Will make net estimates on weighted blinds or on special designs from architects' details.

DIRECTIONS FOR ORDERING.

Give the exact measurement of the opening which the blinds are to fill. Where guideways take the place of stops, state distance from face of casing to inner face of lower sash. If windows are circle head or segment inside, send exact pattern or give radius. Full information for adjusting these blinds accompany each order.

VENETIAN BLINDS.

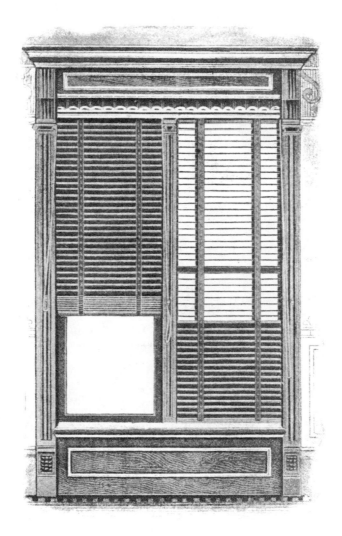

Above cut shows the blinds as used in a Double or Mullion Window.

In the left hand window the blind is partly raised, the slats being arranged to exclude the light.   In the right hand window the blind is lowered, with upper slats arranged to admit light, and the lower ones to exclude it.   In the blind each slat is independent in its action, consequently any number of slats can be closed or left open at will and in any desired part of the blind.   The control of light and air is therefore practically absolute in these blinds.

Give opening size wanted filled.

LIST PRICES VENETIAN BLINDS

CLASSIFICATION OF WOODS.	Price per square foot.	
	2⅜ inch Slats.	2 inch Slats.
Spruce, Whitewood, Linden and Yellow Pine, finished natural, stained to imitate Hardwoods, or painted in dark colors	$0.19	$0.21
Painted in light colors or tints	.21	.23
Painted in enamels	.24	.26
Enameled, rubbed between coats	.38	.40
White Pine, Cypress, Plain Oak, Ash, Elm, Chestnut and ordinary Maple	.21	.23
Plain Birch and Butternut	.22	.24
Quartered Oak and Quartered Sycamore	.24	.26
Cherry, Black Walnut, California Redwood and White Ash	.30	.32
Red Mahogany, Curly Birch, Bird's Eye and White Maple	.38	.40

With the exception of Painted and Enameled work, the above prices are in Varnish Finish. Add to above list for ordinary Rubbed Finish 3 cents per square foot.

No Blind figured to contain less than 15 square feet.

Above prices subject to discount.

Our Venetian Blinds do not require any special frame, are easily applied, and are the most simply constructed on the market. Venetian Blinds do not interfere with curtains or draperies, and are becoming more popular every year.

SWINGING SALOON and CLOSET DOOR DESIGNS.

DOOR BLINDS.

Only carried in stock in pairs.

SIZE.					Thickness.	Price Per Pair.
2	6	x	6	6	$1\frac{1}{8}$	$3.95
2	8	x	6	8	"	4.15
2	10	x	6	10	"	4.40
3	0	x	7	0	"	4.60

$1\frac{3}{8}$ inches thick, add to list price of $1\frac{1}{8}$ inches, 20 per cent.

All Door Blinds made in pairs and rabbeted, same as Window Blinds, unless otherwise ordered.   If made in one piece, 10 per cent extra.

For Blind extras, see page 129.

SWING WATER CLOSET DOORS.

184

184 B

185

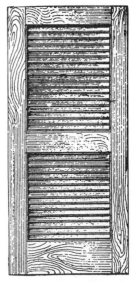

186

SWINGING SALOON and CLOSET DOORS.

We make of Pine or any of the Hardwoods.   In ordering or inquiring prices, give size, number and kind of wood wanted.

STORE FRONTS.

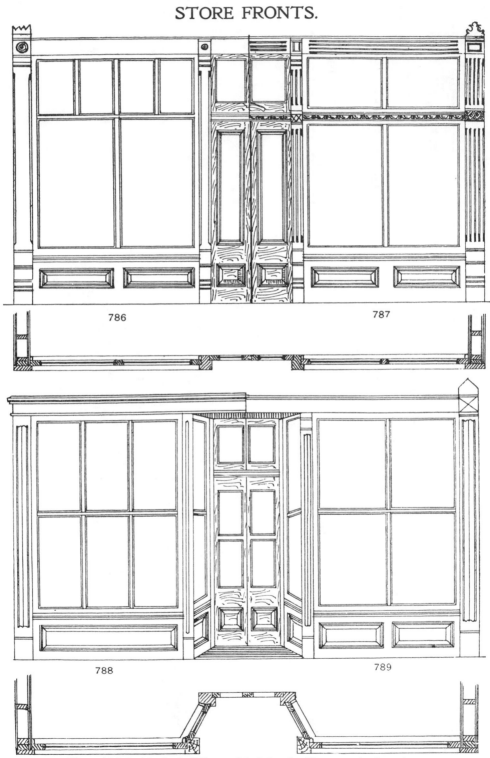

786   787

788   789

Give width inside the building and height of ceiling.   Write for prices.

STORE FRONTS.

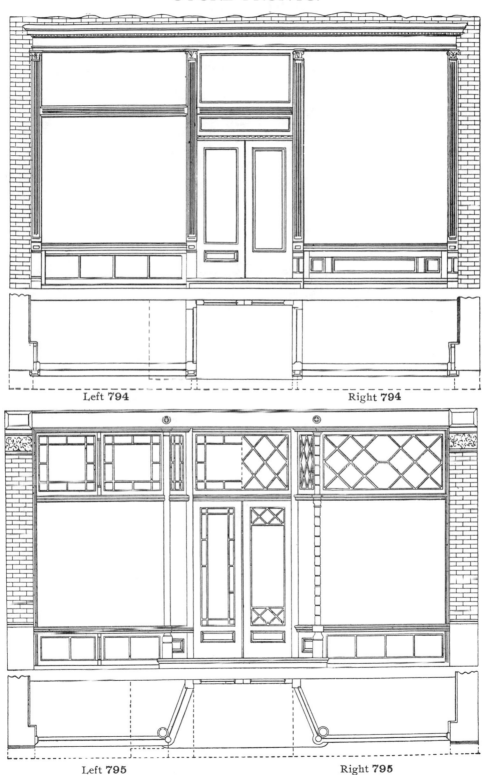

Left **794** Right **794**

Left **795** Right **795**

STORE FRONTS.

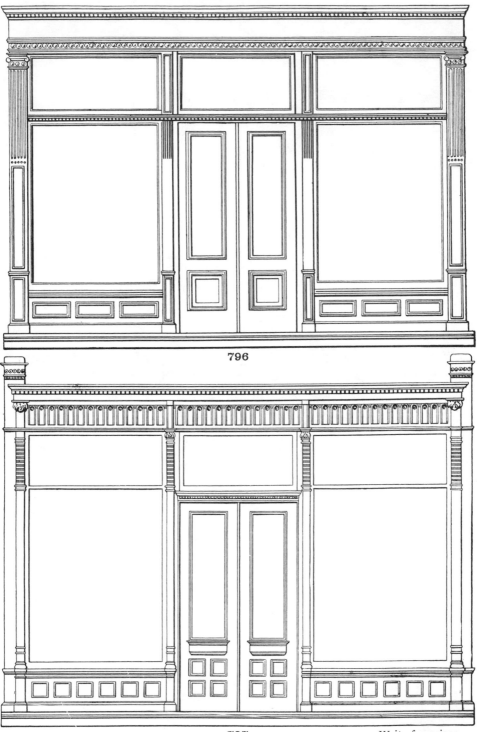

796

797   Write for prices.

STORE FRONTS.

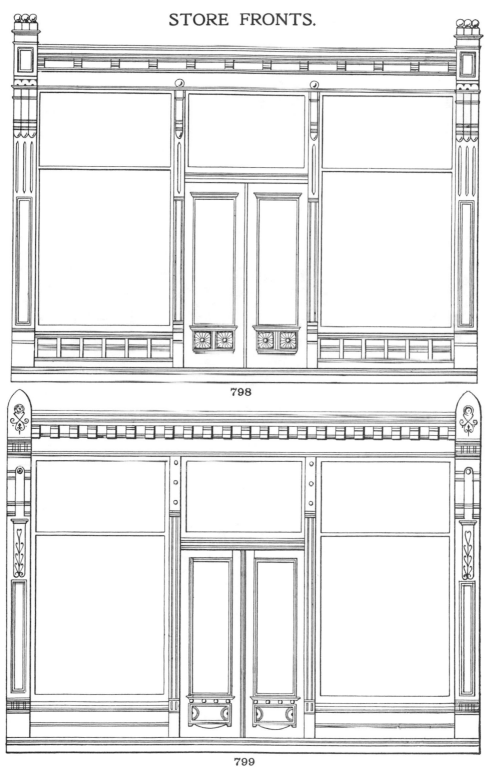

798

799

Give width inside the building and height of ceiling.   Write for prices.

STOCK CORNER BLOCKS.

1⅛ inches Thick.

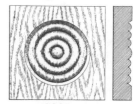

1006
$5.00 per 100

1007
$6.00 per 100

1008
$5.50 per 100

STOCK HEAD BLOCKS.

1⅛ inches Thick.

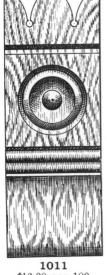

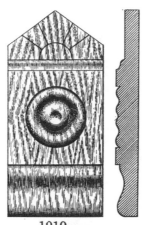

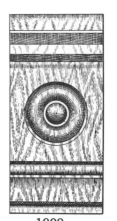

1011
$16.00 per 100

1010
$18.00 per 100

1009
$10.00 per 100

STOCK BASE BLOCKS.

1⅜ inches Thick.

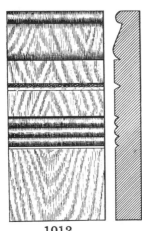

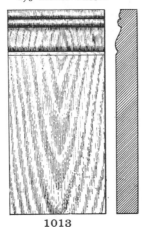

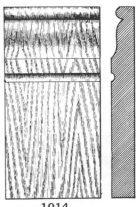

1012
$11.00 per 100

1013
$9.00 per 100

1014
$10.00 per 100

Above **prices** are for **Blocks** not over 5⅝ inches wide. Always specify width of casing when ordering.

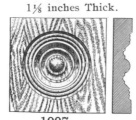

CORNER BLOCKS.

1⅛ inches Thick.

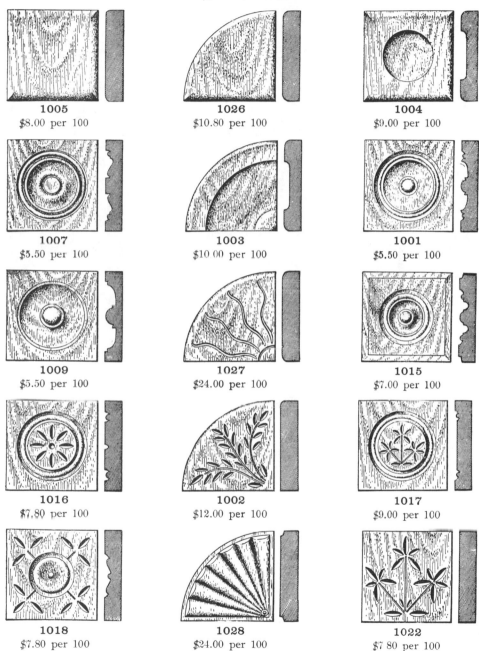

1005
$8.00 per 100

1026
$10.80 per 100

1004
$9.00 per 100

1007
$5.50 per 100

1003
$10 00 per 100

1001
$5.50 per 100

1009
$5.50 per 100

1027
$24.00 per 100

1015
$7.00 per 100

1016
$7.80 per 100

1002
$12.00 per 100

1017
$9.00 per 100

1018
$7.80 per 100

1028
$24.00 per 100

1022
$7 80 per 100

Above prices cover Blocks up to 5½ inches square. Larger sizes, extra price.

HEAD BLOCKS.

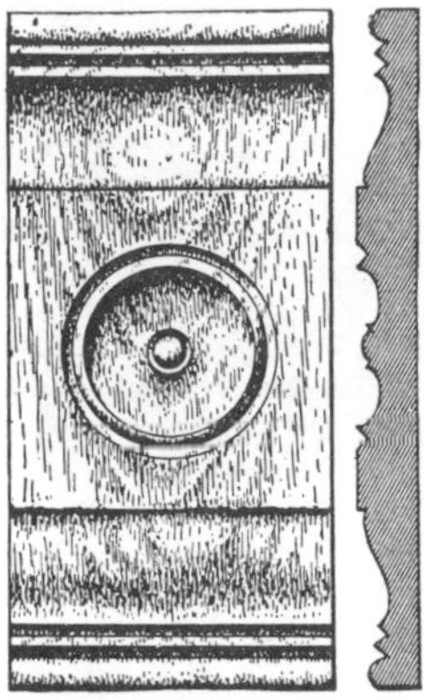

1067
$10.00 per 100

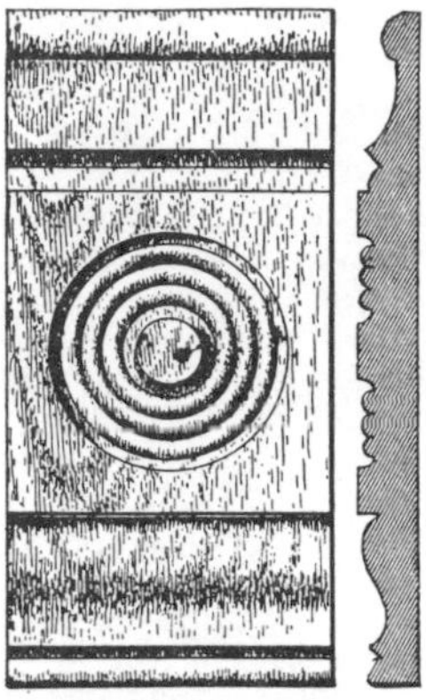

1065
$10.00 per 100

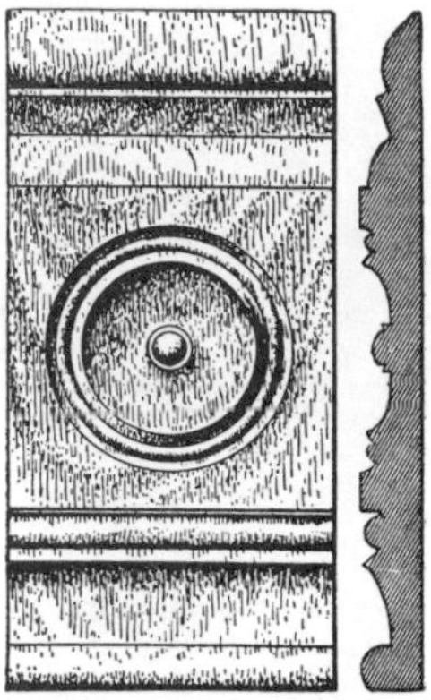

1069
$10.00 per 100

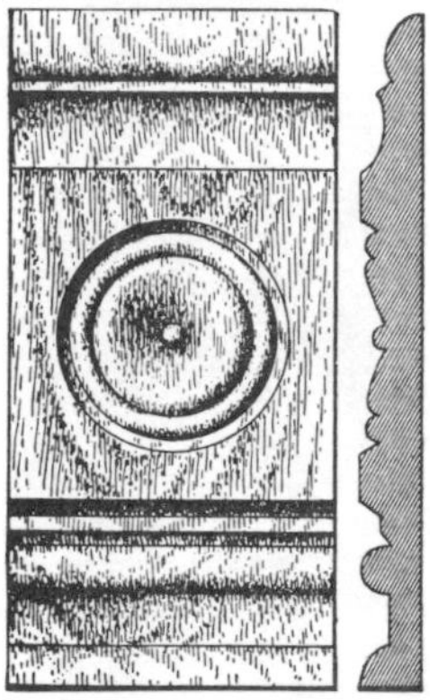

1064
$10.00 per 100

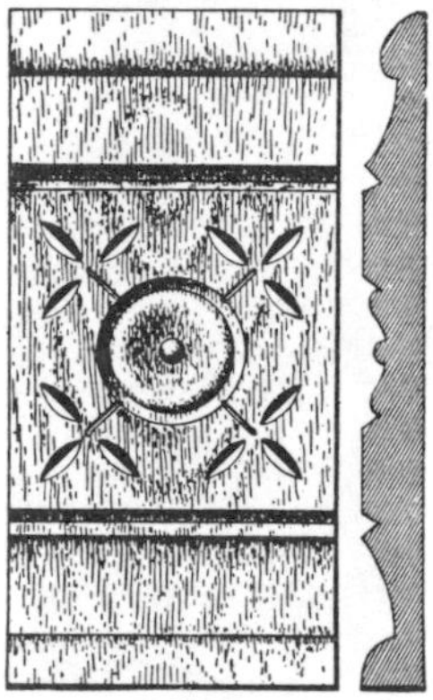

1032
$13.20 per 100

1093
$14.40 per 100

1068
$21.60 per 100

1037
$40.00 per 100

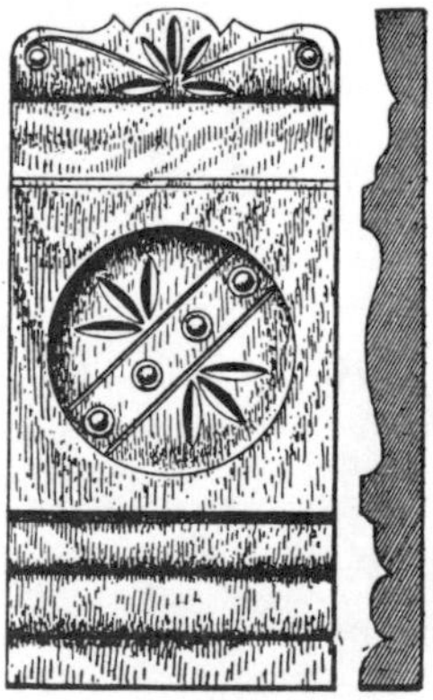

1070
$20.40 per 100

Above prices cover Blocks up to 5½ inches wide, 10 inches long, 1⅛ inches thick.
Larger sizes, extra price.

BASE BLOCKS.

1101
$10.50 per 100

1099
$10.00 per 100

1098
$10.50 per 100

1044
$16.80 per 100

1097
$11.00 per 100

1040
$16.80 per 100

1041
$16.80 per 100

1047
$24.00 per 100

1045
$16.80 per 100

Above prices cover Blocks up to 5½ inches wide, 11 inches long, 1⅜ inches thick.
Larger sizes, extra price.

PRICES on CORNER and PLINTH BLOCKS.

————ADOPTED BY————

Wholesale Sash, Door and Blind Manufacturers' Association
OF THE NORTHWEST.

EFFECTIVE SEPTEMBER 5th 1901.

No.	Price.
1006	$ 5.00
1007	6.00
1008	5.50
1009	10.00
1010	18.00
1011	19.20
1012	11.00
1013	10.00
1014	10.00
1015	7.00
1016	7.80
1017	9.00
1018	7.80
1019	9.60
1020	14.40
1021	8.40
1022	6.60
1023	6.60
1024	9.60
1025	7.20
1026	10.80
1027	24.00
1028	24.00
1029	22.00
1030	14.40
1031	16.80
1032	13.20
1033	26.40
1084	15.60
1035	24.00
1036	15.60
1037	40.00
1038	45.00
1039	21.60
1040	16.80
1041	16.80
1042	16.80
1043	16.80
1044	16.80
1045	16.80
1046	16.80
1047	24.00
2706 4½ to 6 in. x 1⅛	5.00
2707 " " "	5.00
2708 " " "	5.50
2709 " " "	5.50
2710 " " "	5.00
2711 " " "	5.00
2712 " " "	5.00
2713 " " "	5.50
2714 " " "	5.50
2715 " " "	5.00
2716 " " "	6.00
2717 " " "	5.00
2718 " " "	6.00
2719 " " "	5.00
2720 " " "	5.50
2721 " " "	6.00
2722 " " "	6.00
2723 " " "	5.50
2724 " " "	12.00
2725 " " "	12.00
2726 " " "	8.40
2727 " " "	8.40
2728 " " "	24.00
2729 " " "	24.00
2730 " " "	8.40
2731 " " "	7.80
2732 " " "	6.60
2733 " " "	24.00
2734 " " "	24.00
2735 " " "	6.60
2736 " " "	7.80
2737 " " "	7.80
2738 " " "	6.60

No.	Price.
2739 4½ to 6 in. x 1⅛	$ 7.80
2740 " " "	5.50
2741 " " "	30.00
2742 " " "	10.20
2743 " " "	7.00
2744 " " "	132.00
2745 " " "	7.80
2747 " " "	30.00
2748 " " "	21.60
2749 " " "	5.00
2750 " " "	5.50
2751 " " "	6.00
2752 4½ to 5¾ in. sq. x 1⅛	18.00
2752 6 6¾ " x 1⅛	21.60
2752 5 5¾ " x 1⅜	21.60
2752 6 6¾ " x 1⅜	24.00
2754 1⅝ x 8 in	32.00
2755 2¾ x 4½ in	36.00
2755 3⅛ x 2½ in	26.00
2759 5 to 6 in. sq. x 1⅛	30.00
2759 6 to 6¾ " x 1⅜	36.00
2759 7 to 8½ " x 1⅜	42.00
2759 6 to 6¾ " x 1¾	42.00
2759 7 to 8¼ " x 1¾	45.60
2760 4 in. diameter	36.00
2761 3¾ in. sq	48.00
2761 4¾ "	68.00
2762 2¾ x 6 in	56.00
2762 3¾ x 8 in	80.00
2763 1 in. diameter	7.00
2763 1¼ " "	8.00
2763 1½ " "	9.00
2763 1¾ " "	10.00
2763 2 " "	12.00
2763 2¼ " "	14.00
2763 2½ " "	16.00
2763 2¾ " "	18.00
2763 3¼ " "	20.00
2764 1 " "	8.00
2764 1¼ " "	10.00
2764 1½ " "	12.00
2764 1¾ " "	13.00
2764 2 " "	14.00
2765 2⅜ in. sq	16.00
2766 1⅞ "	13.00
2767 1¾ in. diameter	10.00
2768 1⅞ in sq	13.00
2768 2⅜ "	16.00
2768 3¼ "	32.00
2769 1¾ "	12.00
2770 1¾ in. diameter	10.00
2770 2½ "	18.00
2771 1⅛ " "	8.00
2771 1⅜ " "	9.00
2771 1⅝ "	10.00
2771 2⅞ "	14.00
2772 4½ to 6 in. sq. x 1⅛	5.50
2773 4½ to 6 " x 1⅛	7.00
2776 4½ to 6 " x 1⅜	10.80
2777 4½ to 6 " x 1⅜	18.00
2778 4½ to 6 " x 1⅜	12.00
2779 4½ to 6 " x 1⅜	24.00
2780 4½ to 6 " x 1⅛	5.00
2787 5 to 6 " x 1⅜	22.00
2788 5 to 6 " x 1⅜	30.00
2790 5 to 6 " x 1⅛	12.00
2791 5 to 6 " x 1⅛	12.00
2792 5 to 6 " x 1⅛	8.40
2793 5 to 6 " x 1⅛	8.40
2794 5 to 6 " x 1⅛	7.80
2795 5 to 6 " x 1⅛	9.00
2796 5 to 6 " x 1⅛	7.20
2800 5½ x 8 x 1⅛	9.00
2801 5½ x 7 x 1⅛	9.60
2802 5½ x 10 x 1⅛	10.00

No.	Price.
2803 5½ x 10 x 1⅛	$18.00
2804 5½ x 10 x 1⅛	10.00
2805 5½ x 10 x 1⅛	12.00
2806 5½ x 11 x 1⅛	18.00
2807 5½ x 11 x 1⅛	19.20
2808 5½ x 10 x 1⅛	14.40
2809 5½ x 10 x 1⅛	10.00
2810 5½ x 10 x 1⅛	10.00
2811 5½ x 12 x 1⅛	14.00
2812 5½ x 12 x 1⅛	16.00
2813 5½ x 12 x 1⅛	14.00
2814 5½ x 11 x 1⅛	15.60
2815 5½ x 11 x 1⅛	13.20
2816 5½ x 11 x 1⅛	13.20
2817 5½ x 10 x 1⅛	14.40
2818 5½ x 10 x 1⅛	13.20
2819 5½ x 12 x 1⅛	14.40
2820 5½ x 12 x 1⅛	18.00
2821 5½ x 9½ x 1⅛	14.40
2822 5½ x 10 x 1⅛	36.00
2823 5½ x 10 x 1⅛	20.40
2824 5½ x 10 x 1⅛	14.40
2825 5½ x 11 x 1⅛	144.00
2826 5½ x 10 x 1⅛	14.40
2827 5½ x 10½ x 1⅛	11.00
2828 5½ x 10 x 1⅛	13.20
2829 5½ x 10½ x 1⅛	36.00
2830 5½ x 11 x 1⅛	24.00
2831 5½ x 10½ x 1⅛	14.00
2832 5 in. to 5¾ x 9 x 1⅜	48.00
2832 6 in. to 6¾ x 10 x 1⅜	54.00
2833 5 in. to 5¾ x 13 x 1⅜	60.00
2833 6 in. to 6¾ x 13 x 1⅜	72.00
2833 7 in. to 8 x 13 x 1⅜	90.00
2834 5½ x 12½ x 1⅜	72.00
2835 5½ x 11½ x 1⅛	15.60
2836 5½ x 12 x 1⅛	28.80
2837 5½ x 12 x 1⅛	60.00
2838 5½ x 10 x 1⅛	10.00
2839 5½ x 12½ x 1⅜	30.00
2844 5½ x 12 x 1⅛	66.00
2853 5½ x 11 x 1⅛	10.00
2855 5½ x 11 x 1⅜	60.00
2856 5½ x 10 x 1⅜	18.00
2900 5½ x 10 x 1⅜	11.00
2901 5½ x 9 x 1⅜	9.00
2902 5½ x 9 x 1⅜	9.00
2903 5½ x 8 x 1⅜	9.00
2904 5½ x 10 x 1⅜	11.00
2905 5½ x 10 x 1⅜	9.00
2906 5½ x 10 x 1⅜	11.00
2907 5½ x 10 x 1⅜	10.00
2908 5½ x 10 x 1⅜	10.00
2909 5½ x 12 x 1⅜	14.40
2910 5½ x 10 x 1⅜	10.00
2911 5½ x 10 x 1⅜	10.00
2912 5½ x 10 x 1⅜	10.00
2913 5½ x 10 x 1⅜	11.00
2914 5½ x 12 x 1⅜	24.00
2915 5½ x 11 x 1⅜	11.00
2916 5½ x 11 x 1⅜	11.00
2917 5½ x 11 x 1⅜	13.00
2918 5½ x 12 x 1⅜	13.00
2929 5½ x 12 x 1⅜	13.00
2935 5½ x 10 x 1⅜	9.00
2936 5½ x 12 x 1⅜	24.00
2937 5½ x 10 x 1⅜	9.00
2938 5½ x 10 x 1⅜	10.00
2940 5½ x 11 x 1⅜	9.50
2941 5½ x 10 x 1⅜	9.00
2942 5½ x 11 x 1⅜	9.00
2944 5½ x 11 x 1⅜	9.00
2949 5½ x 10 x 1⅜	9.00
2950 5½ x 12 x 1⅜	9.50

STAIR RAIL.

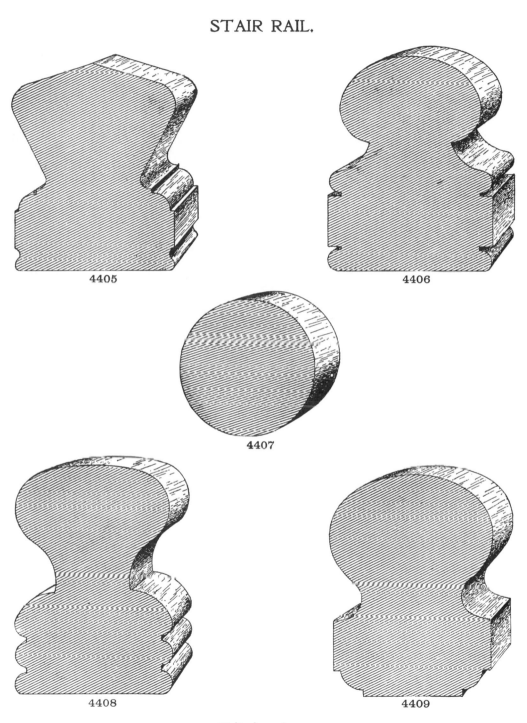

4405

4406

4407

4408

4409

Write for prices.

STAIR RAIL.

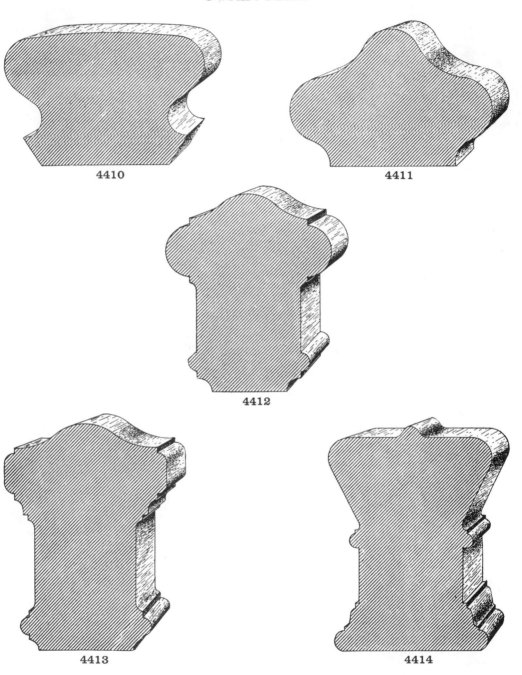

4410

4411

4412

4413

4414

Write for prices.

BUILT UP STAIR RAIL.

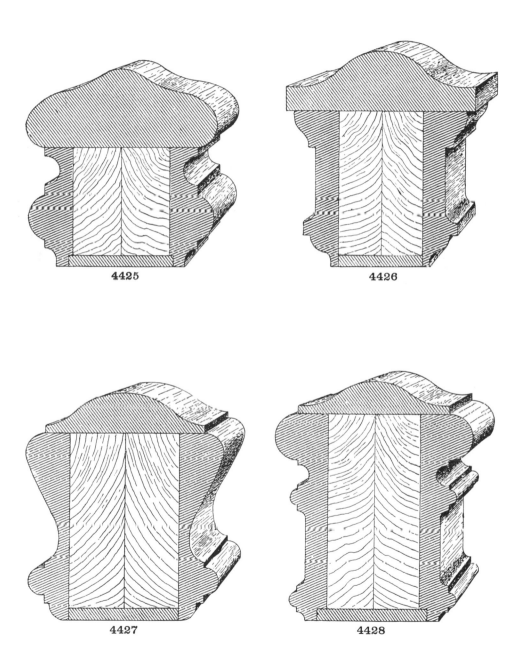

4425   4426

4427   4428

Write for prices.

STAIR BALUSTERS.

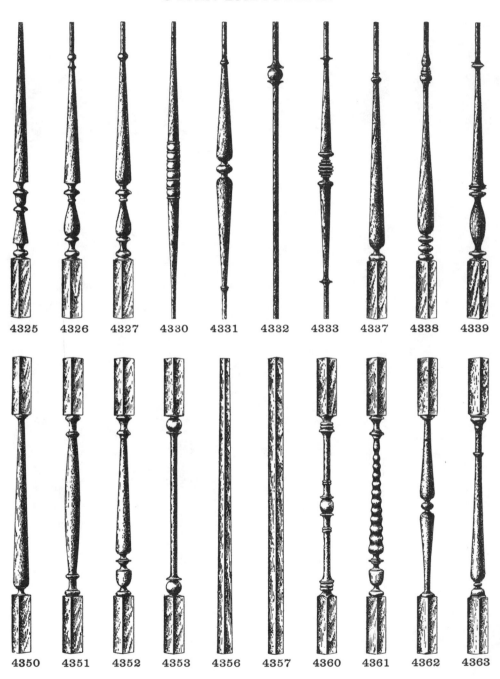

4325 4326 4327 4330 4331 4332 4333 4337 4338 4339

4350 4351 4352 4353 4356 4357 4360 4361 4362 4363

Write for prices.

STAIR ELEVATIONS.

The line drawing that was in this space was missing from the original copy.

1140

1141

1142

Before asking prices or ordering stairways read carefully page 157.

WRITE FOR PRICES.

STAIR ELEVATIONS.

The line drawing that was in this space was missing from the original copy.

1143

1145   1146

Before asking prices or ordering stairways read carefully page 157.
WRITE FOR PRICES.

STAIR ELEVATIONS.

1147

1148

1149

1150

Before asking prices or ordering stairways read carefully page 157.

WRITE FOR PRICES.

STAIR ELEVATIONS.

1151

1152

1153

1154

Before asking prices or ordering stairways read carefully page 157.

WRITE FOR PRICES.

STAIR ELEVATIONS.

4014

Before asking prices or ordering stairways read carefully page 157.

STAIR ELEVATIONS.

4012

Before asking prices or ordering stairways read carefully page 157.

STAIR ELEVATIONS.

4085

Before asking prices or ordering stairways read carefully page 157.

STAIR ELEVATIONS.

4040

Before asking prices or ordering stairways read carefully page 157.

STAIR GROUND PLANS.

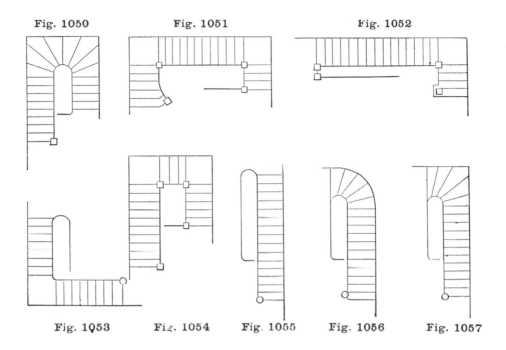

Fig. 1050   Fig. 1051   Fig. 1052

Fig. 1053   Fig. 1054   Fig. 1055   Fig. 1056   Fig. 1057

DIRECTIONS NECESSARY FOR ORDERING STAIRS and STAIR RAILING.

When a flight of stairs is wanted, we should know the height of story from floor to floor, width of joists in second story, width and run of stairs, the size of cylinder, style of base used in the hall, with rough sketch showing about the shape of stairs wanted.

For STAIR RAILING—Straight Flight.

We require the width of rise and step as sawed out on string board, the number of risers, the size of cylinder from face to face of string or face board, which way it turns at head of stairs, and the number of feet of straight rail required at landing. Unless we receive plan showing otherwise, we always suppose the top riser for a straight flight of stairs to be placed at the edge or spring of cylinder.·

For CIRCULAR or WINDING STAIRS.

We should have an exact plan of stairs as built, giving the width of rise and step, the location of risers in cylinder, etc.; and, when there are straight steps below or above the cylinder, always give the distance from the first square riser to the edge or spring line of cylinder, on the face of string or face board. *Always write your address in full on the plans.*

STAIR RAILS.

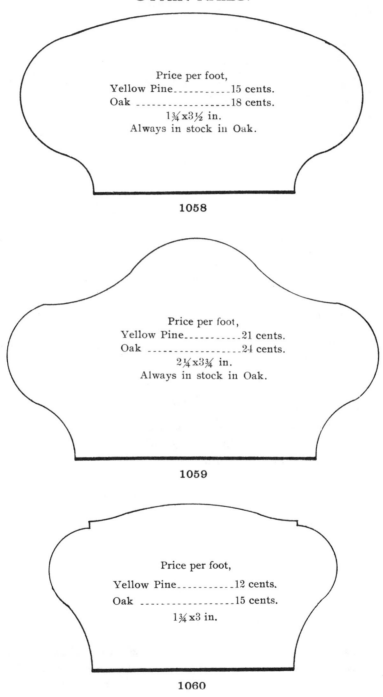

Price per foot,
Yellow Pine_____15 cents.
Oak _____18 cents.
1¾ x 3½ in.
Always in stock in Oak.

1058

Price per foot,
Yellow Pine_____21 cents.
Oak _____24 cents.
2¼ x 3¾ in.
Always in stock in Oak.

1059

Price per foot,
Yellow Pine_____12 cents.
Oak _____15 cents.
1¾ x 3 in.

1060

Above prices subject to discount.

STAIR RAILS

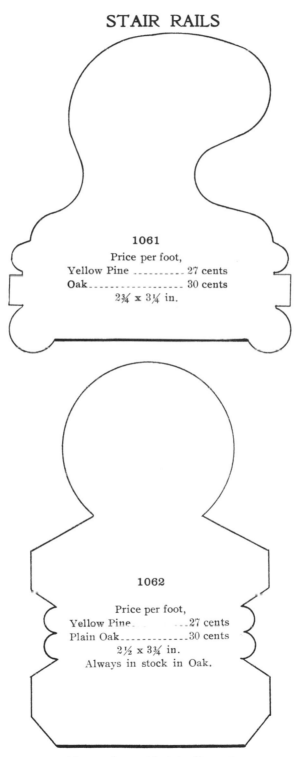

1061

Price per foot,
Yellow Pine _____ 27 cents
Oak _____ 30 cents
2¾ x 3¼ in.

1062

Price per foot,
Yellow Pine _____ 27 cents
Plain Oak _____ 30 cents
2½ x 3¾ in.
Always in stock in Oak.

Above prices subject to discount.

STAIR RAILS.

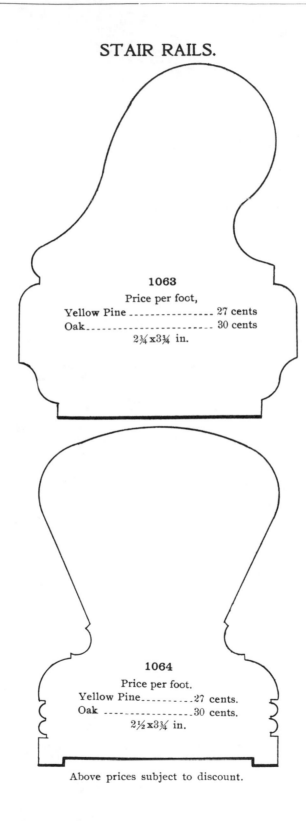

1063

Price per foot,

Yellow Pine _____ 27 cents

Oak _____ 30 cents

2¾ x 3¾ in.

1064

Price per foot.

Yellow Pine _____ 27 cents.

Oak _____ 30 cents.

2½ x 3¾ in.

Above prices subject to discount.

STAIR RAILS.

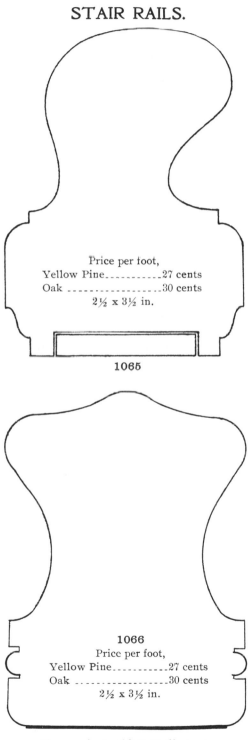

Price per foot,
Yellow Pine_____27 cents
Oak _____30 cents
2½ x 3½ in.

1065

1066
Price per foot,
Yellow Pine_____27 cents
Oak _____30 cents
2½ x 3½ in.

Above prices subject to discount.

PRICES OF STAIR BALUSTERS AND NEWELS.

1¾ to ¾ and ⅞ as shown on page 163.

No.	Yellow Pine	Oak	No.	Yellow Pine	Oak
900	$0.18	$0.21	914	$0.21	$0.24
901	.18	.21	915	.27	.30
902	.24	.20	916	.21	.24
903	.18	.21	917	.21	.24
904	.18	.21	918	.40	.42
905	.18	.21	919	.40	.42
906	.21	.24	920	.33	.36
907	.24	.27	921	.33	.36
908	.15	.18	922	.42	.45
909	.42	.45	923	.39	.42
910	.42	.45	924	.39	.42
911	1.75	1.88	925	1.17	1.20
912	.27	.30	926	1.17	1.20
913	2.10	2.25			

STAIR STARTING NEWELS.

6 inch shaft as shown on pages 164-165.

No.	Yellow Pine	Oak	No.	Yellow Pine	Oak
927	$7.13	$7.50	942	$15.30	$15.40
928	7.13	7.50	943	15.40	15.75
929	9.00	9.75	944	16.50	17.00
930	10.50	10.90	945	12.00	12.40
933	6.00	6.40	946	16.50	17.00
934	12.00	12.40	947	12.75	13.15
935	7.13	7.50	948	15.00	15.75
939	10.50	10.90	949	15.00	15.75
940	15.00	15.40	950	19.50	20.00
941	18.40	18.75			

ANGLE AND LANDING POSTS.

5 inch shaft as shown on page 164.

No.	Yellow Pine	Oak	No.	Yellow Pine	Oak
931	$4.50	$4.90	937	$5.25	$5.65
932	9.00	9.40	938	7.50	7.90
936	9.75	10.05			

Above prices are for Plain Red Oak.   For other woods write for price.

STAIR BALUSTERS.

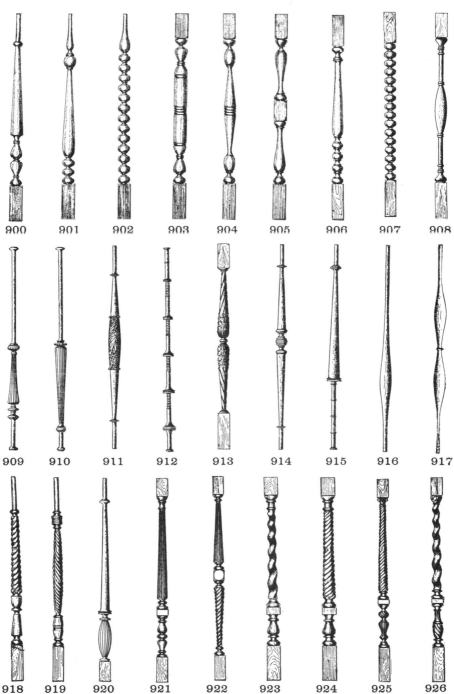

900 901 902 903 904 905 906 907 908

909 910 911 912 913 914 915 916 917

918 919 920 921 922 923 924 925 926

Made in any of the hardwoods.   For prices see page 162.

MAIN, ANGLE and LANDING NEWELS.

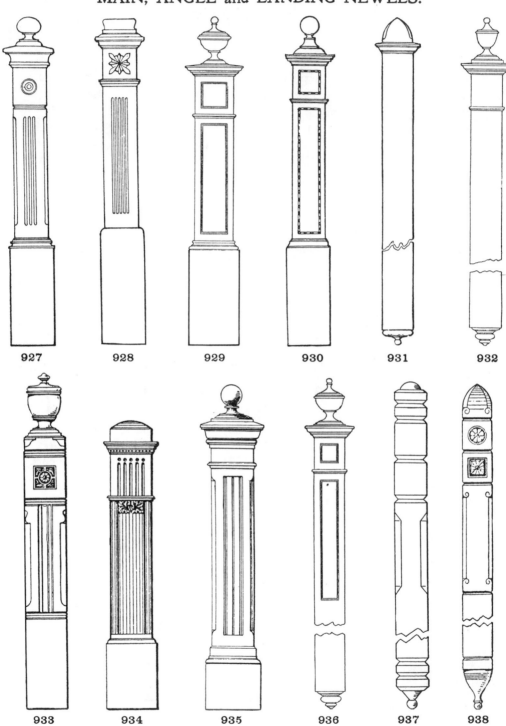

927　　　928　　　929　　　930　　　931　　　932

933　　　934　　　935　　　936　　　937　　　938

Made of Cypress Yellow Pine or Oak.　For list prices see page 162.

MAIN STAIR NEWELS.

939 940 941 942 943 944

945 946 947 948 949 950

Made in any kind of wood. For prices see page 162.

STAIR BRACKETS.

Level Brackets for Stairs, 4 inches wide, ¼ inch thick. Price per foot, Yellow Pine, 6 cents; Oak, 8 cents.

Stair Brackets, 8 to 10 inches long; Oak, 8 cents; Yellow Pine, 6 cents each.

STAIR ELEVATIONS.

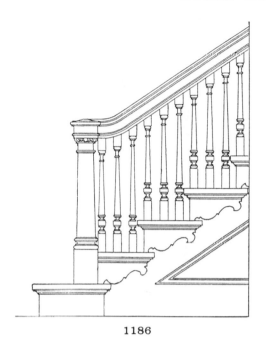

1186

1187

1188

1189

Before asking prices or ordering stairways read carefully page 157.

WRITE FOR PRICES.

STAIR ELEVATIONS.

1190

1191

1192

1193

Before asking prices or ordering stairways read carefully page 157.
Write for prices.

STAIR ELEVATIONS.

1194

1195

1196

1197

Before asking prices or ordering stairways read carefully page 157.

WRITE FOR PRICES.

STAIR INTERIORS.

1155

Before asking prices or ordering stairways read carefully page 157.

STAIR INTERIORS.

1156

Before asking prices or ordering stairways read carefully page 157.

STAIR INTERIORS.

Before asking prices or ordering stairways read carefully page 157.

STAIR INTERIORS.

1158

Before asking prices or ordering stairways read carefully page 157.

PANELED WAINSCOTING—with Cap and Base.

Three feet, six inches high over all.

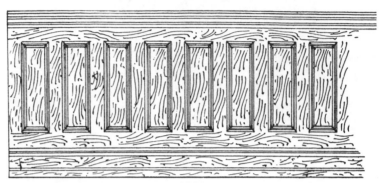

1180

Plain Sawed Oak .... per running foot, $1.50
Quarter " " .... " " 1.75

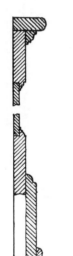

1181

Plain Sawed Oak .... per running foot, $2.00
Quarter " " .... " " 2.25

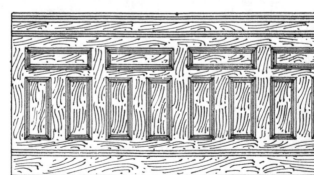

1182

Plain Sawed Oak .... per running foot, $2.00
Quarter " " .... " " 2.25

Subject to Discount.

SPECIAL FINISH for CASED OPENING.

522

This opening can also be filled with any of the grilles shown on pages 240 to 251.

CAPITALS.

FOR INTERIOR OR EXTERIOR USE.

Designs of caps that can be used in connection with above columns.   Write for prices.

WINDOW and DOOR CAPS.

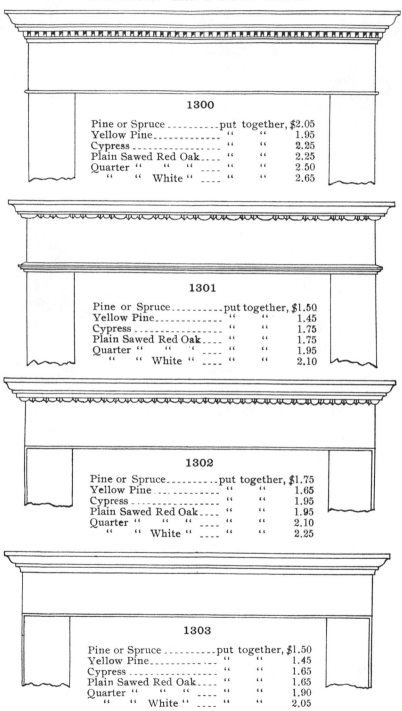

1300

Pine or Spruce	put together,	$2.05
Yellow Pine	" "	1.95
Cypress	" "	2.25
Plain Sawed Red Oak	" "	2.25
Quarter " " "	" "	2.50
" " White "	" "	2.65

1301

Pine or Spruce	put together,	$1.50
Yellow Pine	" "	1.45
Cypress	" "	1.75
Plain Sawed Red Oak	" "	1.75
Quarter " " "	" "	1.95
" " White "	" "	2.10

1302

Pine or Spruce	put together,	$1.75
Yellow Pine	" "	1.65
Cypress	" "	1.95
Plain Sawed Red Oak	" "	1.95
Quarter " " "	" "	2.10
" " White "	" "	2.25

1303

Pine or Spruce	put together,	$1.50
Yellow Pine	" "	1.45
Cypress	" "	1.65
Plain Sawed Red Oak	" "	1.65
Quarter " " "	" "	1.90
" " White "	" "	2.05

All above prices are for Caps of ordinary widths, 3 feet openings and under.

WINDOW and DOOR CAPS with COMPOSITION ORNAMENTS.

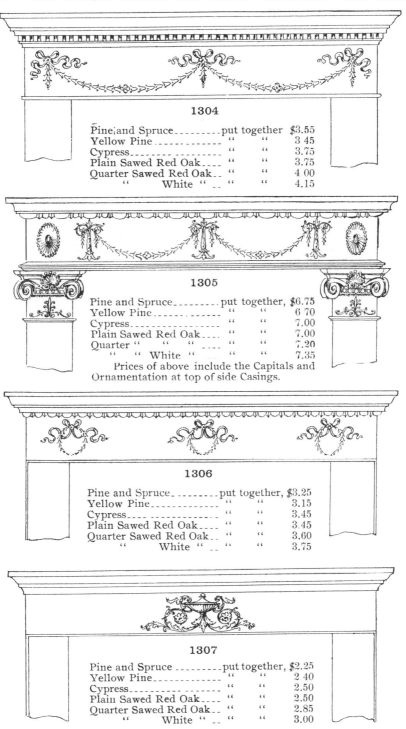

1304

Pine and Spruce	put together	$3.55
Yellow Pine	" "	3 45
Cypress	" "	3.75
Plain Sawed Red Oak	" "	3.75
Quarter Sawed Red Oak	" "	4 00
" White "	" "	4.15

1305

Pine and Spruce	put together,	$6.75
Yellow Pine	" "	6 70
Cypress	" "	7.00
Plain Sawed Red Oak	" "	7.00
Quarter " "	" "	7.20
" " White "	" "	7.35

Prices of above include the Capitals and Ornamentation at top of side Casings.

1306

Pine and Spruce	put together,	$3.25
Yellow Pine	" "	3.15
Cypress	" "	3.45
Plain Sawed Red Oak	" "	3.45
Quarter Sawed Red Oak	" "	3.60
" White "	" "	3.75

1307

Pine and Spruce	put together,	$2.25
Yellow Pine	" "	2 40
Cypress	" "	2.50
Plain Sawed Red Oak	" "	2.50
Quarter Sawed Red Oak	" "	2.85
" White "	" "	3.00

All above prices are for Caps of ordinary widths, 3 feet openings and under.

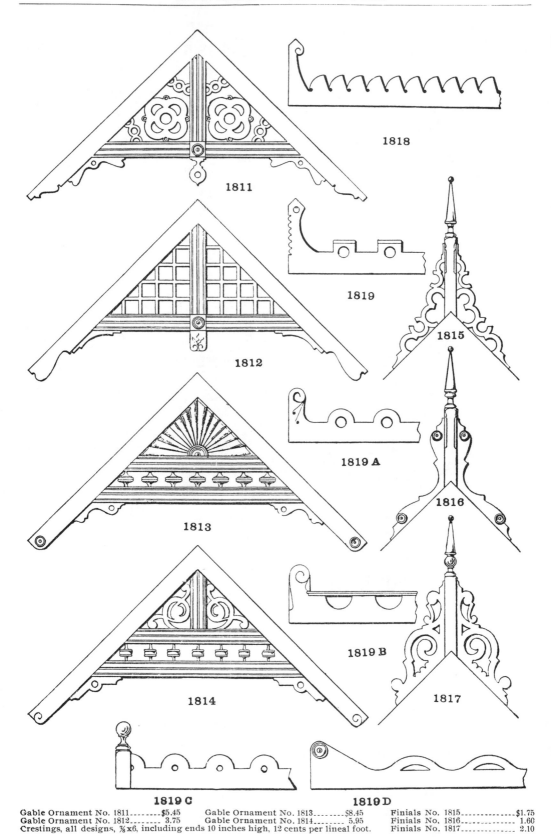

1818

1811

1812

1819

1815

1813

1819 A

1816

1814

1819 B

1817

1819 C

1819 D

Gable Ornament No. 1811_____$5.45   Gable Ornament No. 1813_____$8.45   Finials No. 1815_____$1.75
Gable Ornament No. 1812_____ 3.75   Gable Ornament No. 1814_____ 5.95   Finials No. 1816_____ 1.60
Crestings, all designs, ⅜ x 6, including ends 10 inches high, 12 cents per lineal foot.   Finials No. 1817_____ 2.10

VERGE BOARDS.

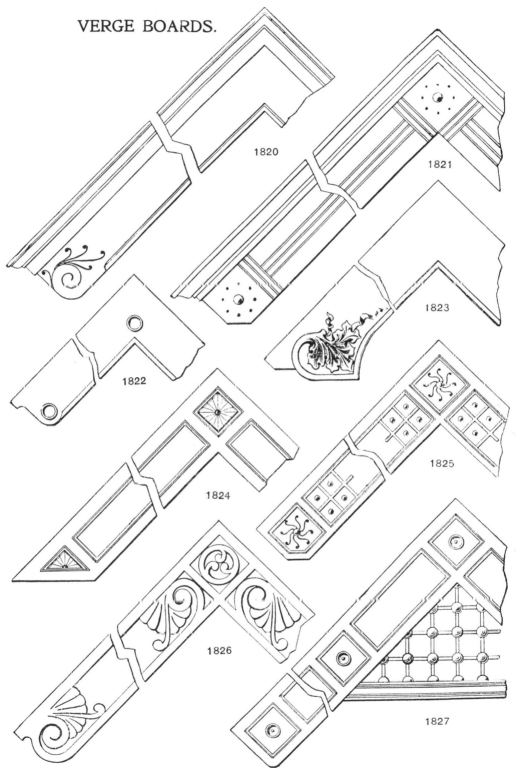

Prices on application. Give thickness, width of board, length of rafter and pitch of roof.

ADJUSTABLE GABLE ORNAMENTS.

Can be Fitted to any Pitch of Roof.

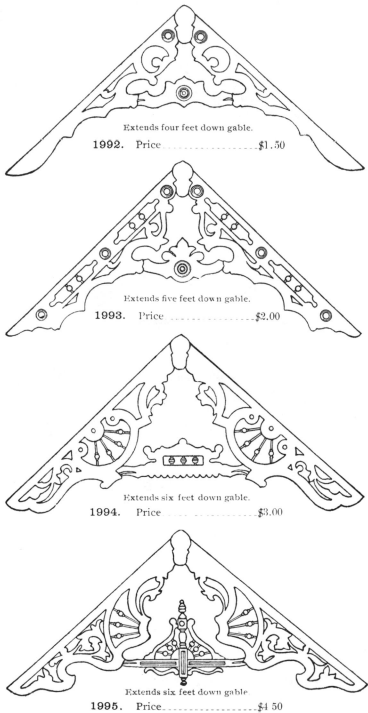

Extends four feet down gable.

1992. Price_____$1.50

Extends five feet down gable.

1993. Price_____$2.00

Extends six feet down gable.

1994. Price_____$3.00

Extends six feet down gable.

1995. Price_____$4 50

Can be Fitted to Either Old or New Houses.

GABLE ORNAMENTS.

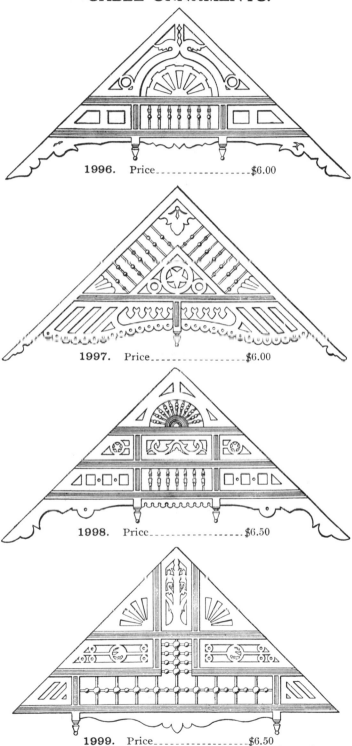

1996. Price_____$6.00

1997. Price_____$6.00

1998. Price_____$6.50

1999. Price_____$6.50

We make these ornaments to fit any size or pitch. Unless otherwise ordered, we make them six feet across at base.

PICKETS, FENCE POSTS and FENCE POST CAPS.

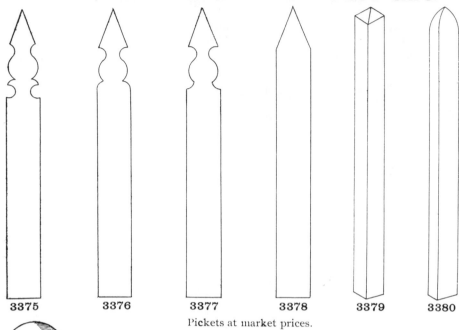

3375   3376   3377   3378   3379   3380

Pickets at market prices.

FENCE POSTS and FENCE POST CAPS.

3381
Cedar Fence Post.
6 inches by 8 feet___$1.40

3382
6 inch_____40c

3383
6 inch_____40c

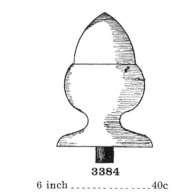

3384
6 inch _____40c

3385
6 inch _____40c

PORCH RAILS.

We carry rails shown on this page in stock—Poplar.

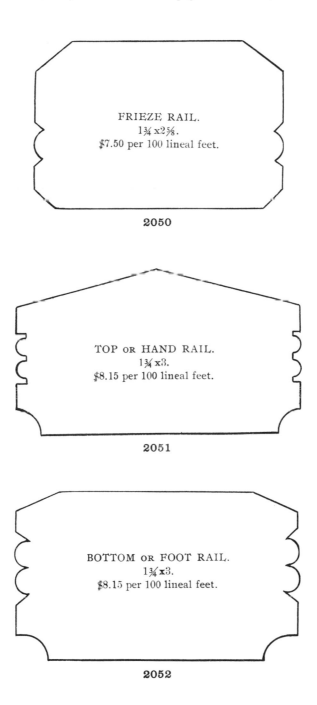

FRIEZE RAIL.
1¾ x2⅝.
$7.50 per 100 lineal feet.

2050

TOP or HAND RAIL.
1¾ x3.
$8.15 per 100 lineal feet.

2051

BOTTOM or FOOT RAIL.
1¾ x3.
$8.15 per 100 lineal feet.

2052

PORCH RAILS.

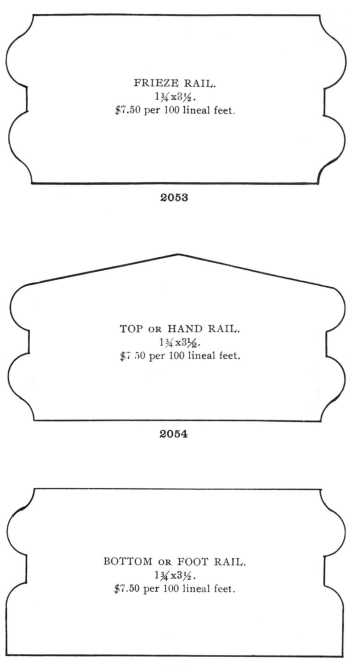

FRIEZE RAIL.
1¾ x 3½.
$7.50 per 100 lineal feet.

2053

TOP or HAND RAIL.
1¾ x 3½.
$7.50 per 100 lineal feet.

2054

BOTTOM or FOOT RAIL.
1¾ x 3½.
$7.50 per 100 lineal feet.

2055

PORCH RAILS and BALUSTER STOCK.

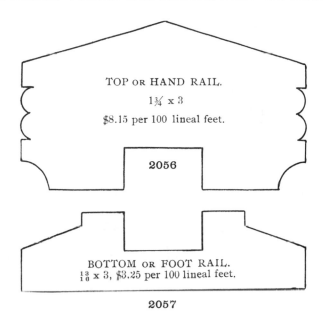

TOP OR HAND RAIL.
1¾ x 3
$8.15 per 100 lineal feet.

2056

BOTTOM OR FOOT RAIL.
1¾₀ x 3, $3.25 per 100 lineal feet.

2057

BALUSTER
STOCK.
1¾ x 1¾.
$5.00 per 100
lineal feet.

2058

BALUSTER
STOCK.
1⅜ x 1⅜.
$2.70 per 100
lineal feet.

2059

BALUSTER STOCK.
1¾ x 1¾
$5.00 per 100 lineal feet.

2060

BALUSTER STOCK
1⅜ x 1⅜
$2.70 per 100 lineal ft.

2061

BRACKETS.

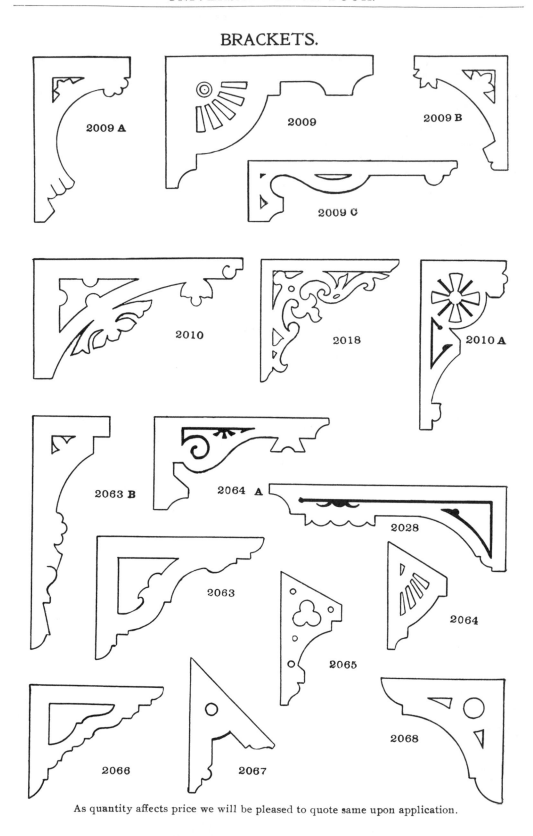

2009 A

2009

2009 B

2009 C

2010

2018

2010 A

2063 B

2064 A

2028

2063

2064

2065

2066

2067

2068

As quantity affects price we will be pleased to quote same upon application.

BRACKETS.

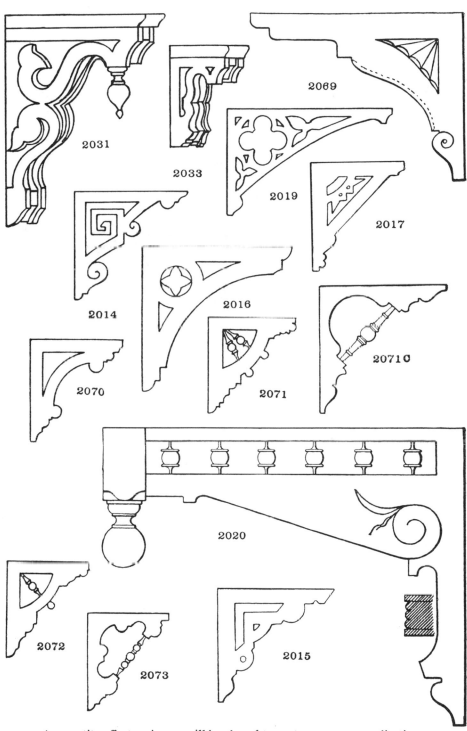

As quantity affects price we will be pleased to quote same upon application.

BRACKETS.

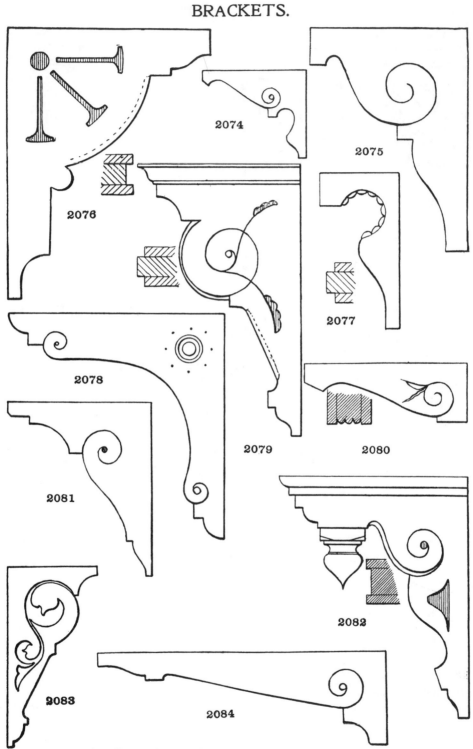

As quantity affects price we will be pleased to quote same upon application.

BRACKETS.

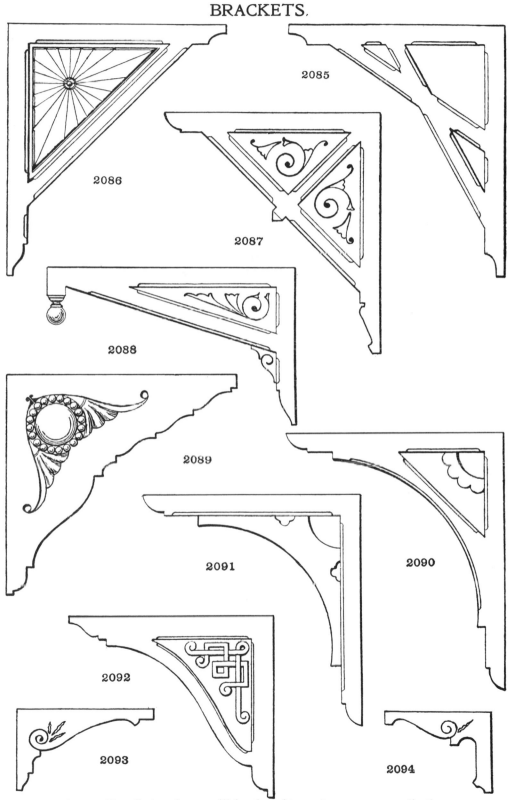

As quantity affects price we will be pleased to quote same upon application.

PORCH BALUSTERS.

HEAVY TURNED BALUSTERS.

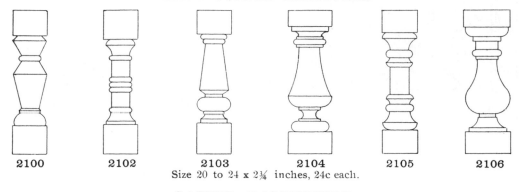

| 2100 | 2102 | 2103 | 2104 | 2105 | 2106 |

Size 20 to 24 x 2¾ inches, 24c each.

SAWED BALUSTERS.

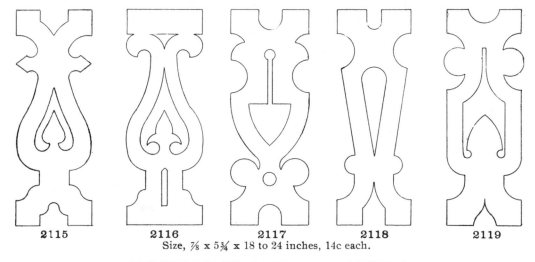

| 2115 | 2116 | 2117 | 2118 | 2119 |

Size, ⅞ x 5¾ x 18 to 24 inches, 14c each.

ORDINARY TURNED BALUSTERS.

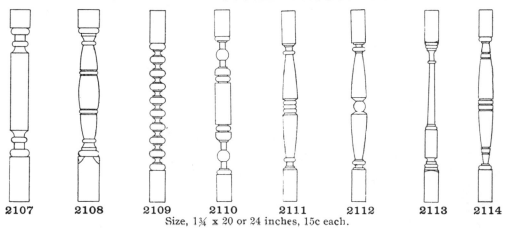

| 2107 | 2108 | 2109 | 2110 | 2111 | 2112 | 2113 | 2114 |

Size, 1¾ x 20 or 24 inches, 15c each.

PORCH SPINDLES.

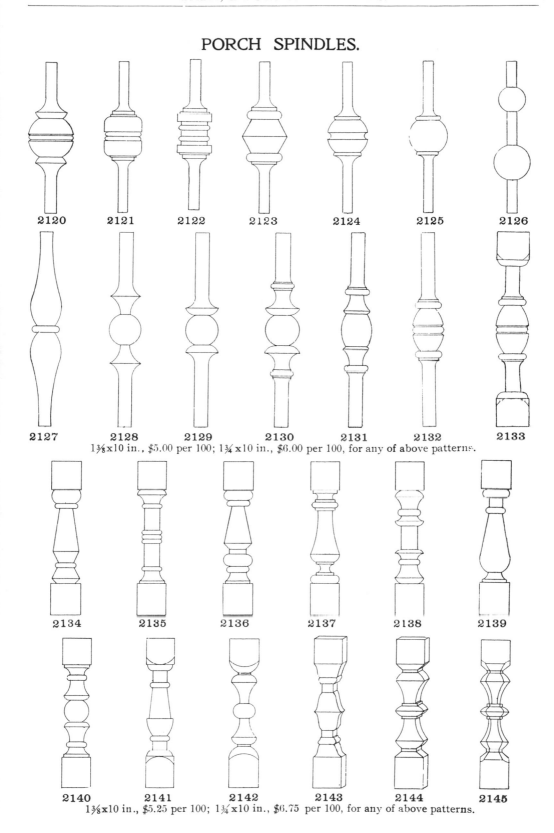

2120   2121   2122   2123   2124   2125   2126

2127   2128   2129   2130   2131   2132   2133

1⅜x10 in., $5.00 per 100; 1¾x10 in., $6.00 per 100, for any of above patterns.

2134   2135   2136   2137   2138   2139

2140   2141   2142   2143   2144   2145

1⅜x10 in., $5.25 per 100; 1¾x10 in., $6.75 per 100, for any of above patterns.

PORCH COLUMNS.

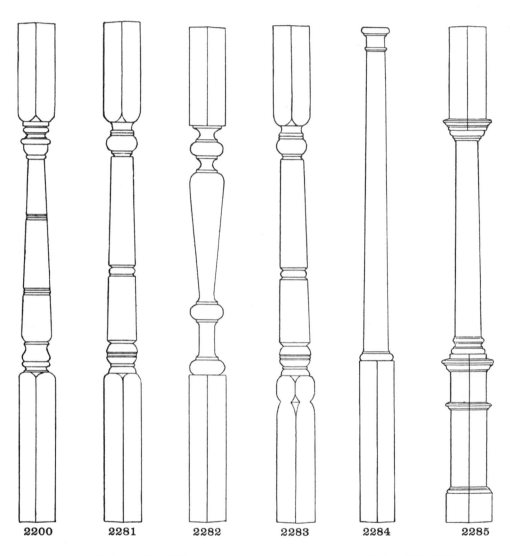

| 2200 | 2281 | 2282 | 2283 | 2284 | 2285 |

Price of No. 2200.   Price of No. 2285.

4x4,	8 ft., $0.90	5x5,	8 ft., $1.45	6x6,	8 ft., $1.90	5x5,	8 ft., $2.00	6x6,	8 ft., $2.40
4x4,	9 ft., 1.00	5x5,	9 ft., 1.60	6x6,	9 ft., 2.20	5x5,	9 ft., 2.15	6x6,	9 ft., 2.60
4x4,	10 ft., 1.10	5x5,	10 ft., 1.75	6x6,	10 ft., 2.40	5x5,	10 ft., 2.35	6x6,	10 ft., 2.75

For columns No. 2281, 2282 and 2283, add 10 cents net to price of No. 2200. For column No. 2284, add 20 cents net to price of No. 2200. Made of No. 1 Poplar, nice stock and smooth workmanship.

Prices subject to discount.

PORCH COLUMNS.

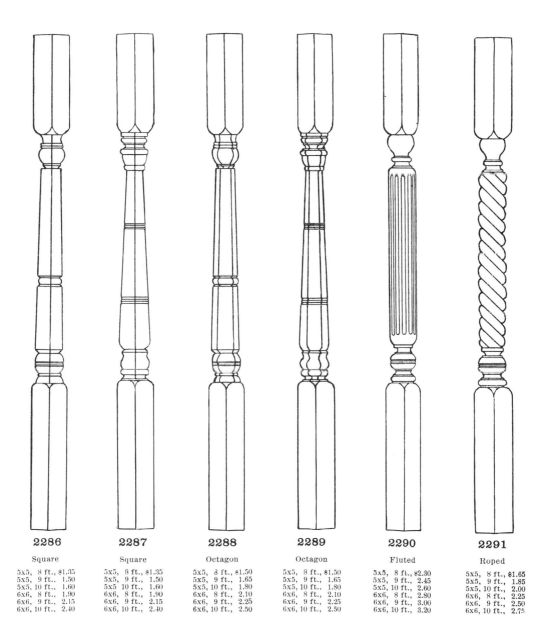

2286	2287	2288	2289	2290	2291
Square	Square	Octagon	Octagon	Fluted	Roped

5x5, 8 ft., $1.35	5x5, 8 ft., $1.35	5x5, 8 ft., $1.50	5x5, 8 ft., $1.50	5x5, 8 ft., $2.30	5x5, 8 ft., $1.65
5x5, 9 ft., 1.50	5x5, 9 ft., 1.50	5x5, 9 ft., 1.65	5x5, 9 ft., 1.65	5x5, 9 ft., 2.45	5x5, 9 ft., 1.85
5x5, 10 ft., 1.60	5x5 10 ft., 1.60	5x5, 10 ft., 1.80	5x5, 10 ft., 1.80	5x5, 10 ft., 2.60	5x5, 10 ft., 2.00
6x6, 8 ft., 1.90	6x6, 8 ft., 1.90	6x6, 8 ft., 2.10	6x6, 8 ft., 2.10	6x6, 8 ft., 2.80	6x6, 8 ft., 2.25
6x6, 9 ft., 2.15	6x6, 9 ft., 2.15	6x6, 9 ft., 2.25	6x6, 9 ft., 2.25	6x6, 9 ft., 3.00	6x6, 9 ft., 2.50
6x6, 10 ft., 2.40	6x6, 10 ft., 2.40	6x6, 10 ft., 2.50	6x6, 10 ft., 2.50	6x6, 10 ft., 3.20	6x6, 10 ft., 2.75

Made of No. 1 Poplar, nice stock and smooth workmanship.

PORCH COLUMNS and NEWELS.

2216

6x 6, 8 ft___$4.50
7x 7, 8 ft___ 5.10
8x 8, 8 ft___ 5.70
10x10, 8 ft___ 9.45
12x12, 8 ft___12.50

2217

6x 6, 8 ft___$4.50
7x 7, 8 ft___ 5.10
8x 8, 8 ft___ 5.70
10x10, 8 ft___ 9.45
12x12, 8 ft___12.50

2218

6x 6, 8 ft___$5.35
7x 7 8 ft___ 6.75
8x 8, 8 ft___ 7.00
10x10, 8 ft___12.50

2219

6x 6, 8 ft___$4.50
7x 7, 8 ft___ 5.10
8x 8, 8 ft___ 5.70
10x10, 8 ft___ 9.45
12x12, 8 ft___12.50

2216	2217	2218	2219

2220	2221	2222	2223	2224	2225

For price of Nos. 2220, 2221 and 2222
see our discount sheet.

2223
5x5, 4 feet,
$1.60

2224
5x5, 4 feet,
$1.60

2225
5x5, 4 feet,
$1.50

PORCH COLUMNS and NEWELS.

A 2238
7¾ in. shaft, 8 ft. long
$7.50

B2238
7¾ in. shaft, 8 ft. long
$11.65

2240
7¾ in. shaft, 8 ft. long
$10.50

2239
7¾ in. shaft, 8 ft. long
$14.25

2294
5x5 in., 4 ft.
long, $1.50

2295
5x5 in., 4 ft.
long, $2 65

2296
5x5 in., 4 ft.
long, $3.00

2297
5x5 in., 4 ft.
long, $3.75

2298
5x5 in., 4 ft.
long, $6.00

2299
5x5 in., 4 ft.
long, $6.40

STAVED UP COLONIAL COLUMNS with COMPOSITION CAP.

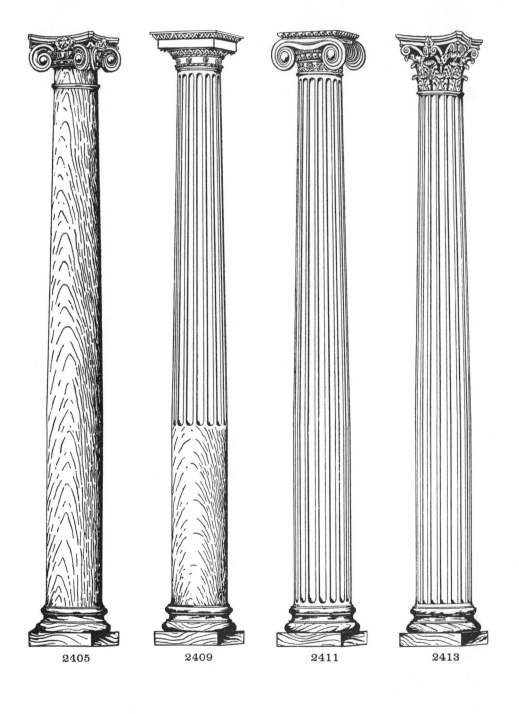

2405   2409   2411   2413

BOXED COLONIAL PILASTERS with COMPOSITION CAP.

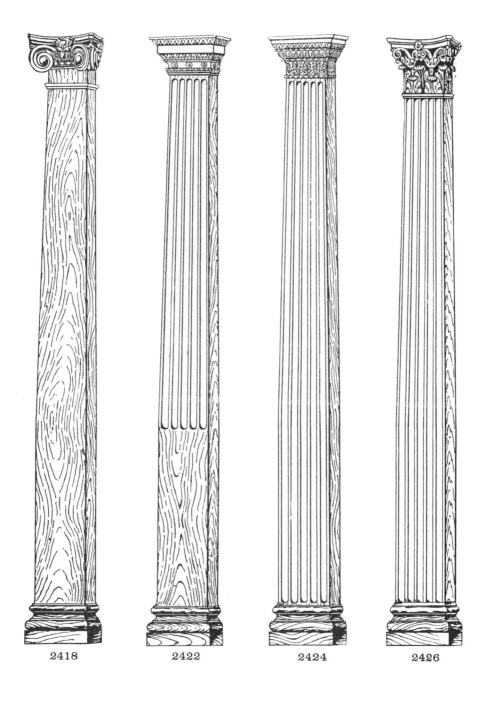

2418   2422   2424   2426

TWIN COLUMNS on PEDESTALS.

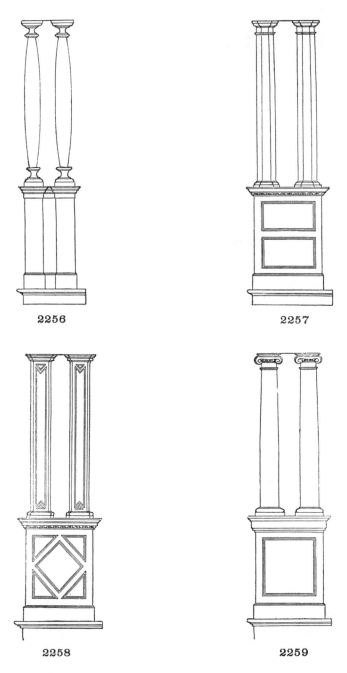

2256

2257

2258

2259

Designs offering suggestions for Porch Columns resting on Pedestals.

DIMENSION SHINGLES.

For Porch and Roof Gables.

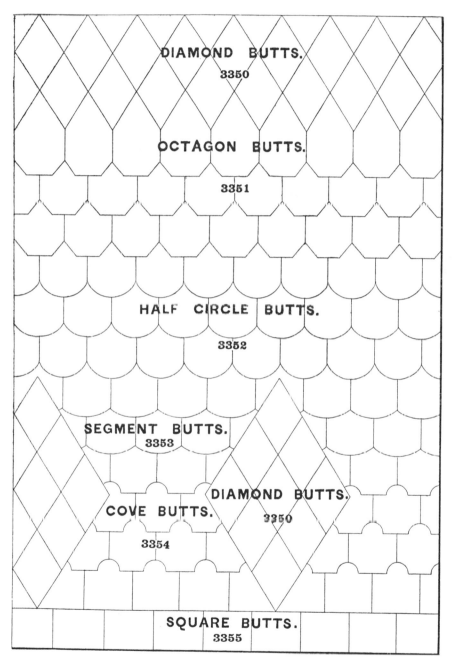

We are prepared to furnish Ornamental Shingles, cut to any shape desired, and can offer inducements in prices. Write for quotations.

PORCH DESIGNS.

Design O 1.   Design O 2.   Design O 3.

Design O 4.   Design O 5.   Design O 6.

Made from stock patterns of Columns, Newels, Balusters, Rails, Spindles and Brackets shown on preceding pages.

PORCH DESIGNS.

Design A

Design B

Design C

Design D

Write for prices.

PORCH DESIGNS.

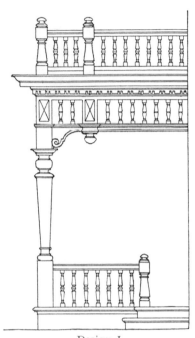

Design I.

Design J.

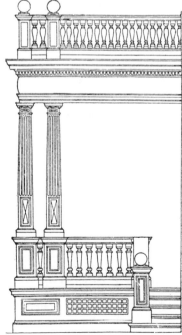

Design K.

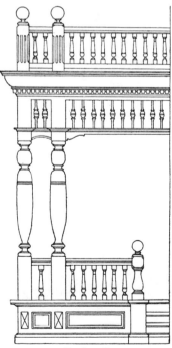

Design L.

WRITE FOR PRICES.

PORCH DESIGNS.

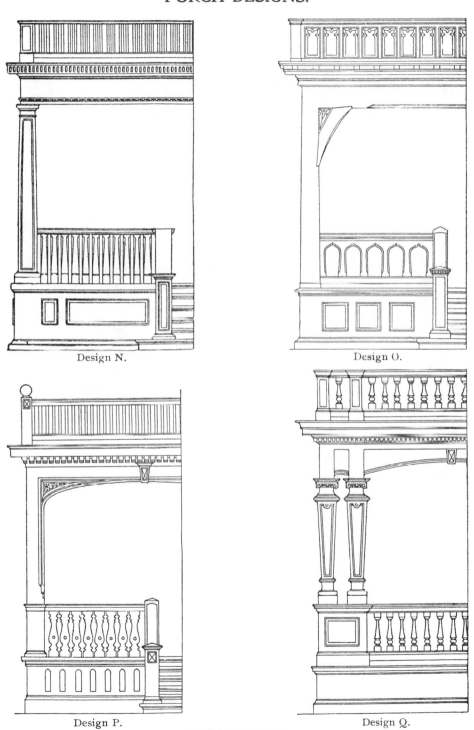

Design N.

Design O.

Design P.

Design Q.

WRITE FOR PRICES.

PORCH VIEWS.

2266. Write for prices. Send ground plan with size of porch and number and location of columns, and show space left open for entrance.

PORCH VIEWS.

2267 Write for prices. Send ground plan with size of porch and number and location of columns, and show space left open for entrance.

PORCH VIEWS.

2268. Write for prices. Send ground plan with size of porch and number and location of columns, and show space left open for entrance.

PORCH VIEWS.

2269. Write for prices. Send ground plan with size of porch and number and location of columns and show space left open for entrance.

PORCH VIEWS.

2270.   Write for prices.   Send ground plan with size of porch and number and location of columns, and show space left open for entrance.

PORCH VIEWS.

2271. Write for prices. Send ground plan with size of porch and number and location of columns, and show space left open for entrance.

PORCH VIEWS.

2272.　Write for prices.　Send ground plan with size of porch and number and location of columns, and show space left open for entrance.

PORCH VIEWS.

2273. Write for prices. Send ground plan with size of porch and number and location of columns, and show space left open for entrance.

WINDOW FRAMES for FRAME BUILDINGS.

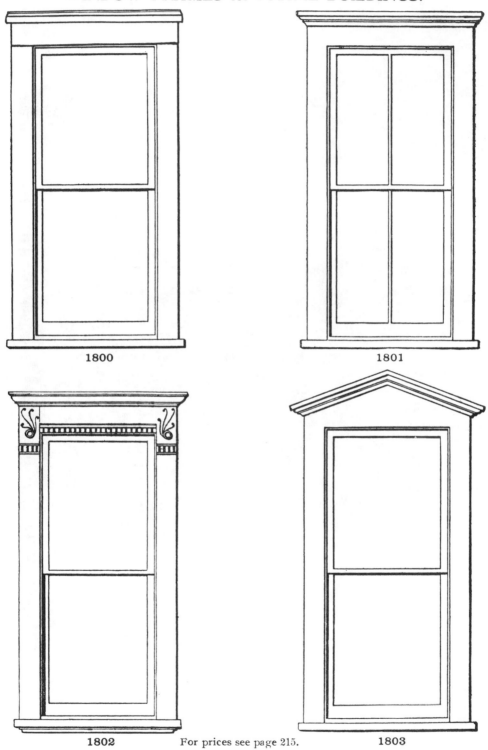

1800

1801

1802

For prices see page 215.

1803

WINDOW FRAMES for FRAME BUILDINGS.

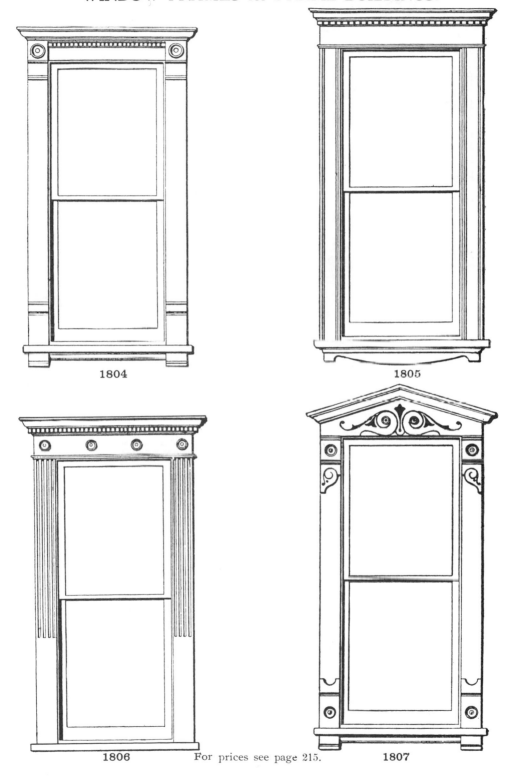

1804

1805

1806   For prices see page 215.   1807

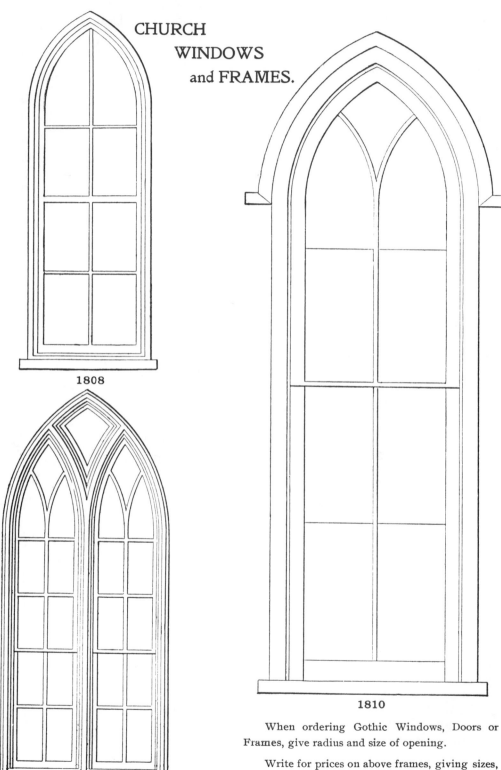

CHURCH WINDOWS and FRAMES.

1808

1809

1810

When ordering Gothic Windows, Doors or Frames, give radius and size of opening.

Write for prices on above frames, giving sizes, width of jambs and full information.

PRICE LIST of WINDOW and DOOR FRAMES.

FRAMES for WOOD BUILDINGS.

Window Frames, 4 inch Studding, ordinary sizes up to 2 lt. 30 x 40.

No.			Knock Down	Put Together
1800.	Plain Drip Cap, with pulleys		$2.05	$2.35
1801.	Crown Mould Cap,	"	2.45	2.70
1802.	Fancy Cap,	"	3.70	4.30
1803.	"	"	2.70	3.00
1804.	"	"	3.70	4.30
1805.	"	"	4.40	4.95
1806.	"	"	4.80	5.20
1807.	"	"	5.00	5.55

OUTSIDE DOOR FRAMES.

Ordinary Sizes.

1⅜ inch Rabbeted Jambs for 4 inch Studding.

No.		Knock Down	Put Together
1800.	Plain Drip Cap	$2.55	$2.70
1801.	Crown Mould Cap	2.95	3.20
1802.	Fancy Cap	4.20	4.70
1803.	"	3.25	3.65
1804.	"	4.20	4.70
1805.	"	4.95	5.30
1806.	"	5.30	6.80
1807.	"	5.55	6.00

OUTSIDE DOOR FRAMES for TRANSOM.

Ordinary Sizes.

1⅜ inch Rabbeted Jambs, for 4 inch Studding, 1800, 1801 _____ add 50c.
1⅜ " " " 4 " " 1802, 1803, 1804, 1805, 1806, 1807 _____ " $1.05

FRAMES for BRICK BUILDINGS.

	Knock Down	Put Together
Box Window Frames, with pulleys, ordinary sizes up to 2 lt., 30 x 40	$2.70	$2.95
Outside Door Frames, 1¾ inch Jamb Rabbeted for 13 inch wall, ordinary sizes	2.55	2.70
" " " " " " transom	3.05	3.30

INSIDE DOOR FRAMES, Knock Down.

		Price
Ordinary sizes, ⅞ x 5¾ inch Jamb,	White Pine	$0.95
" " " " "	Yellow Pine	.80
" " " " "	Cypress	.95
" " " " "	Plain Red Oak	1.25
" " " " "	for Transom, with 1¾ inch Transom Bar, White Pine	1.30
" " " " "	" " " " " " Yellow "	1.00
" " " " "	" " " " " " Cypress	1.30
" " " " "	" " " " " " Plain Red Oak	1.75
Ordinary sizes, 1⅛ x 5¾ inch Jamb,	White Pine	1.05
" " " " "	Yellow "	.95
" " " " "	Cypress	1.05
" " " " "	Plain Red Oak	1.45
" " " " "	for Transom, with 1¾ inch Transom Bar, White Pine	1.55
" " " " "	" " " " " " Yellow "	1.20
" " " " "	" " " " " " Cypress	1.55
" " " " "	" " " " " " Plain Red Oak	2.95

GABLE SASH FRAMES for FRAME BUILDINGS.

No.		Price
3047.	For 2-0 x 2-5 Sash for 4 inch Studding, put together	$1.90
3048.	" " " " " " " "	1.55
3050.	" " " " " " " "	2.40
3053.	" " " " " " " "	2.65
3049.	For Sash, 2 ft. diam. circle outside, square inside, for 4 inch Studding, put together	2.65
3051.	" " " " " " " " " " "	2.65

No Window or Door Stops included with price of frames.   Prices of frames subject to discount.

TURNED BEADS.

White or Yellow Pine, Oak, Birch, or woods of equal value.

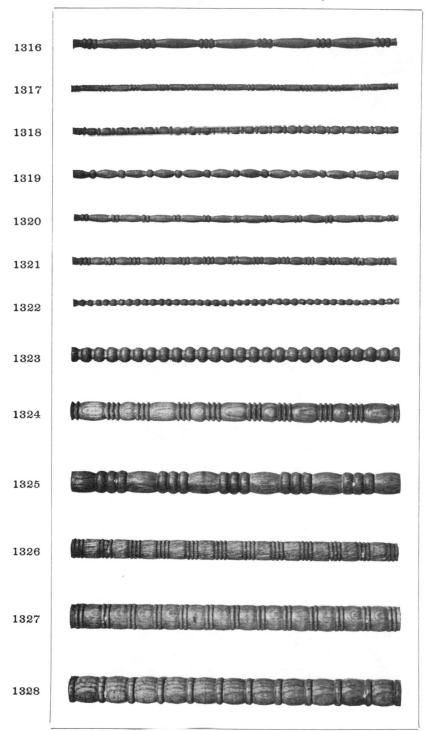

1316
1317
1318
1319
1320
1321
1322
1323
1324
1325
1326
1327
1328

Furnished any diameter up to 2 inches—specify diameter when ordering. Price up to and including ⅞ inch diam. Full Round, $4.50 per 100 lineal feet. Add for quartering, $1.20 per 100 lineal feet. Add for halving, 60c per 100 lineal feet. For over ⅞ inch diameter send for prices, stating quantity wanted. For large quantity will make special prices.

TURNED BEADS.

White or Yellow Pine, Oak, Birch, or woods of equal value.

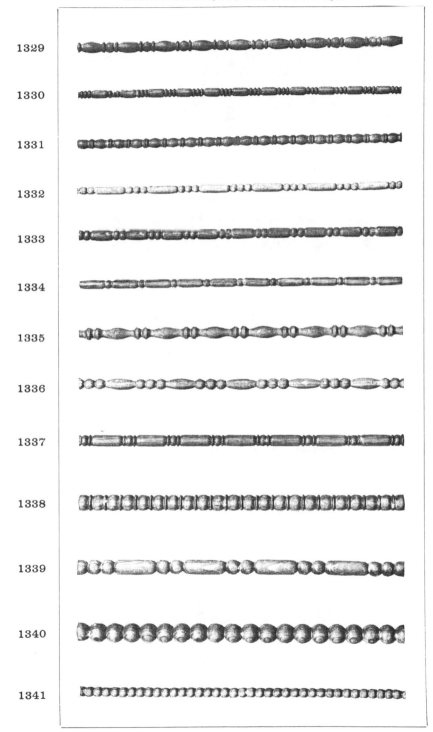

1329

1330

1331

1332

1333

1334

1335

1336

1337

1338

1339

1340

1341

Furnished any diameter up to 2 inches—specify diameter when ordering. Price up to and including ⅞ inch. diam. Full Round, $4.50 per 100 lineal feet. Add for quartering, $1.20 per 100 lineal feet. Add for halving, 60c per 100 lineal feet. For over ⅞ inch diameter send for prices, stating quantity wanted. For large quantity will make special prices.

EMBOSSED PICTURE MOULDINGS.

White or Yellow Pine, Oak, Birch, or woods of equal value.

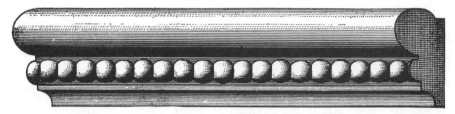

1342.   Two-thirds size, ⅞x1½, $4.00 per 100 lineal feet.

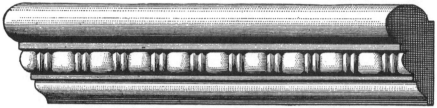

1343.   Two-thirds size, ⅞x1½, $4.00 per 100 lineal feet.

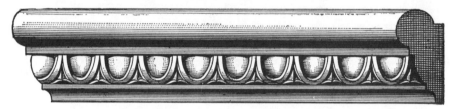

1344.   Two-thirds size, ⅞x1½, $4.00 per 100 lineal feet.

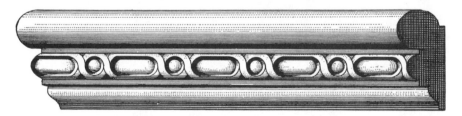

1345.   Two-thirds size, ⅞x1½, $4.00 per 100 lineal feet.

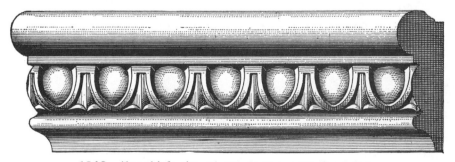

1346.   Two-thirds size, ⅞x2¼, $4.50 per 100 lineal feet.

EMBOSSED MOULDINGS.

White or Yellow Pine, Oak, Birch, or woods of equal value.

1349.   Full size, ⅜ x ½, $2.25 per 100 lineal feet.

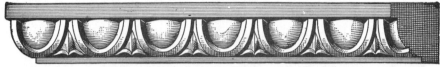

1350.   Full size, ⅜ x ⅝, $2.25 per 100 lineal feet.

1351.   Full size, ½ x 1⅟₁₆, $2.50 per 100 lineal feet.

1352.   Full size, ⅝ x ¾, $2.50 per 100 lineal feet.

1388.   Size, ⅞ x 3 inches.   Price, $5.00 per 100 lineal feet.
1389.   Size, ⅞ x 2½ inches.   Price, $4.50 per 100 lineal feet.
1390.   Size, ¾ x 2 inches.   Price, $4.00 per 100 lineal feet.

EMBOSSED MOULDINGS.

White or Yellow Pine, Oak, Birch, or woods of equal value.

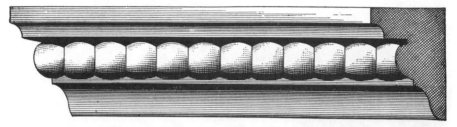

1354.   Full size, ¾ x 1⅛, $3.25 per 100 lineal feet.

1355.   Two-thirds size, ¾ x 1½, $3.50 per 100 lineal feet.

1356.   Full size, ½ x 1¼, $3.25 per 100 lineal feet.

1357.   Two-thirds size, ⅝ x 2½, $4.50 per 100 lineal feet.

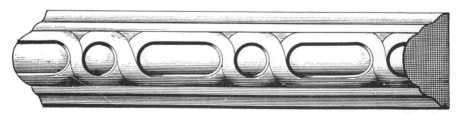

1358.   Full size, ½ x 1, $2.75 per 100 lineal feet.

Prices subject to discount.

EMBOSSED MOULDINGS.

White or Yellow Pine, Oak, Birch, or woods of equal value.

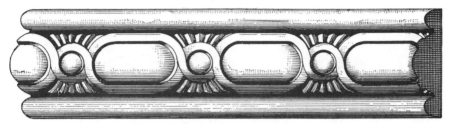

1359. Two-thirds size, ⅜x1⅝, $3.25 per 100 lineal feet.

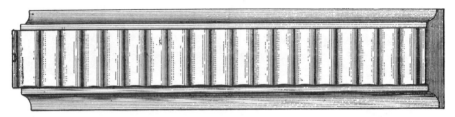

1360. Two-thirds size, ⅜x1½, $3.25 per 100 lineal feet.

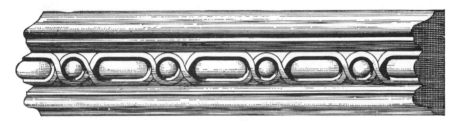

1361. Two-thirds size, ½x1¾, $4.00 per 100 lineal feet.

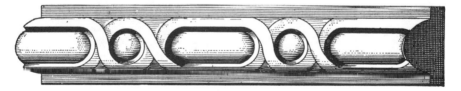

1362. Full size, ½x¾, $2.50 per 100 lineal feet.

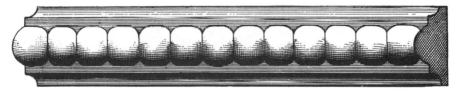

1363. Full size, ⅜x⅞, $2.25 per 100 lineal feet.

Prices Subject to Discount.

EMBOSSED MOULDINGS.

White or Yellow Pine, Oak, Birch, or woods of equal value.

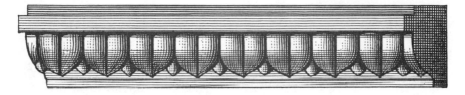

1359½.   Size, ½ x ⅞ inches.   Price, $2.50 per 100 lineal feet.

1360½.   Size, ⅜ x ½ inch   Price, $2.25 per 100 lineal feet.

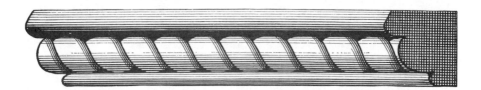

1361½.   Size, 1¾₆ x 1¾₆ inches.   Price, $2.75 per 100 lineal feet.

1362½.   Size, ⅜ x ¾ inches.   Price, $2.75 per 100 lineal feet.

1363½.   Size, ₅⁄₁₆ x ⅝ inches.   Price, $2.50 per 100 lineal feet.

Prices Subject to Discount.

EMBOSSED MOULDINGS.

White or Yellow Pine, Oak, Birch, or woods of equal value.

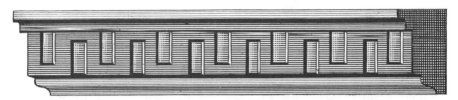

1364. Size, ½ x ⅞ inches, $2.50 per 100 lineal feet.

1365. Size, $\frac{5}{16}$ x ⅞ inches, $2.50 per 100 lineal feet.

1366. Size, ⅝ x 1⅛ inches, $3.00 per 100 lineal feet.

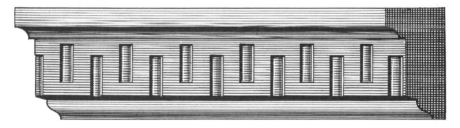

1367. Size, ⅝ x 1⅛ inches, $3 00 per 100 lineal feet.

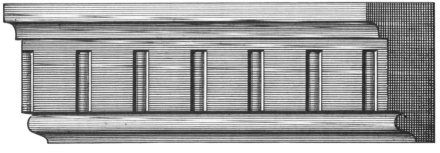

1368. Size, ¾ x 1½ inches, $3.50 per 100 lineal feet.

Prices Subject to Discount.

EMBOSSED MOULDINGS.

White or Yellow Pine, Oak, Birch, or woods of equal value.

1369.   Size, ½ x ⅞ inches, $2.50 per 100 lineal feet.

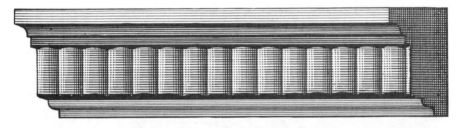

1370.   Size, ⅝ x 1⅛ inches, $3.00 per 100 lineal feet.

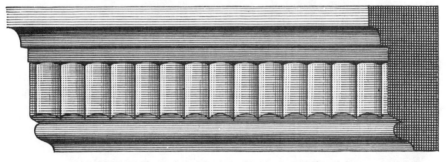

1371.   Size, ¾ x 1½ inches, $3.50 per 100 lineal feet.

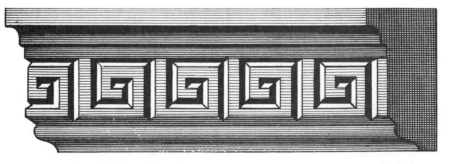

1372.   Size, ¾ x 1½ inches, $3.50 per 100 lineal feet.

Prices Subject to Discount.

EMBOSSED MOULDINGS.

White or Yellow Pine, Oak, Birch, or woods of equal value.

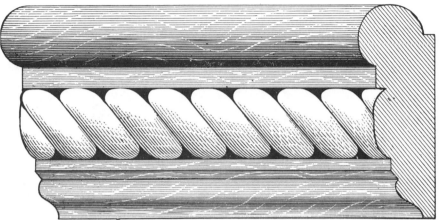

1374. Size, ⅞x2¼ inches, $4.50 per 100 lineal feet.

1375. Size, ⅞x2 inches, $4.00 per 100 lineal feet.

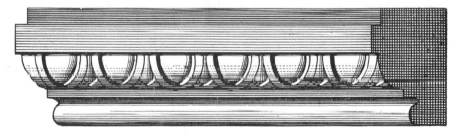

1376. Size, ¾x1¼ inches, $3.00 per 100 lineal feet.

1378. Size, $\frac{5}{16}$x½ inches, $2.50 per 100 lineal feet.
Prices Subject to Discount.

EMBOSSED MOULDINGS.

White or Yellow Pine, Oak, Birch or woods of equal value.

1379. Size, $\frac{5}{16}$x$1\frac{3}{16}$ inches, $2.25 per 100 lineal feet.

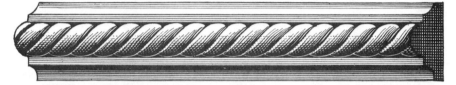

1380. Size, $\frac{3}{8}$x$\frac{7}{8}$ inches, $2.50 per 100 lineal feet.

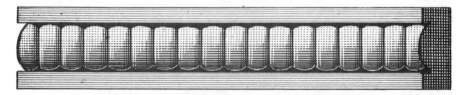

1381. Size, $\frac{3}{8}$x$\frac{7}{8}$ inches, $2.25 per 100 lineal feet.

1382. Size, $\frac{5}{16}$x$1\frac{1}{8}$ inches, $2.75 per 100 lineal feet

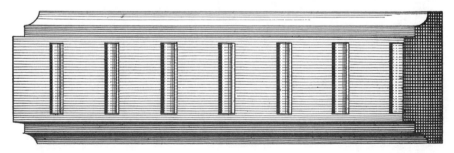

1383. Size, $\frac{3}{8}$x$1\frac{1}{2}$ inches, $3.25 per 100 lineal feet

Prices Subject to Discount.

EMBOSSED MOULDINGS.

White or Yellow Pine, Oak, Birch, or woods of equal value.

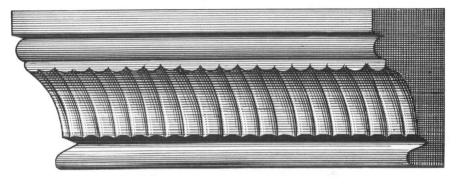

1384   Size, $\frac{5}{16}$ x $\frac{7}{8}$ inches, $2.50 per 100 lineal feet.

1385   Size, $\frac{3}{4}$ x 1 $\frac{5}{8}$ inches, $3.75 per 100 lineal feet.

1386½   Size, ½ x 1 ½ inches, $3.25 per 100 lineal feet.

1387½   Size, $\frac{3}{4}$ x 1 $\frac{5}{8}$ inches, $3.75 per 100 lineal feet.

Prices Subject to Discount.

CHURCH DOORS.

1765

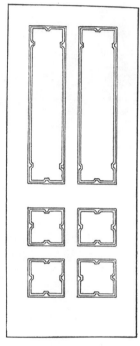

1766

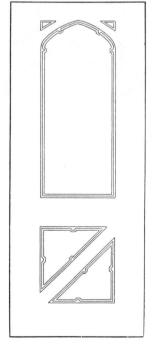

1767

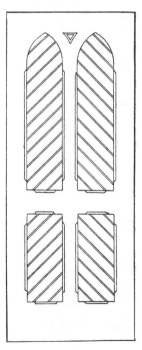

1768

WRITE FOR PRICES.

MULLION CHURCH WINDOWS.

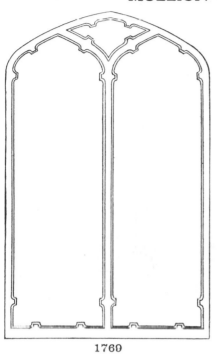

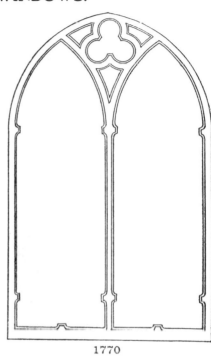

1769

1770

CHURCH DOORS.

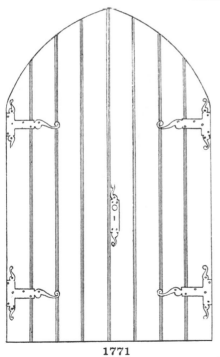

1771

1772

Write for prices.

CHURCH FURNISHINGS.

ALTAR RAIL.

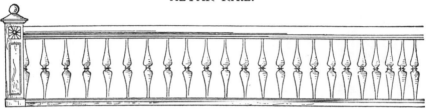

1773

Price per lineal foot of Rail and Balusters__$0.75   Posts, each._____$3.75

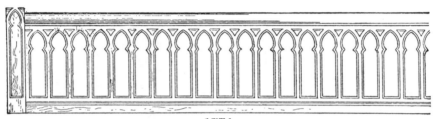

1774

Price per lineal foot of Rail and Balusters_$1.20   Posts, each._____$4.00

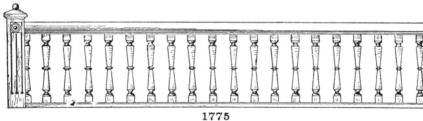

1775

Price per lineal foot of Rail and Balusters__$0.60   Posts, each._____$3.50

1776

Price per lineal foot of Rail and Balusters_$1.50   Posts, each _____$4.00

    Price is based on Oak or woods of equal value, not filled or varnished.   Usual height of rail, 24 inches.   For pine or poplar for paint work, deduct 10 per cent.   For circle or segment shaped railing, write for prices.

PEW ENDS for CHURCHES.

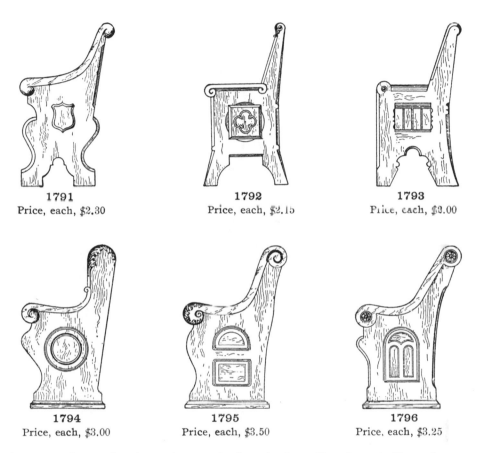

1791
Price, each, $2.30

1792
Price, each, $2.15

1793
Price, each, $3.00

1794
Price, each, $3.00

1795
Price, each, $3.50

1796
Price, each, $3.25

The above prices are based on oak or woods of equal value. Plowed out inside ready to **receive** seats and backs. For pew ends made of poplar for paint work, deduct 10 per cent.

CUTS OF PEW BODIES.

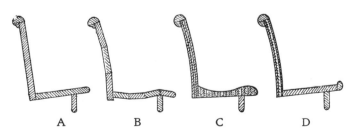

A   B   C   D

The above cuts show the different styles of pew bodies we manufacture. Style "A" is the **most** reasonable in price and the style in most common use.

CHURCH SEATS.

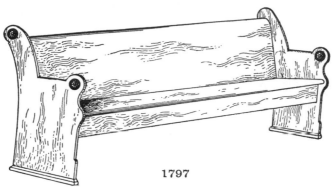

1797

Price complete, including pew ends, as shown.

8 foot seats, not filled or varnished, per lineal foot_____$1.75
10 "   "   "   "   "   "   "   ------ 1.15
12 "   "   "   "   "   "   "   ------ 1.00

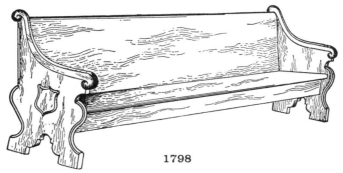

1798

Price complete including pew ends, as shown.

8 foot seats, not filled or varnished, per lineal foot_____$1.50
10 "   "   "   "   "   "   "   ------ 1.35
12 "   "   "   "   "   "   "   ------ 1.25

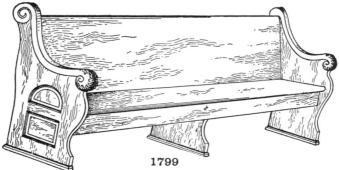

1799

Price complete including pew ends, as shown.

8 foot seats, not filled or varnished, per lineal foot_____$1.80
10 "   "   "   "   "   "   "   ------ 1.65
12 "   "   "   "   "   "   "   ------ 1.50

The usual size of church seats made, is: Back, 18 inches high; seat, 14 inches wide; height of seat, 16½ inches. Pew ends, 1¼ inch thick. Above prices are based on oak or woods of equal value. For church seats made of pine or poplar, for paint work, deduct 10 per cent from above prices. If finished in oil and varnished, add 20 per cent. Above prices are for style "A" back and seat, as shown on page 231.

CHURCH PULPITS.

1777

Price, $20.75

Usual size made: Top, 20x24 inches. Height, 42 inches.

1788

Price, $22.50

Usual size made; 24x36 inches. Bible ¼top, 18x22 inches. Height to top of bible top, 42 inches.

1789

Price, $24.00

Usual size made; 22x32 inches. Bible top, 18x22 inches. Height to top of bible top, 42 inches.

1790

Price, $26.25

Usual size made; 24x36 inches. Bible top, 18x22 inches. Height to top of bible top, 42 inches.

Above prices are based on Oak or woods of equal value. If made of Poplar or Pine for paint work, deduct 10 per cent. If finished in oil and varnish, add 20 per cent.

SINK and TABLE LEGS.

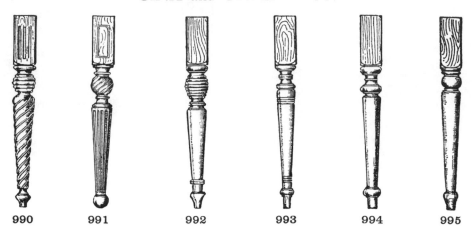

990   991   992   993   994   995

Table and Sink legs usually made 1¾, 2¼ and 3¾ inches square. Write for prices, giving size kind of wood and quantity.

BASE ANGLE BEADS.

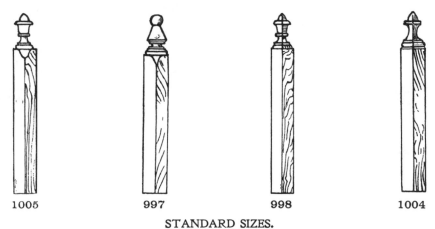

1005   997   998   1004

STANDARD SIZES.

1⅜ x 1⅜ inches, 12 and 14 inches long.

CORNER BEADS.

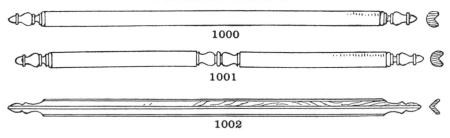

1000

1001

1002

STANDARD SIZES.

1⅛ x 1⅛ inches, 4 feet long.   1⅜ x 1⅜ inches, 4 feet long.   1¾ x 1¾ inches, 4 feet long.

TURNED ROSETTES.

CYPRESS, WHITE PINE, YELLOW PINE OR OAK.

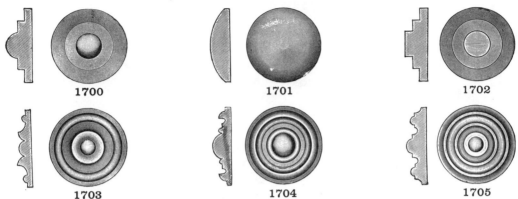

Write for prices, giving size of diameter, quantity, and kind of wood.

TURNED DOWELS, BALLS and DROPS

IN SOFT WOODS.

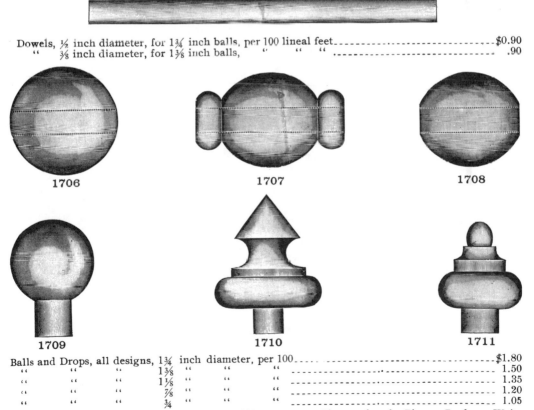

Dowels, ½ inch diameter, for 1¾ inch balls, per 100 lineal feet_____$0.90
   "   ⅜ inch diameter, for 1⅜ inch balls,   "   "   " _____ .90

Balls and Drops, all designs, 1¾ inch diameter, per 100_____ _____$1.80
  "   "   "   1⅜ "   "   " _____ 1.50
  "   "   "   1⅛ "   "   " _____ 1.35
  "   "   "   ⅞   "   "   " _____ 1.20
  "   "   "   ¾   "   "   " _____ 1.05

If balls are cross-bored, add 25 cents per 100 net extra.   Above prices for Pine or Poplar.   Write for prices in hardwood.

Prices subject to discount.

WOOD CARVINGS.

1308   Price, $2.25

1309   Price, $2.25

1310   Price, $2.25

1311   Price, $2.25

1312   Price, $2.25

1312½   Price, $2.25

White or Yellow Pine, Oak, Birch, or woods of equal value.

Sizes, 4 x 37½ inches to 4 x 43½ inches.

RAISED WOOD CARVINGS.

Made ¼ inch thick unless otherwise ordered.

142

5x24, 90c.   5x30, $1.13.   5x36, $1.35

143

4½x18, 38c.   4½x24, 53c.

144

5x30, 98c.   5x36, $1.13.

145

3½x18, 24c.   3½x28, 30c.

146

3½x18, 27c.   3½x24, 35c.

147   3x11, 18c.

148   2x10, 15c.

RAISED WOOD CARVINGS.

Made ¼ inch thick unless otherwise ordered.

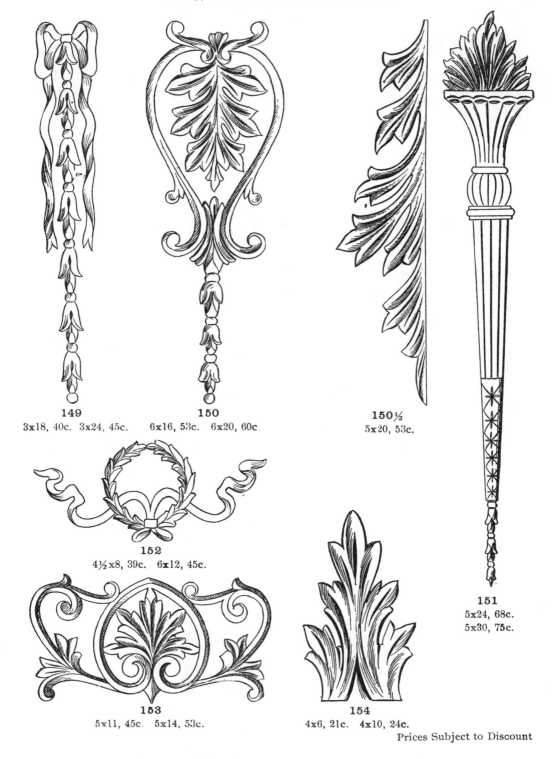

149
3x18, 40c. 3x24, 45c.

150
6x16, 53c. 6x20, 60c.

150½
5x20, 53c.

152
4½x8, 39c. 6x12, 45c.

151
5x24, 68c.
5x30, 75c.

153
5x11, 45c. 5x14, 53c.

154
4x6, 21c. 4x10, 24c.

Prices Subject to Discount

RAISED WOOD CARVINGS.
Made ¼ inch thick unless otherwise ordered.

155
2¾ x12 inches. Price, 24c.
2¾ x16   "   "   30c.

156
4x6½ inches. Price, 18c.

157
3½x7 inches.   Price, 18c.

158
3x5 inches.   Price, 12c.
4x7   "   "   15c.

159
4x4 inches.   Price, 9c.

160
8x8 inches.   Price, 38c.
6x6   "   "   30c.

161
5x5 inches.   Price, 23c.

Prices Subject to Discount.

INSIDE GRILLES.

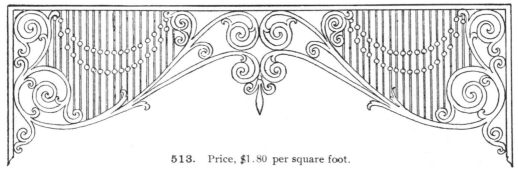

512.   Price, $2.00 per square foot.

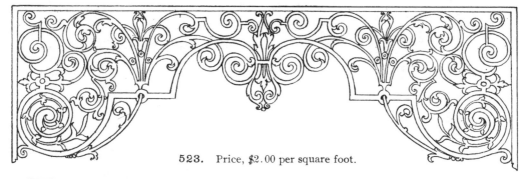

513.   Price, $1.80 per square foot.

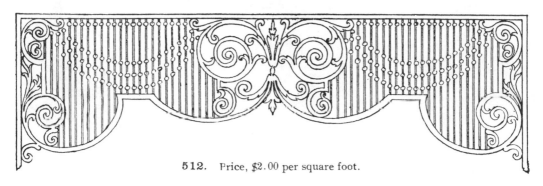

523.   Price, $2.00 per square foot.

500.   Price, $2.50 per square foot.

INSIDE GRILLES.

529. Price, $2.00 per square foot.

528. Price, $2.00 per square foot.

522. Price, $2.25 per square foot.

588. Price, $2.00 per square foot.

INSIDE GRILLES.

593.   Price, $2.25 per square foot

524.   Price, $2.50 per square foot.

508.   Price, $1.80 per square foot.

594.   Price, $2.25 per square foot.

INSIDE GRILLES.

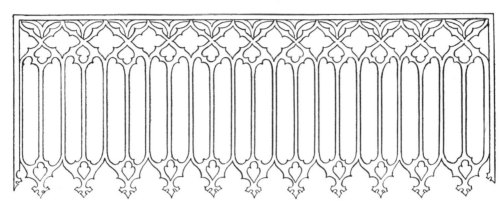

518   Price, $1.70 per square foot.

595.   Price, $2.25 per square foot

592.   Price, $2.25 per square foot.

506.   Price, $1.80 per square foot.

INSIDE GRILLES.

559. $2.00 per square foot.

545. $1.80 per square foot.

INSIDE GRILLES.

544. Price, $2.25 per square foot.

543. Price, $2.00 per square foot.

INSIDE GRILLES.

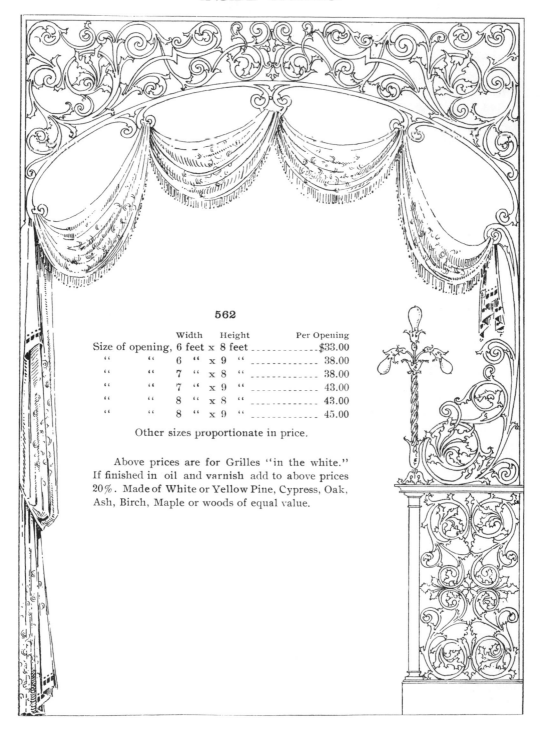

562

	Width	Height		Per Opening
Size of opening,	6 feet	x 8 feet	------------	$33.00
"	" 6 "	x 9 "	------------	38.00
"	" 7 "	x 8 "	------------	38.00
"	" 7 "	x 9 "	------------	43.00
"	" 8 "	x 8 "	------------	43.00
"	" 8 "	x 9 "	------------	45.00

Other sizes proportionate in price.

Above prices are for Grilles "in the white."
If finished in oil and varnish add to above prices
20%. Made of White or Yellow Pine, Cypress, Oak,
Ash, Birch, Maple or woods of equal value.

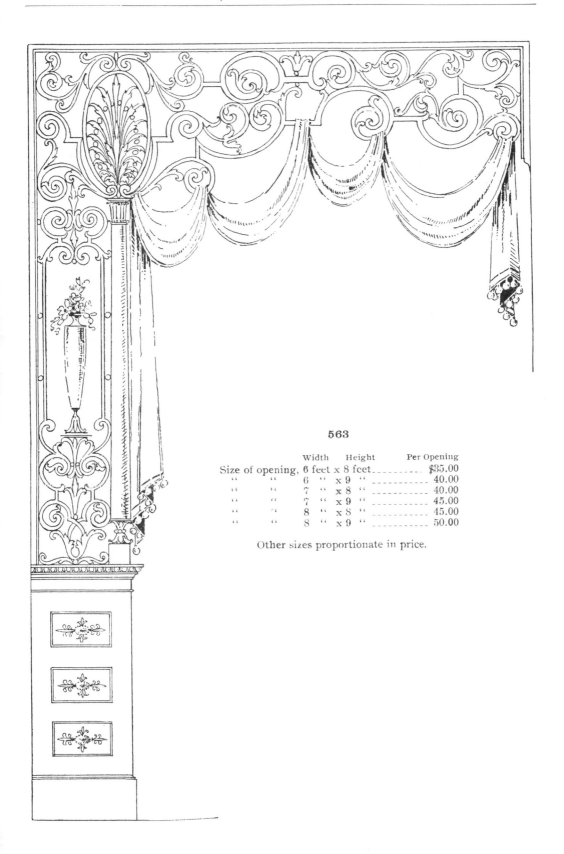

563

		Width	Height	Per Opening
Size of opening,	6 feet	x 8 feet	_____	$35.00
"	"	6 "	x 9 "	_____ 40.00
"	"	7 "	x 8 "	_____ 40.00
"	"	7 "	x 9 "	_____ 45.00
"	"	8 "	x 8 "	_____ 45.00
"	"	8 "	x 9 "	_____ 50.00

Other sizes proportionate in price.

INSIDE GRILLES.

577

For opening 6 feet x 8 feet $45.00
    "   7 " x 8 " 50.00
    "   7 " x 9 " 55.00
    "   8 " x 8 " 55.00
    "   8 " x 9 " 60.00

Above prices are for Grilles "in the white."   If finished in oil and varnish add to above prices 20%.
Made of White or Yellow Pine, Cypress, Oak, Ash, Birch, Maple or woods of equal value.

INSIDE GRILLES.

582

For opening 6 feet x 8 feet........... $45.00
" 7 " x 8 " 50.00
" 7 " x 9 " 55.00
" 8 " x 8 " 55.00
" 8 " x 9 " 60.00

Above prices are for Grilles "in the white." If finished in oil and varnish add to above prices 20%.
Made of White or Yellow Pine, Cypress, Oak, Ash, Birch, Maple or woods of equal value.

INSIDE GRILLES.

560

For opening, 6 feet wide x 8 feet high _____$55.00
"   7 "   "   x 8 "   "   _____ 60.00
"   7 "   "   x 9 "   "   _____ 65.00
'   8 "   "   x 8 "   "   _____ 65.00
"   8 "   "   x 9 "   "   _____ 70.00

Above prices are for Grilles "in the white."   If finished in oil and varnish add to above prices 20%.
Made in White or Yellow Pine, Cypress, Oak, Ash, Birch, Maple or woods of equal value.

INSIDE GRILLES.

564

For opening, 7 feet x 8 feet	$70.00
" 7 " x 9 "	76.00
" 8 " x 8 "	82.00

| For opening 8 feet x 9 feet | $88.00 |
| " 9 " x 9 " | 94.00 |

Above prices are for Grilles "in the white." If finished in oil and varnish add to above prices 20%.
Made of White or Yellow Pine, Cypress, Oak, Ash, Birch, Maple or woods of equal value.

WOOD MANTELS.

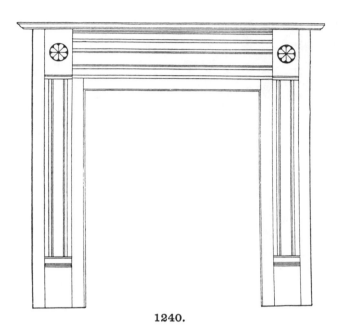

1240.

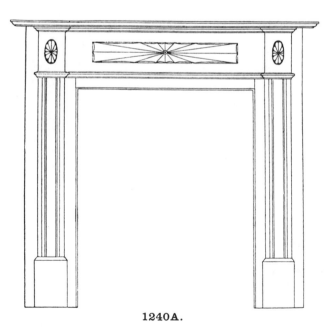

1240A.

In ordering give length and height of shelf and size of fire opening.
Made of pine, yellow pine or cypress, or any of the hardwoods.

WRITE FOR PRICES.

WOOD MANTELS.

1240 B.

1241.

In ordering give length and height of shelf and size of fire opening.
Made of pine, yellow pine or cypress, or any of the hardwoods.

WRITE FOR PRICES.

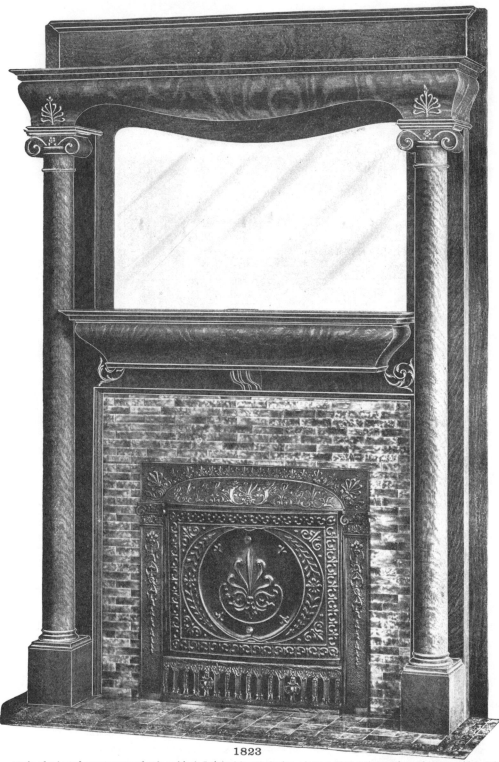

1823

Made of selected quarter sawed oak or birch finished in all shades; piano polish; height, 7 feet 4 inches; width, 5 feet to 5 feet 4 inches; tile opening, 42 x 39 inches; plain French plate mirror, 24 x 40 inches; columns, 4 inches.

Mantel only including mirror, **$78.80**; complete with outfit 20, **$99.80**; 21, **$97.80**; 22 **$96.30**; 23, **$112.30**; 24, **$108.80**; 25, **$115.80**; 26, **$107.80**; 27, **$126.80**. Prices subject to liberal discount.

For full description of outfits, see pages 268 to 272. In ordering, please specify which outfit is wanted with mantel. If mantel is wanted with outfit different from those priced above, write for price on same.

1831

Made of selected quarter sawed oak or birch, finished in all shades, piano polish: height, 7 feet 6 inches; width, 5 feet to 5 feet 4 inches; tile opening, 42x39 inches; columns, 4 inches in diameter; French beveled plate mirror, 20x36 inches; can also be had with 18x36 square mirror at same price.

Mantel only, including mirror, **$82.50** ; Mantel complete with outfit 20, **$103.50** ; 21, **$101.50** ; 22, **$100.00** ; 23, **$116.00** ; 24, **$112.50** ; 25, **$119.50** ; 26, **$111.50** ; 27, **$130.50**.

For full description of outfits, see pages 268 to 272. In ordering, please specify which outfit is wanted with mantel. If mantel is wanted with outfit different from those priced above, write for price on same. Above prices subject to liberal discount.

1742

Made of selected quarter sawed oak or birch, finished in all shades, piano polish; height, 7 feet; width, 5 feet to 5 feet 4 inches; tile opening, 42x39 inches; French bevel plate mirror, 18x36 inches; columns, 3¾ inches.

Mantel only, including mirror_____ ____$52.50	Mantel complete with outfit 24_____$82.50
Mantel complete with outfit 20_____ 73.50	" " " 25_____ 89.50
" " " 21_____ 71.50	" " " 26_____ 81.50
" " " 22_____ 70.00	" " " 27_____100.50
" " " 23_____ 86.00	

For full description of outfits, see pages 268 to 272. In ordering please specify which outfit is wanted with mantel. If mantel is wanted with outfit different from those priced above, write for price on same. Above prices subject to liberal discount.

1739

Made of selected quarter sawed oak or birch, finished in all shades, piano polish; height, 7 feet; width, 5 feet to 5 feet 4 inches; tile opening, 42x39 inches; columns, 3¼ inches; plain French plate mirror, 18x36 inches.

Mantel only, including mirror		$48.80		Mantel complete with outfit 24			$78.80
Mantel complete with outfit 20		69.80		" " " 25			85.80
" " " 21		67.80		" " " 26			77.80
" " " 22		66.30		" " " 27			96.80
" " " 23		82.30					

For full description of outfits, see pages 268 to 272. In ordering please specify which outfit is wanted with mantel. If mantel is wanted with outfit different from those priced above, write for price on same. Above prices subject to liberal discount.

1663

Height, 6 feet 10 inches; width, 4 feet 6 inches to 5 feet; tile projection, 4 inches; French bevel plate mirror, 14x24 inches; opening in mantel, width, 36 inches; height, 36 inches, or width 42 inches; height, 36 inches; made of selected oak superior flowed golden oak finish or birch imitation mahogany finish.

Mantel only, without trimmings, **$23.00**; mantel with outfit 20, **$44.00**; 21, **$42.00**; 22, **$40.50**; 23, **$57.50**; 24, **$53.00**; 25, **$60.00**; 26, **$52.00**; 27, **$71.00**.

Above list prices are subject to liberal discount.

1226

Height, 6 feet 8 inches; width, 4 feet 6 inches to 5 feet; tile projection, 1 inch; Quarter sawed oak columns 3 inches in diameter; French bevel plate mirror, 18 x 36 inches; opening in mantel, width, 36 inches; height, 36 inches. Made of selected Oak, superior flowed, golden oak finish.

Mantel only, without trimmings, **$27.00**; Mantel with outfit 20, **$48.00**; 21, **$46.00**; 22, **$44.50**; 23, **$60.50**; 24, **$64.00**; 25, **$71.00**; 26, **$63.00**; 27, **$82.00.**

Above list prices are subject to liberal discount.

1814

Made of selected quarter sawed oak, or birch, finished all shades, piano polish ; height, 6 feet 9 inches; width, 4 feet 10 inches to 5 feet ; tile opening, 36x39 inches ; French beveled plate mirror, 18x36 inches ; columns, 3 inches.

Mantel only including mirror	$39.50	Mantel complete with outfit 24	$69.50
" complete with outfit 20	60.50	" " " " 25	76.50
" " " " 21	58.50	" " " " 26	68.50
" " " " 22	57.00	" " " " 27	87.50
" " " " 23	73.00		

Above prices subject to liberal discount.

For full description of outfits, see pages 268 to 272. In ordering please specify which outfit is wanted with mantel. If mantel is wanted with outfit different from those priced above, write for price on same.

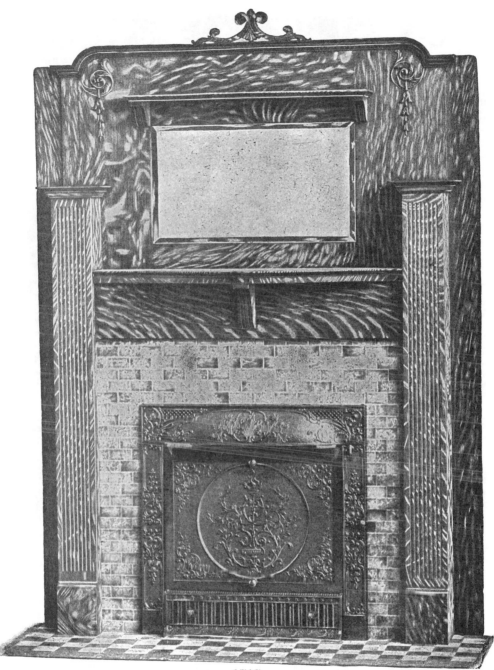

1717

Made of selected quarter sawed oak or birch, finished in all shades, piano polish : height, 6 feet 11 inches; width, 4 feet 10 inches to 5 feet; tile opening, 12x39 inches; French beveled plate mirror, 16x28 inches.

Mantel only, including mirror			$36.50	Mantel complete with outfit 24			$66.50
Mantel complete with outfit 20			57.50	"	"	"	25	73.50
"	"	" 21	55.50	"	"	"	26	65.50
"	"	" 22	54.00	"	"	"	27	84.50
"	"	" 23	70.00					

For full description of outfits, see pages 268 to 272. In ordering, please specify which outfit is wanted with mantel. If mantel is wanted with outfit different from those priced above, write for price on same. Above prices subject to liberal discount.

1841

Made only of selected oak, superior flowed, golden oak finish : height, 6 feet 5 inches; width, 4 feet 10 inches to 5 feet; tile opening, 36x36 inches; columns, 3 inches; French beveled plate mirror, 14x24 inches.

Mantel only, including mirror		$27.50	Mantel complete with outfit 24		$57.50
Mantel complete with outfit 20		48.50	" " " 25		64.50
" " " 21		46.50	" " " 26		56.50
" " " 22		45.00	" " " 27		75.50
" " " 23		61.00			

For full description of outfits, see pages 268 to 272.   In ordering, please specify which outfit is wanted with mantel. If mantel is wanted with outfit different from those priced above, write for price on same. Above prices subject to liberal discount.

1816

Made of selected quarter sawed oak, or birch finished in all shades, piano polish : height, 5 feet 1 inch ; width, 5 feet to 5 feet 4 inches ; tile opening, 42 x 42 inches ; columns, 3½ inches.

Mantel only	$23.00	Mantel complete with outfit 24	$53.00
Mantel complete with outfit 20	44.00	" " " 25	60.00
" " " 21	42.00	" " " 26	52.00
" " " 22	40.50	" " " 27	71.00
" " " 23	56.50		

Above prices subject to liberal discount.

For full description of outfits, see pages 268 to 272. In ordering, please specify which outfit is wanted with mantel. If mantel is wanted with outfit different from those priced above, write for price on same.

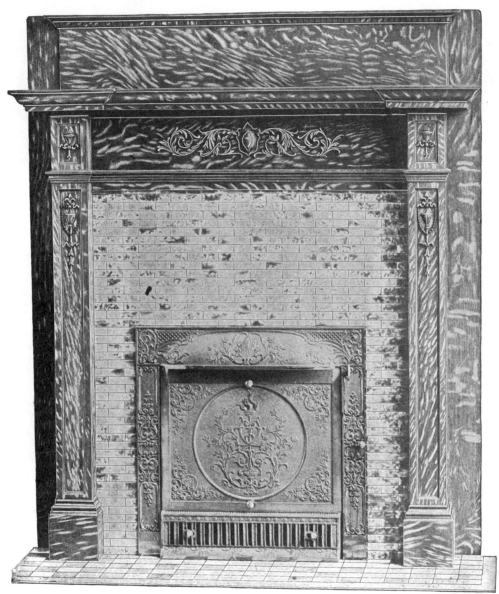

1736

Made of selected quarter sawed oak, or birch, finished in all shades, piano polish; height, 6 feet; width, 5 feet to 5 feet 4 inches; tile opening, 42 x 48 inches.

Mantel only _____	$39.00	Mantel complete with outfit 24 _____ $69.00
Mantel complete with outfit 20 _____	60.00	" " " " 25 __ _____ 76.00
" " " " 21 _____	58.00	" " " " 26 _____ 68.00
" " " " 22 _____	56.50	" " " " 27 _____ 87.00
" " " " 23 _____	72.50	

Above prices subject to liberal discount.

For full description of outfits, see pages 268 to 272. In ordering, please specify which outfit is wanted with mantel. If mantel is wanted with outfit different from those priced above, write for price on same.

1180

Made only of quarter sawed oak, golden oak, polish finish. Height, 83 inches; Width, 4 feet 11 inches to 5 feet 3 inches; tile opening, 42 x 36 or 36 x 36 inches; French bevel plate mirror, 18 x 36 inches; made with 3 inch veneered columns.

Mantel only, including mirror **$30.00**; Mantel complete with outfit 20, **$51.00**; 21, **$49.00**; 22, **$47.50**; 23, **$63.50**; 24, **$60.00**; 25, **$67.00**; 26, **$59.00**; 27, **$78.00**.

Above prices subject to liberal discount.

CONSOL.

1200

Suitable for any room in the house, also appropriate for Ice Cream Parlor, Millinery Store, etc. made only of selected quarter sawed oak, piano polish finish; height, 7 feet 5 inches; width, 5 feet; French bevel plate mirror, 34 x 54 inches.

List price, **$70.40**

Above price subject to mantel discount.

CONSOL.

1210

Suitable for any room in the house; can also be used for Ice Cream Parlor, Millinery Store, etc. made only from selected quarter sawed oak, piano polish finish; height, 7 feet 10 inches; width, 5 feet; heavy French bevel plate mirror 38 x 58 inches.

List price, **$92.90**.

Above price subject to mantel discount.

OUTFITS.

Regarding Outfits--The following Outfits can be furnished with Mantels shown in this catalogue. You will find that each Mantel is priced with the various Outfits. In ordering please be sure and specify which outfit is wanted with each Mantel ordered.

Front View of No. 1366 Virginia Grate, Outfits No. 20 and No. 21.

OUTFIT No. 20 consists of

Fireplace -- No. 1366 Virginia Grate, 30½ inches wide, 30¼ inches high, with 24-inch Fire Pot, 9 inches deep.

Facing -- Best quality enameled tile (any color).

Hearth — 60 x 21 inches; best quality enameled tile (any color).

OUTFIT No. 21 consists of

Fireplace -- No. 1366 Virginia Grate, 24½ inches wide, 30¼ inches high, with Fire Pot 20 inches wide, 9 inches deep.

Facing — Best quality enameled tile (any color).

Hearth — 60 x 21 inches; best quality enameled tile (any color).

Summer Grate can be furnished with Outfits No. 20 and No. 21, for $1.00 net extra.

VIRGINIA GRATE.

OUTFIT No. 22 consists of No. 1366 Frame and Summer Front only, as shown in Outfits 20 and 21. This is the Outfit to use for blind Mantels.

Facing — Best quality enameled tile (any color).

Hearth — 60 x 21 inches; Best quality enameled tile (any color).

✿✿

DESCRIPTION OF VIRGINIA GRATE.

The No. 1366 Virginia grate which we show is undoubtedly one of the handsomest grates of its kind on the market.

The basket is of heavy iron and hangs on the frame, and the fire brick should be built to fit snugly up to the basket. The basket is so made that it is very easy to poke out the ashes. The grate is suitable for burning hard coal, soft coal or wood.

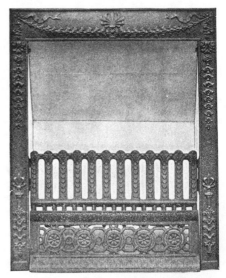

Interior View of No. 1366 Virginia Grate, Outfits No. 21 and No. 22.
Showing how basket hangs on frame.

Regarding Fire Brick—Outfits No. 21 and No. 22 do not include fire brick, as same can usually be bought in your own town for less than the freight would amount to.

OUTFITS—*Continued.*

No. 1045. BUCKEYE GRATE.
Interior View — Outfits 23 and 24.

Outfit 23—30½ in. wide, 30¼ in. high; 24-in. Fire Pot,
12 in. deep.
Outfit 24—24½ in. wide, 30¼ in. high; 20-in. Fire Pot,
12 in. deep.

Side View.

Showing Damper Arrangement, Fire Tile, and General
Construction of No. 1045 Buckeye Grate,
Outfits 23 and 24.

Description of Buckeye Grates.

The Buckeye is undoubtedly the best medium-priced mounted grate on the market.
The body of the grate is cast iron, and is securely bolted to the frame. The sides are also cast iron, and contain an air chamber to insure greater durability.
The fire tile in the back is thick, and is securely attached to the body of grate. (See illustration of side view.)
Buckeye Grates are provided with a dumping bottom that will not clog, and insures the greatest results for the fuel consumed.
They are also provided with double dampers that are operated from the front of the frame. The upper damper is worked in a new manner by a screw and can be regulated to any width and there is no danger of falling, this greatly assists in the operation, and also insures perfect control of the fire.

No. 1045. BUCKEYE GRATE. Outfits 23 and 24
Front View—Showing Summer Front in position

OUTFIT 23 consists of

Fireplace — No. 1045 Plated Buckeye Grate, 30½ in. wide, 30¼ in. high; with 24-in. Fire Pot, 12 in. deep, with summer front.

Facing — Best quality enameled tile (any color).

Hearth—60x21 in., best quality enameled tile (any color).

OUTFIT 24 consists of

Fireplace — No. 1045 Buckeye Grate, 24½ in. wide, 30¼ in. high; with 20-in. Fire Pot, 12 in. deep, with summer front.

Facing — Best quality enameled tile (any color).

Hearth—60x21 in.; best quality enameled tile (any color).

For Front and Side view of Outfits Nos. 23 and 24 see above.

OUTFITS—*Continued.*

Front View No. 1116 Plated Monarch Grate, with summer front in position.

Rear view of No 1116 Monarch Grate Outfit No. **25,** showing damper arrangement.

OUTFIT No. 25 consists of

Fireplace—No. 1116 Plated Monarch Grate, 24½ inches wide, 30¼ inches high. Firepot 20 inches wide, 12 inches deep.

Outfit No. 25 can also be had 30½ x 30¼ inches, with 24 inch firepot, 12 inches deep for $1.50 net extra.

DESCRIPTION OF MONARCH GRATES.

The merits of the Monarch Grate, are so well known that it is not necessary for us to dwell long upon a description of them. They are made like a stove complete, all in one piece. bolted securely together and they do not require the services of a skilled mason to set them. as it is only necessary to push them into the fireplace and they are ready for use. The fire pot in the Monarch is lined with fire clay lining in the back and sides. These grates have a curved top which reflects the heat into the room. They are supplied with double dampers which are operated from the front with knobs (See illustration above). The upper damper is worked in a new manner by a screw and can be regulated any width, and there is no danger of falling. The screw and arm are made of malleable iron. The Monarch Grate is suitable for either hard or soft coal, coke or wood.

OUTFIT No. 26 consists of

Fireplace—No. 975 complete mounted Gas Grate and Summer Front, plated; 24½ inches wide, 30¼ inches high, or 30½ inches wide, 30¼ inches high. This grate has copper reflecting sides and base; made with five-row steel burner; double hood; damper full width of back; operated by handle on top of grate. Has double ventilating back, which takes cold and foul air from the floor, and passes through opening in back of chimney.

Facing—Best quality plain enameled tile.

Hearth—60x21 inches. Best quality plain enameled tile.

With fifteen feet of gas per hour you can keep a room fourteen feet square to a temperature of seventy degrees when the thermometer stands at twenty above zero. It will never burn out. It makes a good ventilator. It burns absolutely odorless. In ordering state whether natural or artificial gas will be used.

975

GAS GRATE with Summer Front in place.
30½x30¼ and 24½x30¼; five-row steel burner; deep or shallow back.

OUTFITS—*Continued.*

488. NEW COLUMBIAN GRATE (Louis XIV design). 30½ inches wide, 30¼ inches high; 24-inch plated basket with shaking and dumping bottom.

OUTFIT No. 27 consists of

Fireplace.—No. 488 Plated New Columbian Grate, 30½ inches wide, 30¼ inches high, with 24-inch plated basket and plated summer front.

Facing.—Best quality enameled tile (any color).

Hearth.—60x21 inches; best quality enameled tile (any color).

Outfit No. 27 can also be had 24½ inches wide, 30¼ inches high, with fire pot 20 inches wide for $1.50 net less.

NOTE.—Read carefully full description of New Columbian Grates on page 272.

SPARK GUARDS.

Our No. 1 and 2 Spark Guards as here shown are designed to answer every purpose for which they are intended. As a protection from falling sparks they are guaranteed, the fine wire cloth with which they are lined practically preventing any sparks from coming through. As a preventative to keep small children from falling into the fire, an article of this kind is invaluable, as it stands solid on the hearth and absolutely covers any fire place up to 31 x 31 inches, the exact size of guard. The value of first feature mentioned will at once be apparent, when one considers the danger to life and property from the many fires originating from just such causes as a spark falling from open grate or fire place. A very small spark quite often does the damage.

DESCRIPTION.—Made of the best coppered steel wire and full lined with finely woven bright wire cloth. Not like the ordinary unlined black wire guard seen in your hardware store, but a very pretty and ornamental piece of fire place furniture.

No. 1 Coppered Fine Wire Lining 24 inches wide, 30 inches high, List........................$2.00

No. 2 Coppered Fine Wire Lining 30 inches wide, 30 inches high, List............................ 3.00

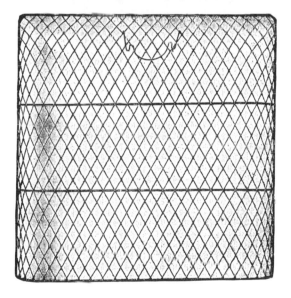

AUTOMATIC NEW YORK ASH TRAPS.

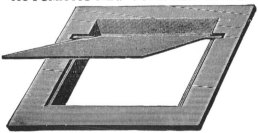

List Price. 7x10 inches; 9x11 inches. Each, 70c.

ASH PIT DOOR—HINGED DOOR.

Made of Heavy Malleable Iron.

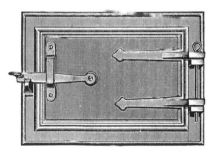

Opening, 8 x 12, 10 x 12, 12 x 12, 12 x 16, or 14 x 20.
List price. Each.....................................$4.00

Prices subject to **Mantel Discount.**

OUTFITS—*Continued*.

Side View

**IMPROVED COLUMBIAN
VENTILATING GRATE**

Showing Damper Arrangement, Fire Tile and General
Construction of Nos. 1 and 2 Improved
Columbian Ventilating Grates.

Interior View

**IMPROVED COLUMBIAN
VENTILATING GRATE**

IMPROVED COLUMBIAN VENTILATING GRATES

For Hard Coal, Soft Coal, Coke or Wood

Nothing but the Very Best Materials and Workmanship
enter into their construction

WHAT THEY WILL DO

The Damper system, as applied to the Improved Columbian Ventilating Grates, gives the user absolute control of the fire, thereby providing an easy way to increase or lessen the heat as required. This is an important feature that can not be accomplished in any other make of grates; we except none. It also affords an excellent system of ventilation, as well as collecting the cold air from the floor and carrying the same into the air chamber back of the fire tile, where it becomes superheated and passes above the line of fire, producing perfect combustion of the gases which otherwise would escape into the flue unconsumed. This consumption of the gases adds very materially to the heating qualities as well as to the economy, cheerfulness, and cleanliness.

We would call your special attention to the position occupied by the top tile, which acts as a check and prevents the heat from passing direct into the flue. It also insures the passing of the superheated air directly over the line of the fire, producing greater benefit for the fuel consumed. By opening the lower damper when shaking the grate, all the dust is drawn into the chamber back of the fire and then discharged into the main flue.

The upper damper is controlled by regulating device, which can be set at any point to meet the requirements of the flue to which the grate is attached. It can be closed absolutely tight when not in use, thereby preventing soot or other dirt from entering the room.

The Improved Columbian Ventilating Grates are constructed in parts and bolted firmly together, with a view of providing for the necessary expansion and contraction. This is an important feature that is never adopted in cheap grates, and where provision is not made for expansion, it very often causes the displacement of the tile facing.

All linings used in the Improved Columbian Ventilating Grates are made with a view of great durability; they are carefully set in asbestos cement, which insures an absolutely tight fire chamber. Special provision is also made for the easy and convenient replacing of the tile lining when required.

BRASS AND IRON ANDIRONS.

541	**526**	**372**
18 inches high.	16½ inches high.	19 inches high.
List Price, per pair___$12.00	List Price, per pair___$4.50	List Price, per pair___$8.50

POLISHED BRASS FIRE SETS.

890	**892**	**895**
List Price, per set ___$12.50	List Price, per set___$16.00	List Price, per set___ $21.00

POLISHED BRASS FENDER.

608

With plain or fancy rail, 36 or 42 inches long _____$19.00

Prices subject to Mantel discount.

Explanation and Instructions for Composition Capitals.

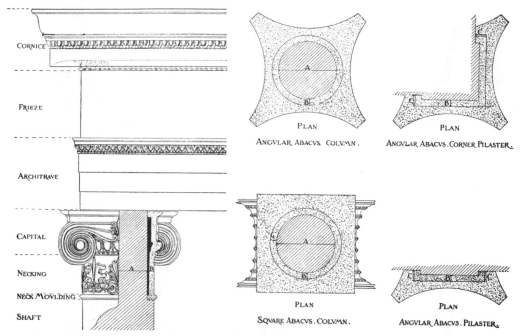

The above plate illustrates one of our modern Ionic Capitals with necking (Empire), as applied to a column showing the wood shaft and core running through the Capital supporting the entablature above. The plans of the different abacus forms as given will serve as a further illustration of the relative position of shaft and our material.

"A" indicates the core or extended shaft running through Capital.

"B" shows thickness of our material.

"C" indicates the return of Pilaster Capital; which always must be mentioned in ordering Pilaster Capitals.

All our Capitals are furnished as shown in the Catalogue, each Capital having a complete finish to connect with shaft. The diameter given in Catalogue represents the top of Column. The width represents the top of Pilaster. The height given is the exact height of Capital. Always allow a trifle more height for your core so the weight will rest on shaft and not on Capital, $\frac{1}{8}$ of an inch up to a 10-inch diameter; $\frac{1}{4}$ of an inch above that size will be sufficient to insure a safe application.

The thickness of our material is one inch up to a 10-inch diameter Capital, making the core of a 10-inch diameter Capital 8 inches, of an 8-inch Capital 6 inches. Above 10 inches allow $\frac{1}{8}$ of an inch more for the thickness of material for every two inches of increased size, making core for a 14-inch diameter Capital $11\frac{1}{2}$ inches, a 16-inch Capital $13\frac{1}{4}$ inches, etc.

In ordering Capital, give name, number and size of diameter or width; also state material wanted, viz: whether Exterior Composition, warranted to stand in any climate, or Interior Composition, made with grain to match any wood; (Interior Composition having a solid wood body requires no core on Column. Always state the kind of wood and finish.)

The sizes of our brackets given are:

    1st   The entire width across abacus moulding.

    2d   Width of face on body.

    3d   Drop or length.

    4th   Projection.

The increasing demand for Capitals, both Column and Pilaster in composition instead of wood warrants us, we believe, in making this class of work a feature of our new catalogue. We show on the following pages a number of designs in different styles of architecture suitable for either inside or outside use. And we also include a large and varied list of the sizes in which they can be furnished. We recommend them as follows :

Composition Capitals and Brackets

In beauty they easily surpass wood carvings, the detail in execution being brought to a fineness impossible in wood

In durability they are the equal of wood, and for outside use they are specially prepared and guaranteed to stand any conditions of climate.

In cost they are very much cheaper than wood.

Write us for prices or any desired information.

We can furnish these Capitals with our Colonial Columns. When ordering always give diameter of neck of column.

ITALIAN RENAISSANCE IONIC (Scamozzi).

COLUMN CAPITAL.

EXTERIOR.

Number.	Diameter, Inches.	Height, Inches.	Prices, Each.
1426	4	2¼	$ 2.00
1427	5	2⅞	2.50
1428	5½	3⅛	2.75
1429	6	3⅜	3.00
1430	6½	3⅝	3.25
1431	7	3¾	3.50
1432	7½	4¼	3.75
1433	8	4⅝	4.00
1434	8½	4¾	4.25
1435	9	5⅛	4.50
1436	9½	5⅜	4.75
1437	10	5¾	5.00
1438	10½	5⅞	5.50
1439	11	6¼	6.00
1440	12	6¾	7.00
1441	13	7½	8.00
1442	14	7⅞	9.50
1443	15	8⅜	10.50
1444	16	9	12.00
1445	17	9¾	13.00
1446	18	10⅛	14.00
1447	20	11⅜	18.00
1448	22	12½	22.00
1449	24	13½	25.00
1450	28	16	35.00
1451	31	17¾	45.00

INTERIOR.

Number.	Diameter, Inches.	Height, Inches.	Prices, Each.
1476	1	$\frac{9}{16}$	$ 0.60
1477	1½	⅞	.70
1478	2	1⅛	.80
1479	2½	1⅜	.90
1480	3	1¾	1.00
1481	3½	2	1.20
1482	4	2¼	1.40
1483	4½	2½	1.60
1484	5	2⅞	1.80
1485	5½	3⅛	2.00
1486	6	3⅜	2.25
1487	6½	3⅝	2.50
1488	7	3¾	3.00
1489	7½	4¼	3.50
1490	8	4⅝	4.50
1491	9	5⅛	6.00
1492	10	5¾	7.50
1493	11	6¼	9.00
1494	12	6¾	11.00
1495	14	7⅞	15.00

PILASTER CAPITAL.

EXTERIOR.

Number.	Width, Inches.	Height, Inches.	Prices, Each.
1526	4	2¼	$ 1.25
1527	5	2⅞	1.50
1528	5½	3⅛	1.50
1529	6	3⅜	1.75
1530	6½	3⅝	1.75
1531	7	3¾	2.00
1532	7½	4¼	2.00
1533	8	4⅝	2.25
1534	8½	4¾	2.25
1535	9	5⅛	2.50
1536	9½	5⅜	2.50
1537	10	5¾	2.75
1538	10½	5⅞	2.75
1539	11	6¼	3.00
1540	12	6¾	3.75
1541	13	7½	4.25
1542	14	7⅞	5.00
1543	15	8⅜	6.00
1544	16	9	7.00
1545	17	9¾	8.00
1546	18	10⅛	9.00
1547	20	11⅜	10.00
1548	22	12½	11.50
1549	24	13½	13.00
1550	28	16	18.00
1551	31	17¾	25.00

INTERIOR.

Number.	Width, Inches.	Height, Inches.	Prices Each.
1576	1	$\frac{9}{16}$	$ 0.40
1577	1½	⅞	.50
1578	2	1⅛	.60
1579	2½	1⅜	.70
1580	3	1¾	.80
1581	3½	2	.90
1582	4	2¼	1.00
1583	4½	2½	1.25
1584	5	2⅞	1.30
1585	5½	3⅛	1.45
1586	6	3⅜	1.60
1587	6½	3⅝	1.80
1588	7	3¾	2.10
1589	7½	4¼	2.50
1590	8	4⅝	3.00
1591	9	5⅛	3.75
1592	10	5¾	4.50
1593	11	6¼	5.00
1594	12	6¾	6.00
1595	14	7⅞	8.00

See page 274 for explanations and instructions.

ITALIAN RENAISSANCE IONIC (Scamozzi).

COLUMN CAPITAL.

COPY'D 1899.   DECORATORS SUP'Y CO.

PILASTER CAPTIAL.

COPY'D 1899.   DECORATORS SUP'Y CO

ROMAN CORINTHIAN (Pantheon)

COLUMN CAPITAL.

EXTERIOR.

Number.	Diameter, Inches.	Height, Inches.	Prices, Each.
301	5	7	$ 4.00
302	6	9	5.00
303	7	10½	6.00
304	8	12	6.50
305	9	12½	7.00
306	10	14⅝	8.00
307	11	15⅜	9.00
308	12	16¾	10.00
309	13	18	11.00
310	14	19½	12.00
311	15	21	14.00
312	16	22⅜	16.00
313	18	25	20.00
314	20	28	25 00
315	24	33½	40.00

INTERIOR.

Number.	Diameter, Inches.	Height, Inches.	Prices, Each.
326	1	1⅜	1.25
327	1½	2	1.50
328	2	2⅝	1.75
329	2½	3⅜	2.25
330	3	4	3.00
331	3½	4¾	3.50
332	4	5½	4.00
333	4½	6¼	4.50
334	5	7	5.00
335	5½	7¾	6.00
336	6	9	7.00
337	8	12	10.00

PILASTER CAPITAL.

EXTERIOR.

Number.	Width, Inches.	Height, Inches.	Prices, Each.
351	5	7	$ 2.50
352	6	9	3.00
353	7	10½	3.50
354	8	12	3.75
355	9	12½	4.00
356	10	14⅝	4.50
357	11	15⅜	5.00
358	12	16¾	6.00
359	13	18	7.00
360	14	19½	8.00
361	15	21	8.50
362	16	22⅜	9.00
363	18	25	11.00
364	20	28	15.00
365	24	33½	25.00

INTERIOR.

Number.	Width, Inches.	Height, Inches.	Prices, Each.
376	1	1⅜	$0.80
377	1½	2	1.00
378	2	2⅝	1.25
379	2½	3⅜	1.50
380	3	4	1.75
381	3½	4¾	2.25
382	4	5½	2.50
383	4½	6¼	3.00
384	5	7	4.00
385	5½	7¾	4.50
386	6	9	5.25
387	8	12	6.50

See page 274 for explanations and instructions.

ROMAN CORINTHIAN (Pantheon).
COLUMN CAPITAL.

COPY'D 1899.   DECORATORS SUP'Y CO.

PILASTER CAPITAL.

COPY'D 1899.   DECORATORS SUP'Y CO.

GREEK IONIC (Erechtheum).

COLUMN CAPITAL

EXTERIOR.

Number.	Diameter, Inches.	Height, Inches.	Prices, Each.
1	4	3⅝	$ 2.25
2	5	4½	2.50
3	6	5½	3.00
4	7	6⅜	4.00
5	8	7	5.00
6	9	8¼	6.00
7	10	9⅛	7.00
8	11	10	8.00
9	12	11	9.00
10	14	12¾	12.00
11	16	14⅝	16.00
12	17	16¼	18.00
13	18	16½	20.00

INTERIOR.

Number.	Diameter, Inches.	Height, Inches.	Prices, Each.
25	3	2¾	$ 2.50
26	3½	3⅛	3.00
27	4	3⅝	3.50
28	4½	4	4.00
29	5	4½	4.50
30	5½	5	5.00
31	6	5½	5.50
32	6½	5⅞	6.00
33	7	6⅜	7.00
34	8	7	8.00

PILASTER CAPITAL.

EXTERIOR.

Number.	Width, Inches.	Height, Inches.	Prices, Each.
51	5	4⅜	$ 1.50
52	5½	4¼	2.00
53	6	5⅛	2.25
54	7	4½	2.50
55	8	8	3.00
56	9¾	9½	3.50
57	10	8	4.00
58	11	7⅛	4.50
59	12	7¾	5.00
60	14	9	5.50
61	16	10⅜	6.50
62	18	11⅝	8.00

INTERIOR.

Number.	Width, Inches.	Height, Inches.	Prices Each
76	3	2	$ 1.50
77	3½	2¼	1.50
78	4	2½	2.00
79	4½	3	2.00
80	5	3¼	2.50
81	5½	3⅝	2.50
82	6	4	3.00
83	6½	4¼	3.00
84	7	4½	3.50
85	8	5	4.00

See page 274 for instructions and explanations.

GREEK IONIC (Erechtheum).

COLUMN CAPITAL.

COPY'D 1899. DECORATORS SUP'Y CO.

PILASTER CAPITAL.

COPY'D 1899. DECORATORS SUP'Y CO.

MODERN IONIC with NECKING (Empire).

COLUMN CAPITAL.

	EXTERIOR.				INTERIOR.		
Number.	Diameter. Inches.	Height, Inches.	Prices, Each.	Number.	Diameter, Inches.	Height, Inches.	Prices, Each.
1051	4	5	$2.50	1101	1	1¼	$0.70
1052	5	6¼	3.00	1102	1½	1⅞	.85
1053	6	7½	3 25	1103	2	2½	1.00
1054	6½	7¾	3.75	1104	2½	3⅛	1.20
1055	7	8⅞	4.00	1105	3	3¾	1.50
1056	7½	9⅜	4.50	1106	3½	4⅜	1.75
1057	8	10¼	5.00	1107	4	5	2.00
1058	8½	10½	5.50	1108	4½	5⅝	2.30
1059	9	11½	6.00	1109	5	6¼	2.70
1060	9½	11⅞	6.50	1110	5½	6⅞	3.00
1061	10	12½	7.50	1111	6	7½	4.00
1062	11	13¾	8.00	1112	7	8⅞	5.00
1063	12	15	8.50	1113	8	10¼	7.00
1064	14	17½	9.50	1114	9	11½	9.00
1065	15	18¾	10.50	1115	10	12½	11.00
1066	16	20	13.00	1116	11	13¾	13.50
1067	17	21¼	14.50	1117	12	15	15.00
1068	18	22½	17.00	1118	14	17½	20.00
1069	21	26¼	22.00	1119	15	18¾	25.00
				1120	16	20	30.00
				1121	17	21¼	38.00
				1122	18	22½	45.00

PILASTER CAPITAL.

	EXTERIOR.				INTERIOR.		
Number.	Width, Inches.	Height, Inches.	Prices, Each.	Number	Width, Inches.	Height, Inches.	Prices, Each.
1151	4	5	$1.50	1201	1	1¼	$0.50
1152	5	6¼	1.75	1202	1½	1⅞	.60
1153	6	7½	2.00	1203	2	2½	.70
1154	6½	7¾	2.25	1204	2½	3⅛	.80
1155	7	8⅞	2.50	1205	3	3¾	.90
1156	7½	9⅜	2.75	1206	3½	4⅜	1.00
1157	8	10¼	3.00	1207	4	5	1.25
1158	8½	10½	3.25	1208	4½	5⅝	1.50
1159	9	11½	3.50	1209	5	6¼	1.75
1160	9½	11⅞	3.75	1210	5½	6⅞	2.00
1161	10	12½	4.00	1211	6	7½	2.50
1162	11	13¾	4.50	1212	7	8⅞	3 00
1163	12	15	5.00	1213	8	10¼	4.00
1164	14	17½	5.50	1214	9	11½	5.00
1165	15	18¾	6.25	1215	10	12½	6.00
1166	16	20	7.50	1216	11	13¾	7.25
1167	17	21¼	8.75	1217	12	15	8.50
1168	18	22½	9.50	1218	14	17½	11.00
1169	21	26¼	12.50	1219	15	18¾	14.00
				1220	16	20	16.50
				1221	17	21¼	20.00
				1222	18	22½	25.00

See page 274 for instructions and explanations.

MODERN IONIC with NECKING (Empire).
COLUMN CAPITAL.

COPY'D 1899   DECORATORS SUP'Y CO.

PILASTER CAPITAL.

COPY D 1899.   DECORATORS SUP'Y CO.

ITALIAN RENAISSANCE CORINTHIAN (Sansovino).

COLUMN CAPITAL.

EXTERIOR.

Number.	Diameter, Inches.	Height, Inches.	Prices, Each.
1626	5	7	$ 2.50
1627	6	8⅜	3.50
1628	7	9⅝	4.50
1629	8	11	5.50
1630	9	12½	6.50
1631	10	13⅞	7.50
1632	12	16¾	9.00
1633	14	19½	11.00
1634	16	22¼	14.00
1635	18	25	17.00

INTERIOR.

Number.	Diameter, Inches.	Height, Inches.	Prices, Each.
1676	1	1⅜	$ 0.70
1677	1½	2	.80
1678	2	2¾	1.00
1679	2½	3½	1.20
1680	3	4⅛	1.50
1681	3½	4¾	1.80
1682	4	5½	2.20
1683	4½	6¼	2.60
1684	5	7	3.00
1685	5½	7¾	3.50
1686	6	8⅜	4.50
1687	6½	9	5.00
1688	7	9⅝	6.00

PILASTER CAPITAL.

EXTERIOR.

Number.	Width, Inches.	Height, Inches.	Prices, Each.
1726	5	7	$ 1.50
1727	6	8⅜	2.00
1728	7	9⅝	2.50
1729	8	11	3.00
1730	9	12½	3.50
1731	10	13⅞	4.00
1732	12	16¾	5.00
1733	14	19½	6.00
1734	16	22¼	7.50
1735	18	25	9.00

INTERIOR.

Number.	Width, Inches.	Height Inches.	Prices, Each.
1776	1	1⅜	$0.50
1777	1½	2	.60
1778	2	2¾	.70
1779	2½	3½	.90
1780	3	4⅛	1.10
1781	3½	4¾	1.25
1782	4	5½	1.50
1783	4½	6¼	1.75
1784	5	7	2.00
1785	5½	7¾	2.25
1786	6	8⅜	2.50
1787	6½	9	3.00
1788	7	9⅝	3.50

See page 274 for instructions and explanations.

ITALIAN RENAISSANCE CORINTHIAN (Sansovino).
COLUMN CAPITAL.

COPY'D 1899.   DECORATORS SUP'Y CO.

PILASTER CAPITAL.

COPY'D 1899.   DECORATORS SUP'Y CO.

GREEK ANGULAR IONIC (Minerva Polias).

COLUMN CAPITAL.

EXTERIOR.

Number	Diameter, Inches.	Height, Inches.	Prices, Each,
201	5	$3\frac{1}{8}$	$ 2.50
202	6	$3\frac{3}{8}$	3.00
203	$6\frac{1}{2}$	4	3.25
204	7	$4\frac{1}{8}$	3.50
205	$7\frac{1}{2}$	$4\frac{1}{4}$	3.75
206	8	5	4 50
207	$8\frac{1}{2}$	$5\frac{1}{4}$	4.75
208	9	$5\frac{5}{8}$	5.00
209	$9\frac{1}{2}$	6	5.50
210	10	$6\frac{1}{4}$	6.00
211	11	$6\frac{7}{8}$	6.75
212	12	$7\frac{1}{2}$	7.50
213	14	$8\frac{3}{4}$	9.00
214	15	$9\frac{3}{8}$	10.00
215	18	$11\frac{1}{4}$	14.00
216	21	$13\frac{1}{8}$	18.00
217	25	$14\frac{3}{8}$	30.00

INTERIOR.

Number.	Diameter, Inches.	Height, Inches.	Prices. Each.
226	$1\frac{1}{2}$	$1\frac{5}{16}$	$1.00
227	2	$1\frac{1}{4}$	1.10
228	$2\frac{1}{2}$	$1\frac{9}{16}$	1.20
229	3	$1\frac{7}{8}$	1.30
230	$3\frac{1}{2}$	$2\frac{3}{16}$	1.40
231	4	$2\frac{1}{2}$	1.60
232	$4\frac{1}{2}$	$2\frac{13}{16}$	1.80
233	5	$3\frac{1}{8}$	2.00
234	$5\frac{1}{2}$	$3\frac{7}{16}$	2.50
235	6	$3\frac{3}{4}$	3.00
236	7	$4\frac{1}{8}$	4.00
237	$7\frac{1}{2}$	$4\frac{1}{4}$	5.00

PILASTER CAPITAL.

EXTERIOR.

Number.	Width, Inches.	Height, Inches.	Prices, Each.
251	5	$3\frac{1}{8}$	$ 1.75
252	6	$3\frac{3}{8}$	2.00
253	$6\frac{1}{2}$	4	2.10
254	7	$4\frac{1}{8}$	2.25
255	$7\frac{1}{2}$	$4\frac{1}{4}$	2.50
256	8	5	2.75
257	$8\frac{1}{2}$	$5\frac{1}{4}$	3.00
258	9	$5\frac{5}{8}$	3.25
259	$9\frac{1}{2}$	6	3.50
260	10	$6\frac{1}{4}$	3.75
261	11	$6\frac{7}{8}$	4.00
262	12	$7\frac{1}{2}$	4.25
263	14	$8\frac{3}{4}$	5.00
264	15	$9\frac{3}{8}$	5.50
265	18	$11\frac{1}{4}$	8.00
266	21	$13\frac{1}{8}$	10.00
267	25	$14\frac{3}{8}$	18.00

INTERIOR.

Number.	Width, Inches.	Height, Inches.	Prices, Each.
276	$1\frac{1}{2}$	$1\frac{5}{8}$	$ .70
277	2	$1\frac{1}{4}$	.80
278	$2\frac{1}{2}$	$1\frac{9}{16}$	.90
279	3	$1\frac{7}{8}$	1 00
280	$3\frac{1}{2}$	$2\frac{3}{16}$	1.10
281	4	$2\frac{1}{2}$	1.20
282	$4\frac{1}{2}$	$2\frac{13}{16}$	1.30
283	5	$3\frac{1}{8}$	1.50
284	$5\frac{1}{2}$	$3\frac{7}{16}$	1.80
285	6	$3\frac{3}{4}$	2.00
286	7	$4\frac{1}{8}$	2.50
287	$7\frac{1}{2}$	$4\frac{1}{4}$	3.00

See page 274 for instructions and explanations.

GREEK ANGULAR IONIC (Minerva Polias).

COLUMN CAPITAL

COPY'D 1899.   DECORATORS SUP'Y CO.

PILASTER CAPITAL.

COPY'D 1899.   DECORATORS SUP'Y CO.

BRACKETS.

ROMAN PANTHEON.

EXTERIOR.

Number.	Abacus Width, Inches.	Face Width, Inches.	Projection, Inches.	Drop, Inches.	Prices, Each.
2351	4	3	6¾	3½	$1.50
2352	5½	4	9	4¾	2.00
2353	6¾	5	11¼	5¾	2.50
2354	8	6	13½	7	3.00
2355	11	8	18	9½	4.00
2356	13	10	22½	11¼	5.00

INTERIOR.

Number.	Abacus Width, Inches.	Face Width, Inches.	Projection, Inches.	Drop, Inches.	Prices, Each.
2376	4	3	6¾	3½	$3.00
2377	5½	4	9	4¾	4.00
2378	6¾	5	11¼	5¾	5.00

MODERN RENAISSANCE (Empire).

EXTERIOR.

Number.	Abacus Width, Inches.	Face Width, Inches.	Projection, Inches.	Drop, Inches.	Prices, Each.
2400	1¼	1	3	1¼	$0.50
2401	1½	1¼	3¾	1½	.60
2402	1⅞	1½	4½	1⅞	.70
2403	2⅛	1¾	5¼	2⅛	.80
2404	2½	2	6	2½	.90
2405	2¾	2¼	6¾	2¾	1.00
2406	3	2½	7½	3	1.15
2407	3⅜	2¾	8¼	3⅜	1.30
2408	3⅝	3	9	3⅝	1.50
2409	4¼	3½	10½	4¼	1.70
2410	5	4	12	5	1.90
2411	5½	4½	13½	5½	2.10
2412	6	5	15	6	2.30
2413	6¾	5½	16½	6¾	2.50
2414	7¼	6	18	7¼	2.80

INTERIOR.

Number.	Abacus Width, Inches.	Face Width, Inches.	Projection, Inches.	Drop, Inches.	Prices, Each.
2426	1¼	1	3	1¼	$0.50
2427	1½	1¼	3¾	1½	.60
2428	1⅞	1½	4½	1⅞	.70
2429	2⅛	1¾	5¼	2⅛	.80
2430	2½	2	6	2½	.90
2431	2¾	2¼	6¾	2¾	1.00
2432	3	2½	7½	3	1.30
2433	3⅜	2¾	8¼	3⅜	1.50
2434	3⅝	3	9	3⅝	1.75
2435	4¼	3½	10½	4¼	2.00
2436	5	4	12	5	2.50

ROMAN VATICAN.

EXTERIOR.

Number.	Abacus Width, Inches.	Face Width, Inches.	Projection, Inches.	Drop, Inches.	Prices, Each.
2651	1⅜	1	1¾	⅞	$0.50
2652	1⅝	1¼	2⅛	1	.60
2653	2	1½	2⅝	1¼	.70
2654	2¼	1¾	3	1½	.80
2655	2⅝	2	3½	1¾	.90
2656	3	2¼	3⅞	2	1.00
2657	3¼	2½	4⅜	2¼	1.15
2658	3⅝	2¾	4¾	2⅜	1.30
2659	4	3	5¼	2⅝	1.50
2660	4½	3½	6	3	1.65
2661	5¼	4	6⅞	3⅜	1.80
2662	6	4⅝	8	4	1.90
2663	6½	5	8⅝	4¼	2.10
2664	7¼	5½	9½	4¾	2.30
2665	8	6	10⅜	5¼	2.50

INTERIOR.

Number.	Abacus Width, Inches.	Face Width, Inches.	Projection, Inches.	Drop, Inches.	Prices, Each.
2701	1⅜	1	1¾	⅞	$0.50
2702	1⅝	1¼	2⅛	1	.60
2703	2	1½	2⅝	1¼	.70
2704	2¼	1¾	3	1½	.80
2705	2⅝	2	3½	1¾	.90
2706	3	2¼	3⅞	2	1.00
2707	3¼	2½	4⅜	2¼	1.25
2708	3⅝	2¾	4¾	2⅜	1.50
2709	4	3	5¼	2⅝	1.75
2710	4½	3½	6	3	2.00
2711	5¼	4	6⅞	3⅜	2.20
2712	6	4⅝	8	4	2.50
2713	6½	5	8⅝	4¼	3.00

BRACKETS.
ROMAN PANTHEON.

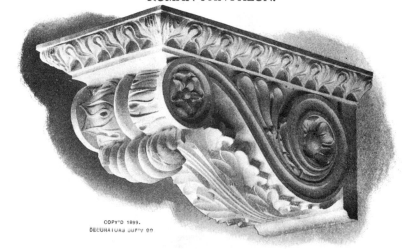

COPY'D 1899.
DECORATORS SUP'Y CO.

MODERN RENAISSANCE (Empire).

COPY'D 1899.
DECORATORS SUP'Y CO.

ROMAN VATICAN.

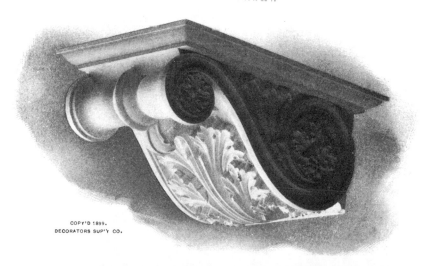

COPY'D 1899.
DECORATORS SUP'Y CO.

CHINA CLOSETS.

1313

1314

In writing for price give opening to fill and depth of shelves. Also state if open or glazed doors.

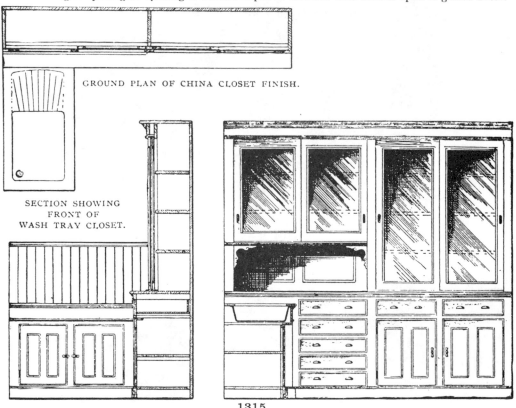

GROUND PLAN OF CHINA CLOSET FINISH.

SECTION SHOWING
FRONT OF
WASH TRAY CLOSET.

1315

In asking price give size of opening to fill, depth of shelves, style of glazing and kind of wood. We make cases of drawers and wardrobes of all kinds. Write for estimates.

HARDWOOD FLOORING.

Plain and Quarter Sawed Oak, (Red or White) Maple Cherry and Walnut.

Dressed and Matched.

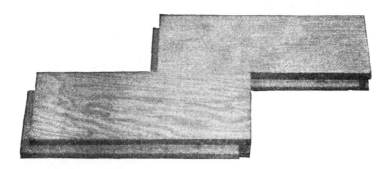

Regular Thickness is ⅜ and ⅞ inches, Length 2 to 16 Feet.

THE STANDARD WIDTHS OF OUR FLOORING ARE AS FOLLOWS:

The 2¾ inch rough is worked 2 inch face
  "   3   "   "   "   2¼ "   "
  "   4   "   "   "   3¼ "   "

Three-quarters of an inch allowed for all matching in flooring ½ inch and thicker.

WEIGHTS OF FLOORING.

⅜ Inch Flooring weighs 1000 pounds per 1000 ft.
½ "   "   "   1200   "   1000 ft.
⅝ "   "   "   1500   "   1000 ft.
¾ "   "   "   2000   "   1000 ft.
⅞ " and thicker "   2500   "   1000 ft.

Hardwood floors are healthful, handsome and economical. With modern appliances, are easily kept clean and the natural beauty of the wood retained. Are cheaper than carpets and when used in connection with rugs, give a very handsome effect in the furnishing of the modern home.

This ⅜-inch dressed and matched flooring takes the place of the old fashioned thick flooring; is cheaper in price, easier laid and wears for all time. With ordinary care given hardwood flooring, you do not even wear through the finishing of the floor, let alone wearing out the floor. Consequently, ⅜-inch flooring is supplanting thick floors and is laid on linings to form new floors in new houses.

But, the special features of the ⅜-inch flooring is its adaptability in covering old floors, doing away with the soft floor and carpets, and giving a strictly "hygienic" floor, attractive, beautiful, lasting and finished in the natural wood.

Our flooring is run with a polished surface, tongued and grooved matched ends and holes bored for blind nailing, so that the question of laying and finishing a hardwood floor is now reduced to a minimum, as it is end matched any lengths, however short, can be utilized and the floor laid as substantially as though in one piece.

Maple flooring has no rival for durability and is used in office buildings, schools, public halls, churches, dwellings stores, etc. Oak flooring, while adapted to all the uses of Maple, is used largely in living rooms, sleeping apartments of the modern house, and is a wood of so much beauty and utility and so well known as to require but little description.

We furnish the Oak flooring in plain and quarter-sawed. Walnut and cherry are handsome woods to lay in conjunction with either Oak or Maple, forming fancy floors, as the cuts on the following pages suggest.

The finishing of hardwood floors is simple and the amount of attention required to keep the floor in perfect order is less than sweeping old fashioned carpets.

For special lengths write us for prices.

WOOD CARPET and PARQUET FLOORING

S NOT, as many people suppose, a temporary floor covering to be laid down and taken up at pleasure, but is a permanent new floor on top of the old one, and is carefully fitted into all the offsets and runs around all the projections of the room, and is firmly nailed down with small brads; and when finished has the effect of a thick European floor. We make it, however, in the same elaborate and beautiful designs, by the process of gluing the wood on cloth instead of to another piece of wood an inch or so thick, and we make it at a much less cost, as we utilize the floor already down, and thus occupy but five-sixteenths of an inch, instead of one inch or more (as with thick parquet).

Where disappointments have arisen from any kind of hardwood floors, it has invariably been from not understanding the proper treatment, or in expecting too much of them. The treatment of floors should be the same as the European.

The common remark "that a bare floor is so cheerless" comes wholly from the impression given by an ordinary pine floor, with its unsightly cracks, and from not having seen the effect of a well-laid Parquet Floor, in combination with the furniture and other articles, in keeping with the character of the room in which it is laid.

WOOD CARPET and PARQUETRY

Is made in the uniform thickness of five-sixteenths of an inch. The woods used are all kiln dried and prepared so as to prevent shrinkage Care must be taken to preserve them from dampness until the floor is laid and finished. The straight carpeting, 36 and 28 inches wide, rolls up like an oilcloth, and is thus readily shipped. The borders and strips are twelve feet long, and the Parquet Flooring comes in sheets 2x6 feet, and make a solid package for shipping.

RUGS

Are being extensively used, on account of their healthfulness and convenience in keeping the room clean and free from dust. They are generally used on the middle part of the room, leaving a margin of about two feet around sides of the room for furniture to stand on. The floor upon which they lie should be a good one, with some degree of ornamentation, and free from joints and cracks. The dust on the floor is easily removed with a damp cloth or brush, and the rug can be rolled up at pleasure, and be taken out to be freed from dust. Rugs are now made to order at a very moderate cost, and of any desired shape and size.

ESTIMATES

Free of charge for floors or borders, with full instructions and working drawing, will be cheerfully given to parties sending us a sketch of the ground plan, with measurements of the space desired to be covered. State what class of room it is for, also if a cheap or ornamented floor is desired. Our floors vary from $1.25 to $18.00 per yard. It is better to say how expensive a floor is desired, and the design will be made in accordance.

PARQUET BORDERS.

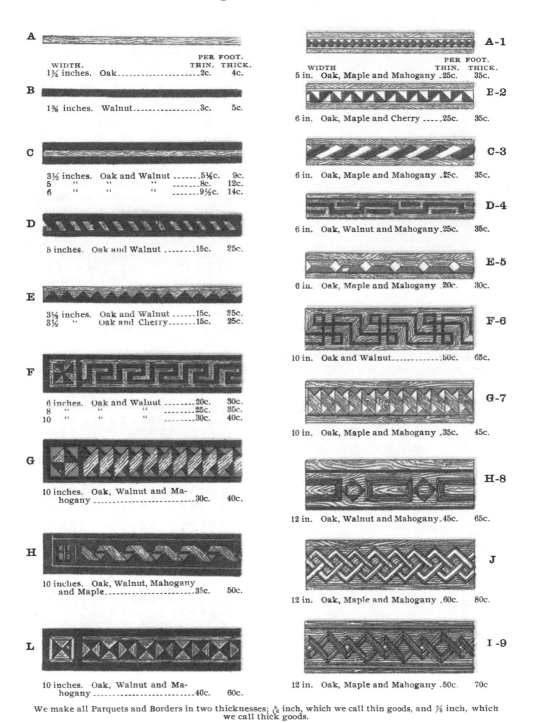

A

PER FOOT.

WIDTH.		THIN.	THICK.
1¾ inches.	Oak	2c.	4c.

B

| 1⅜ inches. | Walnut | 3c. | 5c. |

C

3½ inches.	Oak and Walnut	5½c.	9c.
5 "	" "	8c.	12c.
6 "	" "	9½c.	14c.

D

| 5 inches. | Oak and Walnut | 15c. | 25c. |

E

| 3½ inches. | Oak and Walnut | 15c. | 25c. |
| 3½ " | Oak and Cherry | 15c. | 25c. |

F

6 inches.	Oak and Walnut	20c.	30c.
8 "	" "	25c.	35c.
10 "	" "	30c.	40c.

G

| 10 inches. | Oak, Walnut and Mahogany | 30c. | 40c. |

H

| 10 inches. | Oak, Walnut, Mahogany and Maple | 35c. | 50c. |

L

| 10 inches. | Oak, Walnut and Mahogany | 40c. | 60c. |

A-1

PER FOOT.

WIDTH		THIN.	THICK.
5 in.	Oak, Maple and Mahogany	25c.	35c.

E-2

| 6 in. | Oak, Maple and Cherry | 25c. | 35c. |

C-3

| 6 in. | Oak, Maple and Mahogany | 25c. | 35c. |

D-4

| 6 in. | Oak, Walnut and Mahogany | 25c. | 35c. |

E-5

| 6 in. | Oak, Maple and Mahogany | 20c. | 30c. |

F-6

| 10 in. | Oak and Walnut | 50c. | 65c. |

G-7

| 10 in. | Oak, Maple and Mahogany | 35c. | 45c. |

H-8

| 12 in. | Oak, Walnut and Mahogany | 45c. | 65c. |

J

| 12 in. | Oak, Maple and Mahogany | 60c. | 80c. |

I-9

| 12 in. | Oak, Maple and Mahogany | 50c. | 70c |

We make all Parquets and Borders in two thicknesses; $\frac{5}{16}$ inch, which we call thin goods, and ⅞ inch, which we call thick goods.

PARQUET CENTERS and WOOD CARPETS.

<table>
<tr><td>M</td><td>PARQUET CENTERS.</td><td>R</td></tr>
</table>

For price of Borders see preceding page.

Price of Centers, strips in 12 foot lengths, not glued on canvas per square yard, $1.00.

Parquet designs in rich cabinet woods, made to order for floors, wainscot, center pieces, borders, etc., at from 30 cents to $1.50 per square foot.

Inform us as to your requirements and we will submit special designs in natural color of wood.

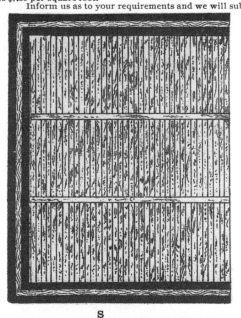
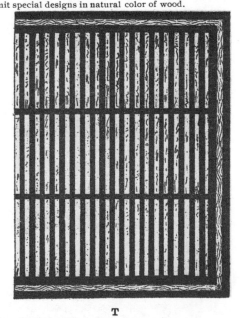

<table>
<tr><td>S</td><td></td><td>T</td></tr>
</table>

WOOD CARPET.—Standard Goods.

36 inches wide ⁵⁄₈ inches thick all oak or maple				per yard $1.25
28 " " " "				" 1.15
36 " " " " oak and walnut or cherry, or gum and maple				" 1.50
28 " " " " " " " "				" 1.25

The straight carpeting, 36 and 28 inches wide, rolls up like an oilcloth, and is thus readily shipped.

PARQUET CENTERS and BORDERS.

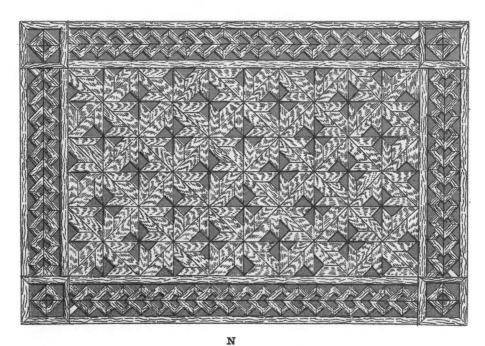

N

MAHOGANY and OAK.

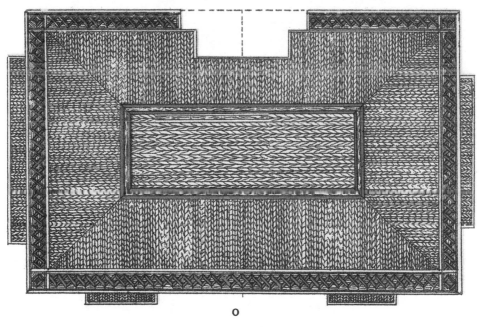

O

MAHOGANY and OAK.

Write for prices, giving ground plan and dimensions of room.

PARQUET CENTERS.

P

ALL OAK.

Thin. 25 cents per square foot.
Thick. 40   "   "   "   "

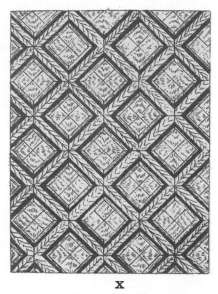

X

OAK and WALNUT.

Thin, 35 cents per square foot
Thick, 50   "   "   "   "

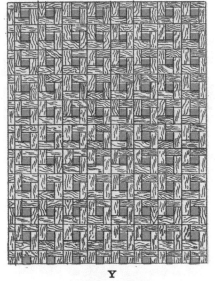

Y

OAK and CHERRY.

Thin, 35 cents per square foot.
Thick, 50   "   "   "   "

Z

OAK and CHERRY.

Thin, 35 cents per square foot.
Thick, 50   "   "   "   "

LOOK TO THE INTERIOR.
PARQUET THICK OR THIN
PLAIN OR ORNAMENTAL FLOORS.
FINISHING SUPPLIES.

PARQUET FLOORS

Consists of strips and blocks of hardwood fastened together at edges and on backs, in slabs of convenient size for laying. They are made a solid part of the floor by being nailed down to the under floor. They are then finished with Wax or Parquet-lac, so as to heighten the natural beauty of the wood.

They are made beautiful by the contrasting color of the different woods employed, and the weaving effects produced by changing the direction of the grain in the perfectly made joints.

They have been made after this method in Europe for centuries and are no experiment.

They are established here, and have come to stay.

To those interested we will mail small sample, so that they may understand the work we offer.

All prices named are for goods $\frac{5}{16}$-inch thick, uncut and measured before laid. Prices for any design in $\frac{7}{8}$-inch thick will be given on application.

We make no charge for plans or estimates furnished, if returned to us. Mail us outlines and measurements of such rooms, which you may have to cover.

DESIGNS for PARQUET FLOORS and BORDERS.

SCALE HALF AN INCH TO THE FOOT.

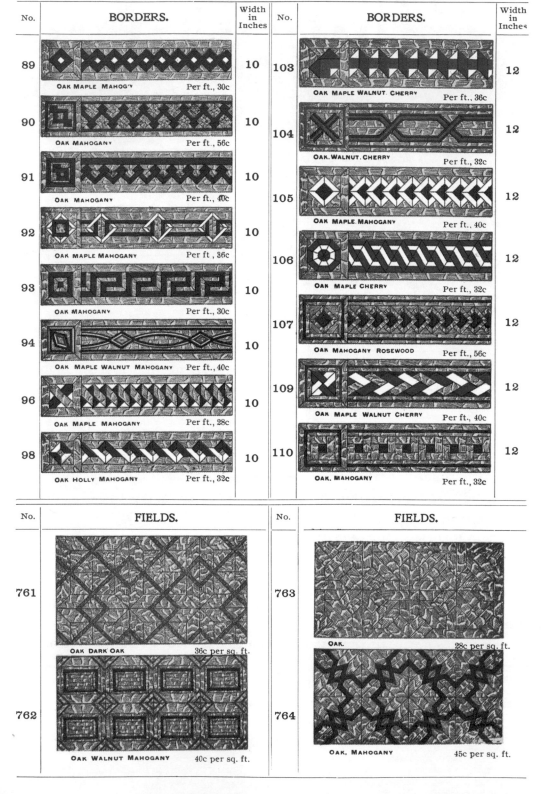

No.	BORDERS.	Width in Inches	No.	BORDERS.	Width in Inches
89	OAK MAPLE MAHOG'Y Per ft., 30c	10	103	OAK MAPLE WALNUT. CHERRY Per ft., 36c	12
90	OAK MAHOGANY Per ft., 56c	10	104	OAK. WALNUT. CHERRY Per ft., 32c	12
91	OAK MAHOGANY Per ft., 40c	10	105	OAK MAPLE MAHOGANY Per ft., 40c	12
92	OAK MAPLE MAHOGANY Per ft, 36c	10	106	OAK MAPLE CHERRY Per ft., 32c	12
93	OAK MAHOGANY Per ft., 30c	10	107	OAK MAHOGANY ROSEWOOD Per ft., 56c	12
94	OAK MAPLE WALNUT MAHOGANY Per ft., 40c	10	109	OAK MAPLE WALNUT CHERRY Per ft., 40c	12
96	OAK MAPLE MAHOGANY Per ft., 28c	10	110	OAK. MAHOGANY Per ft., 32c	12
98	OAK HOLLY MAHOGANY Per ft., 32c	10			

No.	FIELDS.	No.	FIELDS.
761	OAK DARK OAK 36c per sq. ft.	763	OAK. 28c per sq. ft.
762	OAK WALNUT MAHOGANY 40c per sq. ft.	764	OAK. MAHOGANY 45c per sq. ft.

DESIGNS for PARQUET FLOORS.

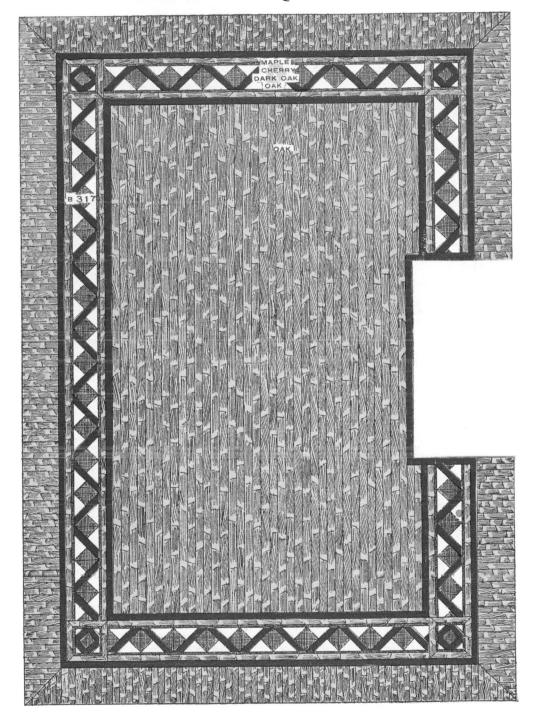

Design No. AA
Made to fit room of any size or shape.   List price as shown, per square foot, 18 cents.

DESIGNS for PARQUET FLOORS.

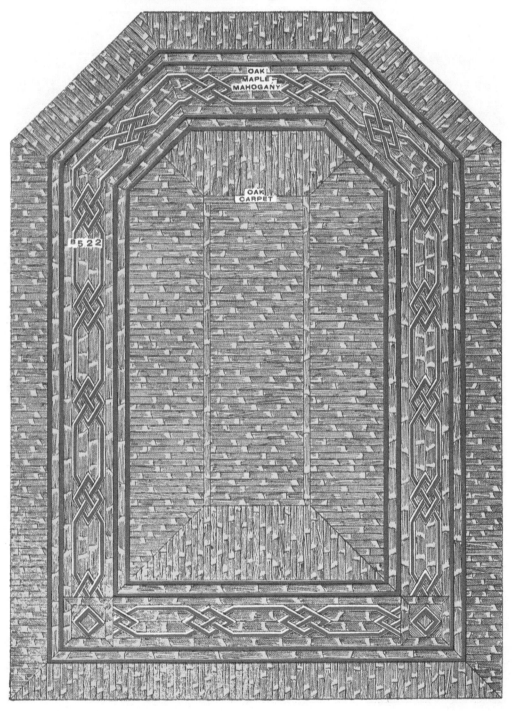

Design No. BB
Made to fit room of any size or shape.   List price as shown, per square foot, 21 cents.

DESIGNS for PARQUET FLOORS.

Design No. CC
Made to fit room of any size or shape.   List price as shown, per square foot, 25 cents.

DESIGNS for PARQUET FLOORS.

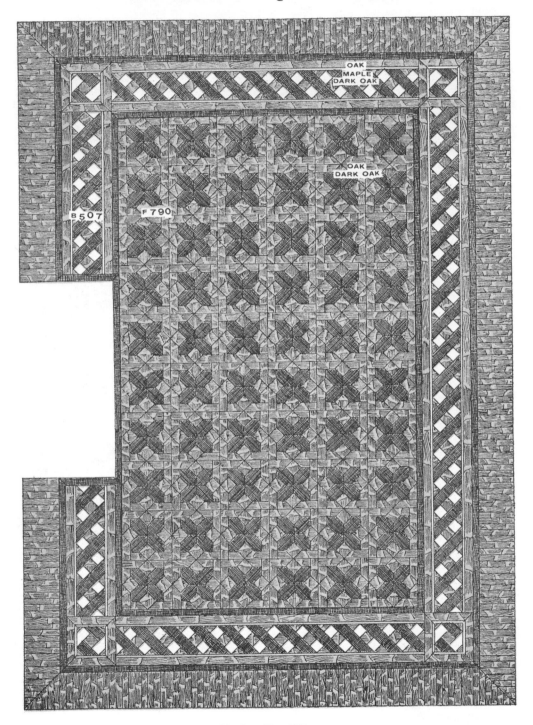

Design No. DD

Made to fit room of any size or shape.   List price as shown, per square foot, 30 cents.

DESIGNS for PARQUET FLOORS.

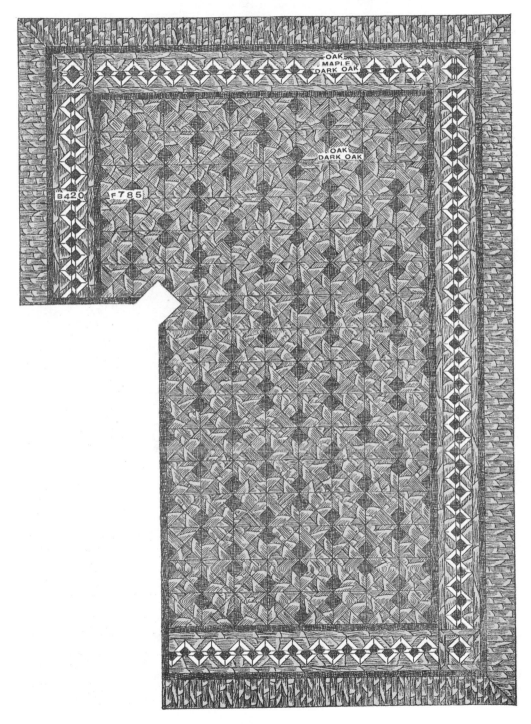

Design No. EE

Made to fit room of any size or shape.　　List price as shown, per square foot, 36 cents.

DESIGNS for PARQUET FLOORS.

Design No. FF
Made to fit room of any size or shape.   List price as shown, per square foot, 42 cents.

We handle and constantly carry in stock all the ordinary sizes of Window Glass, and can furnish promptly all sizes of Plate Glass and the various designs of Fancy Glass shown herein. · . · . We can also supply you with any of the varieties of Glass in ordinary use, such as Ground, Chipped, Enamel, Figured, Wire Glass for skylights, and the different kinds of Colored Glass, viz: Cathedral, Ondoyant, Venetian, etc.

Write us for any desired information and we will be pleased to be of service to you. ❧ ❧

AMERICAN WINDOW GLASS.

Official List Prices, October 1st, 1903.

United Inches.	BRACKET. SIZES.	SINGLE. AA.	A.	B.	C.	DOUBLE. AA.	A.	B.
25	6x 8 to 10x15	$32.00	$26.75	$25.50	$25.00	$42.75	$37.50	$35.50
34	11x14 } 12x13 } to 14x20	33.50	28 00	26.75	26.00	46.75	41.50	38.75
40	10x26 to 16x24	36.00	30.00	28.00	27.00	52.00	45.50	41.50
50	18x22 } 20x20 } to 20x30	37.50	31.75	29.50	------	56.00	49.50	46.00
54	15x36 to 24x30	38.75	32.75	30.00	------	57.50	50.75	46.75
60	26x28 to 24x36	40.00	34.75	31.00	------	58.75	52.00	47.50
70	26x34 } 28x32 } to 30x40 30x30 }	42.75	38.50	33.75	------	62.75	56.00	50.75
80	32x38 } 34x36 } to 30x50	48.75	44.50	38.50	------	68 00	61.50	55.50
84	30x52 to 30x54	52.00	47.50	41.75	------	69.50	62.75	56.75
90	------	------	------	------	------	73.50	66.75	61.50
'94	------	------	------	------	------	74.75	68.00	62.75
100	------	------	------	------	------	88.00	80.00	74.75
105	------	------	------	------	------	94.75	86.75	80.00
110	------	------	------	------	------	105.50	97.50	90.75
115	------	------	------	------	------	118.75	108.00	101.50
120	------	------	------	------	------	140.00	126.75	120.00
125	------	------	------	------	------	153.50	140.25	133.50
130	------	------	------	------	------	167 00	153.75	147.00

An additional 10 per cent. will be charged for all Glass more than 40 inches wide. All sizes over 52 inches in length and not making more than 81 united inches, will be charged in the 84 united inches bracket. All glass 54 inches wide or wider, not making more than 116 united inches, will be charged in the 100 united inches bracket.

AMERICAN WINDOW GLASS.
Official List Prices, October 1st, 1903.

PRICE PER BOX OF FIFTY FEET.						SIZES.	PRICE PER SINGLE LIGHT.						No. Lights per Box
SINGLE.			DOUBLE.				SINGLE.			DOUBLE.			
AA	A	B	AA	A	B		AA	A	B	AA	A	B	
32.00	26.75	25.50	42.75	37.50	35.50	6x 8	.25	.21	.20	.33	.29	.28	150
"	"	"	"	"	"	7x 9	.32	.27	.26	.43	.38	.36	115
"	"	"	"	"	"	8x10	.41	.35	.33	.55	.48	.46	90
"	"	"	"	"	"	12	.50	.42	.40	.66	.58	.55	75
"	"	"	"	"	"	13	.54	.45	.43	.72	.63	.60	69
"	"	"	"	"	"	14	.58	.49	.46	.77	.68	.64	64
"	"	"	"	"	"	15	.62	.52	.49	.82	.72	.69	60
"	"	"	"	"	"	16	.66	.55	.53	.88	.78	.73	56
33.50	28.00	26.75	46.75	41.50	38.75	18	.78	.65	.62	1.08	.96	.90	50
"	"	"	"	"	"	20	.86	.72	.69	1.20	1.07	1.00	45
32.00	26.75	25.50	42.75	37.50	35.50	9x11	.51	.43	.41	.68	.60	.56	73
"	"	"	"	"	"	12	.55	.46	.44	.74	.65	.61	67
"	"	"	"	"	"	13	.59	.50	.48	.80	.70	.66	62
"	"	"	"	"	"	14	.65	.54	.52	.87	.76	.72	57
"	"	"	"	"	"	15	.70	.59	.56	.93	.82	.78	53
"	"	"	"	"	"	16	.74	.62	.59	.99	.87	.82	50
33.50	28.00	26.75	46.75	41.50	38.75	18	.86	.72	.69	1.20	1.07	1.00	45
"	"	"	"	"	"	20	.97	.81	.77	1.35	1.20	1.12	40
"	"	"	"	"	"	22	1.07	.90	.86	1.50	1.33	1.24	36
32.00	26.75	25.50	42.75	37.50	35.50	10x12	.62	.52	.49	.82	.72	.69	60
"	"	"	"	"	"	13	.67	.56	.54	.90	.79	.75	55
"	"	"	"	"	"	14	.71	.59	.57	.95	.83	.79	52
"	"	"	"	"	"	15	.77	.65	.62	1.03	.90	.86	48
33.50	28.00	26.75	46.75	41.50	38.75	16	.87	.72	.69	1.20	1.07	1.00	45
"	"	"	"	"	"	18	.97	.81	.77	1.35	1.20	1.12	40
"	"	"	"	"	"	19	1.02	.85	.81	1.42	1.26	1.18	38
"	"	"	"	"	"	20	1.07	.90	.86	1.50	1.33	1.24	36
"	"	"	"	"	"	22	1.17	.97	.94	1.63	1.45	1.36	33
"	"	"	"	"	"	24	1.29	1.07	1.03	1.80	1.60	1.49	30
36.00	30.00	28.00	52.00	45.50	41.50	26	1.48	1.24	1.15	2.14	1.87	1.71	28
"	"	"	"	"	"	28	1.60	1.33	1.24	2.30	2.02	1.84	26
"	"	"	"	"	"	30	1.74	1.44	1.35	2.50	2.19	1.99	24
37.50	31.75	29.50	56.00	49.50	46.00	32	1.88	1.59	1.48	2.80	2.48	2.30	23
"	"	"	"	"	"	34	2.06	1.74	1.62	3.07	2.72	2.52	21
"	"	"	"	"	"	36	2.16	1.83	1.70	3.22	2.85	2.65	20
"	"	"	"	"	"	38	2.27	1.93	1.79	3.39	3.00	2.79	19
"	"	"	"	"	"	40	2.40	2.03	1.89	3.58	3.17	2.94	18
38.75	32.75	30.00	57.50	50.75	46.75	42	2.63	2.22	2.03	3.99	3.44	3.17	17
"	"	"	"	"	"	44	2.79	2.36	2.16	4.14	3.65	3.37	16
40.00	34.75	31.00	58.75	52.00	47.50	46	2.88	2.50	2.23	4.23	3.74	3.42	16
"	"	"	"	"	"	48	3.07	2.67	2.38	4.51	3.99	3.65	15
"	"	"	"	"	"	50	3.29	2.86	2.55	4.83	4.28	3.91	14
32.00	26.75	25.50	42.75	37.50	35.50	11x12	.67	.56	.54	.90	.79	.75	55
33.50	28.00	26.75	46.75	41.50	38.75	14	.82	.69	.66	1.15	1.02	.95	47
"	"	"	"	"	"	15	.88	.74	.70	1.23	1.09	1.02	44
"	"	"	"	"	"	16	.94	.79	.76	1.32	1.15	1.09	41
"	"	"	"	"	"	18	1.05	.88	.84	1.46	1.29	1.21	37
"	"	"	"	"	"	19	1.14	.95	.91	1.59	1.41	1.32	34
"	"	"	"	"	"	20	1.17	.98	.94	1.63	1.45	1.36	33
"	"	"	"	"	"	22	1.29	1.08	1.03	1.80	1.60	1.49	30
36.00	30.00	28.00	52.00	45.50	41.50	24	1.54	1.28	1.20	2.22	1.94	1.77	27
"	"	"	"	"	"	26	1.66	1.38	1.29	2.40	2.10	1.91	25
"	"	"	"	"	"	28	1.80	1.50	1.40	2.60	2.28	2.08	23
37.50	31.75	29.50	56.00	49.50	46.00	30	1.96	1.66	1.55	2.93	2.59	2.41	22
"	"	"	"	"	"	32	2.16	1.83	1.70	3.22	2.85	2.65	20
"	"	"	"	"	"	34	2.27	1.93	1.79	3.39	3.00	2.79	19
"	"	"	"	"	"	36	2.40	2.03	1.89	3.58	3.17	2.94	18
"	"	"	"	"	"	38	2.54	2.15	2.00	3.79	3.35	3.12	17
38.75	32.75	30.00	57.50	50.75	46.75	40	2.79	2.00	2.10	4.11	3.65	3.07	16
"	"	"	"	"	"	42							16
40.00	34.75	31.00	58.75	52.00	47.50	44	3.07	2.67	2.39	4.51	3.99	3.65	15
"	"	"	"	"	"	46	3.29	2.86	2.55	4.83	4.28	3.91	14
"	"	"	"	"	"	48							14
42.75	38.50	33.75	62.75	56.00	50.75	50	3.79	3.41	2.99	5.56	4.96	4.49	13
32.00	26.75	25.50	42.75	37.50	35.50	12x12	.74	.62	.59	.99	.87	.82	50
33.50	28.00	26.75	46.75	41.50	38.75	13	.84	.70	.67	1.17	1.04	.98	46
"	"	"	"	"	"	14	.90	.75	.72	1.26	1.11	1.04	43
"	"	"	"	"	"	15	.97	.81	.77	1.35	1.20	1.12	40
"	"	"	"	"	"	16	1.01	.85	.81	1.42	1.26	1.18	38
"	"	"	"	"	"	18	1.14	.95	.91	1.59	1.41	1.32	34
"	"	"	"	"	"	19	1.21	1.01	.97	1.69	1.50	1.40	32
"	"	"	"	"	"	20	1.29	1.08	1.03	1.80	1.60	1.49	30
"	"	"	"	"	"	22	1.43	1.20	1.14	2.00	1.77	1.66	27
36.00	30.00	28.00	52.00	45.50	41.50	24	1.66	1.38	1.29	2.40	2.10	1.91	25
"	"	"	"	"	"	26	1.80	1.50	1.40	2.60	2.28	2.08	23
"	"	"	"	"	"	28	1.89	1.57	1.47	2.72	2.38	2.17	22
37.50	31.75	29.50	56.00	49.50	46.00	30	2.16	1.83	1.70	3.22	2.85	2.65	20
"	"	"	"	"	"	32	2.27	1.93	1.79	3.39	3.00	2.79	19
"	"	"	"	"	"	34	2.40	2.03	1.89	3.58	3.17	2.94	18
"	"	"	"	"	"	36	2.54	2.15	2.00	3.79	3.35	3.12	17
"	"	"	"	"	"	38	2.70	2.29	2.13	4.03	3.56	3.31	16
38.75	32.75	30.00	57.50	50.75	46.75	40	2.97	2.52	2.30	4.41	3.90	3.59	15
"	"	"	"	"	"	42	3.19	2.69	2.47	4.73	4.17	3.85	14

AMERICAN WINDOW GLASS.

Official List Prices, October 1st, 1903.

PRICE PER BOX OF FIFTY FEET.						SIZES.	PRICE PER SINGLE LIGHT.						No. Lights per Box
SINGLE.			DOUBLE.				SINGLE.			DOUBLE.			
AA	A	B	AA	A	B		AA	A	B	AA	A	B	
40.00	34.75	31.00	58.75	52.00	47.50	12x44	3.29	2.86	2.55	4.83	4.28	3.91	14
"	"	"	"	"	"	46	3.54	3.08	2.75	5.20	4.60	4.21	13
						48							13
42.75	38.50	33.75	62.75	56.00	50.75	50	4.10	3.69	3.24	6.02	5.37	4.87	12
						52							12
52.00	47.50	41.75	69.50	62.75	56.75	54	5.44	4.97	4.36	7.27	6.57	5.94	11
						56							11
"	"	"	"	"	"	58	5.98	5.47	4.80	8.00	7.22	6.53	10
						60							10
33.50	28.00	26.75	46.75	41.50	38.75	13x15	1.05	.88	.84	1.46	1.29	1.21	37
"	"	"	"	"	"	16	1.11	.92	.88	1.54	1.37	1.28	35
"	"	"	"	"	"	18	1.25	1.04	1.00	1.74	1.54	1.44	31
						20	1.38	1.15	1.10	1.93	1.71	1.60	28
36.00	30.00	28.00	52.00	45.50	41.50	22	1.66	1.38	1.29	2.40	2.10	1.91	25
						24	1.80	1.50	1.40	2.60	2.28	2.08	23
"	"	"	"	"	"	26	1.98	1.64	1.54	2.85	2.50	2.28	21
37.50	31.75	29.50	56.00	49.50	46.00	28	2.16	1.83	1.70	3.22	2.85	2.65	20
"	"	"	"	"	"	30	2.27	1.93	1.79	3.39	3.00	2.79	19
"	"	"	"	"	"	32	2.54	2.15	2.00	3.79	3.35	3.12	17
"	"	"	"	"	"	34	2.70	2.29	2.12	4.03	3.56	3.31	16
"	"	"	"	"	"	36	2.88	2.44	2.27	4.30	3.80	3.53	15
38.75	32.75	30.00	57.50	50.75	46.75	38	2.97	2.51	2.30	4.41	3.90	3.59	15
40.00	34.75	31.00	58.75	52.00	47.50	40	3.19	2.69	2.47	4.73	4.17	3.85	14
"	"	"	"	"	"	42	3.54	3.08	2.75	5.20	4.60	4.21	13
						44							13
42.75	38.50	33.75	62.75	56.00	50.75	46	3.84	3.38	2.98	5.64	4.99	4.56	12
"	"	"	"	"	"	48	4.10	3.69	3.23	6.02	5.37	4.87	12
						50	4.47	4.03	3.53	6.57	5.86	5.31	11
33.50	28.00	26.75	46.75	41.50	38.75	14x14	1.05	.88	.84	1.46	1.29	1.21	37
"	"	"	"	"	"	16	1.21	1.01	.97	1.69	1.50	1.40	32
"	"	"	"	"	"	18	1.33	1.12	1.07	1.86	1.65	1.54	29
						20	1.49	1.24	1.19	2.07	1.84	1.72	26
36.00	30.00	28.00	52.00	45.50	41.50	22	1.73	1.44	1.35	2.50	2.19	1.99	24
"	"	"	"	"	"	24	1.88	1.57	1.47	2.72	2.38	2.17	22
						26	2.07	1.73	1.61	2.99	2.62	2.39	20
37.50	31.75	29.50	56.00	49.50	46.00	28	2.27	1.93	1.79	3.39	3.00	2.79	19
"	"	"	"	"	"	30	2.54	2.15	2.00	3.79	3.35	3.12	17
"	"	"	"	"	"	32	2.70	2.29	2.13	4.03	3.56	3.31	16
"	"	"	"	"	"	34	2.88	2.44	2.27	4.30	3.80	3.53	15
"	"	"	"	"	"	36	3.09	2.61	2.43	4.60	4.07	3.78	14
38.75	32.75	30.00	57.50	50.75	46.75	38	3.19	2.69	2.47	4.73	4.17	3.85	14
"	"	"	"	"	"	40	3.43	2.90	2.66	5.09	4.49	4.14	13
40.00	34.75	31.00	58.75	52.00	47.50	42	3.84	3.33	2.98	5.64	4.99	4.56	12
"	"	"	"	"	"	44							12
42.75	38.50	33.75	62.75	56.00	50.75	46	4.19	3.64	3.25	6.15	5.44	4.97	11
						48	4.47	4.03	3.53	6.57	5.86	5.31	11
						50	4.92	4.43	3.88	7.22	6.44	5.84	10
						52							10
52.00	47.50	41.75	69.50	62.75	56.75	54	5.98	5.47	4.81	8.00	7.22	6.53	10
"	"	"	"	"	"	56	6.65	6.07	5.34	8.89	8.02	7.26	9
						58	"	"	"	"	"	"	9
						60							9
33.50	28.00	26.75	46.75	41.50	38.75	15x15	1.21	1.01	.97	1.69	1.50	1.40	32
"	"	"	"	"	"	16	1.29	1.08	1.03	1.80	1.60	1.49	30
"	"	"	"	"	"	18	1.43	1.20	1.14	2.00	1.77	1.66	27
36.00	30.00	28.00	52.00	45.50	41.50	20	1.73	1.44	1.35	2.50	2.19	1.99	24
"	"	"	"	"	"	22	1.89	1.57	1.47	2.72	2.38	2.17	22
						24	2.07	1.73	1.61	2.99	2.62	2.39	20
37.50	31.75	29.50	56.00	49.50	46.00	26	2.27	1.93	1.79	3.39	3.00	2.79	19
"	"	"	"	"	"	28	2.54	2.15	2.00	3.79	3.35	3.12	17
"	"	"	"	"	"	30	2.70	2.29	2.13	4.03	3.56	3.31	16
"	"	"	"	"	"	32	2.88	2.44	2.27	4.30	3.80	3.53	15
						34	3.09	2.61	2.43	4.60	4.07	3.78	14
38.75	32.75	30.00	57.50	50.75	46.75	36	3.43	2.90	2.66	5.09	4.49	4.14	13
						38							13
40.00	34.75	31.00	58.75	52.00	47.50	40	3.84	3.33	2.98	5.64	4.99	4.56	12
"	"	"	"	"	"	42	4.19	3.64	3.25	6.15	5.44	4.97	11
						44							11
42.75	38.50	33.75	62.75	56.00	50.75	46	4.92	4.43	3.88	7.22	6.44	5.84	10
"	"	"	"	"	"	48	"	"	"	"	"	"	10
						50							10
33.50	28.00	26.75	46.75	41.50	38.75	16x16	1.38	1.15	1.10	1.93	1.71	1.60	28
						18	1.55	1.29	1.24	2.16	1.91	1.79	25
36.00	30.00	28.00	52.00	45.50	41.50	20	1.80	1.50	1.40	2.60	2.28	2.08	23
"	"	"	"	"	"	22	1.98	1.65	1.54	2.85	2.50	2.28	21
						24	2.18	1.82	1.70	3.15	2.76	2.52	19
37.50	31.75	29.50	56.00	49.50	46.00	26	2.54	2.15	2.00	3.79	3.35	3.12	17
"	"	"	"	"	"	28	2.70	2.29	2.13	4.03	3.56	3.31	16
"	"	"	"	"	"	30	2.88	2.44	2.27	4.30	3.80	3.53	15
"	"	"	"	"	"	32	3.09	2.61	2.43	4.60	4.07	3.78	14
"	"	"	"	"	"	34	3.32	2.81	2.61	4.96	4.38	4.07	13
38.75	32.75	30.00	57.50	50.75	46.75	36	3.43	2.90	2.66	5.09	4.49	4.14	13
"	"	"	"	"	"	38	3.72	3.14	2.88	5.52	4.87	4.49	12
40.00	34.75	31.00	58.75	52.00	47.50	40	4.19	3.64	3.25	6.15	5.44	4.97	11
"	"	"	"	"	"	42	"	"	"	"	"	"	11

AMERICAN WINDOW GLASS.

Official List Prices, October 1st, 1903.

| PRICE PER BOX OF FIFTY FEET | | | | | | SIZES | PRICE PER SINGLE LIGHT | | | | | | No. Lights per Box |
| SINGLE | | | DOUBLE | | | | SINGLE | | | DOUBLE | | | |
AA	A	B	AA	A	B		AA	A	B	AA	A	B	
40.00	34.75	31.00	58.75	52.00	47.50	16x44	4.60	4.00	3.57	6.76	5.98	5.47	10
42.75	38.50	33.75	62.75	56.00	50.75	46	4.92	4.43	3.88	7.22	6.44	5.84	10
"	"	"	"	"	"	48	5.47	4.92	4.31	8.02	7.16	6.49	9
"	"	"	"	"	"	50	"	"	"	"	"	"	9
						52							9
......	......	......	69.50	62.75	56.75	54	......	......	......	10.00	9.03	8.16	8
......	......	......	"	"	"	56	......	......	......	"	"	"	8
......	......	......	"	"	"	58	......	......	......	"	"	"	8
......	......	......				60	......	......	......				8
......	......	......				62	......	......	......	11.42	10.31	9.33	7
......	......	......	"	"	"	64	......	......	......	"	"	"	7
......	......	......				66	......	......	......				7
......	......	......				68	......	......	......				7
......	......	......	73.50	66.75	61.50	70	......	......	......	14.09	12.80	11.79	6
......	......	......	"	"	"	72	......	......	......	"	"	"	6
......	......	......				74	......	......	......				6
......	......	......	74.75	68.00	62.75	76	......	......	......	14.33	13.04	12.03	6
36.00	30.00	28.00	52.00	45.50	41.50	18x18	1.89	1.57	1.47	2.72	2.38	2.17	22
						20	2.07	1.73	1.61	2.99	2.62	2.39	20
37.50	31.75	29.50	56.00	49.50	46.00	22	2.40	2.03	1.89	3.58	3.17	2.94	18
"	"	"	"	"	"	24	2.54	2.15	2.00	3.79	3.35	3.12	17
"	"	"	"	"	"	26	2.70	2.29	2.13	4.03	3.56	3.31	16
"	"	"	"	"	"	28	3.09	2.01	0.13	1.60	4.07	3.78	14
"	"	"	"	"	"	30							14
"	"	"	"	"	"	32	3.32	2.81	2.61	4.96	4.38	4.07	13
38.75	32.75	30.00	57.50	50.75	46.75	34	3.72	3.14	2.88	5.52	4.87	4.49	12
						36	4.06	3.43	3.14	6.02	5.31	4.89	11
40.00	34.75	31.00	58.75	52.00	47.50	38	4.19	3.64	3.25	6.15	5.44	4.97	11
"	"	"	"	"	"	40	4.60	4.00	3.57	6.76	5.98	5.47	10
						42	"	"	"	"	"	"	10
42.75	38.50	33.75	62.75	56.00	50.75	44	5.47	4.92	4.32	8.02	7.16	6.49	9
"	"	"	"	"	"	46	"	"	"	"	"	"	9
"	"	"	"	"	"	48	6.15	5.54	4.86	9.03	8.05	7.30	8
"	"	"	"	"	"	50	"	"	"	"	"	"	8
						52							8
......	......	......	69.50	62.75	56.75	54	......	......	......	11.42	10.31	9.33	7
......	......	......	"	"	"	56	......	......	......	"	"	"	7
......	......	......	"	"	"	58	......	......	......	"	"	"	7
......	......	......				60	......	......	......				7
......	......	......				62	......	......	......	13.33	12.03	10.88	6
......	......	......	"	"	"	64	......	......	......	"	"	"	6
......	......	......				66	......	......	......				6
......	......	......	73.50	66.75	61.50	68	......	......	......	14.09	12.80	11.79	6
......	......	......	"	"	"	70	......	......	......	"	"	"	6
......	......	......				72	......	......	......				5
......	......	......	74.75	68.00	62.75	74	......	......	......	17.20	15.64	14.44	5
......	......	......				76	......	......	......				5
37.50	31.75	29.50	56.00	49.50	46.00	20x20	2.40	2.03	1.89	3.58	3.16	2.94	18
"	"	"	"	"	"	22	2.70	2.29	2.13	4.03	3.56	3.31	16
"	"	"	"	"	"	24	2.88	2.44	2.27	4.30	3.80	3.53	15
"	"	"	"	"	"	26	3.09	2.61	2.43	4.60	4.07	3.78	14
"	"	"	"	"	"	28	3.32	2.81	2.61	4.96	4.38	4.07	13
						30	3.60	3.05	2.83	5.37	4.75	4.41	12
38.75	32.75	30.00	57.50	50.75	46.75	32	4.06	3.43	3.14	6.02	5.31	4.89	11
						34							11
40.00	34.75	31.00	58.75	52.00	47.50	36	4.60	4.00	3.57	6.76	5.98	5.47	10
						38							10
						40	5.12	4.43	3.97	7.51	6.65	6.07	9
42.75	38.50	33.75	62.75	56.00	50.75	42	5.47	4.92	4.31	8.02	7.16	6.49	9
"	"	"	"	"	"	44	6.15	5.54	4.86	9.03	8.05	7.30	8
"	"	"	"	"	"	46	"	"	"	"	"	"	8
"	"	"	"	"	"	48	"	"	"	"	"	"	8
						50	7.03	6.33	5.55	10.31	9.20	8.34	7
48.75	44.50	38.50	68.00	61.50	55.50	52	8.01	7.32	6.33	11.18	10.11	9.13	7
......	......	......	69.50	62.75	56.75	54	......	......	......	11.42	10.31	9.33	7
......	......	......	"	"	"	56	......	......	......	13.33	12.03	10.88	6
......	......	......	"	"	"	58	......	......	......	"	"	"	6
......	......	......				60	......	......	......				6
......	......	......				62	......	......	......				6
......	......	......				64	......	......	......				6
......	......	......	73.50	66.75	61.50	66	......	......	......	16.91	15.36	14.15	5
......	......	......	"	"	"	68	......	......	......	"	"	"	5
......	......	......				70	......	......	......				5
......	......	......	74.75	68.00	62.75	72	......	......	......	17.20	15.64	14.44	5
......	......	......	"	"	"	74	......	......	......	"	"	"	5
......	......	......	88.00	80.00	74.75	76	......	......	......	20.24	18.40	17.20	5
......	......	......				78	......	......	......	25.30	23.00	21.50	4
......	......	......				80	......	......	......				4
......	......	......	94.75	86.75	80.00	82	......	......	......	27.25	24.95	23.00	4
......	......	......				84	......	......	......				4
......	......	......	105.50	97.50	90.75	86	......	......	......	30.34	28.04	26.10	4
......	......	......	"	"	"	88	......	......	......	"	"	"	4
......	......	......				90	......	......	......				4
37.50	31.75	29.50	56.00	49.50	46.00	22x22	2.88	2.44	2.27	4.30	3.80	3.53	15
"	"	"	"	"	"	24	3.09	2.61	2.43	4.60	4.07	3.78	14
"	"	"	"	"	"	26	3.32	2.81	2.61	4.96	4.38	4.07	13

AMERICAN WINDOW GLASS.

Official List Prices, October 1st, 1903.

PRICE PER BOX OF FIFTY FEET.						SIZES.	PRICE PER SINGLE LIGHT.						No. Lights per Box
SINGLE.			DOUBLE.				SINGLE.			DOUBLE.			
AA	A	B	AA	A	B		AA	A	B	AA	A	B	
37.50	31.75	29.50	56.00	49.50	46.00	22x28	3.60	3.05	2.83	5.37	4.75	4.41	12
38.75	32.75	30.00	57.50	50.75	46.75	30	4.06	3.43	3.14	6.02	5.31	4.89	11
						32	4.46	3.77	3.45	6.62	5.84	5.38	10
40.00	34.75	31.00	58.75	52.00	47.50	34	4.60	4.00	3.57	6.76	5.98	5.47	10
"	"	"	"	"	"	36	5.12	4.44	3.97	7.51	6.65	6.07	9
						38							9
42.75	38.50	33.75	62.75	56.00	50.75	40	6.15	5.54	4.85	9.03	8.05	7.30	8
"	"	"	"	"	"	42							8
"	"	"	"	"	"	44	7.03	6.33	5.55	10.31	9.20	8.34	7
"	"	"	"	"	"	46							7
"	"	"	"	"	"	48	"	"	"	"	"	"	7
48.75	44.50	38.50	68.00	61.50	55.50	50	8.01	7.32	6.33	11.18	10.11	9.13	7
"						52	9.34	8.53	7.38	13.04	11.79	10.64	6
------	------	------	69.50	62.75	56.75	54	------	------	------	13.33	12.03	10.88	6
------	------	------	"	"	"	56	------	------	------	"	"	"	6
------	------	------	"	"	"	58	------	------	------	"	"	"	6
------	------	------	"	"	"	60	------	------	------	15.99	14.44	13.06	5
------	------	------				62	------	------	------				5
------	------	------	73.50	66.75	61.50	64	------	------	------	16.91	15.36	14.15	5
------	------	------	"	"	"	66	------	------	------	"	"	"	5
------	------	------				68	------	------	------				5
------	------	------	74.75	68.00	62.75	70	------	------	------	17.20	15.64	14.44	5
------	------	------				72	------	------	------				
------	------	------	88.00	80.00	74.75	74	------	------	------	25.30	23.00	21.50	4
------	------	------	"	"	"	76	------	------	------	"	"	"	4
------	------	------				78	------	------	------				4
------	------	------	94.75	86.75	80.00	80	------	------	------	27.25	24.95	23.00	4
------	------	------	"	"	"	82	------	------	------	"	"	"	4
------	------	------	105.50	97.50	90.75	84	------	------	------	30.34	28.04	26.10	4
------	------	------	"	"	"	86	------	------	------	"	"	"	4
------	------	------				88	------	------	------	"	"	"	4
------	------	------	118.75	108.00	101.50	90	------	------	------	34.15	31.05	29.19	4
37.50	31.75	29.50	56.00	49.50	46.00	24x24	3.60	3.05	2.83	5.37	4.75	4.41	12
						26	"	"	"	"	"	"	12
38.75	32.75	30.00	57.50	50.75	46.75	28	4.06	3.43	3.14	6.02	5.31	4.89	11
						30	4.46	3.77	3.45	6.62	5.84	5.38	10
40.00	34.75	31.00	58.75	52.00	47.50	32	4.60	4.00	3.57	6.76	5.98	5.47	10
						34	5.12	4.44	3.97	7.51	6.65	6.07	9
						36							9
42.75	38.50	33.75	62.75	56.00	50.75	38	6.15	5.54	4.85	9.03	8.05	7.30	8
"	"	"	"	"	"	40							8
"	"	"	"	"	"	42	7.03	6.33	5.55	10.31	9.20	8.34	7
"	"	"	"	"	"	44							7
"	"	"	"	"	"	46	"	"	"	"	"	"	7
48.75	44.50	38.50	68.00	61.50	55.50	48	9.34	8.53	7.38	13.04	11.79	10.64	6
"	"	"				50							6
						52							6
52.00	47.50	41.75	69.50	62.75	56.75	54	9.97	9.11	8.00	13.33	12.03	10.88	6
"	"	"	"	"	"	56	11.96	10.93	9.61	15.99	14.44	13.06	5
"	"	"				58	"	"	"	"	"	"	5
						60	"	"	"	"	"	"	5
------	------	------	73.50	66.75	61.50	62	------	------	------	16.91	15.36	14.15	5
------	------	------	"	"	"	64	------	------	------	"	"	"	5
------	------	------				66	------	------	------				5
------	------	------	74.75	68.00	62.75	68	------	------	------	21.50	19.55	18.05	4
------	------	------				70	------	------	------				4
------	------	------	88.00	80.00	74.75	72	------	------	------	25.30	23.00	21.50	4
------	------	------	"	"	"	74	------	------	------	"	"	"	4
------	------	------				76	------	------	------				4
------	------	------	94.75	86.75	80.00	78	------	------	------	27.25	24.95	23.00	4
------	------	------				80	------	------	------				4
------	------	------	105.50	97.50	90.75	82	------	------	------	30.34	28.04	26.10	4
------	------	------	"	"	"	84	------	------	------				4
------	------	------				86	------	------	------	40.45	37.38	34.79	3
------	------	------	118.75	108.00	101.50	88	------	------	------	45.53	41.40	38.91	3
------	------	------				90							3
38.75	32.75	30.00	57.50	50.75	46.75	26x26	4.06	3.43	3.14	6.02	5.31	4.89	11
40.00	34.75	31.00	58.75	52.00	47.50	28	4.60	4.00	3.57	6.76	5.98	5.47	1C
"	"	"				30	5.12	4.44	3.97	7.51	6.65	6.07	9
						32							9
42.75	38.50	33.75	62.75	56.00	50.75	34	6.15	5.54	4.85	9.03	8.05	7.30	8
"	"	"	"	"	"	36							8
"	"	"	"	"	"	38	7.03	6.33	5.55	10.31	9.20	8.34	7
"	"	"	"	"	"	40							7
"	"	"	"	"	"	42	"	"	"	"	"	"	7
						44	8.19	7.38	6.47	12.03	10.74	9.73	6
48.75	44.50	38.50	68.00	61.50	55.50	46	9.34	8.53	7.38	13.04	11.79	10.64	6
"	"	"	"	"	"	48							6
"	"	"				50				"	"	"	6
						52	11.21	10.24	8.86	15.64	14.15	12.77	5
------	------	------	69.50	62.75	56.75	54	------	------	------	15.99	14.44	13.06	5
------	------	------				56	------	------	------	"	"	"	5
------	------	------				58	------	------	------				5
------	------	------	73.50	66.75	61.50	60	------	------	------	16.91	15.36	14.15	5
------	------	------	"	"	"	62	------	------	------	21.14	19.20	17.69	4
------	------	------				64	------	------	------				4
------	------	------	74.75	68.00	62.75	66	------	------	------	21.50	19.55	18.05	4

AMERICAN WINDOW GLASS.

Official List Prices, October 1st, 1903.

PRICE PER BOX OF FIFTY FEET.						SIZES.	PRICE PER SINGLE LIGHT.						No. Lights per Box
SINGLE.			DOUBLE.				SINGLE.			DOUBLE.			
AA	A	B	AA	A	B		AA	A	B	AA	A	B	
			74.75	68.00	62.75	26x68				21.50	19.55	18.05	4
			88.00	80.00	74.75	70				25.30	23.00	21.50	4
			"	"	"	72				"	"	"	4
						74							4
			94.75	86.75	80.00	76				27.25	24.95	23.00	4
						78							4
			105.50	97.50	90.75	80				40.45	37.38	34.79	3
						82							3
			"	"	"	84				"	"	"	3
			118.75	108.00	101.50	86				45.53	41.40	38.91	3
						88							3
			140.00	126.75	120.00	90				53.67	48.59	46.00	3
40.00	34.75	31.00	58.75	52.00	47.50	28x28	5.12	4.44	3.97	7.51	6.65	6.07	9
"	"	"	"	"	"	30							9
42.75	38.50	33.75	62.75	56.00	50.75	32	6.15	5.54	4.85	9.03	8.05	7.30	8
"	"	"	"	"	"	34				"	"	"	8
"	"	"	"	"	"	36	7.03	6.33	5.55	10.31	9.20	8.34	7
"	"	"	"	"	"	38							7
"	"	"	"	"	"	40							7
48.75	44.50	38.50	68.00	61.50	55.50	42	8.20	7.38	6.47	12.03	10.74	9.73	6
"	"	"	"	"	"	44	9.34	8.53	7.38	13.04	11.79	10.64	6
"	"	"	"	"	"	46							5
"	"	"	"	"	"	48	11.21	10.24	8.86	15.04	14.15	12.77	5
"	"	"	"	"	"	50							5
52.00	47.50	41.75	69.50	62.75	56.75	52							5
"	"	"	69.50	62.75	56.75	54	11.96	10.93	9.61	15.99	14.44	13.06	5
			73.50	66.75	61.50	56				21.14	19.20	17.69	4
						58							4
			"	"	"	60				"	"	"	4
			74.75	68.00	62.75	62				21.50	19.55	18.05	4
			74.75	68.00	62.75	64				21.50	19.55	18.05	4
			88.00	80.00	74.75	66				25.30	23.00	21.50	1
			88.00	80.00	74.75	68				25.30	23.00	21.50	4
						70							4
			94.75	86.75	80.00	72				36.33	33.26	30.67	3
			94.75	86.75	80.00	74				36.33	33.26	30.67	3
						76							3
			105.50	97.50	90.75	78				40.45	37.38	34.79	3
			"	"	"	80				"	"	"	3
			118.75	108.00	101.50	82				45.53	41.40	38.91	3
			118.75	108.00	101.50	84				45.53	41.40	38.91	3
						86							3
			140.00	126.75	120.00	88				53.67	48.59	46.00	3
						90							3
42.75	38.50	33.75	62.75	56.00	50.75	30x30	6.15	5.54	4.85	9.03	8.05	7.30	8
"	"	"	"	"	"	32	7.03	6.33	5.55	10.31	9.20	8.34	7
"	"	"	"	"	"	34				"	"	"	7
"	"	"	"	"	"	36				"	"	"	7
"	"	"	"	"	"	38				"	"	"	7
48.75	44.50	38.50	68.00	61.50	55.50	40	8.20	7.38	6.47	12.03	10.74	9.73	6
"	"	"	"	"	"	42	9.34	8.53	7.38	13.04	11.79	10.64	6
"	"	"	"	"	"	44							6
"	"	"	"	"	"	46	11.21	10.24	8.86	15.64	14.15	12.77	6
"	"	"	"	"	"	48							5
"	"	"	"	"	"	50	"	"	"	"	"	"	5
52.00	47.50	41.75	69.50	62.75	56.75	52	11.96	10.93	9.61	15.99	14.44	13.06	5
			73.50	66.75	61.50	54	14.95	13.66	12.00	19.99	18.05	16.32	4
						56				21.14	19.20	17.69	4
						58							4
						60				"	"	"	4
			74.75	68.00	62.75	62				21.50	19.55	18.05	4
						64							4
			88.00	80.00	74.75	66				25.30	23.00	21.50	4
						68							4
						70				33.74	30.67	28.66	3
			94.75	86.75	80.00	72				36.33	33.26	30.67	3
			"	"	"	74							3
			105.50	97.50	90.75	76				40.45	37.38	34.79	3
						78							3
			"	"	"	80				"	"	"	3
			118.75	108.00	101.50	82				45.53	41.40	38.91	3
						84							3
			140.00	126.75	120.00	86				53.67	48.59	46.00	3
						88				"	"	"	3
						90							3
42.75	38.50	33.75	62.75	56.00	50.75	32x32	7.03	6.33	5.55	10.31	9.20	8.34	7
"	"	"	"	"	"	34							7
48.75	44.50	38.50	68.00	61.50	55.50	36	8.20	7.38	6.47	12.03	10.74	9.73	6
"	"	"	"	"	"	38	9.35	8.53	7.38	13.04	11.79	10.64	6
"	"	"	"	"	"	40							6
"	"	"	"	"	"	42							6
"	"	"	"	"	"	44	11.21	10.24	8.86	15.64	14.15	12.77	5
"	"	"	"	"	"	46							5
"	"	"	"	"	"	48	"	"	"	"	"	"	5
52.00	47.50	41.75	69.50	62.75	56.75	50	11.96	10.93	9.61	15.99	14.44	13.06	5
						52	14.95	13.66	12.00	19.99	18.05	16.32	4

AMERICAN WINDOW GLASS.

Official List Prices, October 1st, 1903.

| PRICE PER BOX OF FIFTY FEET. | | | | | | SIZES. | PRICE PER SINGLE LIGHT. | | | | | | No. Lights per Box |
| SINGLE. | | | DOUBLE. | | | | SINGLE. | | | DOUBLE. | | | |
AA	A	B	AA	A	B		AA	A	B	AA	A	B	
------	------	------	73.50	66.75	61.50	**32x54**	------	------	------	21.14	19.20	17.69	4
------	------	------	"	"	"	56	------	------	------	"	"	"	4
------	------	------	"	"	"	58	------	------	------	"	"	"	4
------	------	------	74.75	68.00	62.75	60	------	------	------	21.50	19.55	18.05	4
------	------	------	"	"	"	62	------	------	------	"	"	"	4
------	------	------	88.00	80.00	74.75	64	------	------	------	25.30	23.00	21.50	4
------	------	------	"	"	"	66	------	------	------	33.74	30.67	28.66	3
------	------	------	"	"	"	68	------	------	------	"	"	"	3
------	------	------	94.75	86.75	80.00	70	------	------	------	36.33	33.26	30.67	3
------	------	------	"	"	"	72	------	------	------	"	"	"	3
------	------	------	105.50	97.50	90.75	74	------	------	------	40.45	37.38	34.79	3
------	------	------	"	"	"	76	------	------	------	"	"	"	3
------	------	------	"	"	"	78	------	------	------	"	"	"	3
------	------	------	118.75	108.00	101.50	80	------	------	------	45.53	41.40	38.91	3
------	------	------	"	"	"	82	------	------	------	"	"	"	3
------	------	------	140.00	126.75	120.00	84	------	------	------	53.67	48.59	46.00	3
------	------	------	"	"	"	86	------	------	------	"	"	"	3
42.75	38.50	33.75	62.75	56.00	50.75	**34x34**	8.20	7.38	6.47	12.03	10.74	9.73	6
48.75	44.50	38.50	68.00	61.50	55.50	36	9.35	8.53	7.38	13.04	11.79	10.64	6
"	"	"	"	"	"	38	"	"	"	"	"	"	6
"	"	"	"	"	"	40	"	"	"	"	"	"	6
"	"	"	"	"	"	42	11.21	10.24	8.86	15.64	14.15	12.77	5
"	"	"	"	"	"	44	"	"	"	"	"	"	5
"	"	"	"	"	"	46	"	"	"	"	"	"	5
52.00	47.50	41.75	69.50	62.75	56.75	48	11.96	10.93	9.61	15.99	14.44	13.06	5
"	"	"	"	"	"	50	14.95	13.66	12.00	19.99	18.05	16.32	4
------	------	------	73.50	66.75	61.50	52	------	------	------	21.14	19.20	17.69	4
------	------	------	"	"	"	54	------	------	------	"	"	"	4
------	------	------	"	"	"	56	------	------	------	"	"	"	4
------	------	------	74.75	68.00	62.75	58	------	------	------	21.50	19.55	18.05	4
------	------	------	"	"	"	60	------	------	------	"	"	"	3
------	------	------	88.00	80.00	74.75	62	------	------	------	33.74	30.67	28.66	3
------	------	------	"	"	"	64	------	------	------	"	"	"	3
------	------	------	"	"	"	66	------	------	------	"	"	"	3
------	------	------	94.75	86.75	80.00	68	------	------	------	36.33	33.26	30.67	3
------	------	------	"	"	"	70	------	------	------	"	"	"	3
------	------	------	105.50	97.50	90.75	72	------	------	------	40.45	37.38	34.79	3
------	------	------	"	"	"	74	------	------	------	"	"	"	3
------	------	------	"	"	"	76	------	------	------	"	"	"	3
------	------	------	118.75	108.00	101.50	78	------	------	------	45.53	41.40	38.91	3
------	------	------	"	"	"	80	------	------	------	"	"	"	3
------	------	------	140.00	126.75	120.00	82	------	------	------	53.67	48.59	46.00	3
------	------	------	"	"	"	84	------	------	------	"	"	"	3
------	------	------	"	"	"	86	------	------	------	"	"	"	3
48.75	44.50	38.50	68.00	61.50	55.50	**36x36**	9.35	8.53	7.38	13.04	11.79	10.64	6
"	"	"	"	"	"	38	11.21	10.24	8.86	15.64	14.15	12.77	5
"	"	"	"	"	"	40	"	"	"	"	"	"	5
"	"	"	"	"	"	42	"	"	"	"	"	"	5
"	"	"	"	"	"	44	"	"	"	"	"	"	5
52.00	47.50	41.75	69.50	62.75	56.75	46	14.95	13.66	12.00	19.99	18.05	16.32	4
"	"	"	"	"	"	48	"	"	"	"	"	"	4
------	------	------	73.50	66.75	61.50	50	------	------	------	21.14	19.20	17.69	4
------	------	------	"	"	"	52	------	------	------	"	"	"	4
------	------	------	"	"	"	54	------	------	------	"	"	"	4
------	------	------	74.75	68.00	62.75	56	------	------	------	21.50	19.55	18.05	4
------	------	------	"	"	"	58	------	------	------	28.66	26.07	24.06	3
------	------	------	88.00	80.00	74.75	60	------	------	------	33.74	30.67	28.66	3
------	------	------	"	"	"	62	------	------	------	"	"	"	3
------	------	------	"	"	"	64	------	------	------	"	"	"	3
------	------	------	94.75	86.75	80.00	66	------	------	------	36.33	33.26	30.67	3
------	------	------	"	"	"	68	------	------	------	"	"	"	3
------	------	------	105.50	97.50	90.75	70	------	------	------	40.45	37.38	34.79	3
------	------	------	"	"	"	72	------	------	------	"	"	"	3
------	------	------	"	"	"	74	------	------	------	"	"	"	3
------	------	------	118.75	108.00	101.50	76	------	------	------	45.53	41.40	38.91	3
------	------	------	"	"	"	78	------	------	------	"	"	"	3
------	------	------	140.00	126.75	120.00	80	------	------	------	53.67	48.59	46.00	3
------	------	------	"	"	"	82	------	------	------	"	"	"	3
------	------	------	"	"	"	84	------	------	------	"	"	"	3
------	------	------	153.50	140.25	133.50	86	------	------	------	58.85	53.77	51.18	3
------	------	------	68.00	61.50	55.50	**38x38**	------	------	------	15.64	14.15	12.77	5
------	------	------	"	"	"	40	------	------	------	"	"	"	5
------	------	------	"	"	"	42	------	------	------	"	"	"	5
------	------	------	69.50	62.75	56.75	44	------	------	------	19.99	18.05	16.32	4
------	------	------	"	"	"	46	------	------	------	"	"	"	4
------	------	------	73.50	66.75	61.50	48	------	------	------	21.14	19.20	17.69	4
------	------	------	"	"	"	50	------	------	------	"	"	"	4
------	------	------	"	"	"	52	------	------	------	"	"	"	4
------	------	------	74.75	68.00	62.75	54	------	------	------	21.50	19.55	18.05	4
------	------	------	"	"	"	56	------	------	------	28.66	26.07	24.06	3
------	------	------	88.00	80.00	74.75	58	------	------	------	33.74	30.67	28.66	3
------	------	------	"	"	"	60	------	------	------	"	"	"	3
------	------	------	"	"	"	62	------	------	------	"	"	"	3
------	------	------	94.75	86.75	80.00	64	------	------	------	36.33	33.26	30.67	3
------	------	------	"	"	"	66	------	------	------	"	"	"	3
------	------	------	105.50	97.50	90.75	68	------	------	------	40.45	37.38	34.79	3

AMERICAN WINDOW GLASS.

Official List Prices, October 1st, 1903.

| PRICE PER BOX OF FIFTY FEET. | | | | | | SIZES. | PRICE PER SINGLE LIGHT. | | | | | | No. Lights per Box |
| SINGLE. | | | DOUBLE. | | | | SINGLE. | | | DOUBLE. | | | |
AA	A	B	AA	A	B		AA	A	B	AA	A	B	
			105.50	97.50	90.75	38x70				40.45	37.38	34.79	3
			118.75	108.00	101.50	72				45.53	41.40	38.91	3
			140.00	126.75	120.00	74				53.67	48.59	46.00	3
						76							3
			"	"	"	78				"	"	"	3
						80							3
						82							3
			153.50	140.25	133.50	84				58.85	53.77	51.18	3
						86							3
			68.00	61.50	55.50	40x40				15.64	14.15	12.77	5
			69.50	62.75	56.75	42				19.99	18.05	16.32	4
						44							4
			73.50	66.75	61.50	46				21.14	19.20	17.69	4
						48							4
			"	"	"	50							4
			74.75	68.00	62.75	52				28.66	26.07	24.06	3
						54							3
			88.00	80.00	74.75	56				33.74	30.67	28.66	3
						58							3
			"	"	"	60							3
			94.75	86.75	80.00	62				36.33	33.26	30.67	3
						64							3
			105.50	97.50	90.75	66				40.45	37.38	34.79	3
						68							3
			"	"	"	70							3
			118.75	108.00	101.50	72				45.53	41.40	38.91	3
						74							3
			140.00	126.75	120.00	76				53.67	48.59	46.00	3
						78							3
			"	"	"	80				"	"	"	3
			153.50	140.25	133.50	82				58.85	53.77	51.18	3
						84							3
			76.45	69.03	62.43	42x42				21.99	19.85	17.95	4
			80.85	73.63	67.65	44				23.25	21.12	19.46	4
			"	"	"	46							4
						48							
			82.23	74.80	69.03	50				31.53	28.68	26.47	3
						52							3
			96.80	88.00	82.23	54				37.11	33.74	31.53	3
						56							3
			"	"	"	58				"	"	"	3
			104.23	95.43	88.00	60				39.96	36.59	33.74	3
						62							3
			116.05	107.25	99.83	64				44.49	41.12	38.27	3
			"	"	"	66				"	"	"	3
						68							3
			130.63	118.80	111.65	70				50.08	45.54	42.81	3
						72							3
			154.00	139.43	132.00	74				59.04	53.45	50.60	3
						76							3
			"	"	"	78				"	"	"	3
			168.85	154.28	146.85	80				64.73	59.15	56.30	3
			80.85	73.63	67.65	44x44				23.25	21.12	19.46	4
						46							4
			82.23	74.80	69.03	48				31.53	28.68	26.47	3
						50							3
			96.80	88.00	82.23	52				37.11	33.74	31.53	3
						54							3
			"	"	"	56							3
			104.23	95.43	88.00	60				39.96	36.59	33.74	3
			116.05	107.25	99.83	62				44.49	41.12	38.27	3
						64							3
			"	"	"	66				"	"	"	3
			130.63	118.80	111.65	68				50.08	45.54	42.81	3
						70							3
			154.00	139.43	132.00	72				59.04	53.45	50.60	3
						74							3
			"	"	"	78				"	"	"	3
			168.85	154.28	146.85	78				64.73	59.15	56.30	3
						80							3
			82.23	74.80	69.03	46x46				31.53	28.68	26.47	3
						48							3
			96.80	88.00	82.23	50				37.11	33.74	31.53	3
						52							3
			"	"	"	54				"	"	"	3
			104.23	95.43	88.00	56				39.96	36.59	33.74	3
						58							3
			116.05	107.25	99.83	60				44.49	41.12	38.27	3
						62							3
						64							3
			130.63	118.80	111.65	66				50.08	45.54	42.81	3
						68							3
			154.00	139.43	132.00	70				59.04	53.45	50.60	3
			"	"	"	72				"	"	"	3

AMERICAN WINDOW GLASS.

Official List Prices, October 1st, 1903.

PRICE PER BOX OF FIFTY FEET.						SIZES.	PRICE PER SINGLE LIGHT.						No. Lights per Box
SINGLE.			DOUBLE.				SINGLE.			DOUBLE.			
AA	A	B	AA	A	B		AA	A	B	AA	A	B	
------	------	------	154.00	139.43	132.00	46x74	------	------	------	59.04	53.45	50.60	3
------	------	------	168.85	154.28	146.85	76	------	------	------	64.73	59.15	56.30	3
------	------	------				78	------	------	------	"	"	"	3
------	------	------	183.70	169.13	161.70	80	------	------	------	70.42	64.84	61.99	3
------	------	------	96.80	88.00	82.23	48x48	------	------	------	37.11	33.74	31.53	3
------	------	------				50	------	------	------				3
------	------	------	"	"	"	52	------	------	------	"	"	"	3
------	------	------	104.23	95.43	88.00	54	------	------	------	39.96	36.59	33.74	3
------	------	------	"	"	"	56	------	------	------	"	"	"	3
------	------	------	116.05	107.25	99.83	58	------	------	------	44.49	41.12	38.27	3
------	------	------				60	------	------	------				3
------	------	------	"	"	"	62	------	------	------	"	"	"	3
------	------	------	130.63	118.80	111.65	64	------	------	------	50.08	45.54	42.81	3
------	------	------				66	------	------	------				3
------	------	------	154.00	139.43	132.00	68	------	------	------	59.04	53.45	50.60	3
------	------	------				70	------	------	------				3
------	------	------	"	"	"	72	------	------	------	"	"	"	3
------	------	------	168.85	154.23	146.85	74	------	------	------	64.73	59.15	56.30	3
------	------	------				76	------	------	------				3
------	------	------	183.70	169.13	161.70	78	------	------	------	70.42	64.84	61.99	3
------	------	------				80	------	------	------				3
------	------	------	96.80	88.00	82.23	50x50	------	------	------	37.11	33.74	31.53	3
------	------	------	104.23	95.43	88.00	52	------	------	------	39.96	36.59	33.74	3
------	------					54	------	------	------				3
------	------		116.05	107.25	99.83	56	------	------	------	44.49	41.12	38.27	3
------	------		"	"	"	58	------	------	------	"	"	"	3
------	------					60	------	------	------				3
------	------		130.63	118.80	111.65	62	------	------	------	50.08	45.54	42.81	3
------	------					64	------	------	------				3
------	------		154.00	139.43	132.00	66	------	------	------	59.04	53.45	50.60	3
------	------		"	"	"	68	------	------	------	"	"	"	3
------	------					70	------	------	------				3
------	------		168.85	154.28	146.85	72	------	------	------	64.73	59.15	56.30	3
------	------					74							
------	------	------	104.23	95.43	88.00	52x52	------	------	------	39.96	36.59	33.74	3
------	------	------	116.05	107.25	99.83	54	------	------	------	44.49	41.12	38.27	3
------	------		"	"	"	56	------	------	------				3
------	------					58	------	------	------				3
------	------		130.63	118.80	111.65	60	------	------	------	50.08	45.54	42.81	3
------	------					62	------	------	------				3
------	------		154.00	139.43	132.00	64	------	------	------	59.04	53.45	50.60	3
------	------		"	"	"	66	------	------	------	"	"	"	3
------	------					68	------	------	------				3
------	------		168.85	154.28	146.85	70	------	------	------	64.73	59.15	56.30	3
------	------					72	------	------	------				3
------	------	------	154.00	139.43	132.00	54x54	------	------	------	59.04	53.45	50.60	3
------	------		"	"	"	56	------	------	------	"	"	"	3
------	------		"	"	"	58	------	------	------	"	"	"	3
------	------		"	"	"	60	------	------	------	"	"	"	3
------	------		"	"	"	62	------	------	------	"	"	"	3
------	------		"	"	"	64	------	------	------	"	"	"	3
------	------		"	"	"	66	------	------	------	"	"	"	3
------	------		168.85	154.28	146.85	68	------	------	------	64.73	59.15	56.30	3
------	------		"	"	"	70	------	------	------	"	"	"	3
------	------		183.70	169.13	161.70	72	------	------	------	70.42	64.84	61.99	3
------	------		154.00	139.43	132.00	56x56	------	------	------	59.04	53.45	50.60	3
------	------		"	"	"	58	------	------	------	"	"	"	3
------	------		"	"	"	60	------	------	------	"	"	"	3
------	------		"	"	"	62	------	------	------	"	"	"	3
------	------		"	"	"	64	------	------	------	"	"	"	3
------	------		168.85	154.28	146.85	66	------	------	------	64.73	59.15	56.30	3
------	------		"	"	"	68	------	------	------	"	"	"	3
------	------		183.70	169.13	161.70	70	------	------	------	70.42	64.84	61.99	3
------	------					72							3
------	------	------	154.00	139.43	132.00	58x58	------	------	------	59.04	53.45	50.60	3
------	------	------	"	"	"	60	------	------	------	"	"	"	3
------	------					62	------	------	------				3
------	------	------	168.85	154.28	146.85	64	------	------	------	64.73	59.15	56.30	3
------	------					66	------	------	------				3
------	------	------	183.70	169.13	161.70	68	------	------	------	70.42	64.84	61.99	3
------	------		"	"	"	70	------	------	------	"	"	"	3
------	------					72							
------	------	------	154.00	139.43	132.00	60x60	------	------	------	59.04	53.45	50.60	3
------	------	------	168.85	154.28	146.85	62	------	------	------	64.73	59.15	56.30	3
------	------					64	------	------	------				3
------	------	------	183.70	169.13	161.70	66	------	------	------	70.42	64.84	61.99	3
------	------	------	"	"	"	68	------	------	------	"	"	"	3
------	------	------				70	------	------	------				3

POLISHED PLATE GLASS

ODD and fractional parts of inches are charged at the price of the next highest even number. Irregular shaped glass, or glass cut to pattern, will be charged as it squares. No special thickness guaranteed; but when heavy plate is required, and so ordered, care will be exercised in selecting the heaviest in stock at the time.

Discounts apply to "glazing quality" only, and to glass of ordinary thickness. Selected glass and special thickness charged at special prices.

Glass exceeding the sizes comprised in the tables will be furnished at special prices.

On all orders amounting to less than $100 net, or for less than three plates of whatever value, boxing will be charged at the rate of 8 cents per square foot, lid measurement. Said measurement to be six inches larger each way than the widest and longest plates in the case.

To Approximate Weight of Polished Plate Glass Boxed.

Extend the glass at 3½ lbs. per square foot. Weight of box equals the contents of a plate of greatest width and length of those packed therein multiplied by 10.

Thus :

1 plate 36″ x 96″ } =59 ft. x 3½ ....206½ lbs.
1 plate 60″ x 84″ }
Size of box 60″ x 96″=40 ft. x 10........400   "

606½   "

POLISHED PLATE GLASS.

Official List, July, 1895.

Length.	WIDTH.					Length.	WIDTH.--Continued.				
	6	7	8	9	10		6	7	8	9	10
6	$0.30	------	------	------	------	116	$11.60	$18.35	$20.95	$23.55	$26.20
8	.40	$0.50	$0.5ὣ	$0.65	------	118	11.80	18.65	21.30	23.95	26.65
10	.50	.60	.70	.80	$0.85	120	12.00	19.00	21.70	24.40	27.10

Length.	WIDTH.					Length.	WIDTH.			
	6	7	8	9	10		12	14	16	18
12	.60	.75	.85	.95	1.05	12	$1.25	------	------	------
14	.70	.85	1.00	1.10	1.20	14	1.45	$1.70	------	------
16	.80	1.00	1.15	1.25	1.40	16	1.65	1.95	$2.20	------
18	.95	1.10	1.25	1.40	1.55	18	1.90	2.20	2.50	$2.80
20	1.05	1.20	1.40	1.55	1.75	20	2.10	2.45	2.75	3.15
22	1.15	1.35	1.50	1.70	1.95	22	2.30	2.65	3.05	4.15
24	1.25	1.45	1.65	1.90	2.10	24	2.50	2.90	3.35	4.50
26	1.35	1.60	1.80	2.05	2.25	26	2.70	3.15	4.35	4.90
28	1.45	1.70	1.95	2.20	2.45	28	2.90	4.10	4.65	5.25
30	1.55	1.85	2.10	2.35	2.60	30	3.15	4.40	5.00	5.65
32	1.65	1.95	2.25	2.50	2.75	32	3.35	4.65	5.35	6.00
34	1.80	2.10	2.40	2.65	2.95	34	4.25	4.95	5.65	6.40
36	1.90	2.20	2.50	2.80	3.15	36	4.50	5.25	6.00	6.75
38	2.00	2.30	2.60	3.00	3.30	38	4.75	5.55	6.35	7.15
40	2.10	2.45	2.75	3.15	4.15	40	5.00	5.85	6.65	7.50
42	2.20	2.55	2.90	3.30	4.35	42	5.25	6.15	7.00	12.60
44	2.30	2.65	3.05	4.15	4.60	44	5.50	6.40	7.35	13.20
46	2.40	2.80	3.20	4.30	4.80	46	5.75	6.70	12.30	13.80
48	2.50	2.90	3.35	4.50	5.00	48	6.00	7.00	12.80	14.40
50	2.60	3.05	4.20	4.70	5.20	50	6.25	7.30	13.30	15.00
52	2.70	3.20	4.35	4.90	5.40	52	6.50	12.10	13.90	15.60
54	2.80	3.30	4.50	5.10	5.60	54	6.75	12.60	14.40	16.20
56	2.90	4.10	4.65	5.25	5.85	56	7.00	13.10	14.90	16.80
58	3.00	4.25	4.80	5.45	6.05	58	7.25	13.50	15.50	17.40
60	3.15	4.40	5.00	5.65	6.25	60	7.50	14.00	16.00	18.00
62	6.20	7.25	8.25	9.30	10.35	62	12.40	14.50	16.50	18.60
64	6.40	7.45	8.55	9.60	10.65	64	12.80	14.90	17.10	19.20
66	6.60	7.70	8.80	9.90	11.00	66	13.20	15.40	17.60	19.80
68	6.80	7.95	9.05	10 20	11.35	68	13.60	15.90	18.10	20.40
70	7.00	8.15	9.35	10.50	11.65	70	14.00	16.30	18.70	21.00
72	7.20	8.40	9.60	10.80	12.00	72	14.40	16.80	19.20	21.60
74	7.40	8.65	9.85	11.10	16.70	74	14.80	17.30	19.70	22.20
76	7.60	8.85	10.15	11.40	17.15	76	15.20	17.70	20.30	22.80
78	7.80	9.10	10.40	11.70	17.60	78	15.60	18.20	20.80	23.40
80	8.00	9.35	10.65	12.00	18.05	80	16.00	18.70	21.30	24.00
82	8.20	9.55	10.95	16.65	18.50	82	16.40	19.10	21.90	33.30
84	8.40	9.80	11.20	17.05	18.95	84	16.80	19.60	22.40	34.10
86	8.60	10.05	11.45	17.45	19.40	86	17.20	20.10	22.90	34.90
88	8.80	10.25	11.75	17.90	19.85	88	17.60	20.50	23.50	35.80
90	9.00	10.50	12.00	18.30	20 30	90	18.00	21.00	24.00	36.60
92	9.20	10.75	16.60	18.70	20.75	92	18.40	21.50	33.20	37.40
94	9.40	10.95	16.95	19.10	21.20	94	18.80	21.90	33.90	38.20
96	9.60	11.20	17.35	19.50	21.70	96	19.20	22.40	34.70	39.00
98	9.80	11.45	17.70	19.90	22.15	98	19.60	22.90	35.40	39.80
100	10.00	11.65	18.05	20.30	22.60	100	20.00	23.30	36.10	40.60
102	10.20	11.90	18.45	20.70	23.05	102	20.40	23.80	36.90	41.40
104	10.40	16.45	18.80	21.10	23.50	104	20.80	32.90	37.60	42.20
106	10.60	16.75	19.15	21.55	23.95	106	21.20	33.50	38.30	43.10
108	10.80	17.05	19.50	21.95	24.40	108	21.60	34.10	39.00	43.90
110	11.00	17.35	19.85	22.35	24.85					
112	11.20	17.70	20.25	22.75	25.30					
114	11.40	18.00	20.60	23.15	25.75					

POLISHED PLATE GLASS.

Official List, July, 1895.

Length	WIDTH.—Continued.			
	12	14	16	18
110	$22.00	$34.70	$39.70	$44.70
112	22.40	35.40	40.50	45.50
114	22.80	36.00	41.20	46.30
116	23.20	36.70	41.90	47.10
118	23.60	37.30	42.60	47.90
120	24.00	38.00	43.40	48.80
122	33.00	38.60	44.10	49.60
124	33.60	39.20	44.80	50.40
126	34.10	39.80	45.50	51.20
128	34.70	40.50	46.20	52.00
130	35.20	41.10	47.00	52.80
132	35.80	41.70	47.70	53.60
134	36.30	42.30	48.50	54.40
136	36.90	43.00	49.20	55.30
138	37.40	43.70	49.90	56.10
140	38.00	44.30	50.60	56.90
142	38.50	44.90	51.30	57.70
144	39.00	45.50	52.00	58.50
146	39.60	46.10	52.70	59.30
148	40.10	46.80	53.40	60.10
150	40.60	47.40	54.20	60.90
152	41.20	48.00	54.90	61.80
154	41.70	48.70	55.60	62.60
156	42.20	49.30	56.40	63.40
158	42.80	50.00	57.10	64.20
160	43.40	50.60	57.80	65.00
162	43.90	51.20	58.50	68.80
164	44.50	51.80	59.20	69.70
166	45.00	52.50	60.00	70.60
168	45.50	53.10	60.70	71.40
170	46.00	53.70	61.40	72.30

Length	WIDTH.				
	20	22	24	26	28
20	$4.15	......	......		
22	4.60	$5.05	......		
24	5.00	5.50	$6.00	......	
26	5.40	5.95	6 50	$7.05	......
28	5.85	6.40	7.10	12.10	$13.10
30	6.25	6.90	7.50	13.00	14.00
32	6.65	7.35	12.80	13.90	14.90
34	7.10	12.50	13.60	14.70	15.90
36	7.50	13.20	14.40	15.60	16.80
38	12.70	13.90	15.20	16.50	17.70
40	13.30	14.70	16.00	17.30	18.70
42	14.00	15.40	16.80	18.20	19.60
44	14.70	16.10	17.60	19.10	20 50
46	15.30	16.90	18.40	19.90	21.50
48	16.00	17.60	19.20	20.80	22.40
50	16.70	18.30	20.00	21.70	23.30
52	17.30	19.10	20.80	22.50	32.90
54	18.00	19.80	21.60	23.40	34.10
56	18.70	20.50	22.40	32.90	35.40
58	19.30	21.30	23.20	34.00	36.70
60	20.00	22.00	24.00	35.20	37.90

Length	WIDTH.—Continued.				
	20	22	24	26	28
62	$20.70	$22.70	$33.60	$36.40	$39.20
64	21.30	23.50	34.70	37.60	40.50
66	22.00	32.80	35.80	38.70	41.70
68	22.70	33.70	36.90	39.90	43.00
70	23.30	34.70	38.00	41.00	44.30
72	24.00	35.70	39.00	42.20	45.50
74	33.40	36.70	40.10	43.40	46.80
76	34.30	37.70	41.20	44.60	48.10
78	35.20	38.70	42.30	45.80	49.30
80	36.10	39.70	43.40	47.00	50.60
82	37.00	40.70	44.50	48.20	51.90
84	37.90	41.70	45.50	49.30	53.10
86	38.80	42.70	46.60	50.50	54.40
88	39.70	43.70	47.70	51.70	55.70
90	40.60	44.70	48.80	52.80	56.90
92	41.50	45.70	49.90	54.00	58.20
94	42.40	46.70	51.00	55.20	59.50
96	43.40	47.70	52.00	56.40	60.70
98	44.30	48.70	53.10	57.60	62.00
100	45.20	49.70	54.20	58.70	63.30
102	46.10	50.70	55.30	59.90	64.50
104	47.00	51.70	56.40	61.00	68.70
106	47.90	52.60	57.50	62.20	70.10
108	48.80	53.60	58.50	63.40	71.40
110	49.70	54.60	59.60	64.60	72.70
112	50.60	55.60	60.70	68.70	74.10
114	51.50	56.60	61.80	70.00	75.40
116	52.40	57.60	62.90	71.20	76.70
118	53.30	58.60	64.00	72.40	78.00
120	54.20	59.60	65.00	73.70	79.30
122	55.10	60.60	69.10	74.90	80.70
124	56.00	61.60	70.30	76.10	82.00
126	56.90	62.60	71.40	77.40	83.30
128	57.80	63.60	72.50	78.60	84.70
130	58.70	64.60	73.70	79.80	86.00
132	59.60	68.60	74.80	81.10	87.30
134	60.50	69.60	76.00	82.30	88.60
136	61.40	70.70	77.10	83.50	89.90
138	62.30	71.70	78.20	84 80	91.30
140	63.20	72.70	79.30	86.00	92.60
142	64.10	73.80	80.50	87.20	93.90
144	65.00	74.80	81.60	88.40	95.20
146	68.90	75.90	82.70	89.60	96.50
148	69.90	76.90	83.90	90.90	97.80
150	70.90	77.90	85.00	92.10	99.20
152	71.80	79.00	86.10	93.30	101.00
154	72.70	80.00	87.30	94.60	102.00
156	73.70	81.10	88.40	95.80	103.00
158	74.60	82.10	89.50	97.00	104.00
160	75.60	83.10	90.70	98.30	106.00
162	76.50	84.20	91.80	99.50	107.00
164	77.50	85.20	92.90	101.00	108.00
166	78.40	86.20	94.10	102.00	110.00
168	79.30	87.30	95.20	103.00	111.00
170	80.30	88.30	96.30	104.00	112.00

POLISHED PLATE GLASS.

Official List, July, 1895.

Length	WIDTH 30	32	34	36	38
30	$15.00	-	-	-	-
32	16.00	$17.10	-	-	-
34	17.00	18.10	$19.30	-	-
36	18.00	19.20	20.40	$21.60	-
38	19.00	20.30	21.50	22.80	$32.60
40	20.00	21.30	22.70	24.00	34.30
42	21.00	22.40	23.80	34.10	36.00
44	22.00	23.50	33.70	35.80	37.80
46	23.00	33.20	35.30	37.40	39.50
48	24.00	34.70	36.90	39.00	41.20
50	33.80	36.10	38.40	40.60	42.90
52	35.20	37.60	39.90	42.20	44.60
54	36.60	39.00	41.40	43.90	46.30
56	38.00	40.50	43.00	45.50	48.00
58	39.30	41.90	44.50	47.10	49.80
60	40.60	43.40	46.00	48.80	51.50
62	42.00	44.80	47.60	50.40	53.20
64	43.40	46.20	49.20	52.00	54.90
66	44.70	47.70	50.70	53.60	56.60
68	46.00	49.20	52.20	55.30	58.30
70	47.40	50.60	53.70	56.90	60.00
72	48.80	52.00	55.30	58.50	61.80
74	50.10	53.40	56.80	60.10	63.50
76	51.50	54.90	58.30	61.80	68.20
78	52.80	56.40	59.90	63.40	70.00
80	54.20	57.80	61.40	65.00	71.80
82	55.50	59.20	63.00	69.70	73.60
84	56.90	60.70	64.50	71.40	75.40
86	58.20	62.10	69.00	73.10	77.20
88	59.60	63.60	70.70	74.80	79.00
90	60.90	65.00	72.30	76.50	80.80
92	62.30	69.50	73.90	78.20	82.60
94	63.70	71.00	75.50	79.90	84.40
96	65.00	72.50	77.10	81.60	86.20
98	69.40	74.10	78.70	83.30	88.00
100	70.90	75.60	80.30	85.00	89.80
102	72.30	77.10	81.90	86.70	91.60
104	73.70	78.60	83.50	88.40	93.40
106	75.10	80.10	85.10	90.10	95.20
108	76.50	81.60	86.70	91.80	97.00
110	77.90	83.10	88.30	93.50	98.70
112	79.30	84.60	89.90	95.20	101.00
114	80.80	86.10	91.50	96.90	102.00
116	82.20	87.60	93.10	98.60	104.00
118	83.60	89.10	94.70	100.00	106.00
120	85.00	90.70	96.30	102.00	108.00
122	86.40	92.20	98.00	104.00	109.00
124	87.90	93.70	99.50	105.00	111.00
126	89.30	95.20	101.00	107.00	113.00
128	90.70	96.70	103.00	109.00	115.00
130	92.10	98.20	104.00	110.00	117.00
132	93.50	99.70	106.00	112.00	118.00
134	95.00	101.00	108.00	114.00	120.00
136	96.40	103.00	109.00	116.00	122.00
138	97.80	104.00	111.00	118.00	124.00

Length	WIDTH—Continued. 30	32	34	36	38
140	99.20	106.00	112.00	119.00	126.00
142	101.00	107.00	114.00	120.00	127.00
144	102.00	109.00	116.00	122.00	129.00
146	103.00	110.00	117.00	124.00	131.00
148	105.00	112.00	119.00	126.00	133.00
150	106.00	113.00	120.00	127.00	135.00
152	108.00	115.00	122.00	129.00	136.00
154	109.00	116.00	124.00	131.00	138.00
156	110.00	118.00	125.00	133.00	140.00
158	111.00	119.00	127.00	135.00	142.00
160	113.00	121.00	128.00	136.00	144.00
162	115.00	122.00	130.00	137.00	145.00
164	116.00	124.00	132.00	139.00	147.00
166	118.00	126.00	133.00	141.00	149.00
168	119.00	127.00	135.00	143.00	151.00
170	120.00	128.00	136.00	144.00	152.00

Length	WIDTH 40	42	44	46	48
40	$36.10	-	-	-	-
42	37.90	$39.80	-	-	-
44	39.70	41.70	$43.80	-	-
46	41.50	43.60	45.70	$47.80	-
48	43.40	45.50	47.70	49.90	$52.00
50	45.20	47.40	49.70	51.90	54.20
52	47.00	49.30	51.70	54.00	56.40
54	48.80	51.20	53.60	56.10	58.50
56	50.60	53.10	55.60	58.10	60.70
58	52.40	55.00	57.60	60.20	62.90
60	54.20	56.90	59.60	62.30	65.00
62	56.00	58.80	61.60	64.40	70.30
64	57.80	60.70	63.60	69.50	72.50
66	59.60	62.60	68.60	71.70	74.80
68	61.40	64.50	70.70	73.90	77.10
70	63.20	69.40	72.70	76.10	79.30
72	65.00	71.40	74.80	78.20	81.60
74	69.90	73.40	76.90	80.40	83.90
76	71.80	75.40	79.00	82.60	86.10
78	73.70	77.40	81.10	84.80	88.40
80	75.60	79.40	83.10	86.90	90.70
82	77.50	81.40	85.20	89.10	92.90
84	79.40	83.30	87.30	91.30	95.20
86	81.30	85.30	89.40	93.40	97.50
88	83.10	87.30	91.50	95.60	99.70
90	85.00	89.30	93.50	97.80	102.00
92	86.90	91.30	95.60	100.00	104.00
94	88.80	93.20	97.70	102.00	107.00
96	90.70	95.20	99.70	104.00	109.00
98	92.60	97.20	102.00	106.00	111.00
100	94.50	99.20	104.00	109.00	113.00
102	96.40	101.00	106.00	111.00	116.00
104	98.30	103.00	108.00	113.00	118.00
106	100.00	105.00	110.00	115.00	120.00
108	102.00	107.00	112.00	117.00	122.00

POLISHED PLATE GLASS.

Official List, July, 1895.

Length	WIDTH.—*Continued.*					Length	WIDTH.				
	40	42	44	46	48		50	52	54	56	58
110	104.00	109.00	114.00	120.00	125.00	50	56.50	......	......	......	......
112	106.00	111.00	116.00	122.00	127.00	52	58.70	61.00	......	......	......
114	108.00	113.00	118.00	124.00	129.00	54	60.90	63.40	68.80	......	......
116	110.00	115.00	121.00	126.00	131.00	56	63.20	68.70	71.40	74.10	......
118	112.00	117.00	123.00	128.00	134.00	58	68.50	71.20	74.00	76.70	79.40
120	114.00	119.00	125.00	130.00	136.00	60	70.90	73.70	76.50	79.30	82.20
122	115.00	121.00	127.00	132.00	138.00	62	73.20	76.10	79.00	82.00	84.90
124	117.00	123.00	129.00	135.00	141.00	64	75.60	78.60	81.60	84.70	87.70
126	119.00	125.00	131.00	137.00	143.00	66	77.90	81.10	84.20	87.30	90.40
128	121.00	127.00	133.00	139.00	145.00	68	80.30	83.50	86.70	89.90	93.10
130	123.00	129.00	135.00	141.00	147.00	70	82.60	85.90	89.30	92.50	95.80
132	125.00	131.00	137.00	143.00	150.00	72	85.00	88.40	91.80	95.20	98.60
134	126.00	133.00	139.00	146.00	152.00	74	87.40	90.90	94.40	97.90	101.00
136	128.00	135.00	141.00	148.00	163.00	76	89.70	93.30	96.90	101.00	104.00
138	130.00	137.00	143.00	150.00	166.00	78	92.10	95.70	99.40	103.00	107.00
140	132.00	139.00	145.00	152 00	168.00	80	94.50	98.30	102.00	106.00	110.00
142	134.00	141.00	147.00	163.00	170.00	82	96.80	101.00	105.00	108.00	112.00
144	136.00	143.00	150.00	166.00	173.00	84	99.20	103.00	107.00	111.00	115.00
146	138.00	145.00	152.00	168.00	175.00	86	102.00	106.00	110.00	113.00	118.00
148	140.00	147.00	163.00	170.00	178.00	88	104.00	108.00	112.00	116.00	121.00
150	142.00	149.00	165.00	172.00	180.00	90	106.00	110.00	115.00	119.00	123.00
152	144.00	151.00	167.00	175.00	182.00	92	109.00	113.00	117.00	122.00	126.00
154	145.00	153.00	169.00	177.00	185.00	94	111.00	115.00	120.00	124.00	129.00
156	147.00	164.00	172.00	179.00	187.00	96	113.00	118.00	123.00	127.00	131.00
158	149.00	166.00	174.00	182.00	190.00	98	116.00	120.00	125.00	130.00	134.00
160	151.00	168.00	176.00	184.00	192.00	100	118.00	123.00	127.00	132.00	137.00
162	153.00	170.00	178.00	186.00	194.00	102	120.00	125.00	130.00	135.00	140.00
164	164.00	172.00	180.00	189.00	197.00	104	123.00	128.00	133.00	138.00	142.00
166	166.00	174.00	183.00	191.00	199.00	106	125.00	130.00	135.00	140.00	145.00
168	168.00	177.00	185.00	193.00	202.00	108	127.00	133.00	138.00	143.00	148.00
170	170.00	179.00	187.00	195.00	204.00	110	130.00	135.00	140.00	145.00	151.00
172	172.00	181.00	189.00	198.00	206.00	112	132.00	137.00	143.00	148.00	162.00
174	174.00	183.00	191.00	200.00	209.00	114	135.00	140 00	145.00	151.00	165.00
176	176.00	185.00	194.00	202.00	211.00	116	137.00	142.00	148.00	162.00	168.00
178	178.00	187.00	196.00	205.00	214.00	118	139.00	145.00	150.00	165.00	171.00
180	180.00	189.00	198.00	207.00	216.00	120	142.00	147.00	153.00	168.00	174.00
182	202.00	212.00	222.00	232.00	243.00	122	144.00	150.00	165.00	171.00	177.00
184	204.00	215.00	225.00	235.00	246.00	124	146.00	152.00	167.00	174.00	180.00
186	207.00	217.00	227.00	237.00	248.00	126	149.00	164.00	170.00	176.00	183.00
188	209.00	220.00	230.00	240.00	251.00	128	151.00	166.00	173.00	179.00	186.00
190	211.00	222.00	232.00	243.00	253.00	130	162.00	169.00	175.00	182.00	188.00
192	293.00	308.00	323.00	337.00	352.00	132	165.00	172.00	178.00	185.00	191.00
194	297.00	311.00	326.00	340.00	356.00	134	167.00	174.00	181.00	188.00	194.00
196	300.00	315.00	330.00	344.00	360.00	136	170.00	177.00	184.00	190.00	197.00
198	303.00	318.00	333.00	348.00	363.00	138	172.00	179.00	186.00	193.00	200.00
200	306.00	321.00	336.00	352.00	367.00	140	175.00	182.00	189.00	196.00	203.00
202	309.00	325.00	340.00	355.00	370.00	142	177.00	185.00	192.00	199.00	206.00
204	312.00	328.00	343.00	359.00	374.00	144	180.00	187.00	194.00	202.00	209.00
206	315.00	331.00	346.00	362.00	378.00	146	182.00	190.00	197.00	204.00	212.00
208	318.00	334.00	350.00	366.00	381.00	148	185.00	192.00	200.00	207.00	215.00
210	321.00	337.00	353.00	369.00	385.00	150	187.00	195.00	202.00	210.00	218.60
212	324.00	340.00	356.00	373.00	389.00	152	190.00	198.00	205.00	213.00	220.00
214	327.00	343.00	360.00	376.00	393.00	154	192.00	200.00	208.00	216.00	223.00
216	330.00	346.00	363.00	379.00	396.00	156	195.00	203.00	210.00	218.00	226.00
218	333.00	350.00	366.00	383.00	400.00	158	197.00	205.00	213.00	221.00	229.00

POLISHED PLATE GLASS.

Official List, July, 1895.

Length.	50	52	54	56	58
	WIDTH.—Continued.				
160	200.00	208.00	216.00	224.00	232.00
162	202.00	210.00	219.00	227.00	235.00
164	205.00	213.00	221.00	230.00	238.00
166	207.00	216.00	224.00	232.00	241.00
168	210.00	218.00	227.00	235.00	244.00
170	212.00	221.00	229.00	238.00	246.00
172	215.00	224.00	232.00	241.00	249.00
174	217.00	226.00	235.00	244.00	252.00
176	220.00	229.00	238.00	246.00	255.00
178	222.00	231.00	240.00	249.00	258.00
180	225.00	234.00	243.00	252.00	261.00
182	253.00	263.00	273.00	283.00	293.00
184	256.00	266.00	276.00	286.00	297.00
186	258.00	269.00	279.00	290.00	300.00
188	261.00	271.00	282.00	293.00	303.00
190	264.00	274.00	285.00	296.00	306.00
192	367.00	381.00	396.00	411.00	425.00
194	370.00	385.00	400.00	415.00	430.00
196	374.00	389.00	404.00	419.00	434.00
198	378.00	393.00	408.00	424.00	439.00
200	382.00	397.00	412.00	428.00	443.00
202	386.00	401.00	417.00	432.00	447.00
204	389.00	405.00	421.00	437.00	452.00
206	393.00	409.00	425.00	441.00	456.00
208	397.00	413.00	429.00	445.00	460.00
210	400.00	417.00	433.00	449.00	465.00
212	404.00	421.00	437.00	454.00	470.00
214	408.00	425.00	441.00	458.00	474.00
216	413.00	429.00	445.00	462.00	478.00
218	417.00	434.00	450.00	467.00	483.00

Length.	60	62	64	66	68
	WIDTH.				
60	85.00	------	------	------	------
62	88.00	91.00	------	------	------
64	91.00	94.00	97.00	------	------
66	94.00	97.00	100.00	103.00	------
68	96.00	100.00	103.00	106.00	109.00
70	99.00	102.00	106.00	109.00	112.00
72	102.00	105.00	109.00	112.00	116.00
74	105.00	108.00	112.00	115.00	119.00
76	108.00	111.00	115.00	118.00	122.00
78	110.00	114.00	118.00	121.00	125.00
80	113.00	117.00	121.00	125.00	128.00
82	116.00	120.00	124.00	128.00	132.00
84	119.00	123.00	127.00	131.00	135.00
86	122.00	126.00	130.00	134.00	138.00
88	125.00	129.00	133.00	137.00	141.00
90	127.00	132.00	136.00	140.00	144.00
92	130.00	135.00	139.00	143.00	148.00
94	133.00	138.00	142.00	146.00	151.00
96	136.00	141.00	145.00	150.00	163.00
98	139.00	143.00	148.00	153.00	167.00
100	142.00	146.00	151.00	165.00	170.00
102	144.00	149.00	163.00	168.00	173.00

Length.	60	62	64	66	68
	WIDTH.—Continued.				
104	147.00	152.00	166.00	172.00	177.00
106	150.00	164.00	170.00	175.00	180.00
108	153.00	167.00	173.00	178.00	184.00
110	165.00	170.00	176.00	181.00	187.00
112	168.00	174.00	179.00	185.00	190.00
114	171.00	177.00	182.00	188.00	194.00
116	174.00	180.00	185.00	191.00	197.00
118	177.00	183.00	189.00	195.00	201.00
120	180.00	186.00	192.00	198.00	204.00
122	183.00	189.00	195.00	201.00	207.00
124	186.00	192.00	198.00	205.00	211.00
126	189.00	195.00	202.00	208.00	214.00
128	192.00	198.00	205.00	211.00	218.00
130	195.00	201.00	208.00	214.00	221.00
132	198.00	205.00	211.00	218.00	224.00
134	201.00	208.00	214.00	221.00	228.00
136	204.00	211.00	218.00	224.00	231.00
138	207.00	214.00	221.00	228.00	234.00
140	210.00	217.00	224.00	231.00	238.00
142	213.00	220.00	227.00	234.00	241.00
144	216.00	223.00	230.00	238.00	245.00
146	219.00	226.00	234.00	241.00	248.00
148	222.00	229.00	237.00	244.00	252.00
150	225.00	232.00	240.00	247.00	255.00
152	228.00	236.00	243.00	251.00	258.00
154	231.00	239.00	246.00	254.00	262.00
156	234.00	242.00	250.00	257.00	265.00
158	237.00	245.00	253.00	261.00	269.00
160	240.00	248.00	256.00	264.00	272.00
162	243.00	251.00	259.00	267.00	275.00
164	246.00	254.00	262.00	271.00	279.00
166	249.00	257.00	266.00	274.00	282.00
168	252.00	260.00	269.00	277.00	286.00
170	255.00	263.00	272.00	280.00	289.00
172	258.00	267.00	275.00	284.00	292.00
174	261.00	270.00	278.00	287.00	296.00
176	264.00	273.00	282.00	290.00	299.00
178	267.00	276.00	285.00	294.00	303.00
180	270.00	279.00	288.00	297.00	306.00
182	303.00	314.00	324.00	334.00	344.00
184	307.00	317.00	327.00	337.00	347.00
186	310.00	320.00	331.00	341.00	351.00
188	314.00	324.00	334.00	345.00	355.00
190	317.00	327.00	338.00	348.00	359.00
192	440.00	455.00	469.00	484.00	499.00
194	445.00	459.00	474.00	489.00	504.00
196	449.00	464.00	479.00	494.00	509.00
198	454.00	469.00	484.00	499.00	514.00
200	458.00	473.00	489.00	504.00	520.00
202	463.00	478.00	494.00	509.00	525.00
204	468.00	483.00	499.00	514.00	530.00
206	472.00	488.00	504.00	519.00	535.00
208	477.00	492.00	508.00	524.00	540.00
210	481.00	497.00	513.00	529.00	545.00
212	486.00	501.00	518.00	534.00	601.00

POLISHED PLATE GLASS.

Official List, July, 1895.

Length	WIDTH.—Continued.					Length	WIDTH.—Continued.				
	60	62	64	66	68		70	72	74	76	78
214	490.00	506.00	523.00	539.00	606.00	168	294.00	302.00	311.00	319.00	328.00
216	495.00	512.00	528.00	545.00	612.00	170	297.00	306.00	314.00	323.00	331.00
218	500.00	517.00	533.00	550.00	618.00	172	301.00	310.00	318.00	327.00	335.00

Length	WIDTH.					Length	WIDTH.—Continued.				
	70	72	74	76	78		70	72	74	76	78
70	116.00	....	......	......	......	174	304.00	313.00	322.00	331.00	339.00
72	119.00	122.00	......	......	......	176	308.00	317.00	325.00	334.00	343.00
74	122.00	126.00	129.00	......	......	178	311.00	320.00	329.00	338.00	347.00
76	126.00	129.00	133.00	136.00	......	180	315.00	324.00	333.00	342.00	351.00
78	129.00	133.00	136.00	140.00	144.00	182	354.00	364.00	374.00	384.00	394.00
80	132.00	136.00	139.00	144.00	147.00	184	358.00	368.00	378.00	388.00	399.00
82	136.00	139.00	143.00	147.00	151.00	186	362.00	372.00	382.00	393.00	443.00
84	139.00	143.00	147.00	151.00	164.00	188	366.00	376.00	386.00	397.00	448.00
86	142.00	146.00	150.00	163.00	168.00	190	370.00	380.00	391.00	441.00	453.00
88	145.00	150.00	163.00	167.00	172.00	192	513.00	528.00	543.00	608.00	624.00
90	149.00	153.00	166.00	171.00	175.00	194	518.00	534.00	548.00	615.00	631.00
92	152.00	166.00	170.00	175.00	179.00	196	524.00	539.00	604.00	621.00	637.00
94	165.00	169.00	174.00	179.00	183.00	198	529.00	545.00	610.00	627.00	643.00
96	168.00	173.00	178.00	182.00	187.00	200	534.00	550.00	617.00	633.00	650.00
98	171.00	176.00	181.00	186.00	191.00	202	540.00	606.00	623.00	640.00	656.00
100	175.00	180.00	185.00	190.00	195.00	204	545.00	612.00	630.00	646.00	663.00
102	178.00	184.00	189.00	194.00	199.00	206	601.00	618.00	636.00	652.00	669.00
104	182.00	187.00	192.00	198.00	203.00	208	607.00	624.00	642.00	659.00	676.00
106	185.00	191.00	196.00	201.00	207.00	210	612.00	630.00	648.00	665.00	682.00
108	189.00	194.00	200.00	205.00	210.00	212	618.00	636.00	654.00	672.00	689.00
110	192.00	198.00	203.00	209.00	214.00	214	624.00	642.00	660.00	678.00	696.00
112	196.00	202.00	207.00	213.00	218.00	216	630.00	648.00	666.00	684.00	702.00
114	199.00	206.00	211.00	217.00	222.00	218	636.00	654.00	672.00	690.00	708.00

Length	WIDTH.				
	80	82	84	86	88
116	203.00	209.00	215.00	220.00	226.00
118	206.00	212.00	218.00	224.00	230.00
120	210.00	216.00	222.00	228.00	234.00
122	213.00	220.00	226.00	232.00	238.00
124	217.00	223.00	230.00	236.00	242.00
126	220.00	227.00	233.00	239.00	246.00
128	224.00	230.00	237.00	243.00	250.00
130	227.00	234.00	240.00	247.00	253.00
132	231.00	238.00	244.00	251.00	257.00
134	234.00	241.00	248.00	255.00	261.00
136	238.00	245.00	251.00	258.00	265.00
138	241.00	248.00	255.00	262.00	269.00
140	245.00	252.00	259.00	266.00	273.00
142	248.00	256.00	263.00	270.00	277.00
144	252.00	259.00	266.00	274.00	281.00
146	255.00	263.00	270.00	277.00	285.00
148	259.00	266.00	274.00	281.00	289.00
150	262.00	270.00	277.00	285.00	292.00
152	266.00	274.00	281.00	289.00	296.00
154	269.00	277.00	285.00	293.00	300.00
156	273.00	281.00	288.00	296.00	304.00
158	276.00	284.00	292.00	300.00	308.00
160	280.00	288.00	296.00	304.00	312.00
162	283.00	292.00	300.00	308.00	316.00
164	287.00	295.00	303.00	312.00	320.00
166	290.00	299.00	307.00	315.00	324.00

Length	WIDTH.				
	80	82	84	86	88
80	151.00	......	......	......	......
82	164.00	168.00	......	......	......
84	168.00	172.00	176.00	......	......
86	172.00	176.00	181.00	185.00	......
88	176.00	180.00	185.00	189.00	194.00
90	180.00	184.00	189.00	193.00	198.00
92	184.00	189.00	193.00	198.00	202.00
94	188.00	193.00	197.00	202.00	207.00
96	192.00	197.00	202.00	206.00	211.00
98	196.00	201.00	206.00	211.00	216.00
100	200.00	205.00	210.00	215.00	220.00
102	204.00	209.00	214.00	219.00	224.00
104	208.00	213.00	218.00	224.00	229.00
106	212.00	217.00	223.00	228.00	233.00
108	216.00	221.00	227.00	232.00	237.00
110	220.00	225.00	231.00	237.00	242.00
112	224.00	230.00	235.00	241.00	246.00
114	228.00	234.00	239.00	245.00	251.00
116	232.00	238.00	244.00	250.00	255.00
118	236.00	242.00	248.00	254.00	260.00
120	240.00	246.00	252.00	258.00	264.00
122	244.00	250.00	256.00	262.00	268.00
124	248.00	254.00	260.00	267.00	273.00
126	252.00	258.00	265.00	271.00	277.00
128	256.00	262.00	269.00	275.00	282.00
130	260.00	266.00	273.00	279.00	286.00

POLISHED PLATE GLASS.

Official List, July, 1895.

Length	WIDTH.—Continued. 80	82	84	86	88
132	264.00	271.00	277.00	284.00	290.00
134	268.00	275.00	281.00	288.00	295.00
136	272.00	279.00	286.00	292.00	299.00
138	276.00	283.00	290.00	297.00	304.00
140	280.00	287.00	294.00	301.00	308.00
142	284.00	291.00	298.00	305.00	312.00
144	288.00	295.00	302.00	310.00	317.00
146	292.00	299.00	307.00	314.00	321.00
148	296.00	303.00	311.00	318.00	326.00
150	300.00	307.00	315.00	322.00	330.00
152	304.00	312.00	319.00	327.00	334.00
154	308.00	316.00	323.00	331.00	339.00
156	312.00	320.00	328.00	335.00	343.00
158	316.00	324.00	332.00	340.00	348.00
160	320.00	328.00	336.00	344.00	352.00
162	324.00	332.00	340.00	348.00	356.00
164	328.00	336.00	344.00	353.00	401.00
166	332.00	340.00	349.00	357.00	406.00
168	336.00	344.00	353.00	401.00	411.00
170	340.00	348.00	357.00	406.00	416.00
172	344.00	353.00	401.00	411.00	420.00
174	348.00	357.00	406.00	416.00	425.00
176	352.00	401.00	411.00	420.00	430.00
178	356.00	405.00	415.00	425.00	435.00
180	360.00	410.00	420.00	430.00	440.00
182	445.00	456.00	467.00	478.00	489.00
184	450.00	461.00	472.00	483.00	495.00
186	455.00	466.00	477.00	489.00	500.00
188	460.00	471.00	482.00	494.00	506.00
190	464.00	476.00	488.00	500.00	511.00
192	640.00	656.00	672.00	688.00	704.00
194	647.00	663.00	679.00	695.00	711.00
196	653.00	670.00	686.00	703.00	719.00
198	660.00	676.00	693.00	710.00	907.00
200	666.00	683.00	700.00	717.00	917.00
202	673.00	690.00	707.00	905.00	926.00
204	679.00	697.00	714.00	914.00	935.00
206	686.00	704.00	901.00	923.00	944.00
208	693.00	711.00	910.00	932.00	953.00
210	700.00	718.00	918.00	941.00	962.00
212	706.00	905.00	927.00	950.00	972.00
214	713.00	914.00	936.00	959.00	981.00
216	720.00	923.00	944.00	967.00	990.00
218	908.00	931.00	953.00	976.00	999.00

Length	WIDTH. 90	92	94	96
90	202.00	------	------	------
92	207.00	212.00	------	------
94	211.00	216.00	221.00	------
96	216.00	221.00	226.00	230.00
'98	220.00	225.00	230.00	235.00
100	225.00	230.00	235.00	240.00
102	229.00	235.00	240.00	245.00

Length	WIDTH.—Continued. 90	92	94	96
104	234.00	239.00	244.00	250.00
106	238.00	244.00	249.00	254.00
108	243.00	248.00	254.00	259.00
110	247.00	253.00	258.00	264.00
112	252.00	258.00	263.00	269.00
114	256.00	262.00	268.00	274.00
116	261.00	267.00	273.00	278.00
118	265.00	272.00	277.00	283.00
120	270.00	276.00	282.00	288.00
122	274.00	281.00	287.00	293.00
124	279.00	285.00	291.00	298.00
126	283.00	290.00	296.00	302.00
128	288.00	294.00	301.00	307.00
130	292.00	299.00	305.00	312.00
132	297.00	304.00	310.00	317.00
134	301.00	308.00	315.00	322.00
136	306.00	313.00	320.00	326.00
138	310.00	317.00	324.00	331.00
140	315.00	322.00	329.00	336.00
142	319.00	327.00	334.00	341.00
144	324.00	331.00	339.00	346.00
146	328.00	336.00	343.00	350.00
148	333.00	340.00	348.00	355.00
150	337.00	345.00	352.00	360.00
152	342.00	350.00	357.00	405.00
154	346.00	354.00	402.00	411.00
156	351.00	359.00	407.00	416.00
158	355.00	404.00	413.00	421.00
160	360.00	409.00	418.00	427.00
162	405.00	414.00	423.00	432.00
164	410.00	419.00	428.00	437.00
166	415.00	424.00	433.00	443.00
168	420.00	429.00	439.00	448.00
170	425.00	434.00	444.00	453.00
172	430.00	440.00	449.00	459.00
174	435.00	445.00	454.00	464.00
176	440.00	450.00	460.00	469.00
178	445.00	455.00	465.00	475.00
180	450.00	460.00	470.00	480.00
182	500.00	511.00	523.00	758.00
184	506.00	517.00	751.00	767.00
186	511.00	523.00	759.00	775.00
188	517.00	751.00	767.00	783.00
190	522.00	759.00	775.00	792.00
192	720.00	920.00	940.00	960.00
194	909.00	930.00	950.00	970.00
196	919.00	939.00	960.00	980.00
198	928.00	949.00	970.00	990.00
200	937.00	958.00	979.00	1000.00
202	947.00	968.00	989.00	1010.00
204	956.00	977.00	999.00	1020.00
206	965.00	987.00	1009.00	1030.00
208	975.00	997.00	1018.00	1040.00
210	984.00	1006.00	1028.00	1050.00
212	994.00	1016.00	1038.00	1060.00

POLISHED PLATE GLASS.
Official List, July, 1895.

WIDTH.—Continued.

Length	90	92	94	96
214	1003.00	1025.00	1048.00	1070.00
216	1012.00	1035.00	1057.00	1080.00
218	1022.00	1045.00	1067.00	1090.00

WIDTH.

Length	98	100	102	104
98	240.00	------	------	------
100	245.00	250.00	------	------
102	250.00	255.00	260.00	------
104	255.00	260.00	265.00	270.00
106	260.00	265.00	270.00	276.00
108	265.00	270.00	275.00	281.00
110	269.00	275.00	280.00	286.00
112	274.00	280.00	285.00	291.00
114	279.00	285.00	290.00	296.00
116	284.00	290.00	296.00	302.00
118	289.00	295.00	301.00	307.00
120	294.00	300.00	306.00	312.00
122	299.00	305.00	311.00	317.00
124	304.00	310.00	316.00	322.00
126	309.00	315.00	321.00	328.00
128	314.00	320.00	326.00	333.00
130	318.00	325.00	331.00	338.00
132	323.00	330.00	337.00	343.00
134	328.00	335.00	342.00	348.00
136	333.00	340.00	347.00	354.00
138	338.00	345.00	352.00	359.00
140	343.00	350.00	357.00	404.00
142	348.00	355.00	402.00	410.00
144	353.00	360.00	408.00	416.00
146	358.00	406.00	414.00	422.00
148	403.00	411.00	419.00	428.00
150	408.00	417.00	425.00	433.00
152	414.00	422.00	431.00	439.00
154	419.00	428.00	436.00	445.00
156	425.00	433.00	442.00	451.00
158	430.00	439.00	448.00	456.00
160	436.00	444.00	453.00	462.00
162	441.00	450.00	459.00	468.00
164	446.00	456.00	465.00	474.00
166	452.00	461.00	470.00	480.00
168	457.00	467.00	476.00	758.00
170	463.00	472.00	753.00	767.00
172	468.00	478.00	761.00	776.00
174	474.00	755.00	770.00	785.00
176	479.00	764.00	779.00	794.00
178	757.00	773.00	788.00	803.00
180	766.00	781.00	797.00	812.00
182	774.00	790.00	806.00	986.00
184	783.00	799.00	977.00	997.00
186	791.00	807.00	988.00	1007.00
188	800.00	979.00	999.00	1018.00
190	808.00	990.00	1009.00	1029.00
192	980.00	1000.00	1020.00	1040.00
194	990.00	1010.00	1031.00	1051.00

WIDTH.—Continued.

Length	98	100	102	104
196	1000.00	1021.00	1041.00	1062.00
198	1011.00	1031.00	1052.00	1072.00
200	1021.00	1042.00	1062.00	1083.00
202	1031.00	1052.00	1073.00	1094.00
204	1041.00	1062.00	1084.00	1105.00
206	1051.00	1073.00	1094.00	1116.00
208	1062.00	1083.00	1105.00	1314.00
210	1072.00	1094.00	1116.00	1327.00
212	1082.00	1104.00	1314.00	1340.00
214	1092.00	1115.00	1326.00	1352.00
216	1102.00	1125.00	1339.00	1365.00
218	1113.00	1325.00	1351.00	1378.00

WIDTH.

Length	106	108	110	112
106	281.00	------	------	------
108	286.00	292.00	------	------
110	291.00	297.00	302.00	------
112	297.00	302.00	308.00	348.00
114	302.00	308.00	314.00	355.00
116	307.00	313.00	319.00	361.00
118	313.00	319.00	324.00	367.00
120	318.00	324.00	330.00	373.00
122	323.00	329.00	335.00	380.00
124	329.00	335.00	341.00	386.00
126	334.00	340.00	346.00	392.00
128	339.00	346.00	352.00	398.00
130	345.00	351.00	357.00	404.00
132	350.00	356.00	403.00	411.00
134	355.00	402.00	409.00	417.00
136	400.00	408.00	415.00	423.00
138	406.00	414.00	422.00	429.00
140	412.00	420.00	428.00	436.00
142	418.00	426.00	434.00	442.00
144	424.00	432.00	440.00	448.00
146	430.00	438.00	446.00	454.00
148	436.00	444.00	452.00	460.00
150	442.00	450.00	458.00	467.00
152	448.00	456.00	464.00	473.00
154	453.00	462.00	471.00	479.00
156	459.00	468.00	477.00	758.00
158	465.00	474.00	754.00	768.00
160	471.00	480.00	764.00	778.00
162	477.00	759.00	773.00	787.00
164	755.00	769.00	783.00	797.00
166	764.00	778.00	793.00	807.00
168	773.00	787.00	802.00	980.00
170	782.00	797.00	812.00	992.00
172	791.00	806.00	985.00	1003.00
174	801.00	979.00	997.00	1015.00
176	810.00	990.00	1008.00	1027.00
178	983.00	1001.00	1020.00	1038.00
180	994.00	1012.00	1031.00	1050.00
182	1005.00	1024.00	1043.00	1062.00
184	1016.00	1035.00	1054.00	1073.00

POLISHED PLATE GLASS.
Official List, July, 1895.

Length	WIDTH.—Continued.				Length	WIDTH.—Continued.			
	106	108	110	112		114	116	118	120
186	1027.00	1046.00	1066.00	1085.00	182	1081.00	1100.00	1119.00	1327.00
188	1038.00	1057.00	1077.00	1097.00	184	1092.00	1112.00	1319.00	1342.00
190	1049.00	1069.00	1089.00	1108.00	186	1104.00	1124.00	1334.00	1356.00
192	1060.00	1080.00	1100.00	1120.00	188	1116.00	1325.00	1348.00	1371.00
194	1071.00	1091.00	1111.00	1320.00	190	1316.00	1339.00	1362.00	1385.00
196	1082.00	1102.00	1123.00	1334.00	192	1330.00	1353.00	1376.00	1400.00
198	1093.00	1114.00	1323.00	1347.00	194	1344.00	1367.00	1391.00	1415.00
200	1104.00	1125.00	1337.00	1361.00	196	1358.00	1382.00	1405.00	1429.00
202	1115.00	1326.00	1350.00	1375.00	198	1372.00	1396.00	1419.00	1444.00
204	1314.00	1339.00	1364.00	1388.00	200	1385.00	1410.00	1434.00	1458.00
206	1327.00	1352.00	1377.00	1402.00	202	1399.00	1424.00	1448.00	1473.00
208	1340.00	1365.00	1390.00	1416.00	204	1413.00	1438.00	1463.00	1487.00
210	1353.00	1378.00	1404.00	1429.00	206	1427.00	1452.00	1477.00	1502.00
212	1365.00	1391.00	1417.00	1443.00	208	1441.00	1466.00	1491.00	1517.00
214	1378.00	1404.00	1430.00	1456.00	210	1455.00	1480.00	1506.00	1531.00
216	1391.00	1417.00	1444.00	1470.00	212	1469.00	1494.00	1520.00	2208.00
218	1404.00	1431.00	1457.00	1484.00	214	1482.00	1508.00	2192.00	2229.00
					216	1496.00	1522.00	2212.00	2250.00
					218	1510.00	2195.00	2233.00	2271.00

Length	WIDTH.				Length	WIDTH.			
	114	116	118	120		122	124	126	128
114	361.00	------	------	------	122	455.00	------	------	------
116	367.00	374.00	------	------	124	462.00	470.00	------	------
118	374.00	380.00	387.00	------	126	470.00	477.00	485.00	------
120	380.00	387.00	393.00	400.00	128	478.00	485.00	493.00	501.00
122	386.00	393.00	400.00	407.00	130	485.00	493.00	501.00	509.00
124	393.00	400.00	406.00	413.00	132	493.00	501.00	508.00	516.00
126	399.00	406.00	413.00	420.00	134	500.00	509.00	516.00	524.00
128	405.00	412.00	420.00	427.00	136	507.00	516.00	524.00	756.00
130	412.00	419.00	426.00	433.00	138	515.00	523.00	755.00	767.00
132	418.00	425.00	433.00	440.00	140	522.00	753.00	766.00	778.00
134	424.00	432.00	439.00	447.00	142	752.00	764.00	777.00	789.00
136	431.00	438.00	446.00	453.00	144	762.00	775.00	787.00	800.00
138	437.00	445.00	452.00	460.00	146	773.00	786.00	798.00	811.00
140	443.00	451.00	459.00	467.00	148	784.00	796.00	809.00	987.00
142	450.00	457.00	465.00	473.00	150	794.00	807.00	984.00	1000.00
144	456.00	464.00	472.00	480.00	152	805.00	982.00	997.00	1013.00
146	462.00	470.00	479.00	760.00	154	979.00	995.00	1011.00	1027.00
148	469.00	477.00	758.00	771.00	156	991.00	1007.00	1024.00	1040.00
150	475.00	755.00	768.00	781.00	158	1004.00	1020.00	1037.00	1053.00
152	752.00	765.00	778.00	792.00	160	1017.00	1033.00	1050.00	1067.00
154	762.00	775.00	789.00	802.00	162	1029.00	1046.00	1063.00	1080.00
156	772.00	785.00	799.00	812.00	164	1042.00	1059.00	1076.00	1093.00
158	782.00	795.00	809.00	987.00	166	1055.00	1072.00	1089.00	1107.00
160	792.00	805.00	983.00	1000.00	168	1067.00	1085.00	1102.00	1120.00
162	802.00	979.00	996.00	1012.00	170	1080.00	1098.00	1116.00	1322.00
164	812.00	991.00	1008.00	1025.00	172	1093.00	1111.00	1317.00	1338.00
166	986.00	1003.00	1020.00	1037.00	174	1106.00	1124.00	1332.00	1353.00
168	997.00	1015.00	1032.00	1050.00	176	1118.00	1326.00	1347.00	1369.00
170	1009.00	1027.00	1045.00	1062.00	178	1320.00	1341.00	1363.00	1384.00
172	1021.00	1039.00	1057.00	1075.00	180	1334.00	1356.00	1378.00	1400.00
174	1033.00	1051.00	1069.00	1087.00	182	1349.00	1371.00	1393.00	1416.00
176	1045.00	1063.00	1082.00	1100.00	184	1364.00	1386.00	1409.00	1431.00
178	1057.00	1075.00	1094.00	1112.00	186	1379.00	1401.00	1424.00	1447.00
180	1069.00	1087.00	1106.00	1125.00					

POLISHED PLATE GLASS.

Official List, July, 1895.

Length	WIDTH.—Continued.			
	122	124	126	128
188	1394.00	1417.00	1439.00	1462.00
1'0	1408.00	1432.00	1455.00	1478.00
192	1423.00	1447.00	1470.00	1493.00
194	1438.00	1462.00	1485.00	1509.00
196	1453.00	1477.00	1501.00	1524.00
198	1468.00	1492.00	1516.00	2200.00
200	1483.00	1507.00	1531.00	2222.00
202	1497.00	1522.00	2209.00	2244.00
204	1512.00	2196.00	2231.00	2267.00
206	1527.00	2217.00	2253.00	2289.00
208	2203.00	2239.00	2275.00	2311.00
210	2224.00	2260.00	2297.00	2333.00
212	2245.00	2282.00	2319.00	2356.00
214	2266.00	2303.00	2341.00	2378.00
216	2287.00	2325.00	2362.00	2400.00
218	2309.00	2347.00	2384.00	2422.00

Length	WIDTH.—Continued.			
	130	132	134	136
194	2189.00	2223.00	2257.00	2290 00
196	2212.00	2246.00	2280.00	2314.00
198	2234.00	2269.00	2303.00	2337.00
200	2257.00	2292.00	2326.00	2361.00
202	2280.00	2315.00	2350.00	2385.00
204	2302.00	2337.00	2373.00	2408.00
206	2325.00	2360.00	2396.00	2432.00
208	2347.00	2383.00	2419.00	2456.00
210	2370.00	2406.00	2443.00	2479.00
212	2392.00	2429.00	2466.00	------
214	2415.00	2452.00	2489.00	------
216	2437.00	2475.00	------	------
218	2460.00	2498.00		------

Length	WIDTH.			
	138	140	142	144
138	992.00	------	------	------
140	1006.00	1021.00	------	------
142	1021.00	1035.00	1400.00	------
144	1035.00	1050.00	1420.00	1440.00
146	1049.00	1065.00	1440.00	1460.00
148	1064.00	1079.00	1460.00	1480.00
150	1078.00	1094.00	1480 00	1500.00
152	1092.00	1108.00	1500.00	1520.00
154	1107.00	1123.00	1519.00	1540.00
156	1121.00	1327.00	1538.00	1560.00
158	1325.00	1344.00	1558.00	1580.00
160	1342.00	1361.00	1578.00	1600.00
162	1358.00	1378.00	1598.00	1620.00
164	1375.00	1395.00	1617.00	1640.00
166	1392.00	1412.00	1637.00	1660.00
168	1409.00	1429.00	1657.00	1680.00
170	1426.00	1446.00	1676.00	1700.00
172	1442.00	1463.00	1696.00	1720.00
174	1459.00	1480.00	1716.00	1740.00
176	1476.00	1497.00	1736.00	2200.00
178	1493.00	1514.00	2194.00	2225.00
180	1509.00	1531.00	2219.00	2250.00
182	1526.00	2212.00	2243.00	2275 00
184	2204.00	2236.00	2268.00	2300.00
186	2228.00	2260.00	2293.00	2325.00
188	2252.00	2285.00	2317.00	2350.00
190	2276.00	2309.00	2342.00	2375.00
192	2300.00	2333.00	2367.00	2400.00
194	2324.00	2358.00	2391.00	2425.00
196	2348.00	2382.00	2416.00	2450.00
198	2372.00	2406.00	2441.00	2475.00
200	2396.00	2431.00	2465.00	2500.00
202	2420.00	2455.00	2490.00	------
204	2444.00	2479.00	------	------
206	2468.00	------	------	------
208	2492.00	------	------	------

Length	WIDTH.			
	130	132	134	136
130	516.00	------	------	------
132	525.00	847.00	------	------
134	756.00	860.00	873.00	------
136	767.00	873.00	886.00	899.00
138	779.00	886.00	899.00	977.00
140	790.00	898.00	977.00	992.00
142	801.00	976.00	991.00	1006.00
144	812.00	990.00	1005.00	1020.00
146	989.00	1004.00	1019.00	1034.00
148	1002.00	1017.00	1033.00	1048.00
150	1016.00	1031.00	1047.00	1062.00
152	1029.00	1045.00	1061.00	1077.00
154	1043.00	1059.00	1075.00	1091.00
156	1056.00	1072.00	1089.00	1105.00
158	1070.00	1086.00	1103.00	1119.00
160	1083.00	1100.00	1117.00	1322.00
162	1097.00	1114.00	1319.00	1339.00
164	1110.00	1315.00	1335.00	1355.00
166	1124.00	1331.00	1352.00	1372.00
168	1327.00	1347.00	1368.00	1388.00
170	1343.00	1364.00	1384.00	1405.00
172	1359.00	1380.00	1400.00	1421.00
174	1374.00	1396.00	1417.00	1438.00
176	1390.00	1412.00	1433.00	1454.00
178	1406.00	1428.00	1449.00	1471.00
180	1422.00	1444.00	1466.00	1487.00
182	1438.00	1460.00	1482.00	1504.00
184	1453.00	1476.00	1498.00	1521.00
186	1469.00	1492.00	1514.00	2196.00
188	1485.00	1508.00	1531.00	2219.00
190	1501.00	1524.00	2210.00	2243.00
192	1517.00	2200.00	2233.00	2267.00

PATTERNS ENAMEL GLASS.

5016

5017

5018

5019

If semi-obscure D. S. Glass..24 cents per square foot
If full obscure D. S. Glass..30 cents per square foot

ART SAND BLAST GLASS.

5000

$1.00 per square foot.

5001

$1.00 per square foot.

5002

$1.00 per square foot.

5003

$1.00 per square foot.

ART SAND BLAST GLASS.

1425
$1.00 per square foot.

1426
$1.00 per square foot.

1427
$1.00 per square foot.

1428
$1.00 per square foot.

ART SAND BLAST GLASS.

5012

$1.00 per square foot.

5013

$1.00 per square foot.

5014

$1.00 per square foot.

5015

$1.00 per square foot.

ART SAND BLAST GLASS.

5004
$1.00 per square foot.

5005
$1.00 per square foot.

5006
$1.00 per square foot.

5007
$1.00 per square foot.

ART SAND BLAST GLASS.

5008
$1.00 per square foot.

5009
$1.00 per square foot.

5010
$1.00 per square foot.

5011
$1.00 per square foot.

ART SAND BLAST GLASS.

1423
$1.00 per square foot.

1424
$1.00 per square foot.

1446
$1.00 per square foot.

1447
$1.00 per square foot.

BEVELED MITRED MAZE.

1448
$1.05 per square foot.

1449
$1.10 per square foot.

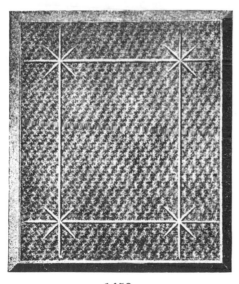

1450
$1.30 per square foot.

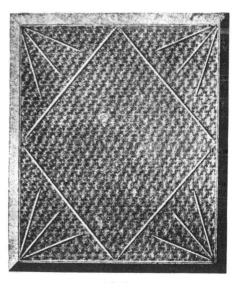

1451
$1.55 per square foot.

ARTISTIC CHIPPED.

Sand Blast Center.

1452
90 cents per square foot.

1453
90 cents per square foot.

1454
90 cents per square foot.

1455
90 cents per square foot.

FIGURED GLASS.

⅛-inch thick.

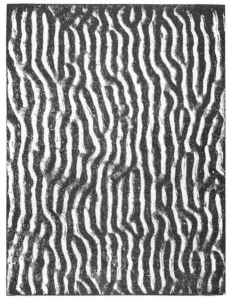

1456
20 cents per square foot cut to size.

1457
20 cents per square foot cut to size.

1458
20 cents per square foot cut to size.

1459
20 cents per square foot cut to size.

Special prices on large quantities.

UNIQUE CHIPPED.

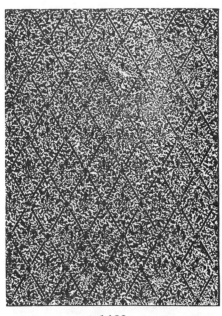

1460
50 cents per square foot cut to size.

1461
50 cents per square foot cut to size.

1462
50 cents per square foot cut to size.

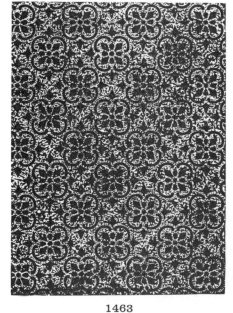

1463
50 cents per square foot cut to size.

All new handsome designs.

Wire Glass made by the new and improved process makes the very best skylights known, and is strongly recommended for the following reasons:

That having a fine wire imbedded midway between its surfaces, the glass will not drop out when, by any accident, it becomes cracked.

Wire Glass requires no netting as protection from falling fragments. It may crack but cannot fall down, and need not necessarily be replaced.

It is also practically Fire Proof, Burglar Proof and Stone Proof, and withal is easier cleaned than when netting is used.

Wire Glass is either Ribbed or Rough Rolled Glass, having wire netting imbedded in its centre during the process of manufacture.

Skylight Glass wired in this manner possesses the combined strength of the wire netting and the glass plate, and the wire being imbedded in the glass is protected from rust or corrosion.

WRITE FOR PRICES.

COLORED and FANCY GLASS.

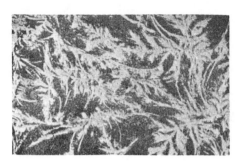

Chipped. Single Process.
22 cents per square foot.

Chipped. Double Process.
24 cents per square foot.

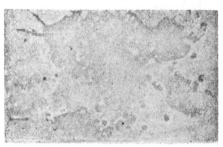

Rolled Cathedral.
24 cents per square foot.

Radiant.
30 cents per square foot.

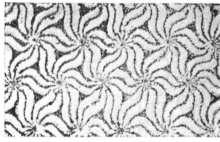

Florentine.
22 cents per square foot.

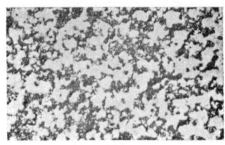

Moss.
30 cents per square foot.

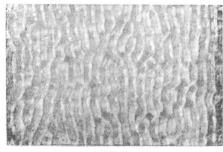

Riffled.
20 cents per square foot,

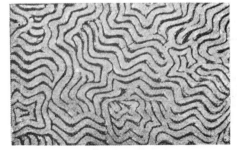

Irridescent.
24 cents per square foot.

Can furnish above in Clear or Assorted Colors.

GEOMETRIC CHIPPED and GROUND GLASS.

1400
90 cents per square foot.

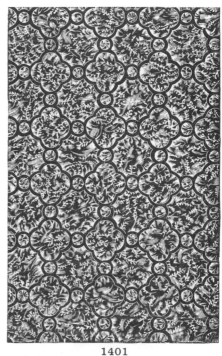

1401
90 cents per square foot.

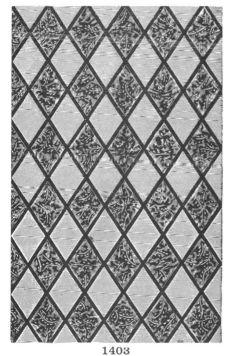

1403
95 cents per square foot.

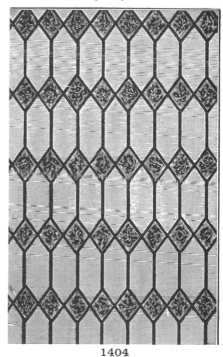

1404
95 cents per square foot.

SPECIAL GLASS DESIGNS.

5016
$1.00 per square foot.

Letters 15c
each,
net extra.

5017
$1.00 per square foot.

5018
$1.00 per square foot.

5019
$1.00 per square foot.

4052. $3.00 per square foot

4048. $1.25 per square foot.

4051. $2.50 per square foot.

LEADED ART GLASS.

4046. $2.00 per square foot.

4047. $2.00 per square foot.

4050. $1.75 per square foot.

4049. $1.25 per square foot.

4057. $1.80 per sq. ft.

4060. $2.75 per square foot.

4054. $1.60 per square foot.

4056. $1.75 per square foot

LEADED COLORED ART GLASS.

4059. $1.50 per sq. ft.

4053. $1.60 per square foot.

4055. $3.00 per square foot.

4058. $1.60 per square foot.

4066. $1.60 per square foot.

4067. $1.50 per square foot.

4068. $1.60 per square foot.

4069. $1.25 per square foot.

4065. $1.20 per sq ft.

4061. $1.75 per square foot.

4062. $1.40 per square foot.

4063. $1.25 per square foot.

4064. $1.60 per square foot.

LEADED COLORED ART GLASS.

4076. 90c per square foot.

4077. $1.00 per square foot

4078. 90c per square foot.

4079. 90c per square foot.

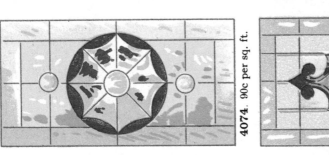

4074. 90c per sq. ft.

4075. $1.20 per sq. ft.

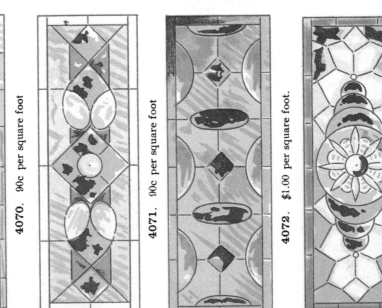

4070. 90c per square foot

4071. 90c per square foot

4072. $1.00 per square foot.

4073. $1.00 per square foot.

LEADED COLORED ART GLASS.

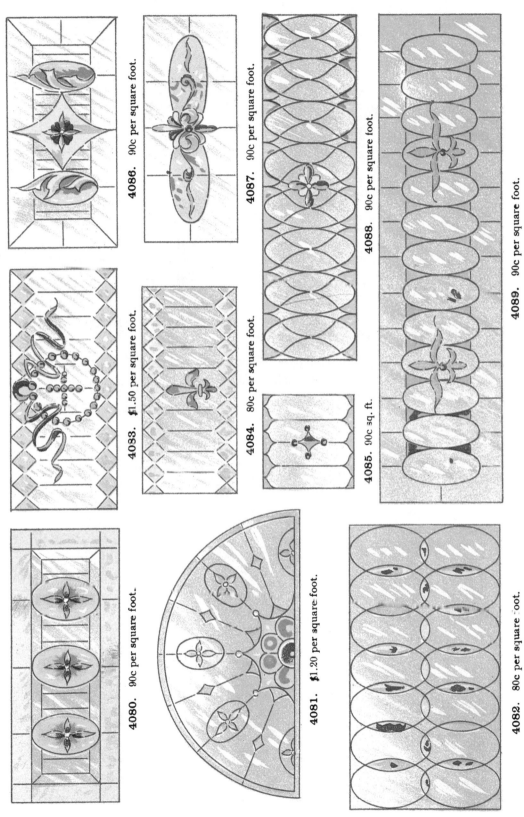

4086. 90c per square foot.

4087. 90c per square foot.

4088. 90c per square foot.

4089. 90c per square foot.

4083. $1.50 per square foot.

4084. 80c per square foot.

4085. 90c sq. ft.

4080. 90c per square foot.

4081. $1.20 per square foot.

4082. 80c per square foot.

LEADED COLORED ART GLASS.

4092. 90c per square foot.

4097. $1.75 per square foot.

4102. $1.40 per square foot.

4101. $1.50 sq. ft.

4091. $1.40 per square foot.

4100. $1.25 per square foot.

LEADED COLORED ART GLASS.

4090. $1.50 per square foot.

4094. $1.60 per square foot.

4095. $1.25 per square foot.

4099. $1.25 per square foot.

4093. $1.10 sq. ft.

4105. $2.00 per sq. ft.

4109. $1.30 per sq. ft.

4104. $2.00 per square foot.

4106. $1.70 per square foot.

4108. $1.50 per square foot.

LEADED COLORED ART GLASS.

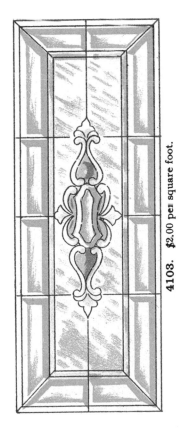

4103. $2.00 per square foot.

4107. $1.90 per square foot.

4116. $2.10 per square foot.

4114. 80c sq. ft.

4115. 80c sq. ft.

4111. $1.40 per square foot.

4113. $2.50 per square foot.

4118. $2.50 per square foot

LEADED COLORED ART GLASS.

4110. $1.60 per square foot.

4112. $1.00 per sq. ft.

4117. $2.00 per square foot.

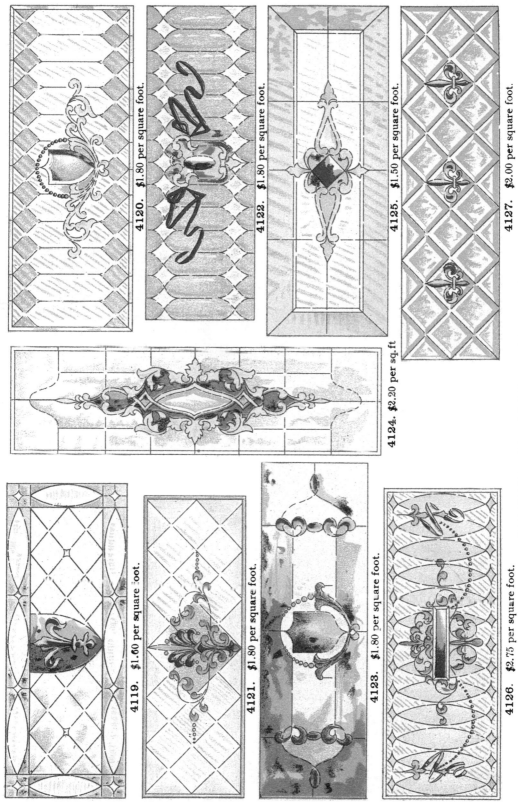

4120. $1.80 per square foot.

4122. $1.80 per square foot.

4125. $1.50 per square foot.

4127. $2.00 per square foot.

4124. $2.20 per sq. ft

4119. $1.60 per square foot.

4121. $1.80 per square foot.

4123. $1.80 per square foot.

4126. $2.75 per square foot.

LEADED COLORED ART GLASS.

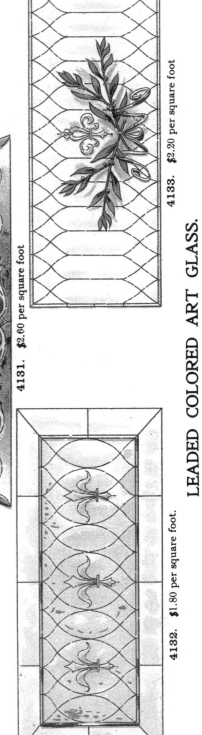

4130. $2.60 per square foot.

4133. $2.20 per square foot

4129. $2.00 per square foot.

4131. $2.60 per square foot

4128. $2.50 per square foot.

4132. $1.80 per square foot.

LEADED COLORED ART GLASS.

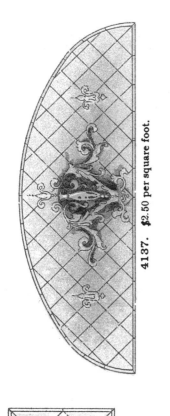

4137. $2.50 per square foot.

4138. $2.60 per square foot.

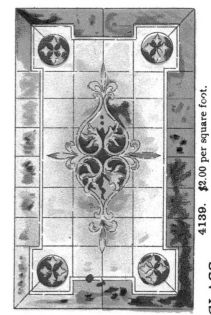

4139. $2.00 per square foot.

4184. $1.60 per square foot

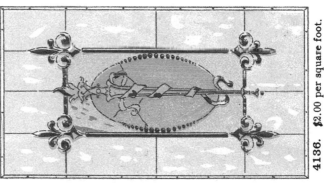

4136. $2.00 per square foot.

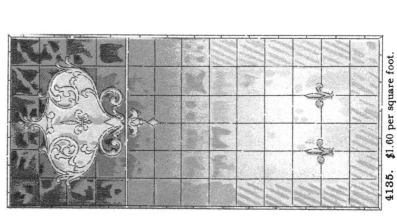

4135. $1.60 per square foot.

LEADED COLORED ART GLASS.

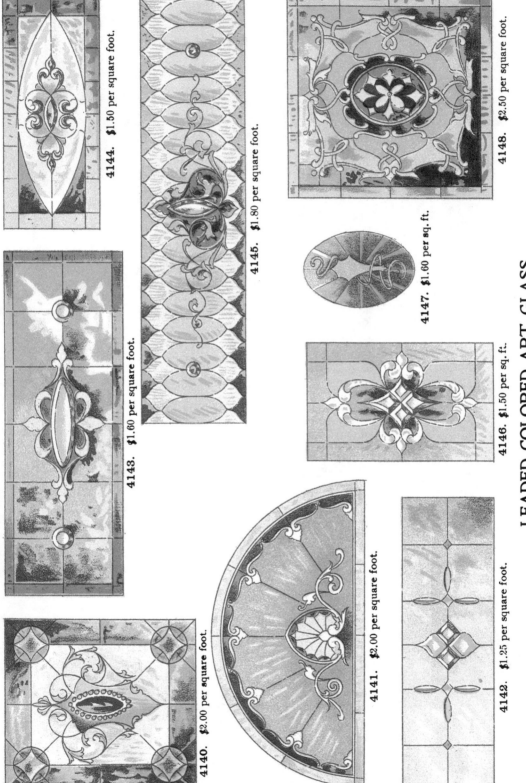

4144. $1.50 per square foot.

4145. $1.80 per square foot.

4148. $2.50 per square foot.

4147. $1.60 per sq. ft.

4143. $1.60 per square foot.

4146. $1.50 per sq. ft.

4141. $2.00 per square foot.

4140. $2.00 per square foot.

4142. $1.25 per square foot.

LEADED COLORED ART GLASS.

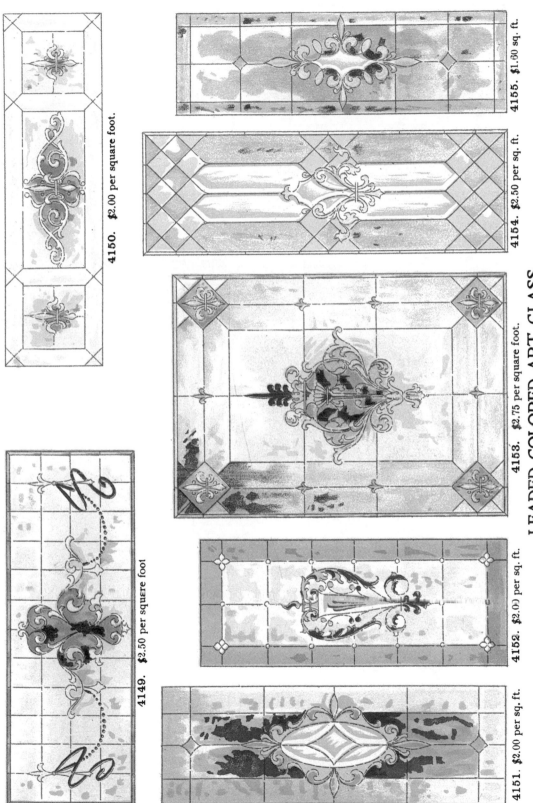

4150. $2.00 per square foot.

4155. $1.50 sq. ft.

4154. $2.50 per sq. ft.

4153. $2.75 per square foot.

4149. $2.50 per square foot

4152. $2.00 per sq. ft.

4151. $2.00 per sq. ft.

LEADED COLORED ART GLASS.

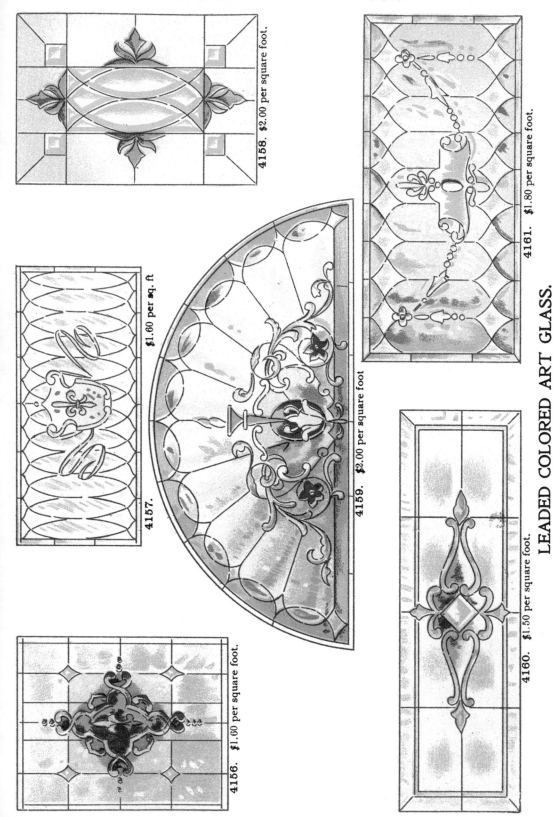

4158. $2.00 per square foot.

4161. $1.80 per square foot.

4157. $1.60 per sq. ft

4159. $2.00 per square foot

4156. $1.60 per square foot.

4160. $1.50 per square foot.

LEADED COLORED ART GLASS.

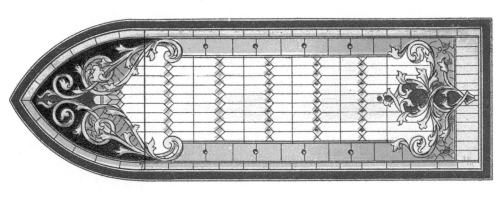

4165.

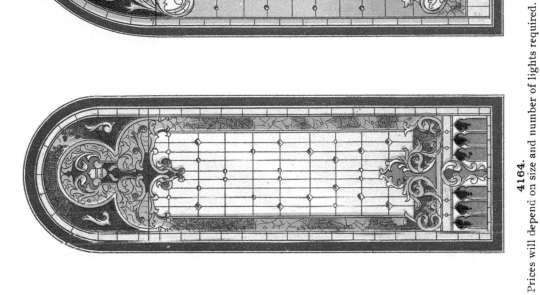

4164.

4163.

4162.

Prices will depend on size and number of lights required.

Special prices furnished on application.

LEADED COLORED ART GLASS for CHURCH WINDOWS.

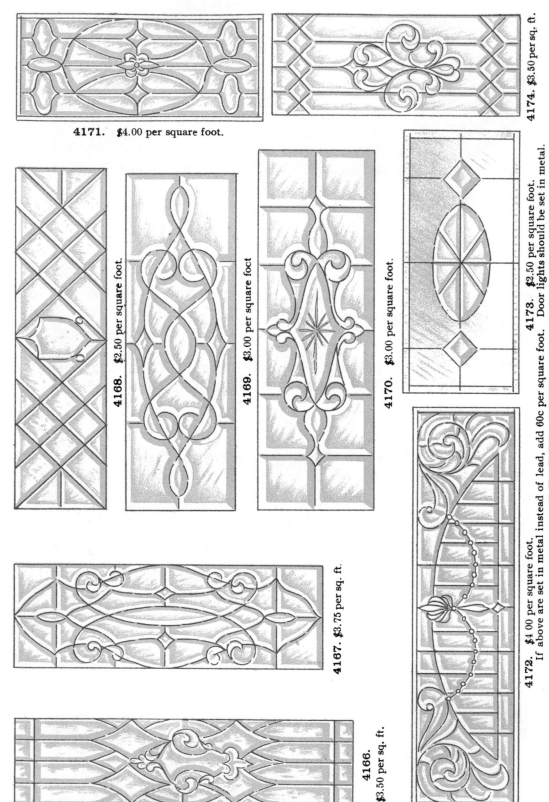

4171. $4.00 per square foot.

4174. $3.50 per sq. ft.

4168. $2.50 per square foot.

4169. $3.00 per square foot

4170. $3.00 per square foot.

4173. $2.50 per square foot.   Door lights should be set in metal.

LEADED BEVEL PLATE.

4167. $3.75 per sq. ft.

4172. $4.00 per square foot.
If above are set in metal instead of lead, add 60c per square foot.

4166.
$3.50 per sq. ft.

4177. $2.10 per sq. ft.

4182. $2.20 per sq. ft.

4176. $1.40 per sq. ft.

4181. $1.60 sq. ft.

4180. $2.50 per sq. ft.

4175. $2.20 per sq. ft.

4179. $1.60 per sq. ft.

4178. $2.50 per sq. ft.

MITRED BEVEL PLATE.

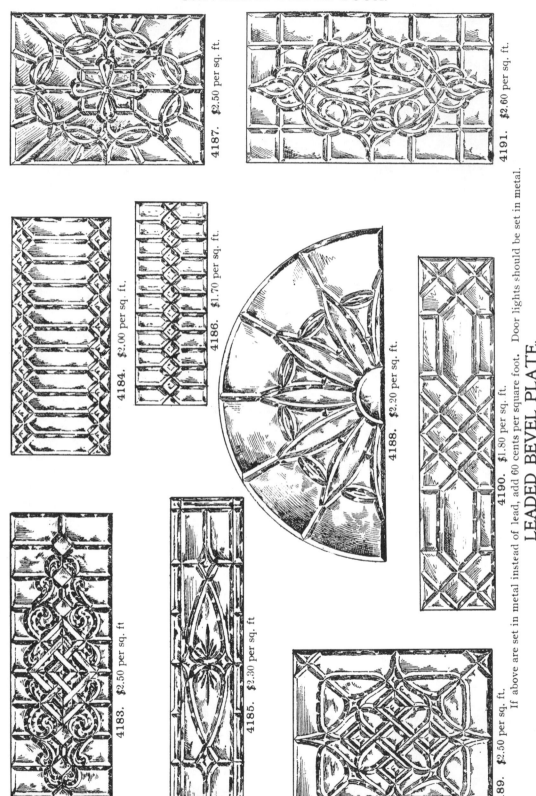

4187. $2.50 per sq. ft.

4191. $2.60 per sq. ft.

4184. $2.00 per sq. ft.

4186. $1.70 per sq. ft.

4188. $2.20 per sq. ft.

Door lights should be set in metal.

4190. $1.80 per sq. ft.

LEADED BEVEL PLATE.

4183. $2.50 per sq. ft

4185. $2.30 per sq. ft

If above are set in metal instead of lead, add 60 cents per square foot.

4189. $2.50 per sq. ft.

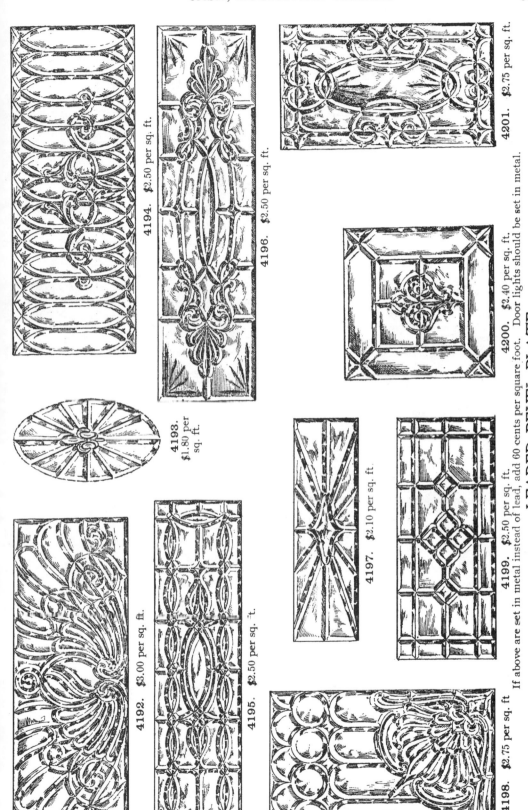

4194. $2.50 per sq. ft.

4196. $2.50 per sq. ft.

4201. $2.75 per sq. ft.

4193. $1.80 per sq. ft.

4200. $2.40 per sq. ft. Door lights should be set in metal.

4192. $3.00 per sq. ft.

4195. $2.50 per sq. ft.

4197. $2.10 per sq. ft.

4199. $2.50 per sq. ft. If above are set in metal instead of lead, add 60 cents per square foot. LEADED BEVEL PLATE.

4198. $2.75 per sq. ft.

4207. $2.75 per sq. ft.

4206. $3.00 per sq. ft. Door lights should be set in metal.

4203. $2.60 per sq. ft

4205. $2.20 per sq. ft.

4204. $3.20 per sq. ft.

4202. $3.10 per sq. ft,

If above are set in metal instead of lead, add 60 cents per square foot.

LEADED BEVEL PLATE.

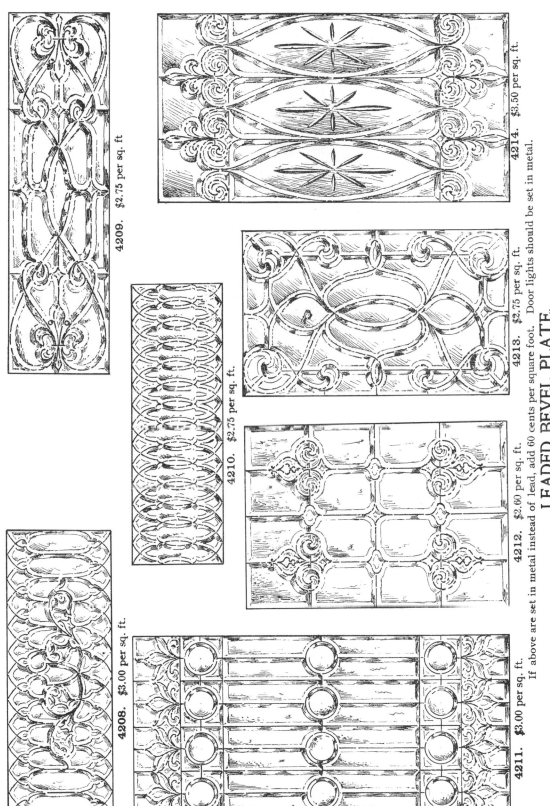

4209. $2.75 per sq. ft

4214. $3.50 per sq. ft.

4213. $2.75 per sq. ft.

4210. $2.75 per sq. ft.

4212. $2.60 per sq. ft.

4208. $3.00 per sq. ft.

4211. $3.00 per sq. ft.

Door lights should be set in metal.

If above are set in metal instead of lead, add 60 cents per square foot.

LEADED BEVEL PLATE.

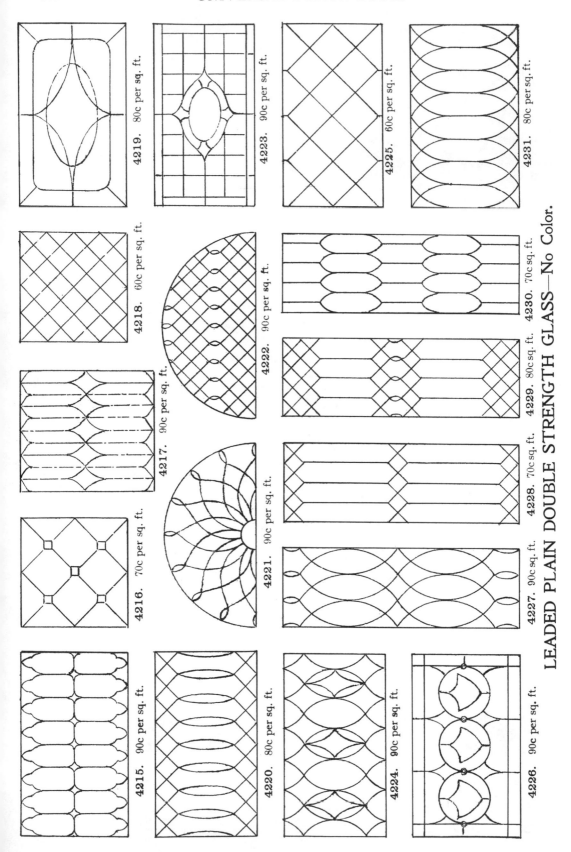

4219. 80c per sq. ft.

4223. 90c per sq. ft.

4225. 60c per sq. ft.

4231. 80c per sq. ft.

4218. 60c per sq. ft.

4222. 90c per sq. ft.

4230. 70c sq. ft.

4217. 90c per sq. ft.

4229. 80c sq. ft.

4228. 70c sq. ft.

4216. 70c per sq. ft.

4221. 90c per sq. ft.

4227. 90c sq. ft.

4215. 90c per sq. ft.

4220. 80c per sq. ft.

4224. 80c per sq. ft.

4226. 90c per sq. ft.

LEADED PLAIN DOUBLE STRENGTH GLASS—No Color.

GLASS MEASUREMENT.

A table giving the number of square feet in glass of given dimensions.

Length	WIDTH of GLASS.														
	6	7	8	9	10	12	14	16	18	20	22	24	26	28	30
20	0⅚	1	1 1/12	1¼	1 5/12	1⅔	1 11/12	2¼	2½	2¾	----	----	----	----	----
22	0 11/12	1 1/12	1¼	1 5/12	1½	1⅚	2 1/6	2 5/12	2¾	3 1/12	3⅓	----	----	----	----
24	1	1 1/6	1⅓	1½	1⅔	2	2⅓	2⅔	3	3⅓	3⅔	4	----	----	----
26	1 1/12	1¼	1 5/12	1⅔	1⅚	2 1/6	2½	2 11/12	3¼	3 7/12	4	4⅓	4⅔	----	----
28	1 1/6	1⅓	1 7/12	1¾	1 11/12	2⅓	2¾	3 1/12	3½	3 11/12	4¼	4⅔	5 1/12	5 5/12	----
30	1¼	1½	1⅔	1 11/12	2 1/12	2½	2 11/12	3⅓	3¾	4 1/6	4 7/12	5	5 5/12	5⅚	6¼
32	1⅓	1 7/12	1¾	2	2¼	2⅔	3 1/12	3 7/12	4	4 5/12	4 11/12	5⅓	5¾	6¼	6⅔
34	1 5/12	1⅔	1 11/12	2 1/6	2⅓	2⅚	3⅓	3¾	4¼	4¾	5 1/6	5⅔	6 1/6	6 7/12	7 1/12
36	1½	1¾	2	2¼	2½	3	3½	4	4½	5	5½	6	6½	7	7½
38	1 7/12	1⅚	2 1/12	2 5/12	2⅔	3 1/6	3⅔	4¼	4¾	5¼	5⅚	6⅓	6⅚	7 5/12	7 11/12
40	1⅔	1 11/12	2¼	2½	2¾	3⅓	3 11/12	4 5/12	5	5 7/12	6 1/12	6⅔	7¼	7¾	8⅓
42	1¾	2 1/12	2⅓	2⅔	2 11/12	3½	4 1/12	4⅔	5¼	5⅚	6 5/12	7	7 7/12	8 1/6	8¾
44	1⅚	2 1/6	2 5/12	2¾	3 1/12	3⅔	4¼	4 11/12	5½	6 1/12	6¾	7⅓	7 11/12	8 7/12	9 1/6
46	1 11/12	2¼	2 7/12	2 11/12	3 1/6	3⅚	4½	5 1/12	5¾	6 5/12	7	7⅔	8⅓	8 11/12	9 7/12
48	2	2⅓	2⅔	3	3⅓	4	4⅔	5⅓	6	6⅔	7⅓	8	8⅔	9⅓	10
50	2 1/12	2 5/12	2¾	3 1/6	3½	4 1/6	4⅚	5 7/12	6¼	6 11/12	7⅔	8⅓	9	9¾	10 5/12
52	2 1/6	2½	2 11/12	3¼	3 7/12	4⅓	5 1/12	5¾	6½	7¼	7 11/12	8⅔	9 5/12	10 1/12	10⅚
54	2¼	2⅔	3	3 5/12	3¾	4½	5¼	6	6¾	7½	8¼	9	9¾	10½	11¼
56	2⅓	2¾	3 1/12	3½	3 11/12	4⅔	5 5/12	6¼	7	7¾	8 7/12	9⅓	10 1/12	10 11/12	11⅔
58	2 5/12	2⅚	3¼	3⅔	4	4⅚	5⅔	6 5/12	7¼	8 1/12	8⅚	9⅔	10½	11¼	12 1/12
60	2½	2 11/12	3⅓	3¾	4 1/6	5	5⅚	6⅔	7½	8⅓	9 1/6	10	10⅚	11⅔	12½
62	2 7/12	3	3 5/12	3 11/12	4⅓	5 1/6	6	6 11/12	7¾	8 7/12	9½	10⅓	11 1/6	12 1/12	12 11/12
64	2⅔	3 1/12	3 7/12	4	4 5/12	5⅓	6¼	7 1/12	8	8 11/12	9¾	10⅔	11 7/12	12 5/12	13⅓
66	2¾	3¼	3⅔	4 1/6	4 7/12	5½	6 5/12	7⅓	8¼	9 1/6	10 1/12	11	11 11/12	12⅚	13¾
68	2⅚	3⅓	3¾	4¼	4¾	5⅔	6 7/12	7 7/12	8½	9 5/12	10 5/12	11⅓	12¼	13¼	14 1/6
70	2 11/12	3 5/12	3 11/12	4 5/12	4⅚	5⅚	6⅚	7¾	8¾	9¾	10⅔	11⅔	12⅔	13 7/12	14 7/12
72	3	3½	4	4½	5	6	7	8	9	10	11	12	13	14	15

OFFICIAL BENDING LIST.

(Adopted March 1st, 1900.)

PLATE AND WINDOW GLASS, NOT EXCEEDING QUARTER CIRCLE.

PLATE GLASS.

	Sq. ft.
Plates where length and width added are less than 76 in. say 34x40	$0.60
Plate of 76 in. or more, but less than 90 united in..	.75
" 90 " " " " 100 " ..	1 00
" 100 " " " " 110 " ..	1.50
" 110 " " " " 120 " ..	2.00
" 120 " " " " 140 " ..	2.50

	Sq. ft.
Plates of 140 in. or more, but less than 160 united in..	3.00
" 160 " " " " 180 " ..	3.50
" 180 " " " " 200 " ..	4.00
" 200 " " " " 210 " ..	4.50
" 210 " " " " 220 " ..	5 00
" 220 " " " " 230 " ..	5 50
" 230 " " " " 240 " ..	6.00

Minimum charge for bending plate is $1.00, irrespective of size.

WINDOW GLASS.

	Sq. ft.
Lights of less than 60 united in.	$0.25
" 60 in. or more, but less than 70 united in..	.30
" 70 " " " " 80 " ..	.40

	Sq. ft.
Lights of 80 in. or more, but less than 90 united in.	$0.50
" 90 " " " " 100 "	.60
" 100 " " " " 110 "	.90

Minimum charge for bending light is 50c, irrespective of size.

Beveled glass, 25 per cent additional and at owner's risk.

Bending on the length where it exceeds the width by more than 6 in., 25 per cent additional.

Odd or fractional parts of inches charged as even inches of next larger size. Sizes containing less than one square foot will be charged as a full foot, and in narrow widths no size will be figured as less than 12 inches wide.

Above prices are for bending only. Boxing extra.

TABLE SHOWING NUMBER OF SQUARE FEET IN DOORS.

HEIGHT / WIDTH	6^8	6^{10}	7	7^2	7^4	7^6	7^8	7^{10}	8	8^2	8^4	8^6	8^8	8^{10}	9
2^2	----	----	----	----	----	----	----	----	17½	18	18	18½	19	19	19½
2^4	----	----	----	----	----	17½	18	18½	19	19	19½	20	20½	21	21
2^6	----	----	17½	18	18½	19	19½	20	20	20½	21	21½	22	22½	22½
2^8	18	18½	19	19½	19½	20	20½	21	21½	22	22½	23	23½	23½	24
2^{10}	19	19½	20	20½	21	21½	22	22½	23	23½	24	24½	24½	25	25½
3	20	20½	21	21½	22	22½	23	23½	24	24½	25	25½	26	26½	27
3^2	21½	22	22½	23	23½	24	24½	25	25½	26	26½	27	27½	28	28½
3^4	22½	23	23½	24	24½	25	25½	26	27	27½	28	28½	29	29½	30
3^6	23½	24	24½	25½	26	26½	27	27½	28	29	29½	30	30½	31	31½
3^8	24½	25	26	26½	27	27½	28½	29	29½	30	30½	31½	32	32½	33
3^{10}	25½	26½	27	27½	28½	29	29½	30	31	31½	32	33	33½	34	34½
4	27	27½	28	29	29½	30	31	31½	32	33	33½	34	35	35½	36
4^2	28	28½	29½	30	30½	31½	32	33	33½	34	35	35½	36½	37	37½
4^4	29	30	30½	31	32	32½	33½	34	35	35½	36½	37	37½	38½	39
4^6	30	31	31½	32½	33	34	34½	35½	36	37	37½	38½	39	40	40½
4^8	31½	32	33	33½	34½	35	36	36½	37½	38½	39	40	40½	41½	42
4^{10}	32½	33	34	35	35½	36½	37	38	39	39½	40½	41½	42	43	43½
5	33½	34½	35	36	37	37½	38½	39½	40	41	42	42½	43½	44½	45
5^2	34½	35½	36½	37	38	39	40	40½	41½	42½	43	44	45	46	46½
5^4	35½	36½	37½	38½	39½	40	41	42	43	43½	44½	45½	46½	47½	48
5^6	37	38	38½	39½	40½	41½	42½	43½	44	45	46	47	48	49	49½
5^8	38	39	40	41	41½	42½	43½	44½	45½	46½	47½	48½	49½	50	51
5^{10}	39	40	41	42	43	44	45	46	47	48	49	50	50½	51½	52½
6	40	41	42	43	44	45	46	47	48	49	50	51	52	53	54
6^2	41½	42½	43½	44½	45½	46½	47½	48½	49½	50½	51½	52½	53½	54½	55½
6^4	42½	43½	44½	45½	46½	47½	48½	50	51	52	53	54	55	56	57
6^6	43½	44½	45½	47	48	49	50	51	52	53½	54½	55½	56½	57½	58½
6^8	44½	45½	47	48	49	50	51½	52½	53½	54½	55½	57	58	59	60
6^{10}	45½	47	48	49	50½	51½	52½	53½	55	56	57	58½	59½	60½	61½
7	47	48	49	50½	51½	52½	54	55	56	57½	58½	59½	61	62	63
7^2	48	49	50½	51½	52½	54	55	56½	57½	58½	60	61	62½	63½	64½
7^4	49	50½	51½	52½	54	55	56½	57½	59	60	61½	62½	63½	65	66
7^6	50	51½	52½	54	55	56½	57½	59	60	61½	62½	64	65	66½	67½
7^8	51½	52½	54	55	56½	57½	59	60	61½	63	64	65	66½	68	69
7^{10}	52½	53½	55	56½	57½	59	60	61½	63	64	65½	67	68	69½	70½
8	53½	55	56	57½	59	60	61½	63	64	65½	67	68	69½	71	72

As labor is the principal item in cost of doors we figure no door less than 17½ square feet.

OFFICIAL

MOULDING BOOK

(ILLUSTRATED)

SHOWING FULL FINISHED SIZE OF

MOULDINGS

WITH EXACT SIZE AND LIST PRICE PER ONE HUNDRED
LINEAL FEET MARKED ON EACH.

ADOPTED MARCH 1, 1897.

REVISED MAY 2, 1901.

PUBLISHED BY

SHATTOCK & McKAY,

180-182 MONROE STREET,

CHICAGO.

List Prices as given are per 100 lineal feet.

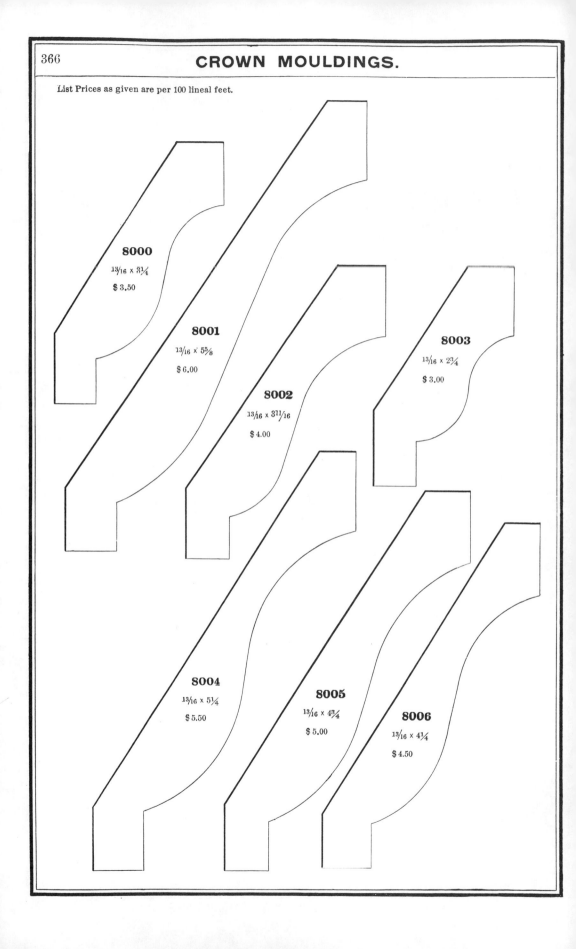

8000

$^{13}/_{16}$ x $3^{1}/_{4}$

$ 3.50

8001

$^{13}/_{16}$ x $5^{5}/_{8}$

$ 6.00

8002

$^{13}/_{16}$ x $3^{11}/_{16}$

$ 4.00

8003

$^{13}/_{16}$ x $2^{3}/_{4}$

$ 3.00

8004

$^{13}/_{16}$ x $5^{1}/_{4}$

$ 5.50

8005

$^{13}/_{16}$ x $4^{3}/_{4}$

$ 5.00

8006

$^{13}/_{16}$ x $4^{1}/_{4}$

$ 4.50

List Prices as given are per 100 lineal feet.

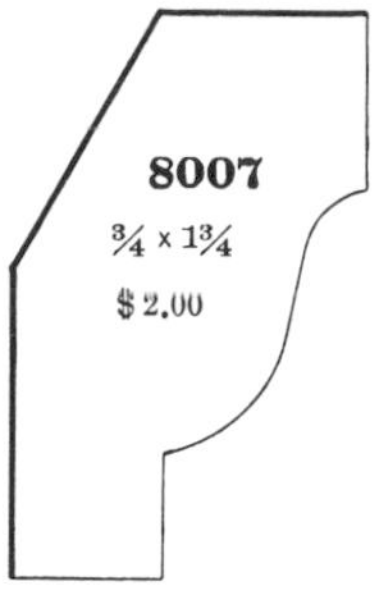

8007
¾ × 1¾
$ 2.00

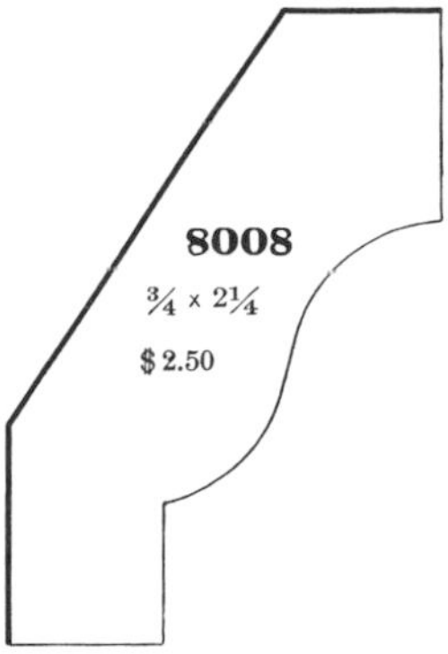

8008
¾ × 2¼
$ 2.50

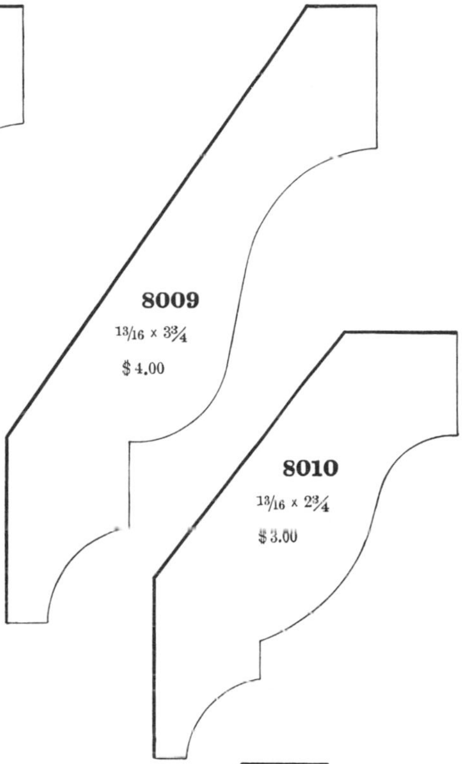

8009
1³⁄₁₆ × 3¾
$ 4.00

8011
¾ × 2¼
$ 2.50

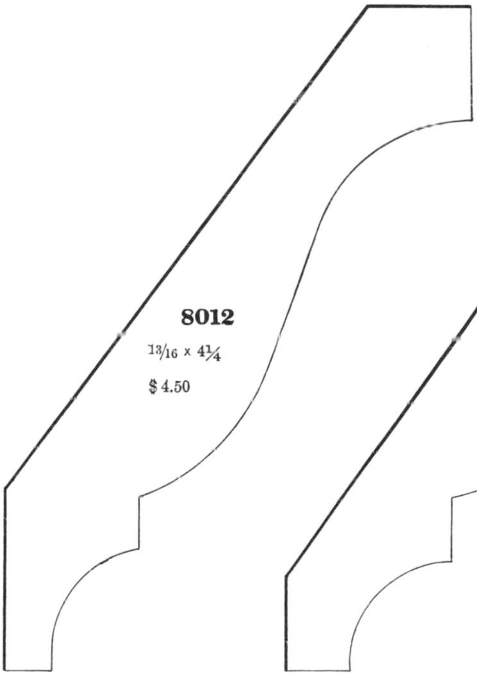

8010
1³⁄₁₆ × 2¾
$ 3.00

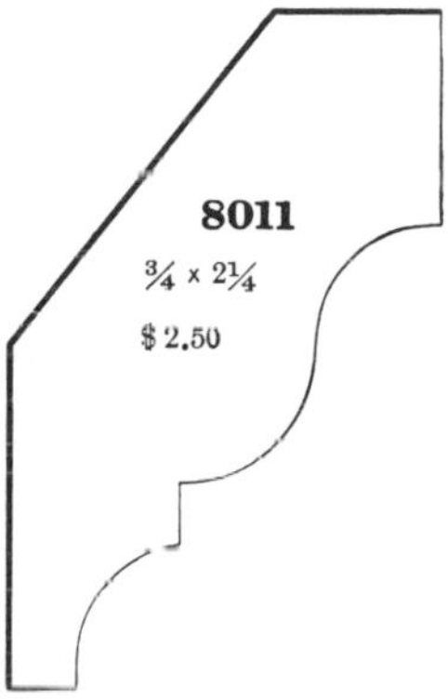

8012
1³⁄₁₆ × 4¼
$ 4.50

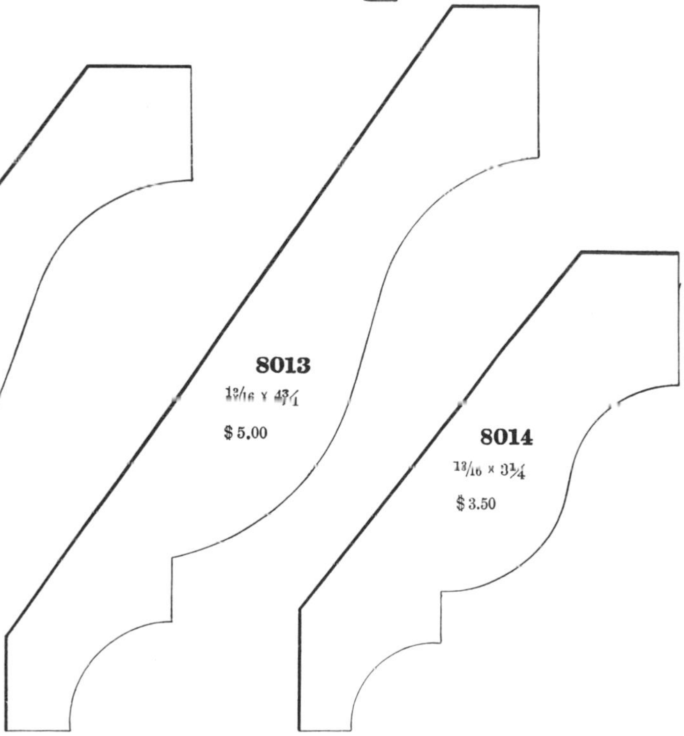

8013
1³⁄₁₆ × 4¾
$ 5.00

8014
1³⁄₁₆ × 3¼
$ 3.50

CROWN MOULDINGS.

List Prices as given are per 100 lineal feet.

8015
13/16 x 1
$ 1.15

8016
13/16 x 1¾
$ 2.00

8017
13/16 x 1½
$ 1.65

8018
¾ x 2¼
$ 2.50

8019
13/16 x 2¾
$ 3.00

8020
13/16 x 3¼
$ 3.50

8021
13/16 x 4¼
$ 4.50

8022
13/16 x 4¾
$ 5.00

8023
13/16 x 3¾
$ 4.00

SPRUNG COVE AND BED MOULDINGS.

List Prices as given are per 100 lineal feet.

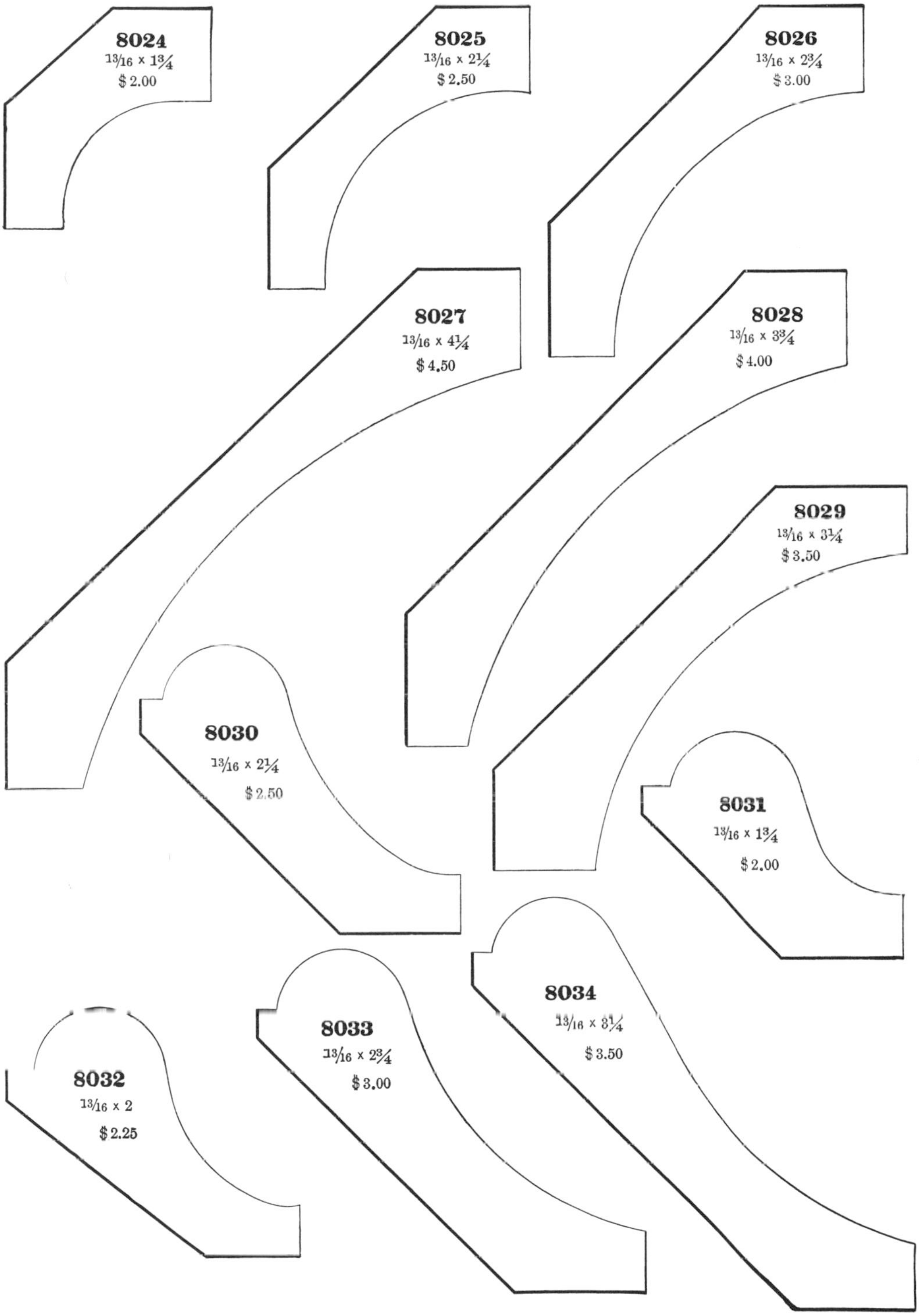

8024
13/16 x 1 3/4
$ 2.00
8025
13/16 x 2 1/4
$ 2.50
8026
13/16 x 2 3/4
$ 3.00
8027
13/16 x 4 1/4
$ 4.50
8028
13/16 x 3 3/4
$ 4.00
8029
13/16 x 3 1/4
$ 3.50
8030
13/16 x 2 1/4
$ 2.50
8031
13/16 x 1 3/4
$ 2.00
8032
13/16 x 2
$ 2.25
8033
13/16 x 2 3/4
$ 3.00
8034
13/16 x 3 1/4
$ 3.50

BED MOULDINGS.

List Prices as given are per 100 lineal feet.

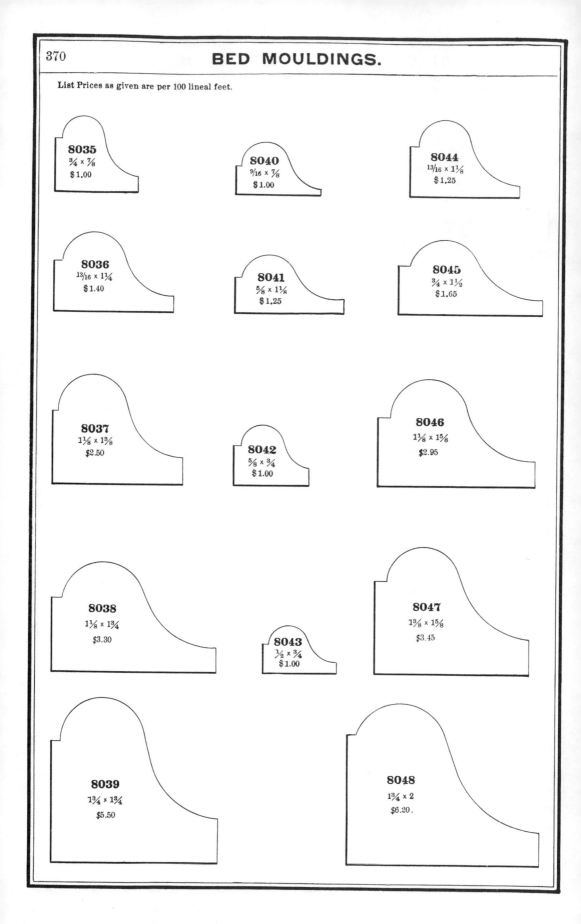

8035
¾ × ⅞
$1.00

8040
⁹⁄₁₆ × ⅞
$1.00

8044
¹³⁄₁₆ × 1⅛
$1.25

8036
¹³⁄₁₆ × 1¼
$1.40

8041
⅝ × 1⅛
$1.25

8045
¾ × 1½
$1.65

8037
1⅛ × 1⅜
$2.50

8042
⅝ × ¾
$1.00

8046
1⅛ × 1⅝
$2.95

8038
1⅛ × 1¾
$3.30

8043
½ × ¾
$1.00

8047
1⅜ × 1⅝
$3.45

8039
1¾ × 1¾
$5.50

8048
1¾ × 2
$6.20 .

List Prices as given are per 100 lineal feet.

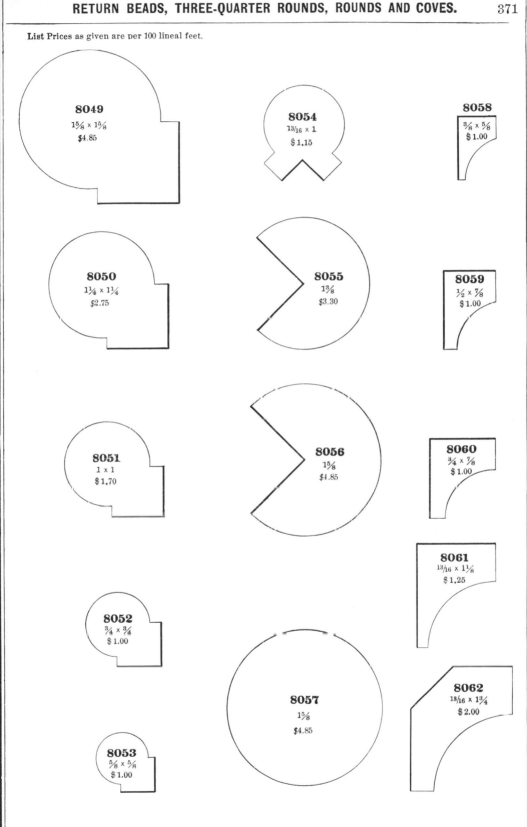

8049
1⅝ × 1⅝
$4.85

8054
13/16 × 1
$1.15

8058
⅜ × ⅝
$1.00

8050
1¼ × 1¼
$2.75

8055
1⅜
$3.30

8059
½ × ⅞
$1.00

8051
1 × 1
$1.70

8056
1⅝
$4.85

8060
¾ × ⅞
$1.00

8061
13/16 × 1⅛
$1.25

8052
¾ × ¾
$1.00

8062
13/16 × 1¾
$2.00

8057
1⅝
$4.85

8053
⅝ × ⅝
$1.00

List Prices as given are per 100 lineal feet.

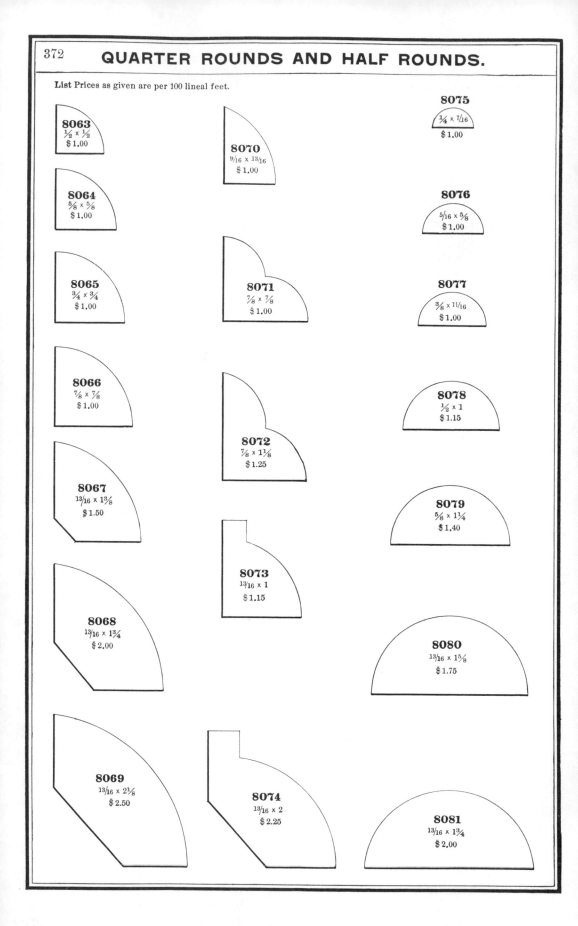

8063
½ x ½
$1.00

8064
⅝ x ⅝
$1.00

8065
¾ x ¾
$1.00

8066
⅞ x ⅞
$1.00

8067
13/16 x 1⅜
$1.50

8068
13/16 x 1¾
$2.00

8069
13/16 x 2⅛
$2.50

8070
9/16 x 13/16
$1.00

8071
⅞ x ⅞
$1.00

8072
⅞ x 1⅛
$1.25

8073
13/16 x 1
$1.15

8074
13/16 x 2
$2.25

8075
¼ x 7/16
$1.00

8076
5/16 x ⅝
$1.00

8077
⅜ x 11/16
$1.00

8078
½ x 1
$1.15

8079
⅝ x 1¼
$1.40

8080
13/16 x 1⅝
$1.75

8081
13/16 x 1¾
$2.00

List Prices as given are per 100 lineal feet.

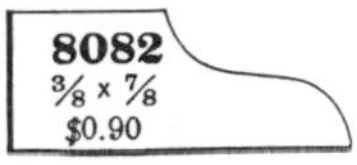

8082
3/8 × 7/8
$0.90

8092
1/2 × 2 1/2
$ 2.25

8083
3/8 × 1 1/8
$1.00

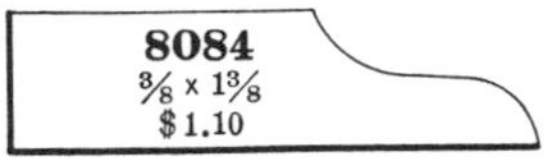

8093
1/2 × 2 1/4
$ 2.00

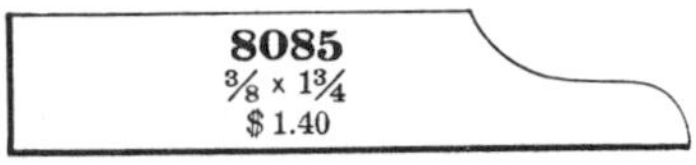

8084
3/8 × 1 3/8
$1.10

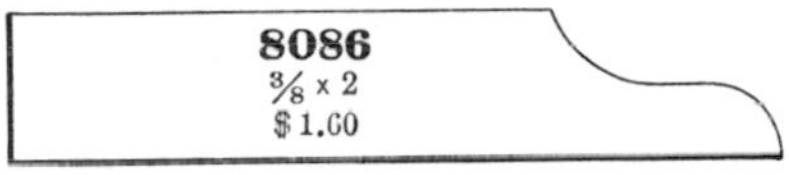

8094
1/2 × 2
$ 1.80

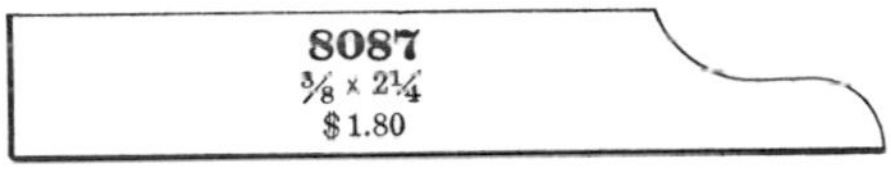

8085
3/8 × 1 3/4
$ 1.40

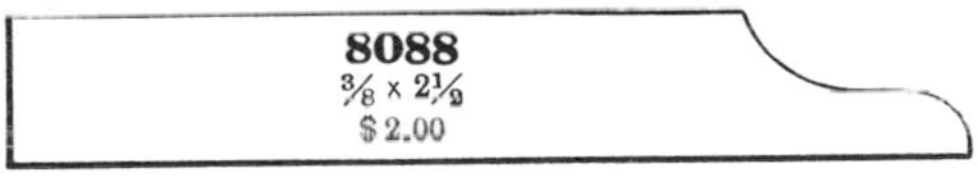

8095
1/2 × 1 3/4
$ 1.60

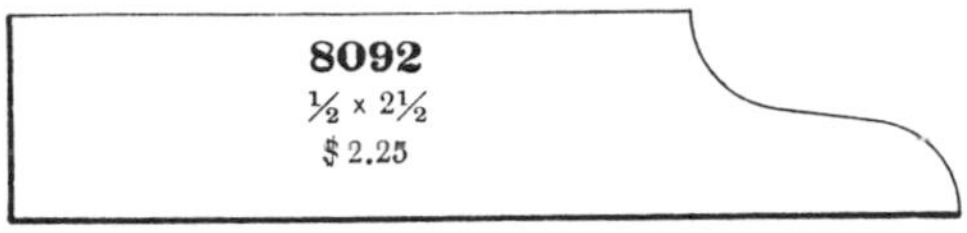

8086
3/8 × 2
$ 1.60

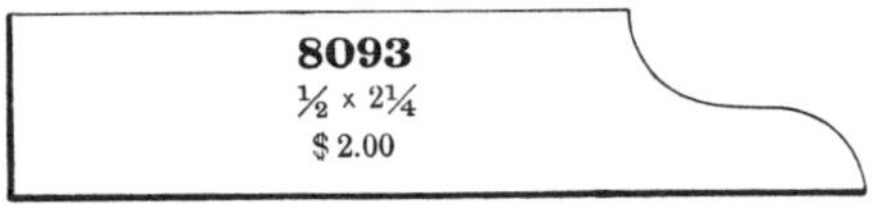

8096
1/2 × 1 3/8
$ 1.20

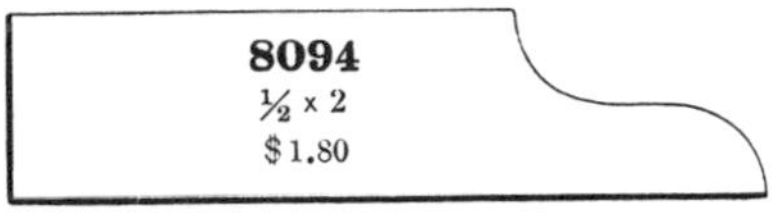

8087
3/8 × 2 1/4
$ 1.80

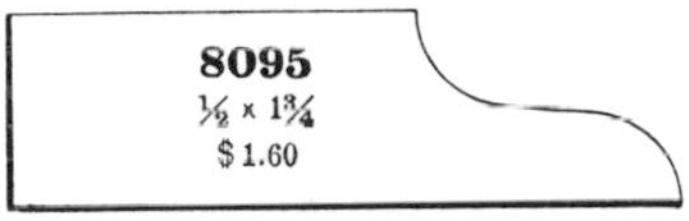

8097
1/2 × 1 1/8
$1.10

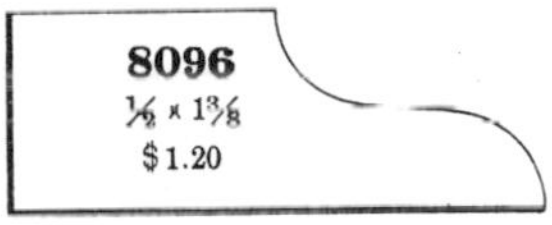

8088
3/8 × 2 1/2
$ 2.00

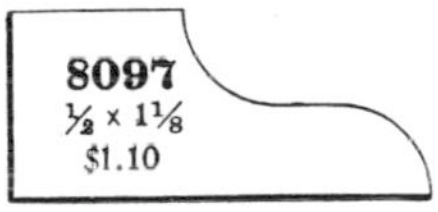

8089
1/2 × 1 1/8
$ 1.15

8098
1/2 × 1 3/8
$ 1.35

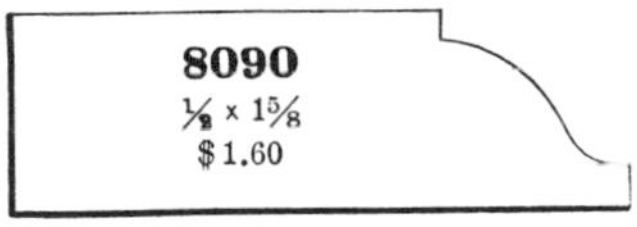

8090
1/2 × 1 5/8
$ 1.60

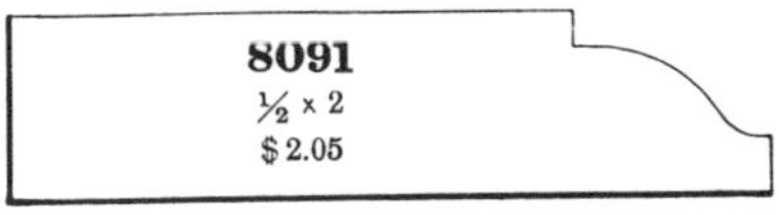

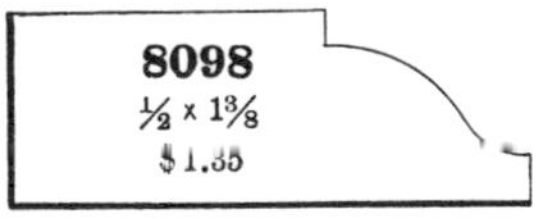

8099
1/2 × 1 3/4
$ 1.80

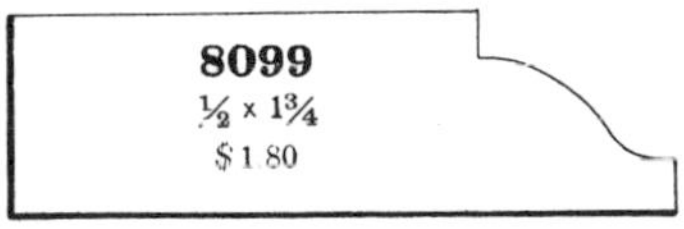

8091
1/2 × 2
$ 2.05

8100
1/2 × 2 1/4
$ 2.25

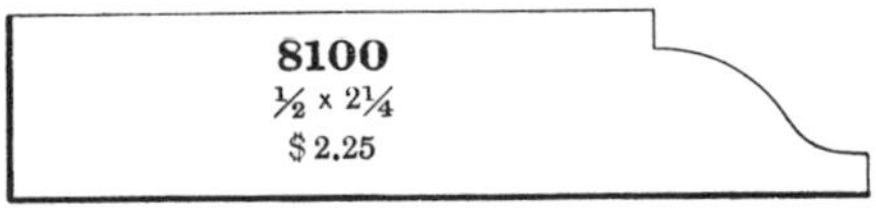

P. G. AND BEAD STOPS.

List Prices as given are per 100 lineal feet.

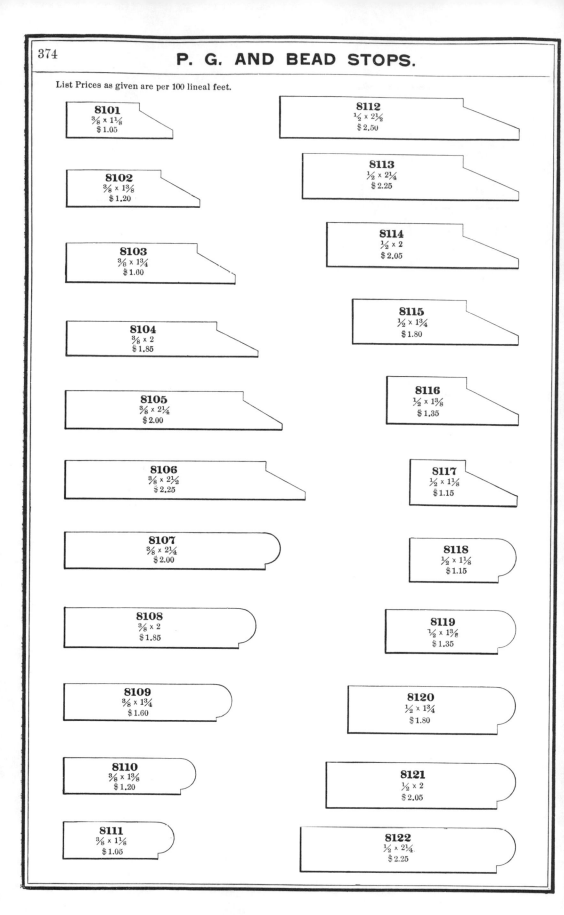

8101
⅜ x 1⅛
$1.05

8102
⅜ x 1⅜
$1.20

8103
⅜ x 1¾
$1.00

8104
⅜ x 2
$1.85

8105
⅜ x 2¼
$2.00

8106
⅜ x 2½
$2.25

8107
⅜ x 2¼
$2.00

8108
⅜ x 2
$1.85

8109
⅜ x 1¾
$1.60

8110
⅜ x 1⅜
$1.20

8111
⅜ x 1⅛
$1.05

8112
½ x 2½
$2.50

8113
½ x 2¼
$2.25

8114
½ x 2
$2.05

8115
½ x 1¾
$1.80

8116
½ x 1⅜
$1.35

8117
½ x 1⅛
$1.15

8118
½ x 1⅛
$1.15

8119
½ x 1⅜
$1.35

8120
½ x 1¾
$1.80

8121
½ x 2
$2.05

8122
½ x 2¼
$2.25

List Prices as given are per 100 lineal feet.

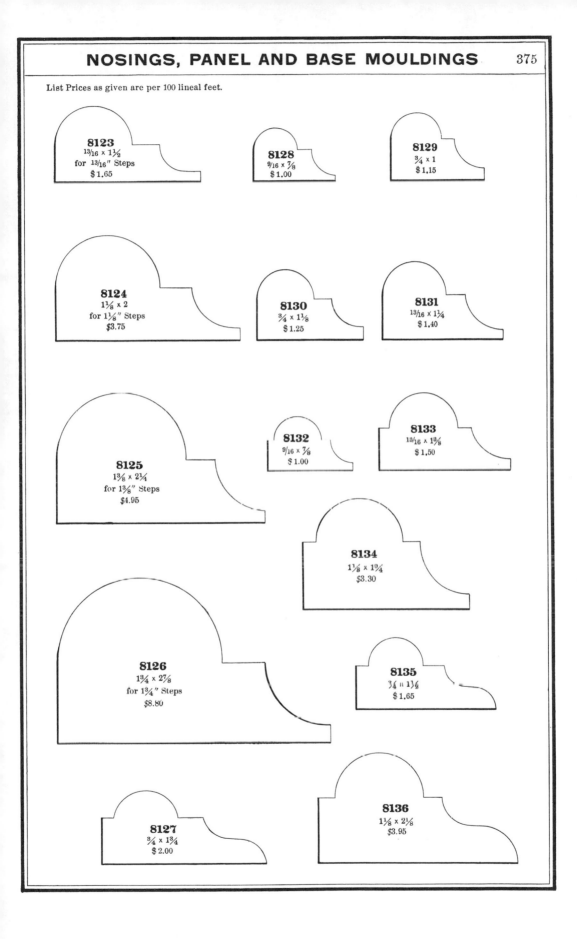

8123
13/16 x 1½
for 13/16" Steps
$1.65

8128
9/16 x 7/8
$1.00

8129
¾ x 1
$1.15

8124
1⅛ x 2
for 1⅛" Steps
$3.75

8130
¾ x 1⅛
$1.25

8131
13/16 x 1¼
$1.40

8125
1⅜ x 2¼
for 1⅜" Steps
$4.95

8132
9/16 x 7/8
$1.00

8133
13/16 x 1⅜
$1.50

8134
1⅛ x 1¾
$3.30

8126
1¾ x 2⅞
for 1¾" Steps
$8.80

8135
¾ x 1½
$1.65

8127
¾ x 1¾
$2.00

8136
1⅛ x 2⅛
$3.95

List Prices as given are per 100 lineal feet.

8137
13/16 x 1¾
$ 2.00

8145
⅜ x ⅝
$ 1.00

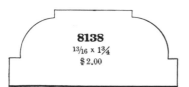

8138
13/16 x 1¾
$ 2.00

8146
7/16 x ¾
$ 1.00

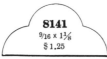

8139
5/16 x ⅝
$ 1.00

8140
⅜ x 13/16
$ 1.00

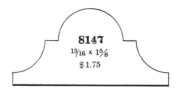

8147
13/16 x 1⅝
$ 1.75

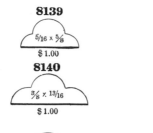

8141
9/16 x 1⅛
$ 1.25

8148
7/16 x 2
$ 2.25

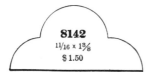

8142
11/16 x 1⅜
$ 1.50

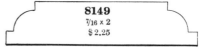

8149
7/16 x 2
$ 2.25

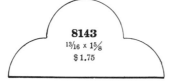

8143
13/16 x 1⅝
$ 1.75

8150
13/16 x 1¾

8144
13/16 x 2
$ 2.25

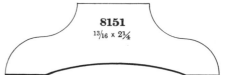

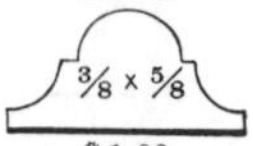

8151
13/16 x 2¼

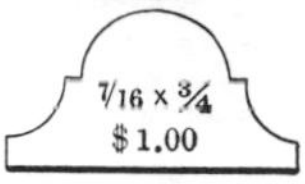

PANEL AND BASE MOULDINGS.

List Prices as given are per 100 lineal feet.

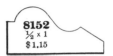

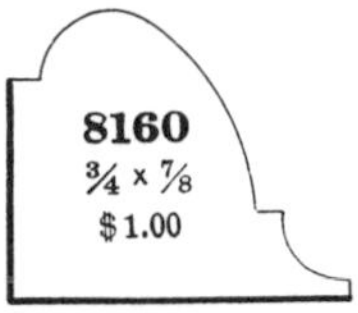

8152
½ x 1
$ 1.15

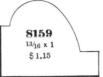

8159
13/16 x 1
$ 1.15

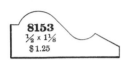

8153
½ x 1⅛
$ 1.25

8160
¾ x ⅞
$ 1.00

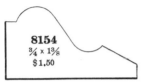

8154
¾ x 1⅜
$ 1.50

8161
¾ x 1
$ 1.15

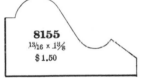

8155
13/16 x 1⅜
$ 1.50

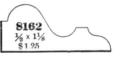

8162
½ x 1⅛
$ 1.25

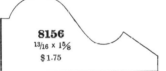

8156
13/16 x 1⅝
$ 1.75

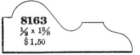

8163
½ x 1⅜
$ 1.50

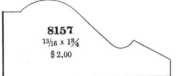

8157
13/16 x 1¾
$ 2.00

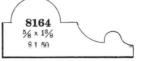

8164
⅝ x 1⅜
$ 1.50

8158
13/16 x 1⅝
$ 1.75

8165
13/16 x 2¼
$ 2.50

List Prices as given are per 100 lineal feet.

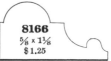

8166
5/8 x 1 1/8
$1.25

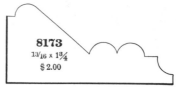

8172
9/16 x 1 3/4
$2.00

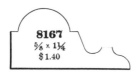

8167
5/8 x 1 1/4
$1.40

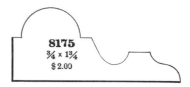

8173
13/16 x 1 3/4
$2.00

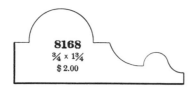

8168
3/4 x 1 3/4
$2.00

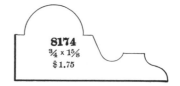

8174
3/4 x 1 5/8
$1.75

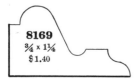

8169
3/4 x 1 1/4
$1.40

8175
3/4 x 1 3/4
$2.00

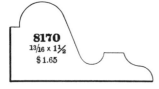

8170
13/16 x 1 1/2
$1.65

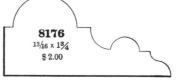

8176
13/16 x 1 3/4
$2.00

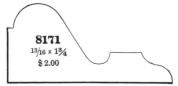

8171
13/16 x 1 3/4
$2.00

8177
13/16 x 2
$2.25

List Prices as given are per 100 lineal feet.

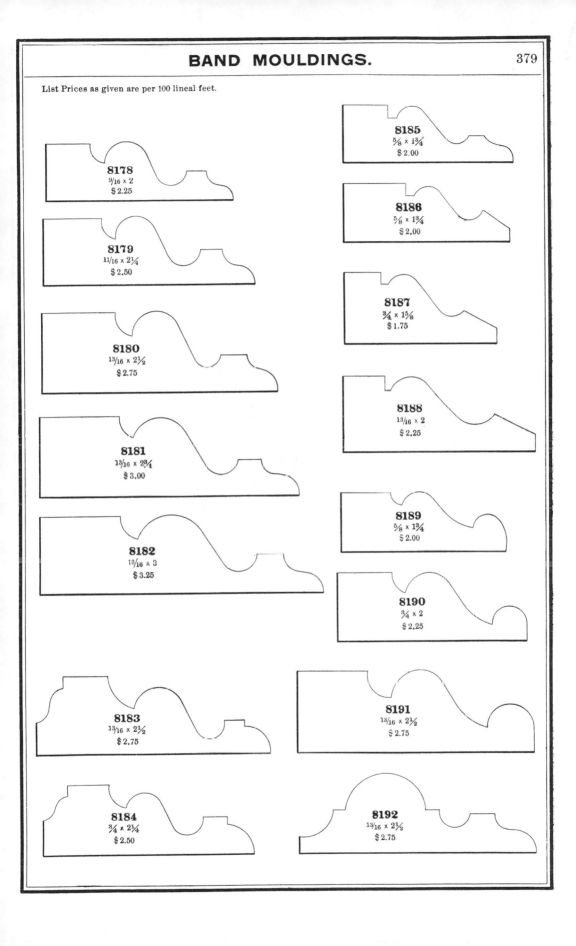

8178
9/16 x 2
$ 2.25

8179
11/16 x 2¼
$ 2.50

8180
13/16 x 2½
$ 2.75

8181
13/16 x 2¾
$ 3.00

8182
13/16 x 3
$ 3.25

8183
13/16 x 2½
$ 2.75

8184
¾ x 2¼
$ 2.50

8185
5/8 x 1¾
$ 2.00

8186
5/8 x 1¾
$ 2.00

8187
¾ x 1⅝
$ 1.75

8188
13/16 x 2
$ 2.25

8189
5/8 x 1¾
$ 2.00

8190
¾ x 2
$ 2.25

8191
13/16 x 2½
$ 2.75

8192
13/16 x 2½
$ 2.75

List Prices as given are per 100 lineal feet.

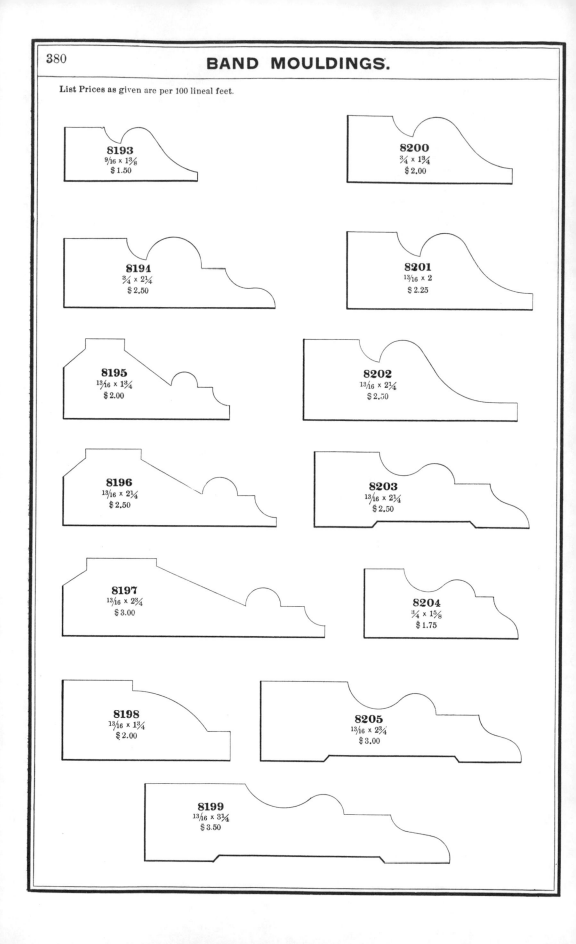

8193
9/16 x 1⅜
$ 1.50

8200
¾ x 1¾
$ 2.00

8194
¾ x 2¼
$ 2.50

8201
13/16 x 2
$ 2.25

8195
13/16 x 1¾
$ 2.00

8202
13/16 x 2¼
$ 2.50

8196
13/16 x 2¼
$ 2.50

8203
13/16 x 2¼
$ 2.50

8197
13/16 x 2¾
$ 3.00

8204
¾ x 1⅝
$ 1.75

8198
13/16 x 1¾
$ 2.00

8205
13/16 x 2¾
$ 3.00

8199
13/16 x 3¼
$ 3.50

List Prices as given are per 100 lineal feet.

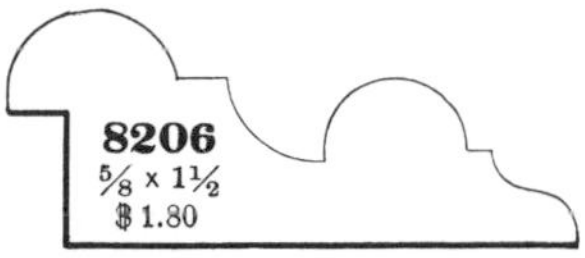

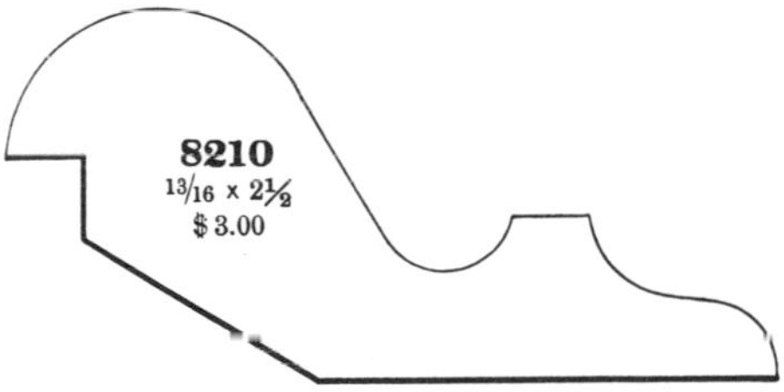

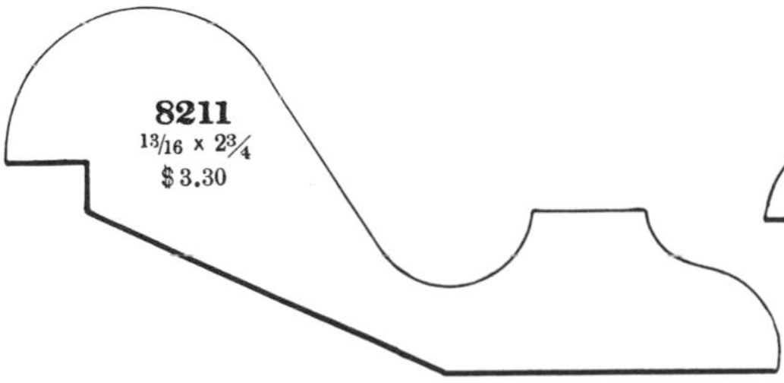

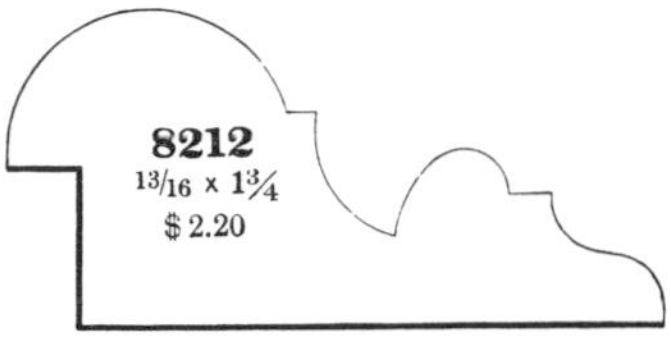

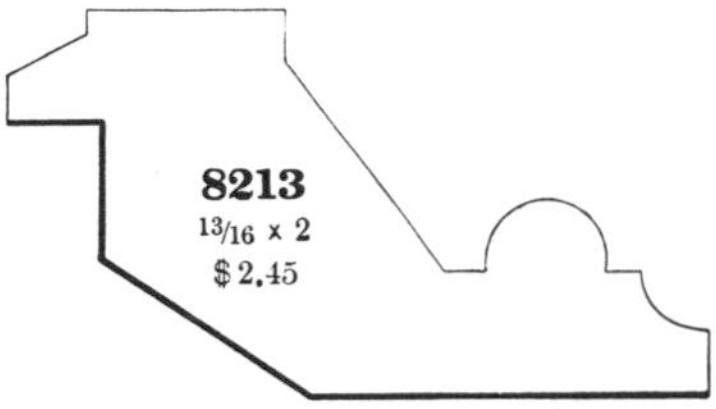

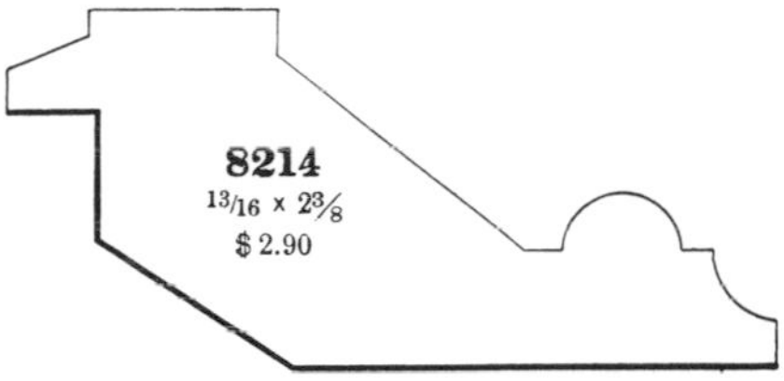

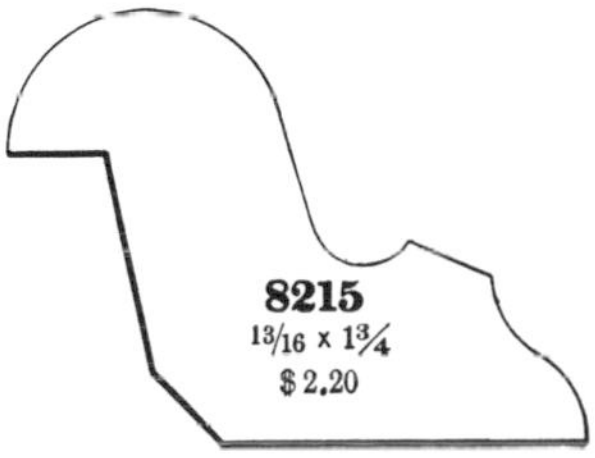

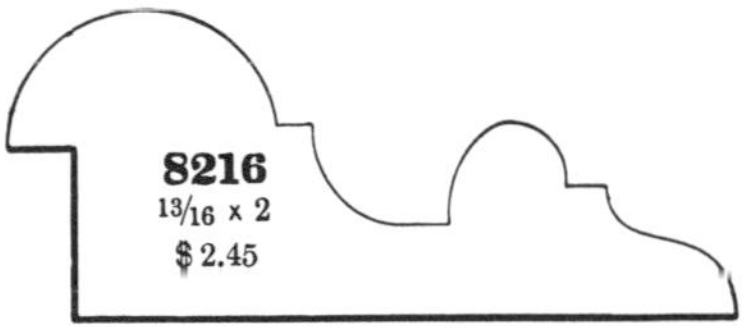

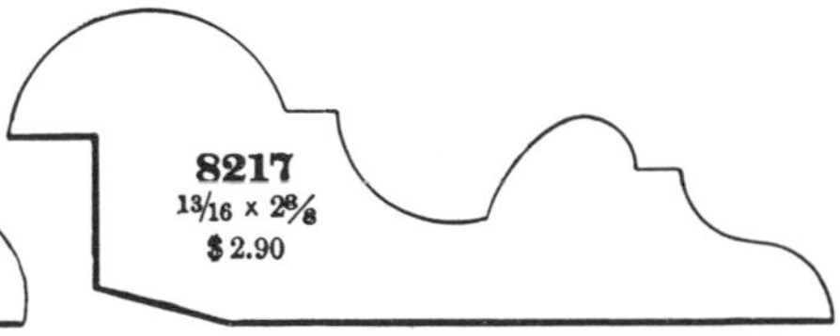

8206
5/8 x 1 1/2
$ 1.80

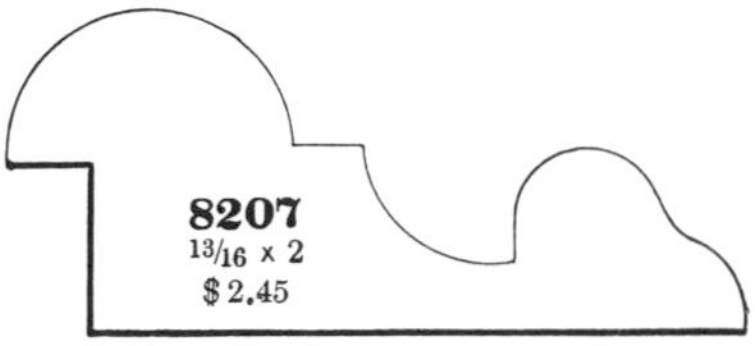

8212
13/16 x 1 3/4
$ 2.20

8207
13/16 x 2
$ 2.45

8213
13/16 x 2
$ 2.45

8208
13/16 x 2 1/2
$ 3.00

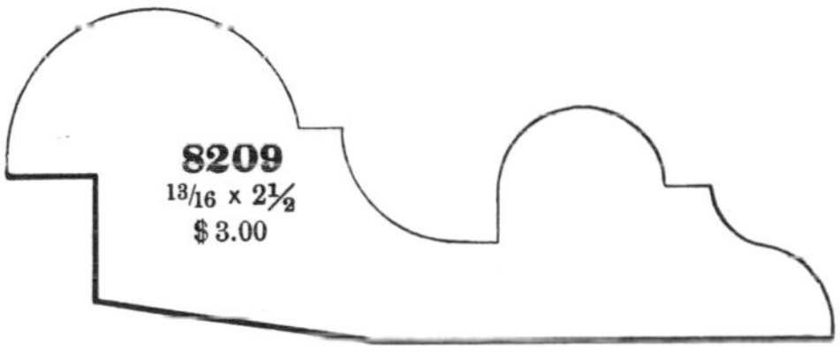

8214
13/16 x 2 3/8
$ 2.90

8209
13/16 x 2 1/2
$ 3.00

8215
13/16 x 1 3/4
$ 2.20

8210
13/16 x 2 1/2
$ 3.00

8216
13/16 x 2
$ 2.45

8211
13/16 x 2 3/4
$ 3.30

8217
13/16 x 2 3/8
$ 2.90

List Prices as given are per 100 lineal feet.

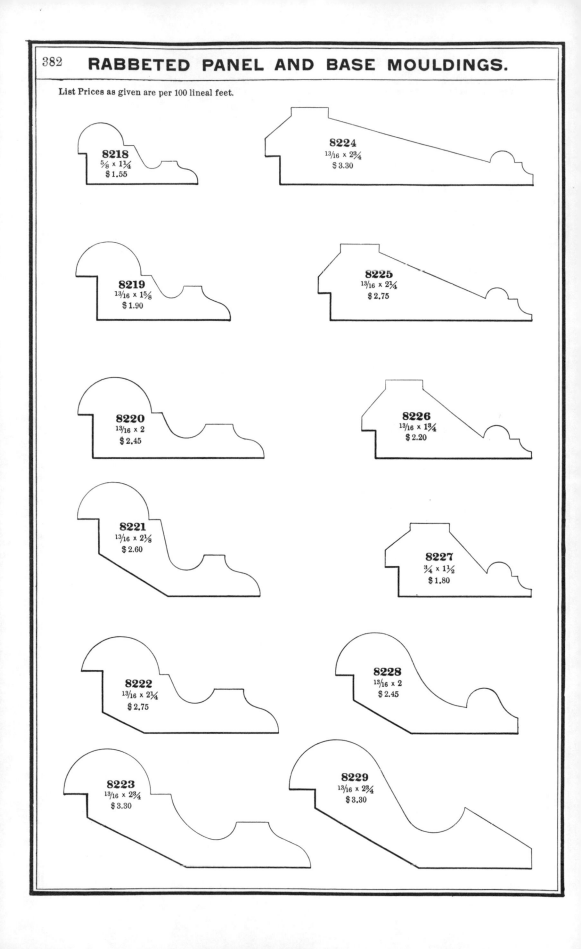

8218
⅝ x 1¼
$ 1.55

8224
¹³⁄₁₆ x 2¾
$ 3.30

8219
¹³⁄₁₆ x 1⅝
$ 1.90

8225
¹³⁄₁₆ x 2¼
$ 2.75

8220
¹³⁄₁₆ x 2
$ 2.45

8226
¹³⁄₁₆ x 1¾
$ 2.20

8221
¹³⁄₁₆ x 2⅛
$ 2.60

8227
¾ x 1½
$ 1.80

8222
¹³⁄₁₆ x 2¼
$ 2.75

8228
¹³⁄₁₆ x 2
$ 2.45

8223
¹³⁄₁₆ x 2¾
$ 3.30

8229
¹³⁄₁₆ x 2¾
$ 3.30

List Prices as given are per 100 lineal feet.

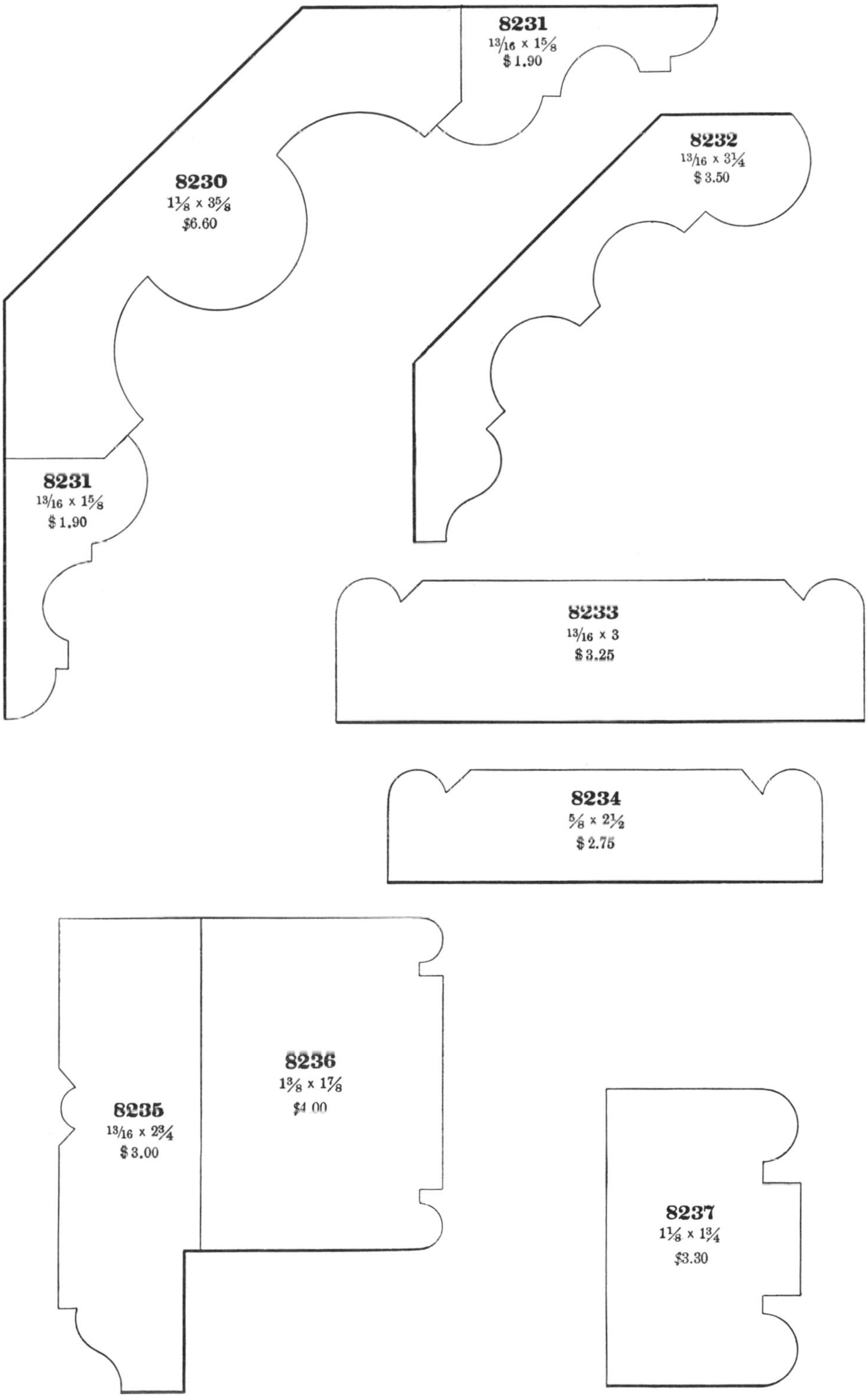
8231
13/16 x 1 5/8
$ 1.90
8230
1 1/8 x 3 5/8
$6.60
8231
13/16 x 1 5/8
$ 1.90
8232
13/16 x 3 1/4
$ 3.50
8233
13/16 x 3
$ 3.25
8234
5/8 x 2 1/2
$ 2.75
8235
13/16 x 2 3/4
$ 3.00
8236
1 3/8 x 1 7/8
$4.00
8237
1 1/8 x 1 3/4
$3.30

List Prices as given are per 100 lineal feet.

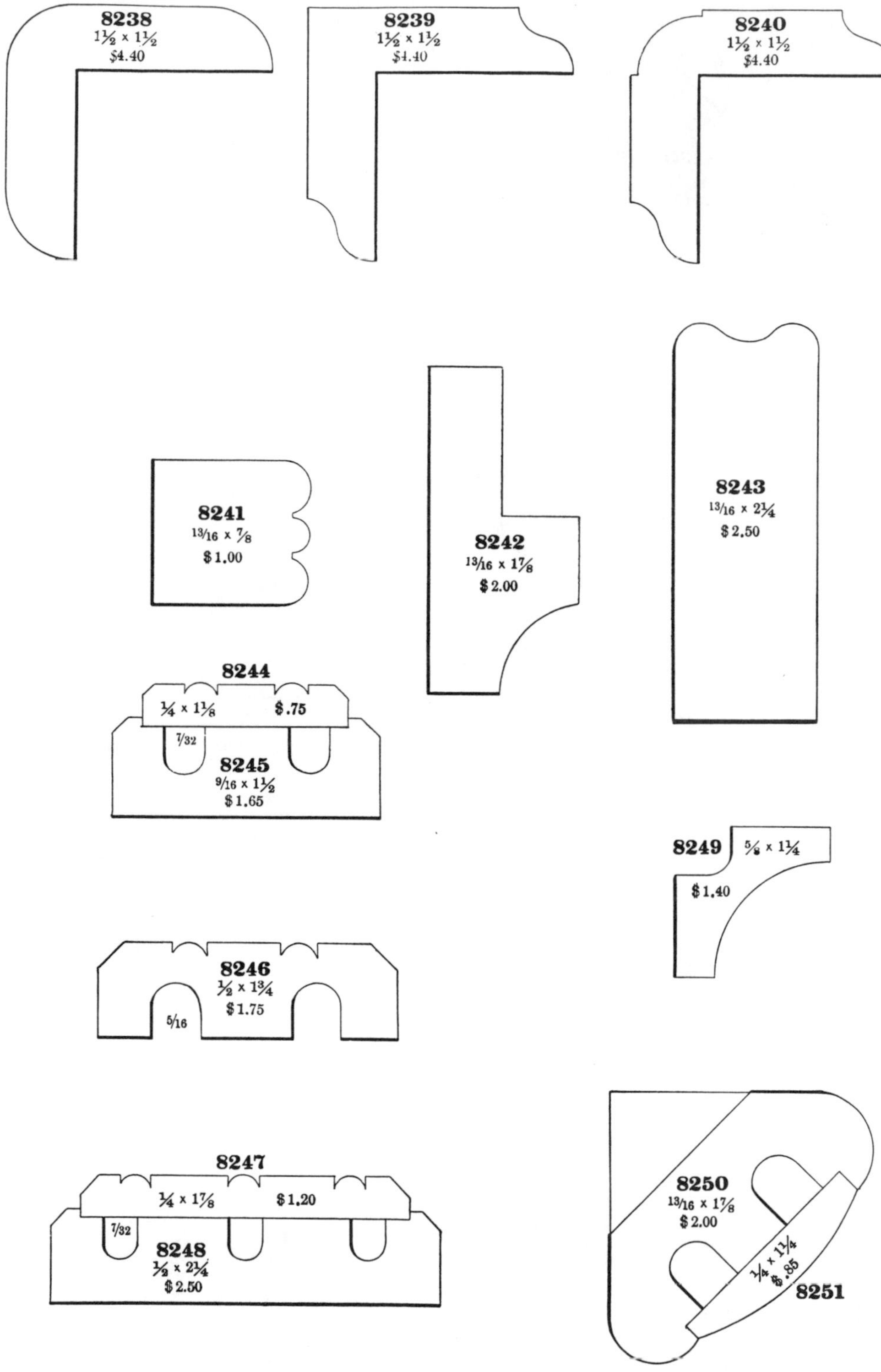
8238
1½ x 1½
$4.40
8239
1½ x 1½
$4.40
8240
1½ x 1½
$4.40
8241
13/16 x 7/8
$1.00
8242
13/16 x 1⅞
$2.00
8243
13/16 x 2¼
$2.50
8244
¼ x 1⅛
$.75
7/32
8245
9/16 x 1½
$1.65
8249
⅝ x 1¼
$1.40
8246
½ x 1¾
$1.75
5/16
8247
¼ x 1⅞
$1.20
7/32
8248
½ x 2¼
$2.50
8250
13/16 x 1⅞
$2.00
¼ x 1¼
$.85
8251

List Prices as given are per 100 lineal feet.

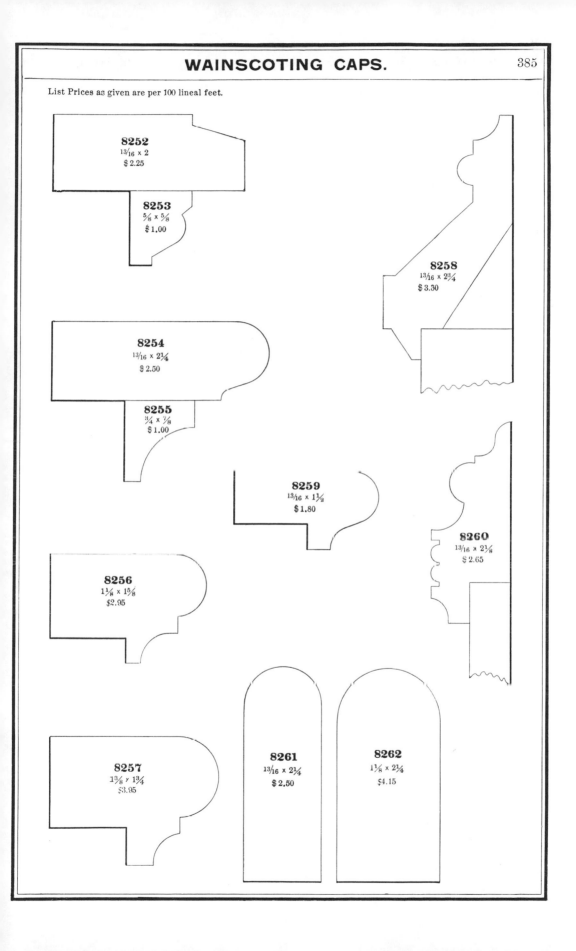

8252
13/16 x 2
$ 2.25

8253
5/8 x 5/8
$ 1.00

8258
13/16 x 2¾
$ 3.30

8254
13/16 x 2¼
$ 2.50

8255
¾ x ⅞
$ 1.00

8259
13/16 x 1½
$ 1.80

8260
13/16 x 2⅛
$ 2.65

8256
1⅛ x 1⅝
$2.95

8257
1⅜ x 1¾
$3.95

8261
13/16 x 2¼
$ 2.50

8262
1⅛ x 2¼
$4.15

List Prices as given are per 100 lineal feet.

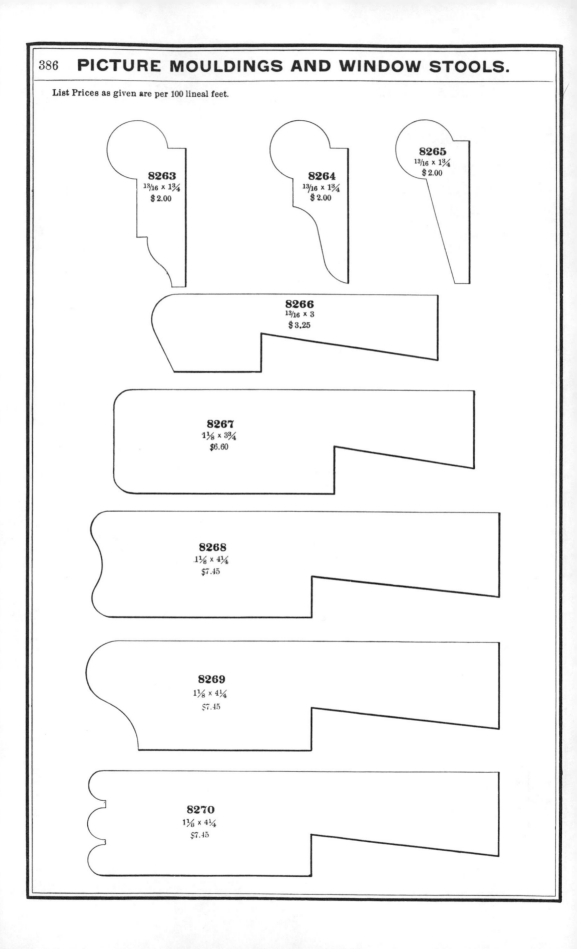

8263
13/16 x 1¾
$ 2.00

8264
13/16 x 1¾
$ 2.00

8265
13/16 x 1¾
$ 2.00

8266
13/16 x 3
$ 3.25

8267
1⅛ x 3¾
$6.60

8268
1⅛ x 4¼
$7.45

8269
1⅛ x 4¼
$7.45

8270
1⅛ x 4¼
$7.45

List Prices as given are per 100 lineal feet.

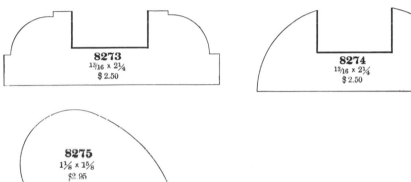

8271
13/16 x 13/4
$ 2.00

8272
11/8 x 2
$3 75

8273
13/16 x 21/4
$ 2.50

8274
13/16 x 21/4
$ 2.50

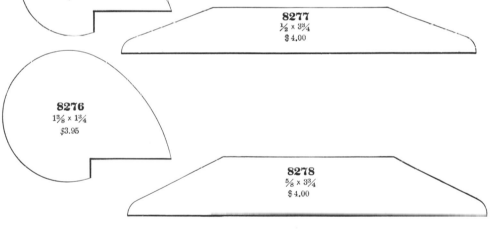

8275
11/8 x 15/8
$2.95

8277
1/2 x 33/4
$ 4.00

8276
13/8 x 13/4
$3.95

8278
5/8 x 33/4
$ 4.00

8279
5/8 x 41/4
$ 4.50

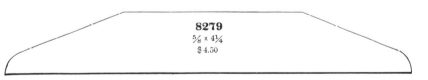

8280
5/16 x 11/8
$0.85

8281
5/16 x 13/8
$1.00

8282
5/16 x 13/4
$1.35

DRIP CAPS FOR WINDOW AND OUTSIDE DOOR FRAMES.

List Prices as given are per 100 lineal feet.

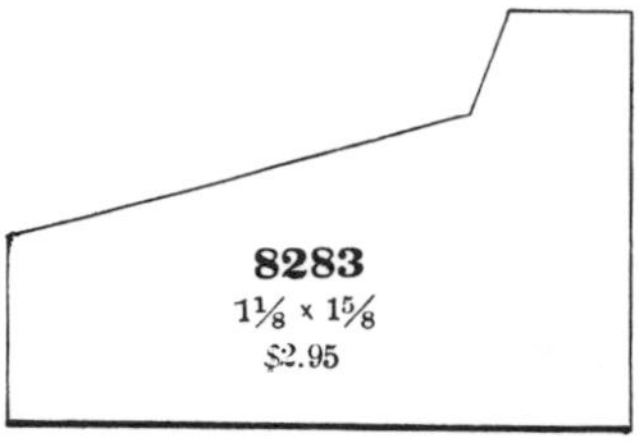

8283
1⅛ x 1⅝
$2.95

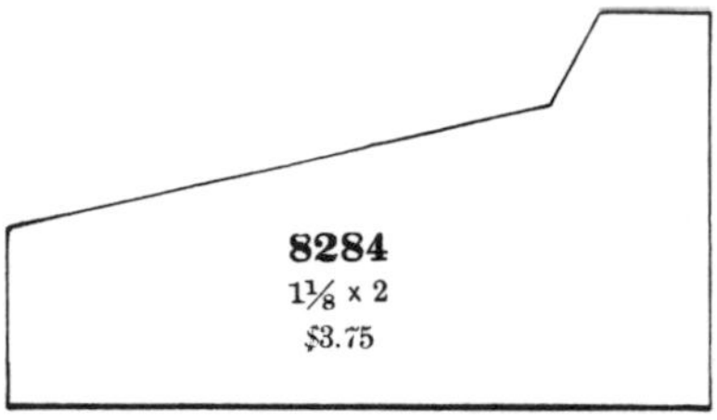

8284
1⅛ x 2
$3.75

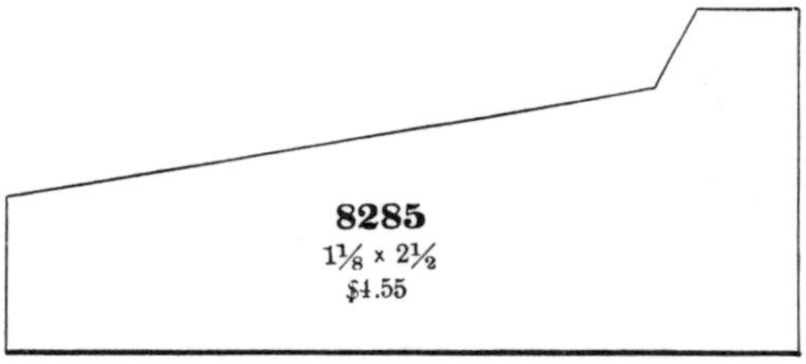

8285
1⅛ x 2½
$4.55

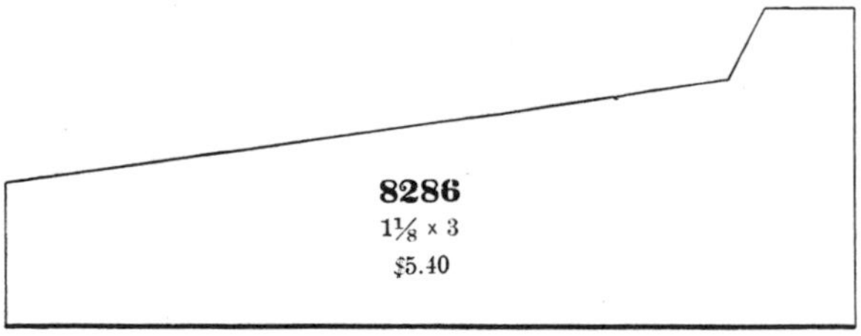

8286
1⅛ x 3
$5.40

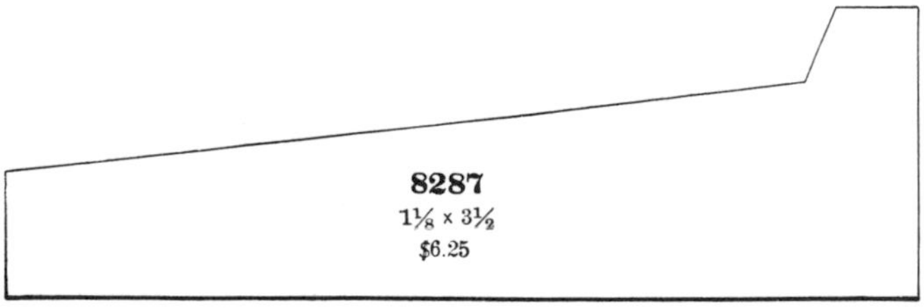

8287
1⅛ x 3½
$6.25

List Prices as given are per 100 lineal feet.

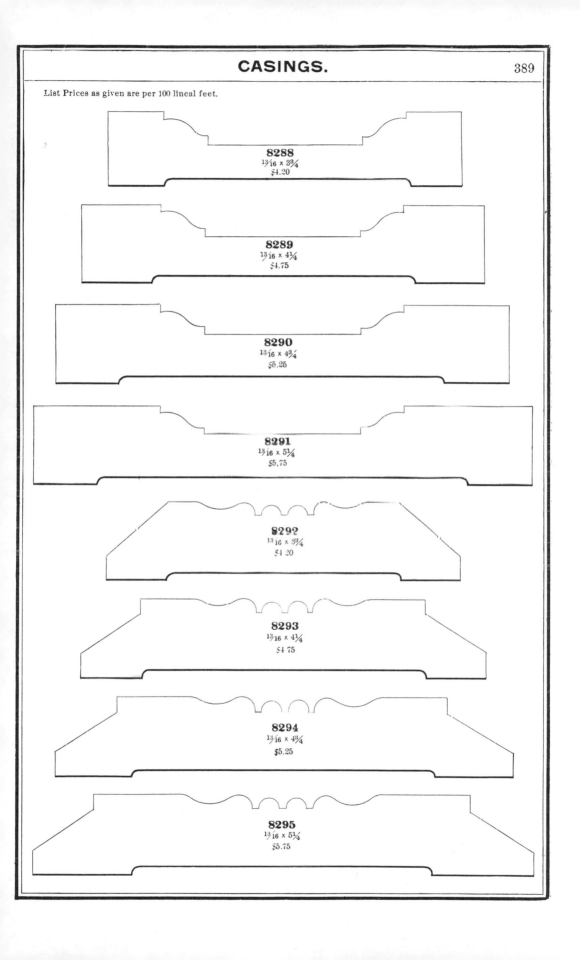

8288
13⁄16 x 3¾
$4.20

8289
13⁄16 x 4¼
$4.75

8290
13⁄16 x 4¾
$5.25

8291
13⁄16 x 5¼
$5.75

8292
13⁄16 x 3¾
$4 20

8293
13⁄16 x 4¼
$4 75

8294
13⁄16 x 4¾
$5.25

8295
13⁄16 x 5¼
$5.75

List Prices as given are per 100 lineal feet.

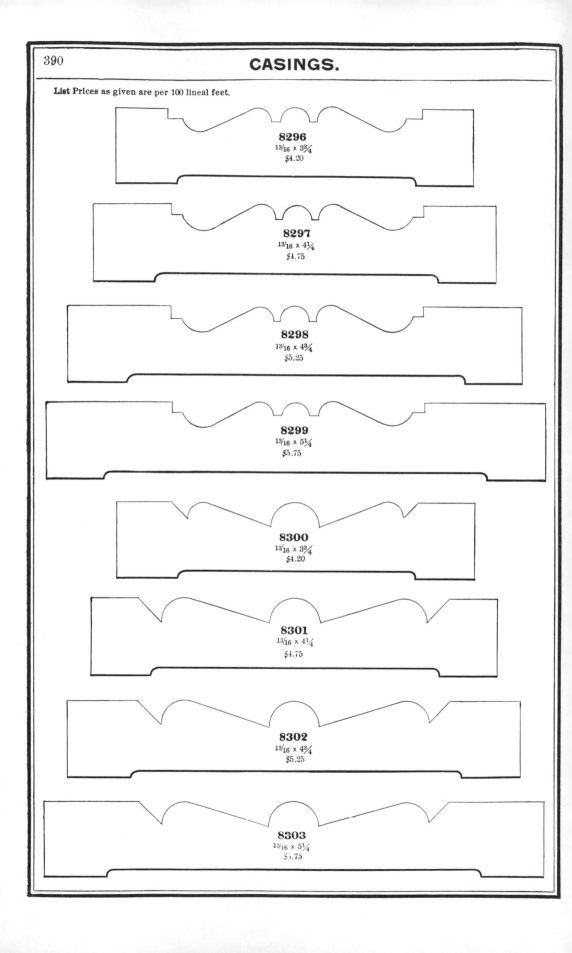

8296
13/16 x 3¾
$4.20

8297
13/16 x 4¼
$4.75

8298
13/16 x 4¾
$5.25

8299
13/16 x 5¼
$5.75

8300
13/16 x 3¾
$4.20

8301
13/16 x 4¼
$4.75

8302
13/16 x 4¾
$5.25

8303
13/16 x 5¼
$5.75

List Prices as given are per 100 lineal feet.

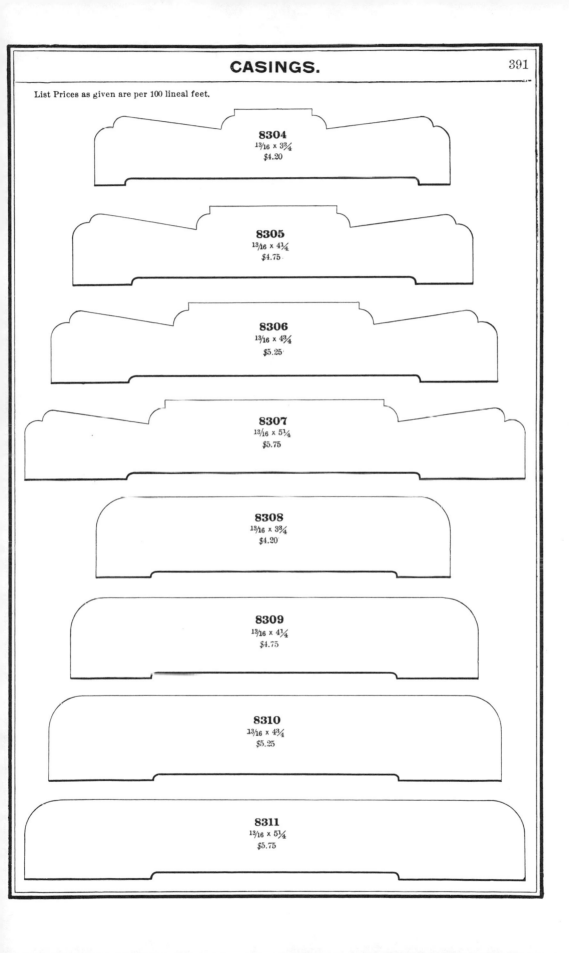

8304
13/16 x 3¾
$4.20

8305
13/16 x 4¼
$4.75

8306
13/16 x 4¾
$5.25

8307
13/16 x 5¼
$5.75

8308
13/16 x 3¾
$4.20

8309
13/16 x 4¼
$4.75

8310
13/16 x 4¾
$5.25

8311
13/16 x 5¼
$5.75

List Prices as given are per 100 lineal feet.

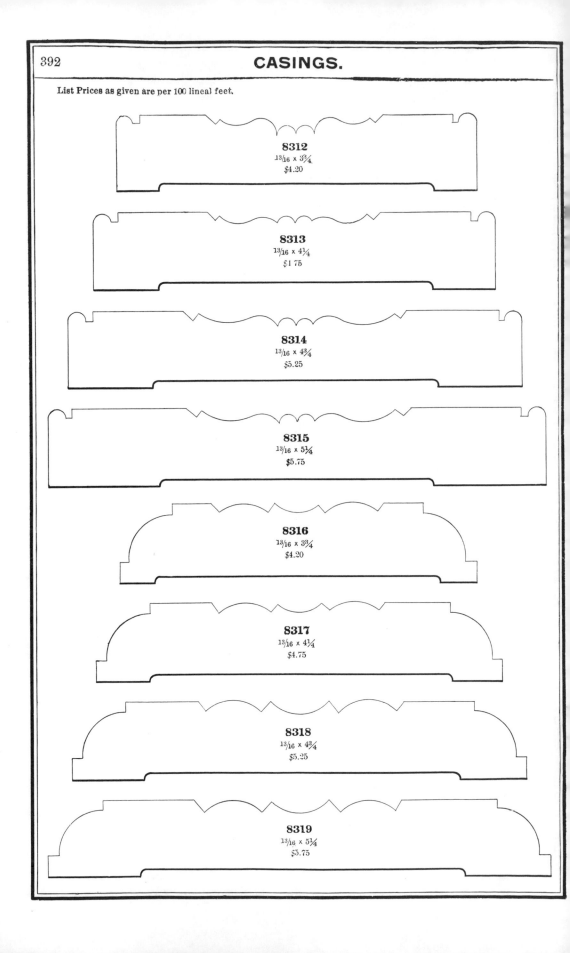

8312
$13/16 \times 3\frac{3}{4}$
$4.20

8313
$13/16 \times 4\frac{1}{4}$
$1 75

8314
$13/16 \times 4\frac{3}{4}$
$5.25

8315
$13/16 \times 5\frac{1}{4}$
$5.75

8316
$13/16 \times 3\frac{3}{4}$
$4.20

8317
$13/16 \times 4\frac{1}{4}$
$4.75

8318
$13/16 \times 4\frac{3}{4}$
$5.25

8319
$13/16 \times 5\frac{1}{4}$
$5.75

List Prices as given are per 100 lineal feet.

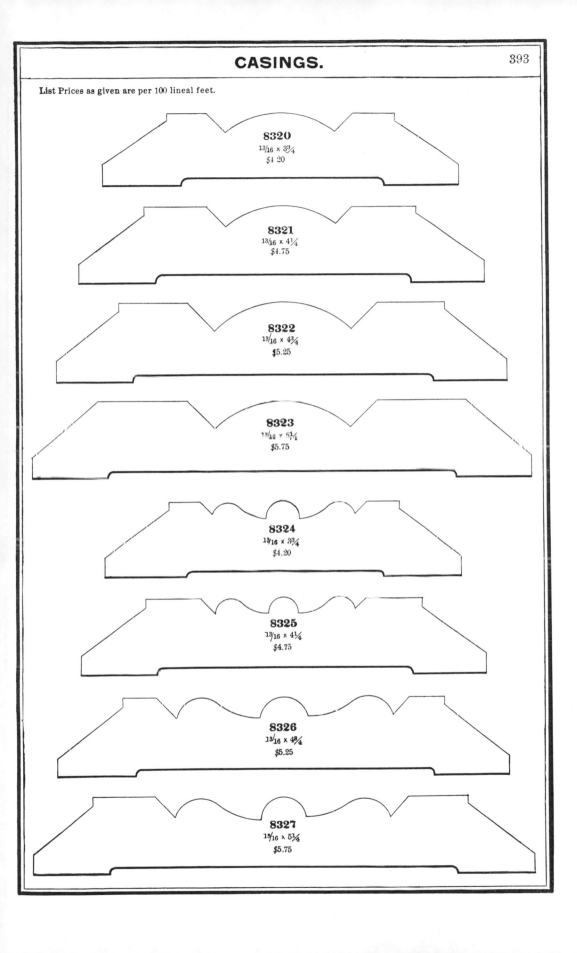

8320
13/16 x 3¾
$4 20

8321
13/16 x 4¼
$4.75

8322
13/16 x 4¾
$5.25

8323
13/16 x 5¼
$5.75

8324
13/16 x 3¾
$4.20

8325
13/16 x 4¼
$4.75

8326
13/16 x 4¾
$5.25

8327
13/16 x 5¼
$5.75

CASINGS.

List Prices as given are per 100 lineal feet.

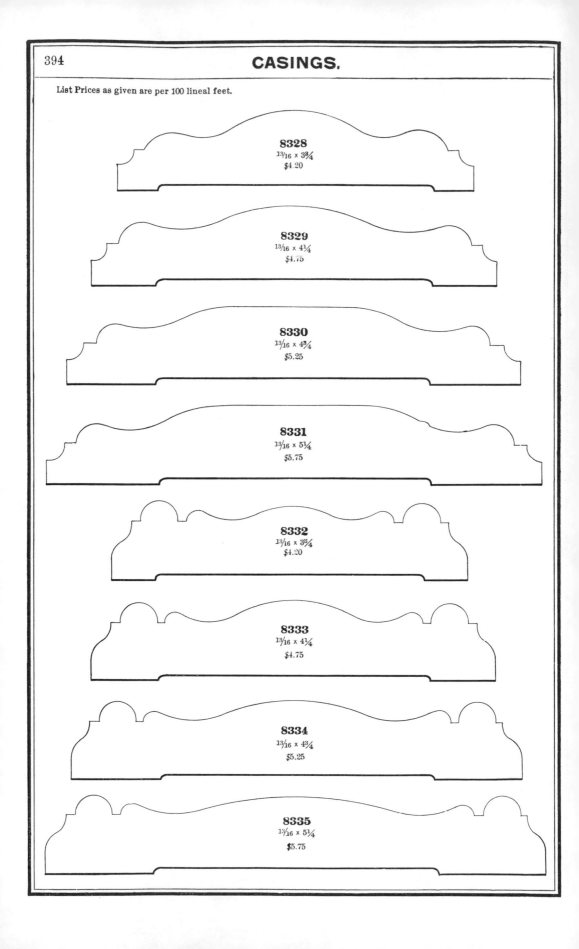

8328
13/16 x 3¾
$4.20

8329
13/16 x 4¼
$4.75

8330
13/16 x 4¾
$5.25

8331
13/16 x 5¼
$5.75

8332
13/16 x 3¾
$4.20

8333
13/16 x 4¼
$4.75

8334
13/16 x 4¾
$5.25

8335
13/16 x 5¼
$5.75

List Prices as given are per 100 lineal feet.

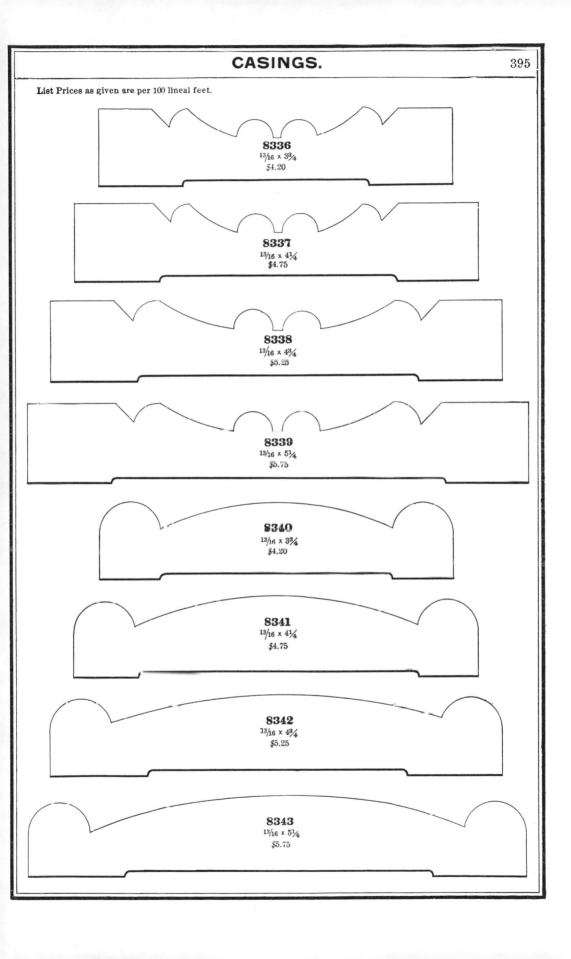

8336
13/16 x 3¾
$4.20

8337
13/16 x 4¼
$4.75

8338
13/16 x 4¾
$5.25

8339
13/16 x 5¼
$5.75

8340
13/16 x 3¾
$4.20

8341
13/16 x 4¼
$4.75

8342
13/16 x 4¾
$5.25

8343
13/16 x 5¼
$5.75

CASINGS.

List Prices as given are per 100 lineal feet.

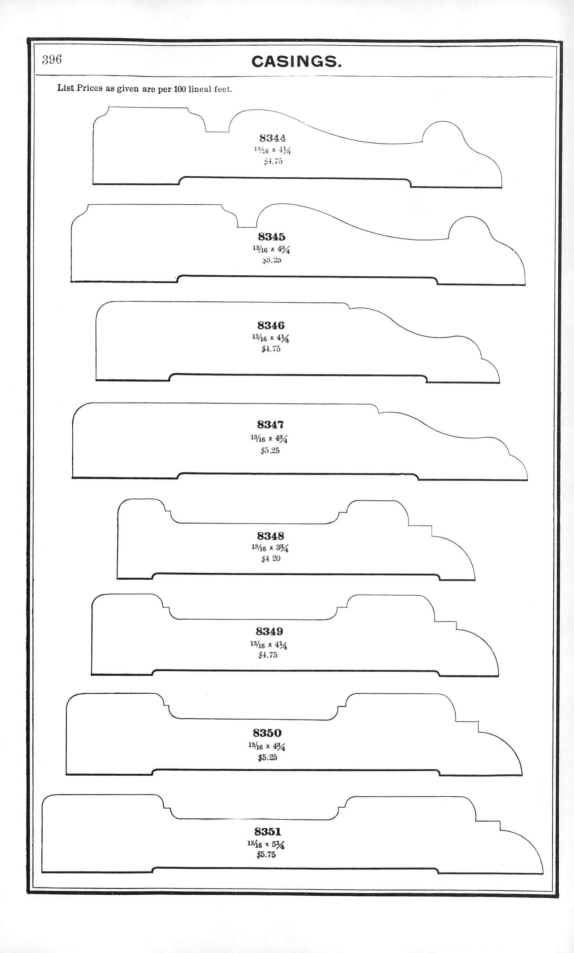

8344
$^{13}\!/_{16}$ x $4\frac{1}{4}$
$4.75

8345
$^{13}\!/_{16}$ x $4\frac{3}{4}$
$5.25

8346
$^{13}\!/_{16}$ x $4\frac{1}{4}$
$4.75

8347
$^{13}\!/_{16}$ x $4\frac{3}{4}$
$5.25

8348
$^{13}\!/_{16}$ x $3\frac{3}{4}$
$4.20

8349
$^{13}\!/_{16}$ x $4\frac{1}{4}$
$4.75

8350
$^{13}\!/_{16}$ x $4\frac{3}{4}$
$5.25

8351
$^{13}\!/_{16}$ x $5\frac{1}{4}$
$5.75

List Prices as given are per 100 lineal feet.

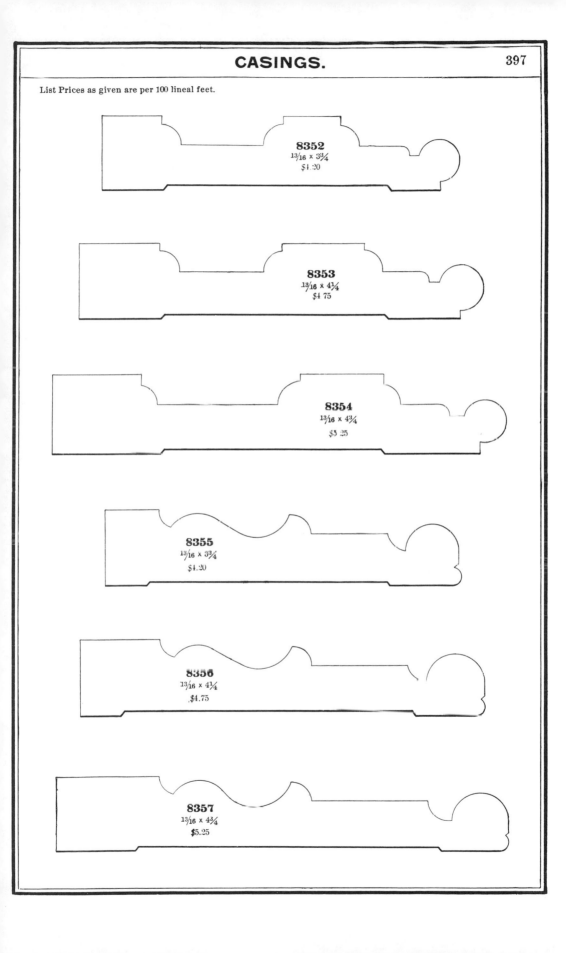

8352
13/16 x 3¾
$4.20

8353
13/16 x 4¼
$4.75

8354
13/16 x 4¾
$5.25

8355
13/16 x 3¾
$4.20

8356
13/16 x 4¼
$4.75

8357
13/16 x 4¾
$5.25

List Prices as given are per 100 lineal feet.

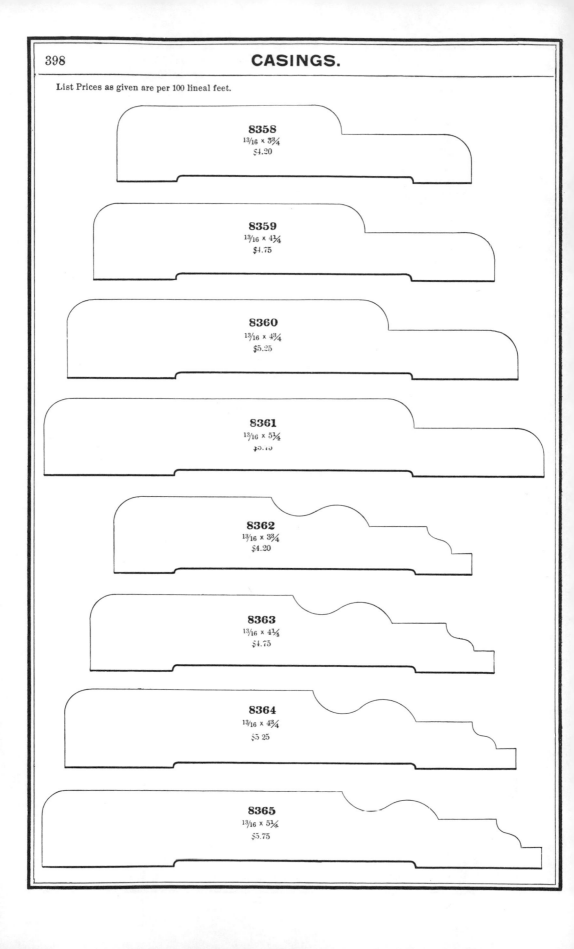

8358
$13/16 \times 3\frac{3}{4}$
$4.20

8359
$13/16 \times 4\frac{1}{4}$
$4.75

8360
$13/16 \times 4\frac{3}{4}$
$5.25

8361
$13/16 \times 5\frac{1}{4}$
$5.75

8362
$13/16 \times 3\frac{3}{4}$
$4.20

8363
$13/16 \times 4\frac{1}{4}$
$4.75

8364
$13/16 \times 4\frac{3}{4}$
$5 25

8365
$13/16 \times 5\frac{1}{4}$
$5.75

List Prices as given are per 100 lineal feet.

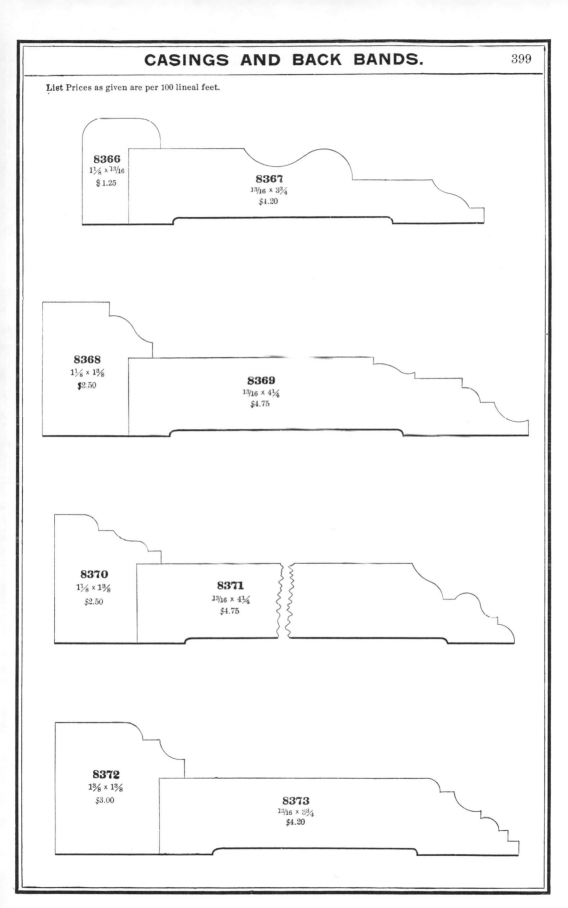

8366
1⅛ x ¹³⁄₁₆
$ 1.25

8367
¹³⁄₁₆ x 3¾
$4.20

8368
1⅛ x 1⅜
$2.50

8369
¹³⁄₁₆ x 4¼
$4.75

8370
1⅛ x 1⅜
$2.50

8371
¹³⁄₁₆ x 4¼
$4.75

8372
1⅜ x 1⅜
$3.00

8373
¹³⁄₁₆ x 3¾
$4.20

List Prices as given are per 100 lineal feet.

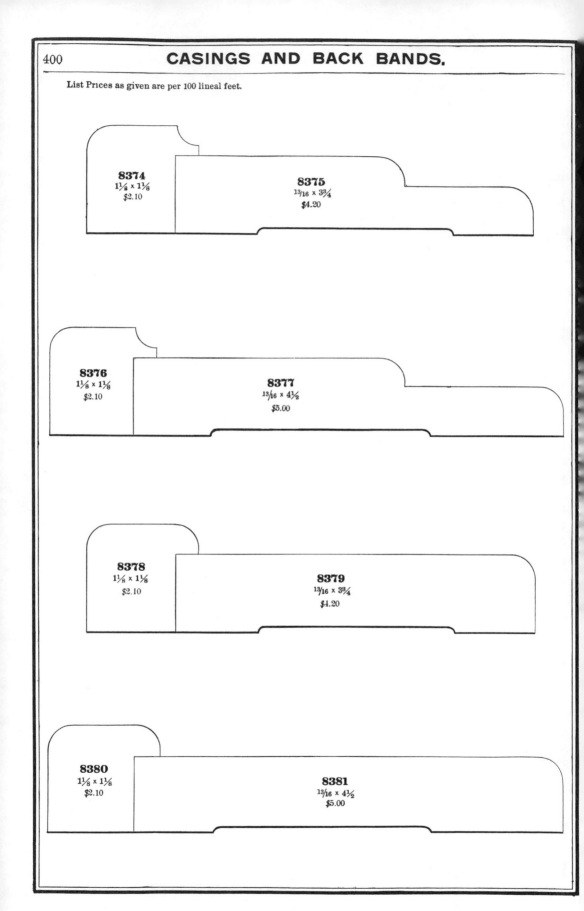

8374
1⅛ x 1⅛
$2.10

8375
13/16 x 3¾
$4.20

8376
1⅛ x 1⅛
$2.10

8377
13/16 x 4½
$5.00

8378
1⅛ x 1⅛
$2.10

8379
13/16 x 3¾
$4.20

8380
1⅛ x 1⅛
$2.10

8381
13/16 x 4½
$5.00

List Prices as given are per 100 lineal feet.

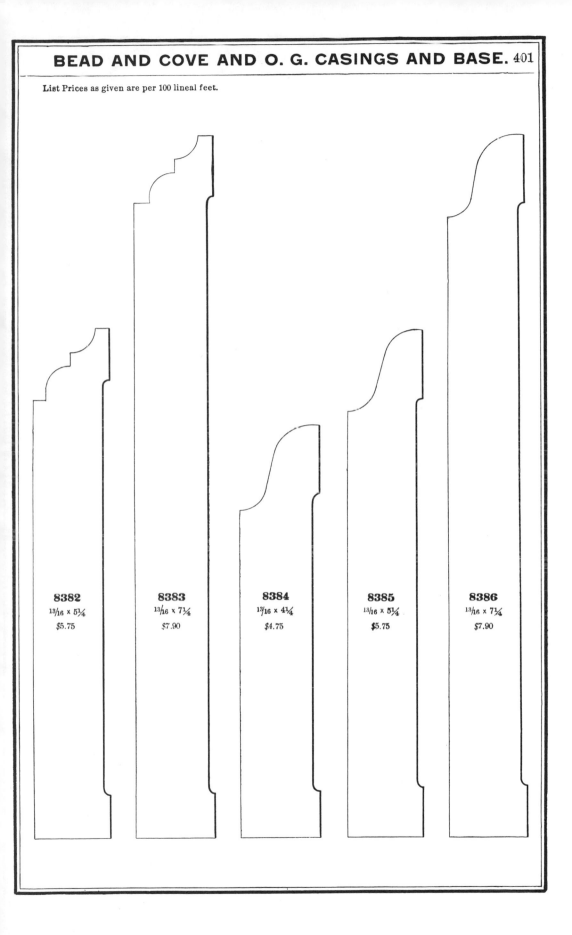

8382
13/16 x 5¼

$5.75

8383
13/16 x 7¼

$7.90

8384
13/16 x 4¼

$4.75

8385
13/16 x 5¼

$5.75

8386
13/16 x 7¼

$7.90

List Prices as given are per 100 lineal feet.

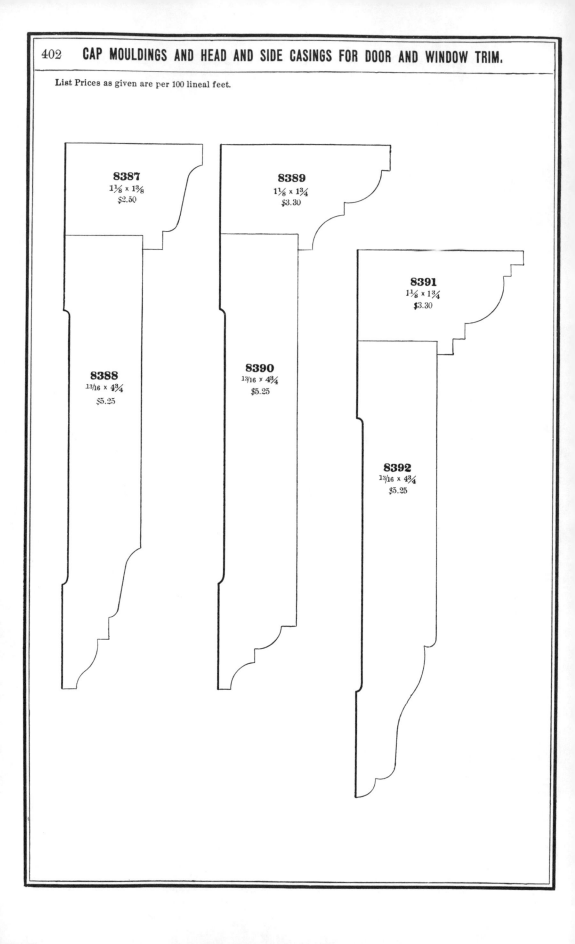

8387
1⅛ × 1⅜
$2.50

8389
1⅛ × 1¾
$3.30

8391
1⅛ × 1¾
$3.30

8388
1³/16 × 4¾
$5.25

8390
1³/16 × 4¾
$5.25

8392
1³/16 × 4¾
$5.25

List Prices as given are per 100 lineal feet.

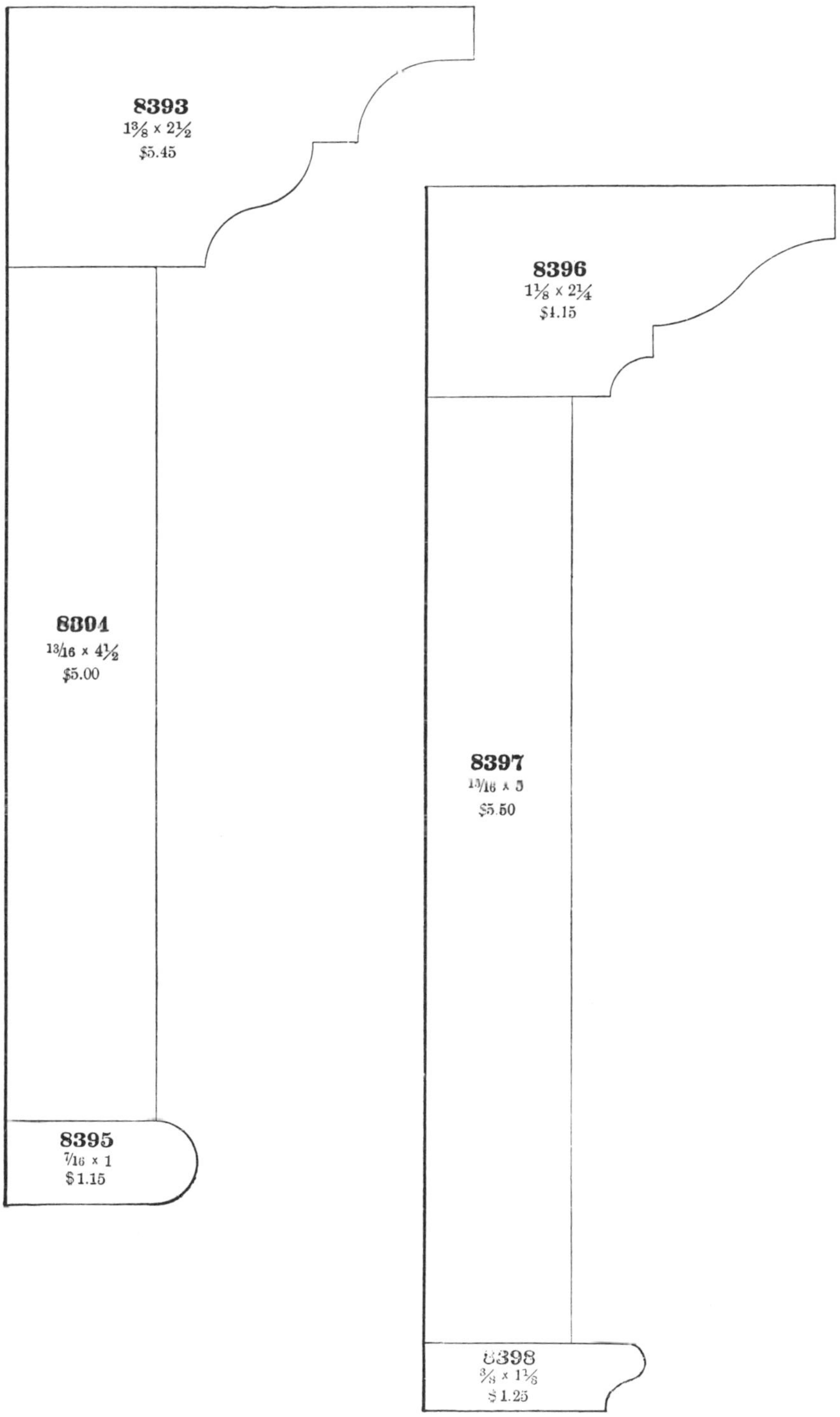

8393
1⅜ x 2½
$5.45

8396
1⅛ x 2¼
$4.15

8394
13/16 x 4½
$5.00

8397
13/16 x 3
$5.50

8395
7/16 x 1
$1.15

8398
¾ x 1⅛
$1.25

List Prices as given are per 100 lineal feet.

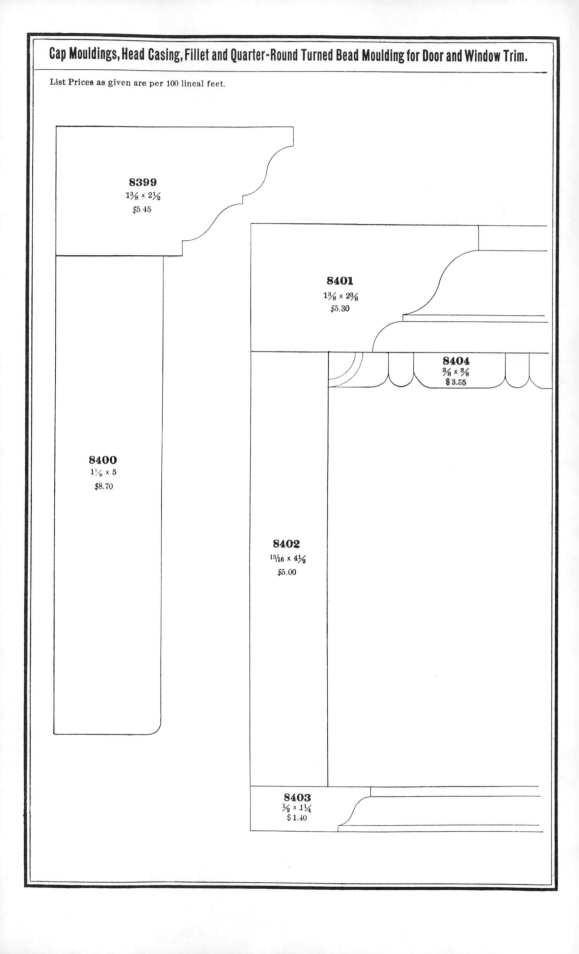

8399
1⅜ × 2½
$5.45

8401
1⅜ × 2⅜
$5.30

8404
⅜ × ⅜
$3.85

8400
1⅛ × 5
$8.70

8402
13⁄16 × 4½
$5.00

8403
½ × 1¼
$1.40

List Prices as given are per 100 lineal feet.

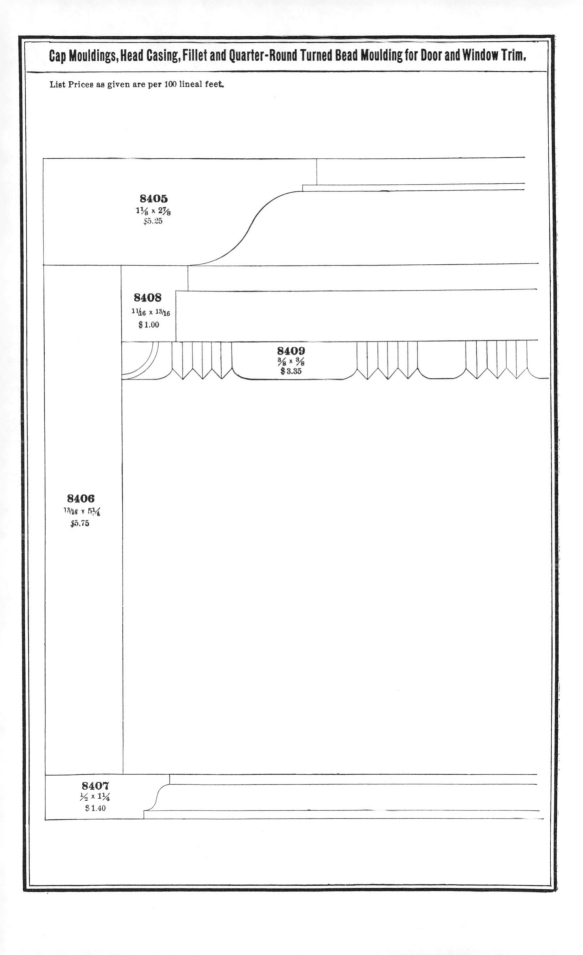

8405
1⅛ x 2⅞
$5.25

8408
1¹⁄₁₆ x 1³⁄₁₆
$1.00

8409
⅜ x ⅜
$3.35

8406
1³⁄₁₆ x 5¼
$5.75

8407
½ x 1¼
$1.40

List Prices as given are per 100 lineal feet.

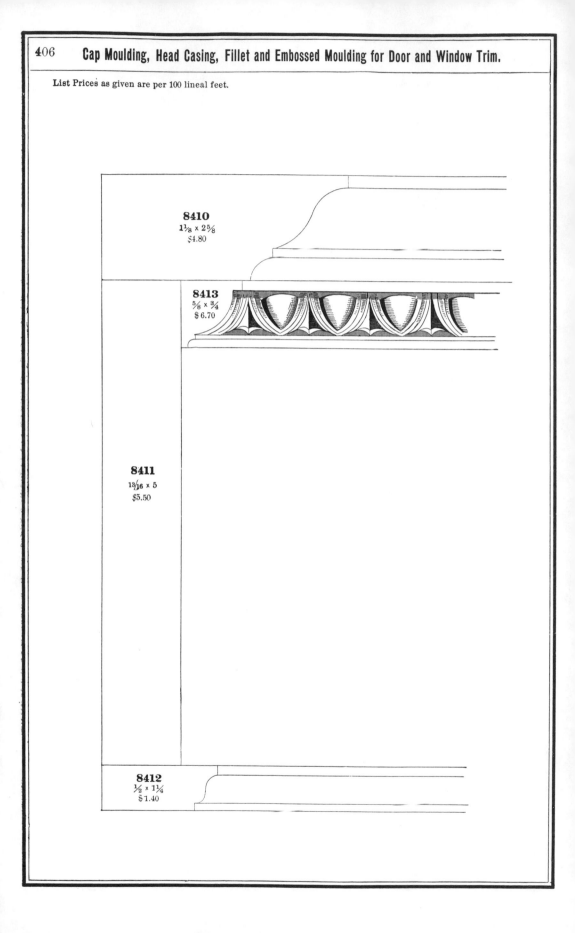

8410
1⅛ x 2⅝
$4.80

8413
⅝ x ¾
$ 6.70

8411
1³⁄₁₆ x 5
$5.50

8412
½ x 1¼
$ 1.40

List Prices as given are per 100 lineal feet.

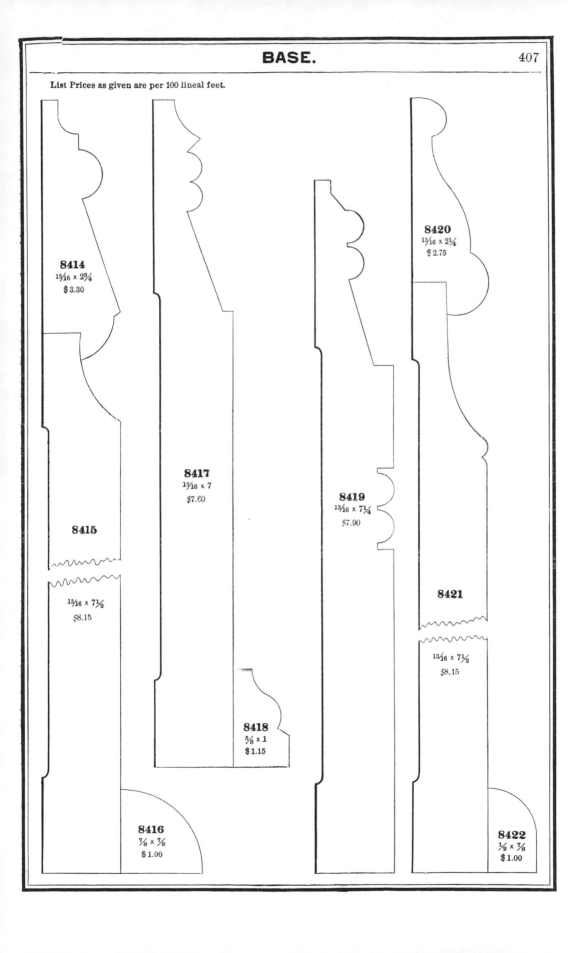

8414
13⁄16 x 2¾
$3.30

8415

13⁄16 x 7½
$8.15

8416
⅞ x ⅞
$1.00

8417
13⁄16 x 7
$7.60

8418
⅝ x 1
$1.15

8419
13⁄16 x 7¼
$7.90

8420
13⁄16 x 2¼
$2.75

8421

13⁄16 x 7½
$8.15

8422
½ x ⅞
$1.00

List Prices as given are per 100 lineal feet.

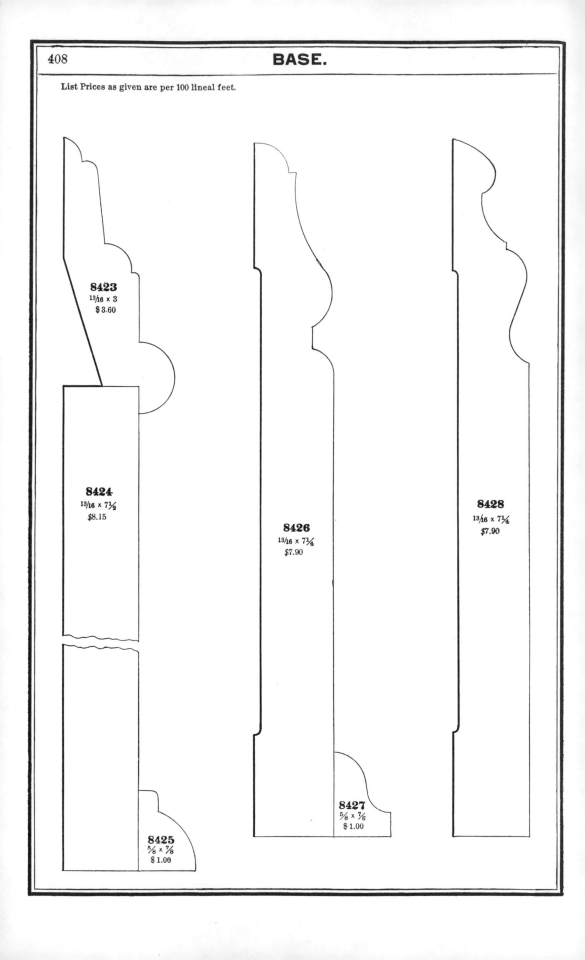

8423
13/16 x 3
$3.60

8424
13/16 x 7½
$8.15

8425
⅝ x ⅞
$1.00

8426
13/16 x 7¼
$7.90

8427
⅝ x ⅞
$1.00

8428
13/16 x 7¼
$7.90

List Prices as given are per 100 lineal feet.

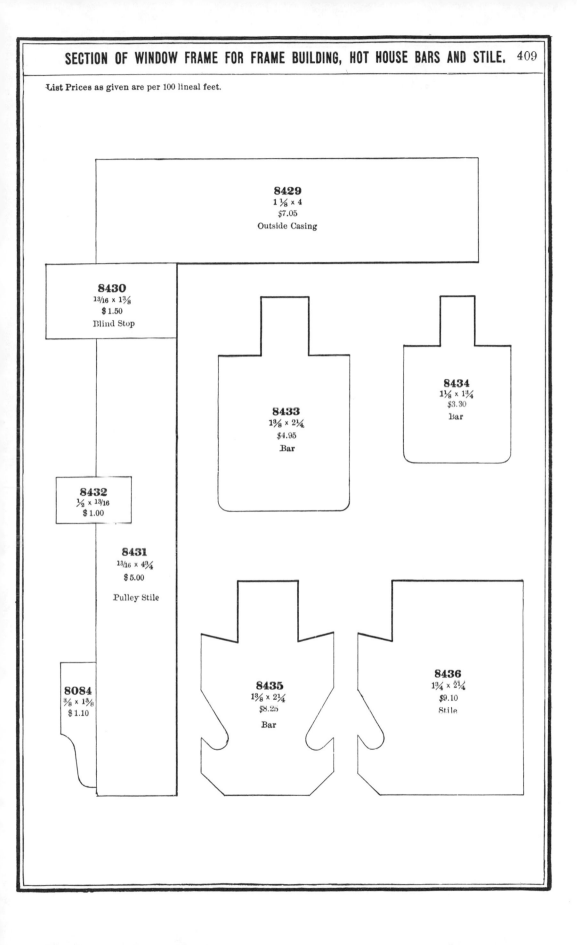

8429
1⅛ × 4
$7.05
Outside Casing

8430
13/16 × 1⅜
$1.50
Blind Stop

8433
1⅜ × 2¼
$4.95
Bar

8434
1⅛ × 1¾
$3.30
Bar

8432
½ × 13/16
$1.00

8431
13/16 × 4¾
$5.00
Pulley Stile

8084
⅜ × 1⅜
$1.10

8435
1⅜ × 2¼
$8.25
Bar

8436
1¾ × 2¼
$9.10
Stile

List Prices as given are per 100 lineal feet.

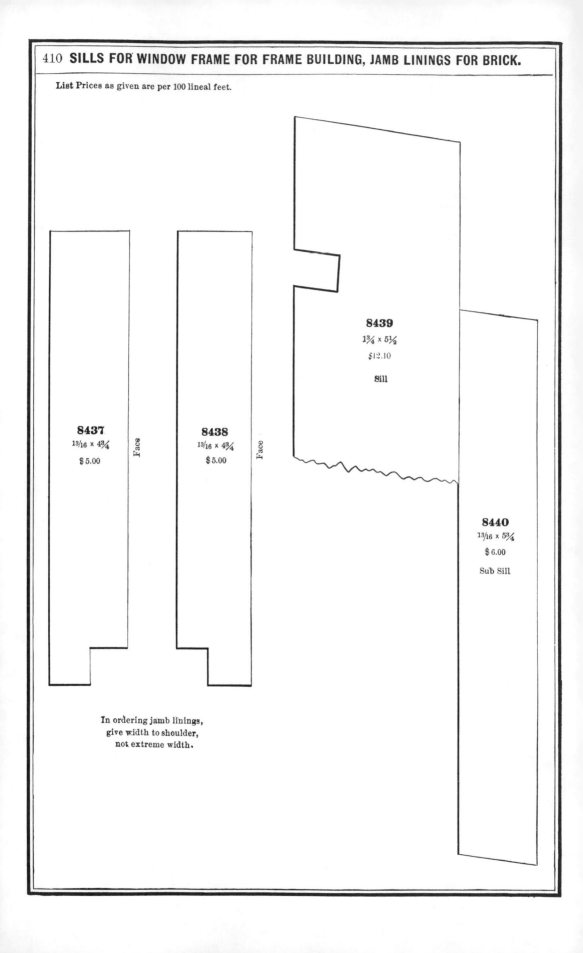

8439

1¾ × 5½

$12.10

Sill

8437

13/16 × 4¾

$ 5.00

Face

8438

13/16 × 4¾

$ 5.00

Face

8440

13/16 × 5¾

$ 6.00

Sub Sill

In ordering jamb linings,
give width to shoulder,
not extreme width.

List Prices as given are per 100 lineal feet.

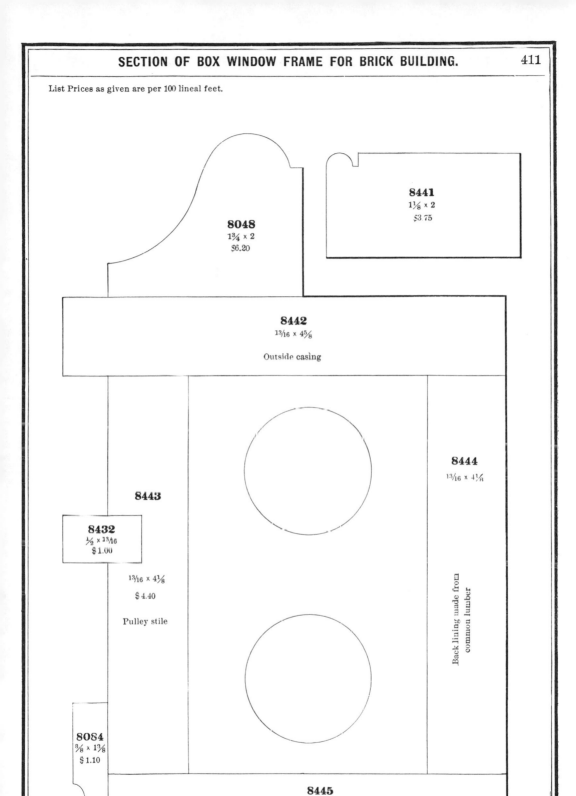

8048
1¾ × 2
$6.20

8441
1⅛ × 2
$3 75

8442
13/16 × 4⅝

Outside casing

8444
13/16 × 4¼

8443

8432
½ × 13/16
$1.00

13/16 × 4⅛

$4.40

Pulley stile

Back lining made from
common lumber

8084
⅜ × 1⅛
$1.10

8445
13/16 × 4⅛

Inside casing of frame

ASTRAGALS FOR SLIDING AND FOLDING DOORS.

8446

1 3/4 Rabbet
1 3/16 x 2 3/8
1 3/16 x 2 3/8

50 Cents per pair Net.

8447

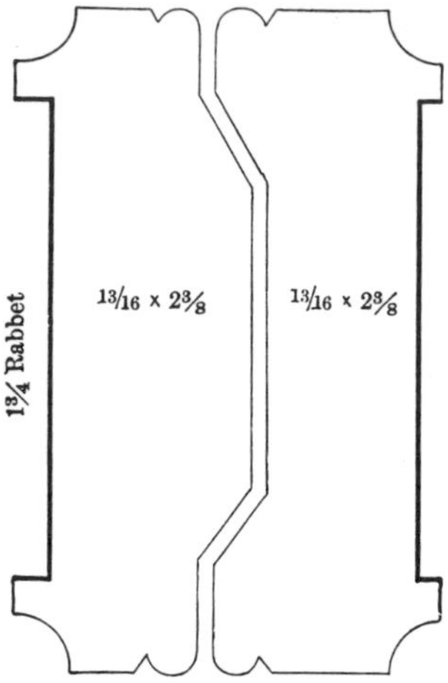

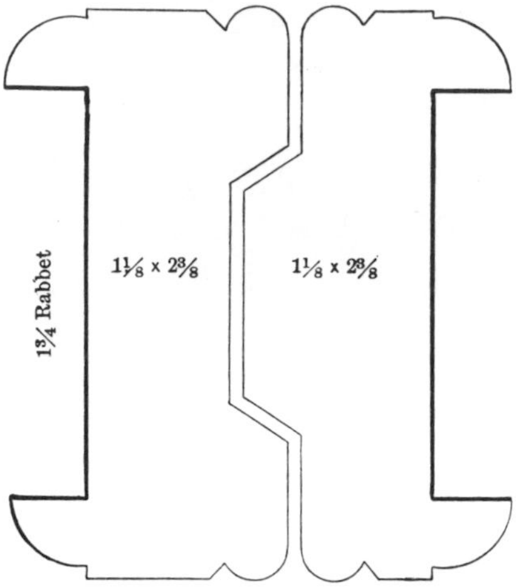

1 3/4 Rabbet
1 1/8 x 2 3/8
1 1/8 x 2 3/8

50 Cents per pair Net.

8448
1 3/4 x 2 1/2

25 Cents each Net.

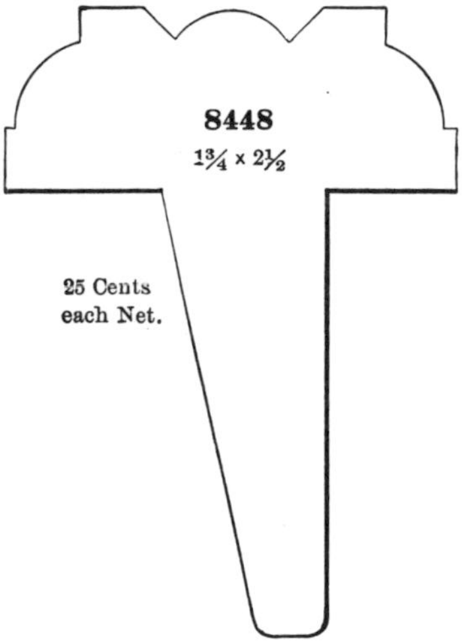

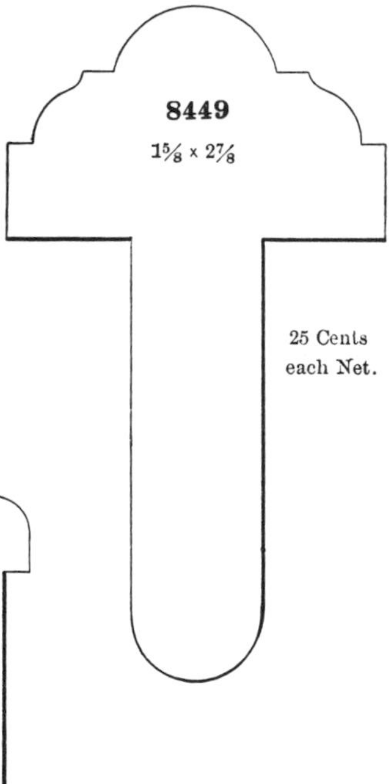

8449
1 5/8 x 2 7/8

25 Cents each Net.

8450

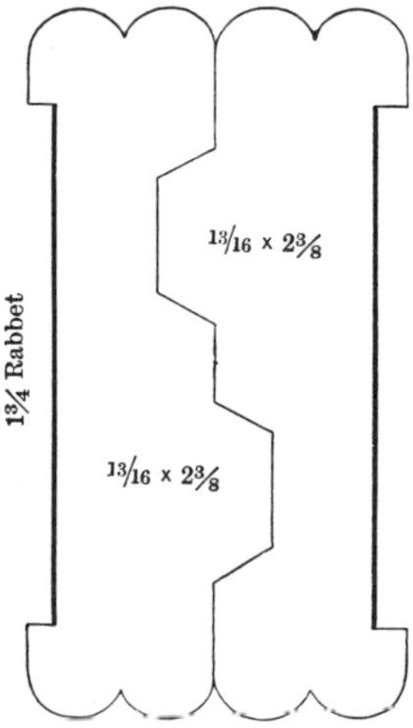

1 3/16 x 2 3/8
1 3/4 Rabbet
1 3/16 x 2 3/8

40 Cents per pair Net.

PORCH RAILS.

List Prices as given are per 100 lineal feet.

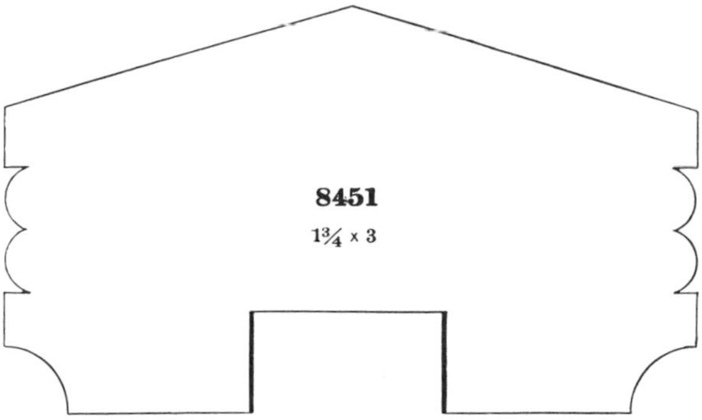
8451
1¾ x 3

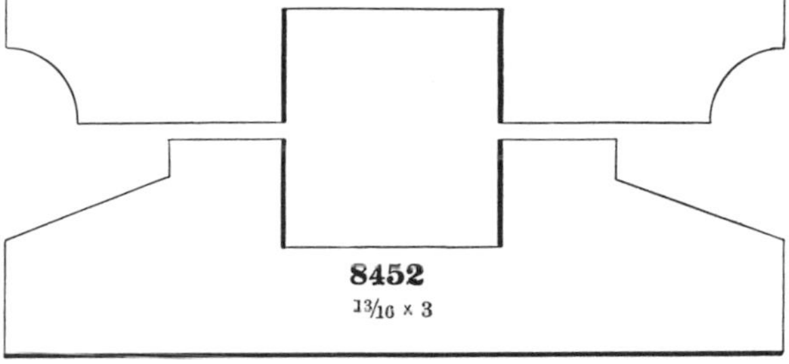
8452
13/16 x 3

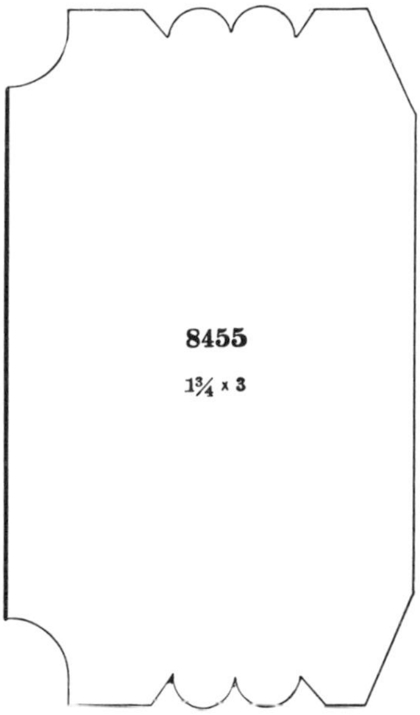
8455
1¾ x 3

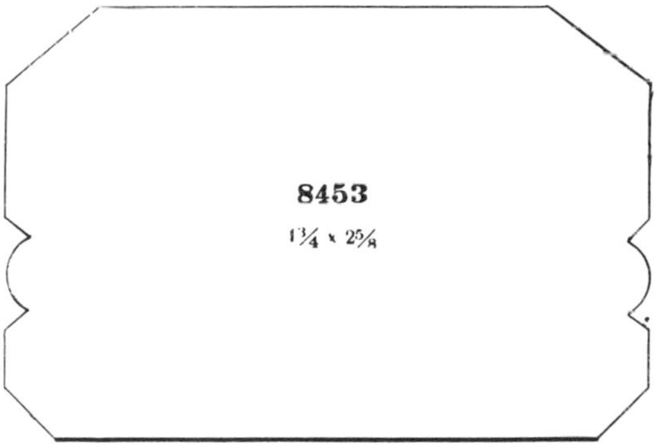
8453
1¾ x 2⅝

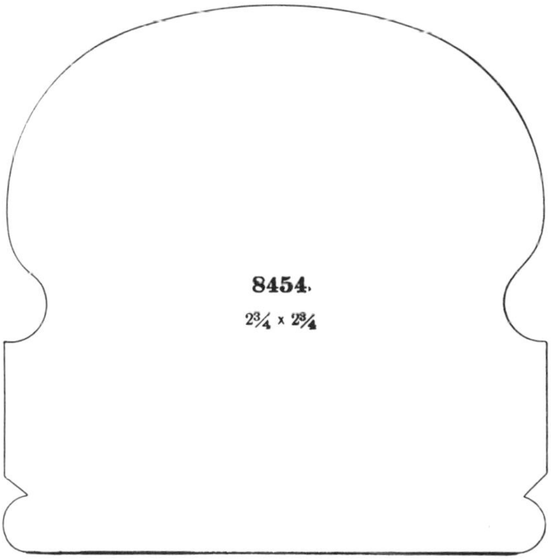
8454
2¾ x 2¾

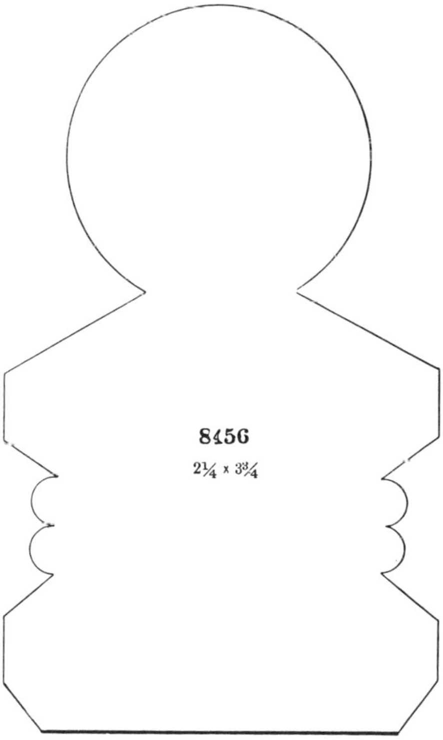
8456
2¼ x 3¾

List Prices as given are per 100 lineal feet.

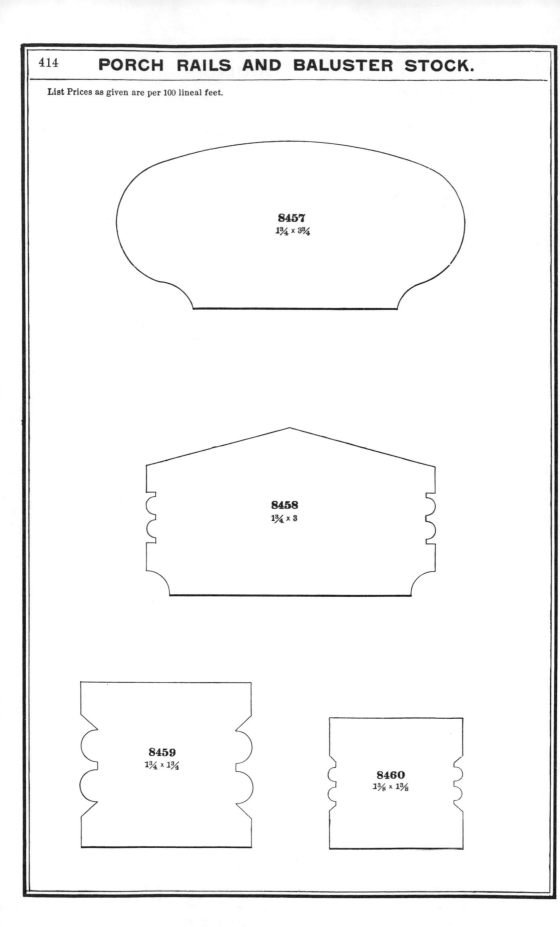

8457
1¾ x 3¾

8458
1¾ x 3

8459
1¾ x 1¾

8460
1⅜ x 1⅜

LIST PRICE OF MOULDINGS.

415

PRICES GIVEN ARE PER 100 LINEAL FEET.

No.	Price	No.	Price	No.	Price	No.	Price	No.	Price
8000	$3.50	8055	$3.30	8110	$1.20	8165	$2.50	8220	$2.45
8001	6.00	8056	4.85	8111	1.05	8166	1.25	8221	2.60
8002	4.00	8057	4.85	8112	2.50	8167	1.40	8222	2.75
8003	3.00	8058	1.00	8113	2.25	8168	2.00	8223	3.30
8004	5.50	8059	1.00	8114	2.05	8169	1.40	8224	3.30
8005	5.00	8060	1.00	8115	1.80	8170	1.65	8225	2.75
8006	4.50	8061	1.25	8116	1.35	8171	2.00	8226	2.20
8007	2.00	8062	2.00	8117	1.15	8172	2.00	8227	1.80
8008	2.50	8063	1.00	8118	1.15	8173	2.00	8228	2.45
8009	4.00	8064	1.00	8119	1.35	8174	1.75	8229	3.30
8010	3.00	8065	1.00	8120	1.80	8175	2.00	8230	6.60
8011	2.50	8066	1.00	8121	2 05	8176	2.00	8231	1.90
8012	4.50	8067	1.50	8122	2.25	8177	2.25	8232	3.50
8013	5.00	8068	2.00	8123	1.65	8178	2.25	8233	3.25
8014	3.50	8069	2.50	8124	3.75	8179	2.50	8234	2.75
8015	1.15	8070	1.00	8125	4.95	8180	2.75	8235	3.00
8016	2.00	8071	1.00	8126	8.80	8181	3.00	8236	4.00
8017	1.65	8072	1.25	8127	2.00	8182	3.25	8237	8.30
8018	2.50	8073	1.15	8128	1.00	8183	2.75	8238	4.40
8019	3.00	8074	2.25	8129	1.15	8184	2.50	8239	4 40
8020	3.50	8075	1.00	8130	1.25	8185	2.00	8240	4.40
8021	4.50	8076	1.00	8131	1.40	8186	2.00	8241	1.00
8022	5.00	8077	1.00	8132	1.00	8187	1.75	8242	2.00
8023	4.00	8078	1.15	8133	1.50	8188	2.25	8243	2.50
8024	2.00	8079	1.40	8134	3.30	8189	2.00	8244	.75
8025	2.50	8080	1.75	8135	1.65	8190	2.25	8245	1.65
8026	3.00	8081	2.00	8136	3.95	8191	2.75	8246	1.75
8027	4.50	8082	.90	8137	2.00	8192	2.75	8247	1.20
8028	4.00	8083	1.00	8138	2.00	8193	1.50	8248	2.50
8029	3.50	8084	1.10	8139	1.00	8194	2.50	8249	1.40
8030	2.50	8085	1.40	8140	1.00	8195	2.00	8250	2.00
8031	2.00	8086	1.60	8141	1.25	8196	2.50	8251	.85
8032	2.25	8087	1.80	8142	1.50	8197	3.00	8252	2.25
8033	3.00	8088	2.00	8143	1.75	8198	2.00	8253	1.00
8034	3.50	8089	1.15	8144	2.25	8199	3.50	8254	2.50
8035	1.00	8090	1.60	8145	1.00	8200	2.00	8255	1.00
8036	1.40	8091	2.05	8146	1.00	8201	2.25	8256	2.95
8037	2.50	8092	2.25	8147	1.75	8202	2.50	8257	3.95
8038	3.30	8093	2.00	8148	2.25	8203	2.50	8258	3.30
8039	5.50	8094	1.80	8149	2.25	8204	1.75	8259	1.80
8040	1.00	8095	1.60	8150	....	8205	3.00	8260	2.65
8041	1.25	8096	1.20	8151	....	8206	1.80	8261	2.50
8042	1.00	8097	1.10	8152	1.15	8207	2.45	8262	4.15
8043	1.00	8098	1.35	8153	1.25	8208	3.00	8263	2.00
8044	1.25	8099	1.80	8154	1.50	8209	3.00	8264	2.00
8045	1.65	8100	2.25	8155	1.50	8210	3.00	8265	2.00
8046	2.95	8101	1.05	8156	1.75	8211	3.30	8266	3.25
8047	3.45	8102	1.20	8157	2.00	8212	2.20	8267	6.60
8048	6.20	8103	1.60	8158	1.75	8213	2.45	8268	7.45
8049	4.85	8104	1.85	8159	1.15	8214	2.90	8269	7.45
8050	2.75	8105	2.00	8160	1.00	8215	2.20	8270	7.45
8051	1.70	8106	2.25	8161	1.15	8216	2.45	8271	2.00
8052	1.00	8107	2.00	8162	1.25	8217	2.90	8272	3.75
8053	1.00	8108	1.85	8163	1.50	8218	1.55	8273	2.50
8054	1.15	8109	1.60	8164	1.50	8219	1.90	8274	2.50

LIST PRICE OF MOULDINGS.

PRICES GIVEN ARE PER 100 LINEAL FEET.

No.	Price	No.	Price	No.	Price	No.	Price	No.	Price
8275	$2.95	8313	$4.75	8351	$5.75	8389	$3.30	8427	$1.00
8276	3.95	8314	5.25	8352	4.20	8390	5.25	8428	7.90
8277	4.00	8315	5.75	8353	4.75	8391	3.30	8429	7.05
8278	4.00	8316	4.20	8354	5.25	8392	5.25	8430	1.50
8279	4.50	8317	4.75	8355	4.20	8393	5.45	8431	5.00
8280	.85	8318	5.25	8356	4.75	8394	5.00	8432	1.00
8281	1.00	8319	5.75	8357	5.25	8395	1.15	8433	4.95
8282	1.35	8320	4.20	8358	4.20	8396	4.15	8434	3.30
8283	2.95	8321	4.75	8359	4.75	8397	5.50	8435	8.25
8284	3.75	8322	5.25	8360	5.25	8398	1.25	8436	9.10
8285	4.55	8323	5.75	8361	5.75	8399	5.45	8437	5.00
8286	5.40	8324	4.20	8362	4.20	8400	8.70	8438	5.00
8287	6.25	8325	4.75	8363	4.75	8401	5.30	8439	12.10
8288	4.20	8326	5.25	8364	5.25	8402	5.00	8440	6.00
8289	4.75	8327	5.75	8365	5.75	8403	1.40	8441	3.75
8290	5.25	8328	4.20	8366	1.25	8404	3.35	8442	....
8291	5.75	8329	4.75	8367	4.20	8405	5.25	8443	4.40
8292	4.20	8330	5.25	8368	2.50	8406	5.75	8444	....
8293	4.75	8331	5.75	8369	4.75	8407	1.40	8445	....
8294	5.25	8332	4.20	8370	2.50	8408	1.00	8446	....
8295	5.75	8333	4.75	8371	4.75	8409	3.35	8447	....
8296	4.20	8334	5.25	8372	3.00	8410	4.80	8448	....
8297	4.75	8335	5.75	8373	4.20	8411	5.50	8449	....
8298	5.25	8336	4.20	8374	2.10	8412	1.40	8450	....
8299	5.75	8337	4.75	8375	4.20	8413	6.70	8451	....
8300	4.20	8338	5.25	6376	2.10	8414	3.30	8452	....
8301	4.75	8339	5.75	8377	5.00	8415	8.15	8453	....
8302	5.25	8340	4.20	8378	2.10	8416	1.00	8454	....
8303	5.75	8341	4.75	8379	4.20	8417	7.60	8455	....
8304	4.20	8342	5.25	8380	2.10	8418	1.15	8456	....
8305	4.75	8343	5.75	8381	5.00	8419	7.90	8457	....
8306	5.25	8344	4.75	8382	5.75	8420	2.75	8458	....
8307	5.75	8345	5.25	8383	7.90	8421	8.15	8459	....
8308	4.20	8346	4.75	8384	4.75	8422	1.00	8460	....
8309	4.75	8347	5.25	8385	5.75	8423	3.60		
8310	5.25	8348	4.20	8386	7.90	8424	8.15		
8311	5.75	8349	4.75	8387	2.50	8425	1.00		
8312	4.20	8350	5.25	8388	5.25	8426	7.90		

IMPORTANT NOTICE.

When moulding is priced by the inch *it is in all cases understood* that the price is based on ripping width of lumber, that is : $\frac{1}{4}$ *of an inch wider than the finished size* of moulding. For example : A $\frac{7}{8}$ inch thick panel moulding if made to finish $1\frac{3}{4}$ inches wide would be charged as 2 inches (being ripping size); to finish full 2 inches, would be charged as $2\frac{1}{4}$ inches, etc.

Approximate weight of Mouldings, 1x1 inch, per 100 lineal feet, 15 pounds.